Ideal and Reality
in Frankish and Anglo-Saxon Society

John Michael Wallace-Hadrill, CBE, FBA, FRHistS, D. Litt.
(*Photograph by James Wallace-Hadrill*)

Ideal and Reality
in Frankish and
Anglo-Saxon Society

Studies presented to
J. M. Wallace-Hadrill

Edited by
Patrick Wormald
with
Donald Bullough *and* Roger Collins

Basil Blackwell

© Basil Blackwell Publisher Limited 1983

First published 1983
Basil Blackwell Publisher Limited
108 Cowley Road, Oxford OX4 1JF, England

British Library Cataloguing in Publication Data

Ideal and reality in Frankish and Anglo-Saxon society.
1. Wallace-Hadrill, J.M.   2. France – History
– To 987 – Addresses, essays, lectures   3. Great
Britain – History – Anglo-Saxon period – Addresses,
essays, lectures
I. Wormald, Patrick   II. Bullough, Donald
III. Collins, Roger   IV. Wallace-Hadrill, J.M.
944.01   DC65

ISBN 0-631-12661-9

Typesetting by Oxford Verbatim Limited
Printed in Great Britain

Contents

Illustrations

J. M. Wallace-Hadrill *frontispiece*

Plates between pages 178 and 179

Foreword

PATRICK WORMALD

This collection of essays is concerned with two main themes in the early history of Europe. One is the parallel development and interdependence of Frankish and Anglo-Saxon history; the other, the complex relationship between the way that men believed that society *should* be and the way that society actually *was* in the early medieval West. The collection is also a *Festschrift* for a scholar who has been the teacher of many of the contributors and the friend of them all. One might say of *Festschriften* what Gibbon said of the title 'Great' inherent in the name Charlemagne: that they have 'been often bestowed and sometimes deserved'. All too rarely are they objective reflections of a scholar's achievement and influence rather than a disconnected series of subjective expressions of gratitude (the proverbial 'Essays from the bottom drawer presented to . . .'). Professor Wallace-Hadrill's achievement and influence are directly assessed elsewhere in this volume (pp. 1–6). Something may perhaps be said here of how they came to inspire the book as a whole.

In assembling the collection we have made no attempt to secure contributions from all those who taught, were taught by, or were colleagues of, Professor Wallace-Hadrill. Tomes of the size that would be necessary are quite beyond the resources of the English component of the Republic of Letters. In making our selection we aimed above all for coherence. Thus, the contributors are almost all well known to one another and intellectually of the same generation. Each has seen the other papers in draft and modified his or her own accordingly, so that cross-references, implicit and explicit, will be found throughout. Within this group, contributions were invited only from specialists in the Frankish and Anglo-Saxon fields, where Professor Wallace-Hadrill has made his major impact. Even the editors, however, had never anticipated that what would result would be so closely interlocking a series of papers that they might almost be the proceedings of a weekend conference on a pre-set theme. It deserves both emphasis and explanation that this book's title emerged only after first drafts had been submitted, yet is obviously a faithful reflection of its contents.

Professor Wallace-Hadrill neither sought nor managed to found a 'school'. His effect on those who have learnt from him is singularly hard to generalize, and would probably be differently described by each. A common theme is his ruthlessly high standards of scholarly enquiry; the most sincere and well-meaning fools were never suffered gladly. But beyond that it could be argued that the two most persistent threads are precisely those worked out in this book. Others before Professor Wallace-Hadrill had of course been aware of the mutual influences between the spheres of British and continental history in the early Middle Ages and beyond: notably Wilhelm Levison, whose great book had something of the status of a Patristic, if not Scriptural, text, both for Professor Wallace-Hadrill and his pupils.[1] But he was, I think, the first to protest the outstanding relevance of the history of the Franks to almost any aspect of that of the Anglo-Saxons, and *vice versa*. The contributors to this book intellectually stand astride the English Channel: our understanding of our subjects has been formed, in principle, by awareness of the wider geographical context. This approach is no longer as new as when Professor Wallace-Hadrill first adopted it in 1949 (p. 317); it could still do with wider application, both in England and on the continent.

A more elusive but perhaps more fundamental theme has been Professor Wallace-Hadrill's ability to ride the crest of historical paradox. It is not simply that one was not permitted to follow fashionable historiographical lines – for example on the 'decadence' of the later Merovingian and Carolingian periods. It was also his ability to hold what Erich Heller called 'the equipoise of suspense' when confronted with the tensions between the cultivated image and the brutal realities of early medieval western society.[2] Professor Wallace-Hadrill insists that one must take seriously and on its own terms what one acquires at such peril to the eyesight in the first 150

[1] W. Levison, *England and the Continent in the Eighth Century* (Oxford, 1946).
[2] E. Heller, *The Disinherited Mind* (London, 4th edn, 1975), p. 87.

volumes of Migne; but he has never thought that *Ideengeschichte*, ancient or modern, was the whole story. The near-contemporary English historians whom he has most admired are Sir Richard Southern and Sir Herbert Butterfield. The essays in this book tend to follow him in his careful cultivation of the boundary between ideal and reality in the world of his 'Barbarian West'. We hear of ways in which learned idealism did affect what happened, of ways in which it failed to and of ways in which its effect was ultimately somewhat other than that intended. The clergy are the architects of national solidarity, moral reform and imperial visions, yet almost absurdly vulnerable to social pressures locally; they are experts in the arcane techniques of late Roman statecraft, yet unwilling or unable to influence so fundamental a religious function (as it seems to us) as family burial; they see kings as like David, yet commend their withdrawal from worldly power; they compose elaborate liturgies solemnizing the office of king alongside sober descriptions of normal political procedures and biting assessments of actual royal performance; a potentially revolutionary ideology of christocentric kingship is formulated by someone who both experienced and depended upon a king's ability to exploit his demesne. The mutual interaction of intellectual ideals and social realities is arguably history's most abiding theme. If this book takes that theme any further, it will be a proper tribute to a historian who never allowed pupils or friends to forget it.

It also seems right to record here the names (alphabetically and without title) of those who might, in an ideal world, have contributed to a *Festschrift* for Professor Wallace-Hadrill and who are, by their own explicit admission, happy to congratulate him on his place in the history of medieval scholarship: Jeremy Adams, Stuart Airlie, Jack Baldwin, Geoffrey Barraclough, Max Beloff, Helmut Beumann, Daniel Binchy, Bernhard Bischoff, Alan Bott, Christopher Brooke, Giles Brown, Peter Brown, Rupert Bruce Mitford, Carl-Richard Brühl, Francis John Byrne, James Campbell, Peter Carter, Henry Chadwick, Christopher Cheney, Mary Cheney, Ralph Davis, Eugen Ewig, Ann Freeman, Horst Fuhrmann, Peter Godman, Walter Goffart, Albert Goodwin, Ida Gordon, Philip Grierson, Bernard Guenée, Karl Hauck, Roger Highfield, Jocelyn Hillgarth, Peregrine Horden, Jean Hutton, Michael Kauffmann, Maurice Keen, Karl Leyser, Trevor Lloyd, Derek Lomax, Heinz Löwe, Gary Lysaght, Jack McManners,

Geoffrey Martin, Donald Matthew, Henry Mayr-Harting, Paul Meyvaert, Arnaldo Momigliano, Lucien Musset, Florentine Mütherich, Noel Myres, Anthony Price, Pierre Riché, John Roberts, David Rollason, Michael Roper, Theodor Schieffer, Julia Smith, Richard Southern, (†) Walter Ullmann, Bryan Ward-Perkins, Chris Wickham and David Winfield; Alfred Smyth perhaps deserves especial mention because he agreed to contribute to the book but was prevented from doing so at the last moment by other commitments.

I wish to thank Roger Collins, Judith McClure and Ian Wood who helped to plan this book as well as contributing to it; Roger Collins also did much of the editorial work and gave valuable assistance with the plates. I must further thank my other co-editor, Donald Bullough, for the prodigious erudition which saved many of us from error, and Janet Nelson for her own exception-ally thorough and generous review of other contributions. Acknowledgements for illustrations are made elsewhere, but special mention should be made of Günther Kotzor and Anne Wallace-Hadrill. Finally, I wish to thank John Davey and Basil Blackwell Publisher for believing in this book and seeing it through, and Jenny Wormald for sharing with me her hard-earned personal experience of the pains and pleasures of an editor's life – the index, not least.

Abbreviations

ASC	*Anglo-Saxon Chronicle*, cited *sub anno* and, where necessary, by the conventional MS sigla, A-G; ed. J. Earle and C. Plummer, *Two of the Saxon Chronicles Parallel* (2 vols Oxford, 1899); trans. D. Whitelock *et al.*, *The Anglo-Saxon Chronicle* (London, 1961), and in *EHD*
ASE	*Anglo-Saxon England*
AU	*Annals of Ulster*, cited *sub anno*, ed. and trans. W. M. Hennessy (4 vols, Dublin, 1887–1901)
BAR	British Archaeological Reports (Oxford)
BCS	W. de Gray Birch, *Cartularium Saxonicum* (3 vols, London, 1885–99)
BL	British Library
BN	Bibliothèque Nationale, Paris
CCSL	*Corpus Christianorum, Series Latina*
CSEL	*Corpus Scriptorum Ecclesiasticorum Latinorum*
DA	*Deutsches Archiv für Erforschung des Mittelalters*
EHD	*English Historical Documents*, ed. D. Whitelock (London, 2nd edn, 1979)
EHR	*English Historical Review*
Gesetze	*Die Gesetze der Angelsachsen*, ed. F. Liebermann (3 vols, Halle, 1903–16)
GCS	*Die griechischen christlichen Schriftsteller der ersten drei Jahrhunderte*
HE	Bede, *Historia Ecclesiastica*, ed. Plummer, (see below)
HR	*Historia Regum*, cited *sub anno*, *Symeoni Monachi Opera, II*, ed. T. Arnold (RS, 1885)
HZ	*Historische Zeitschrift*
Lowe, *CLA*	E. A. Lowe, *Codices Latini Antiquiores* (Oxford, 1934–71)

MGH	Monumenta Germaniae Historica
MGH, AA	MGH, Auctores Antiquissimi
MGH, Capit.	MGH, Capitularia Regum Francorum
MGH, Conc.	MGH, Concilia
MGH, Ep.	MGH, Epistolae
MGH, Ep. Sel.	MGH, Epistolae Selectae in usum scholarum
MGH, Leg.	MGH, Leges (quarto series)
MGH, LC	MGH, Libri Confraternitatum
MGH, Poet.	MGH, Poetae Latini Medii Aevi
MGH, SRG	MGH, Scriptores rerum Germanicarum
MGH, SRL	MGH, Scriptores rerum Langobardicarum
MGH, SRM	MGH, Scriptores rerum Merovingicarum
MGH, SS	MGH, Scriptores (folio series)
MIÖG	Mitteilungen des Instituts für österreichische Geschichtsforschung
PL	Patrologia Latina
Plummer	Baedae Venerabilis Opera Historica (2 vols, Oxford, 1896)
RH	Revue Historique
RS	Rolls Series (London)
S	P. H. Sawyer, Anglo-Saxon Charters: an annotated list and bibliography (London, 1968)
SC	Sources Chrétiennes
SCH	Studies in Church History (Oxford)
Settimane	Settimane di Studio del Centro Italiano di Studi sull' Alto Medioevo (Spoleto)
Stenton, CP	Preparatory to Anglo-Saxon England, being the collected papers of Frank Merry Stenton, ed. D. M. Stenton (Oxford, 1970)
Stenton, ASE	F. M. Stenton, Anglo-Saxon England (Oxford, 3rd edn, 1971)
TRHS	Transactions of the Royal Historical Society
Wallace-Hadrill, LHK	J. M. Wallace-Hadrill, The Long-haired Kings (London, 1962)
Wallace-Hadrill, EGK	J. M. Wallace-Hadrill, Early Germanic Kingship in England and on the Continent (Oxford, 1971)
Wallace-Hadrill, EMH	J. M. Wallace-Hadrill, Early Medieval History (Oxford, 1975)
ZRG	Zeitschrift der Savigny-Stiftung für Rechtsgeschichte

Michael Wallace-Hadrill:
An Appreciation

DONALD BULLOUGH

My first introduction to *topoi* – although the word was then unknown to me – was not through the pages of Curtius' influential book but trying to get approval of 'The Administration of the *regnum Italiae* under the Ottonian Emperors' as a D. Phil. thesis subject in the autumn of 1950. 'It's all been done already'; 'there aren't any sources'; 'you would be far better biting on something solid in the PRO'; and finally, and far more worrying, 'there's no one to supervise you'. A suggested approach to a possible supervisor outside Oxford was politely rebutted. With the appropriate Faculty Board meeting rapidly approaching, Professor Galbraith, appealed to for the third time, said simply: 'Not going to give up are you? Quite right. You'd better go and see Wallace-Hadrill and ask him to take you on.'

As someone who had taken his 'First Public Examination' in the special circumstances of 1946 and had hitherto taken little or no interest in anything earlier than the tenth century, the name was familiar to me only for an attributed sharp comment on candidates answering 'Early Medieval' questions in History Prelims without ever bothering to look at the Early Medieval collections in the Ashmolean Museum. But I had little choice. A letter requesting an appointment brought a reply in what was soon to become a familiar hand, with an equally familiar spareness of words. I have a dim, and conceivably false, memory of climbing stairs in Merton St Albans quadrangle. I have a very clear memory of what followed. The response to a knock on the door was a 'Yes?' which I rightly interpreted as an invitation to enter: a chair in the near corner of an austere room (what was very soon to be a fine scholar's library was, I learnt later, kept at home) was occupied by a slightly slumped figure whose eyes maintained an unnerving straight gaze. I outlined my predicament as briefly as the determination not to be given the answer 'no' allowed. 'I don't know anything about the subject but I can see you need me,' was the reply, given confidently but without arrogance; 'let us try it for six months'. I quickly discovered, not without discomfort, that the merely nominal supervision which most of my contemporaries enjoyed (or suffered from) was not to be my lot: one piece of written work was followed by a demand for another. When, after six months, I wrote to say that clearly it was hopeless to try to understand tenth-century Italy without making the thorough study of the Carolingian period which was conspicuously lacking, the reply was simple and direct: 'I hoped you would decide that.' I had entered on an intellectual and personal relationship from which I have been the gainer over three decades.

It is perhaps characteristic both of that relationship and of the man that I have never learnt at what moment or in what circumstances Michael Wallace-Hadrill decided that he would be the first English scholar after Sir Samuel Dill and O. M. Dalton 'to whom Frankish studies seemed important for themselves'. True, he had been an undergraduate at Corpus, the college of Dill (who was appalled by the Merovingians) and of Plummer; but in the 1930s it was unable to offer teaching in Medieval European History and so (as he recalled in his 1974 Inaugural Lecture) it was to Merton and Geoffrey Barraclough that he was sent for tuition – 'an electrifying experience'. Clearly a remarkable series of lectures by Robin Flower on the Charlemagne legend in twelfth-century Europe proved a powerful inspiration. His Lothian Prize Essay on *The Abbey of St Denis in the Twelfth and Thirteenth Centuries* took him to Paris and the Bibliothèque Nationale – an early rejection of the merely second-hand, which proved fertile ground for the future scholar, although less rewarding to the undergraduate preparing himself for 'Schools'.

Gibbon declared that his time with the Hampshire Militia was not unhelpful to the historian of the Later Roman Empire. A natural reticence, and a military career latterly in one of the more secret areas of interpretative intelligence, prevent our knowing whether Michael Wallace-Hadrill feels that his war-service has been helpful to the historian of the Merovingians, Carolingians and Anglo-Saxons; one of the few occasions on which he has made any public reference to it was in conversation with a distinguished German colleague who had done similar work on the other side. It has indeed been suggested that we should look for a reflection of these years in the novels of John le Carré rather than his own writings. It is permissable to feel that a different experience of war would have produced a different kind of early medieval historian: one who would give more prominence to the stench, the squalor, Dill's 'elemental passions' than find a place even in his more recent writings. One does not need to share all George Steiner's obsessions to feel that 'listening to Venantius Fortunatus' is not entirely convincing as a redemptive element in Merovingian behaviour. Yet it is difficult to doubt that an insistence on never taking apparently self-evident propositions at their face value, on probing behind words and concepts, was powerfully confirmed in the war years.

These qualities, combined with a sense of style, are abundantly evident in everything he wrote in his years as a Tutorial Fellow at Merton College (following a briefly held Research Fellowship at Corpus) and as Professor of Medieval History at Manchester (1956–61): not least in his masterly little book – the result of an inspired invitation from Sir Maurice Powicke – on *The Barbarian West 400–1000*, originally published in 1952. Here the 'new thinking' on Europe's Early Medieval centuries, much of it his own, was made available to a wide audience. His one proclaimed regret was that he had not dared to ignore the contractual limits of length, as Sir Richard Southern was doing; but the steady demand for reprints eventually allowed him to add a chapter on Visigothic Spain, which remains the best short account of that once-neglected region of 'the Barbarian West'. What is not so immediately evident is the wide range of reading in both sources and secondary literature which lies behind the simplest as well as the boldest statement; no colleague across the Channel would dare to throw away the crutch of lengthy footnotes as evidence of his own superior scholarship. True, charters have always been less congenial and less surely handled than narrative sources; and 'previous contributions to the subject' have never seemed particularly important to Michael Wallace-Hadrill. What creates problems for many of his readers is the determination to avoid the obvious, sometimes to a point of perversity. When his notable paper on Gregory of Tours was reprinted in 1962, I observed in a review that, although 'read originally to a non-specialist audience, [it] includes only seven dates, five of them from the twentieth century; and we are nowhere reminded of when Gregory lived or wrote.' If his lectures to Manchester undergraduates shared these characteristics – and I have unhappily no evidence on this point – one feels that they must have been fascinated but baffled.

Clearly, however, younger colleagues who have never been famous for a humble attitude towards their seniors in scholarship or in the university hierarchy responded eagerly to the challenge of his presence and ideas. Moreover, Manchester in the 1950s, although soon to be betrayed by its literary *Guardian*, was a city still proud of its cultural vigour and independence: its professors were and are expected to communicate their learning to a wider public in lectures at the John Ryland's Library. It was in one of these that he asked – and answered – the question, what did blood-feud actually mean to a society that recognized it as an integral part of its own existence? Anthropologists had posed it before; historians had not. His book reviews – largely written, he claimed, during family summer holidays in the Scillies – were marked by a similar ability to ask fundamental questions which had escaped the authors even as they presented the evidence on which the answers would be based. His edition and translation of *The Fourth Book of the Chronicle of Fredegar*, a model treatment of an initially rebarbative but important early medieval chronicle, appeared in 1960. In 1962 came a reprint of his most important papers of the 1950s, together with an entirely new account of Merovingian kings and kingship under the title of *The Long-haired Kings*: described by its publisher as 'probably the only book of its kind in English and possibly in any other European language', it was and is *the* only one.

Fruitful though the Manchester years had been, and particularly congenial when he and his closely-knit family were established in a house on the edge of The Peak, the return to Oxford in 1961 as Senior Research Fellow at Merton, to which was soon to be added the onerous duties of Editor of the *English Historical Review*, was clearly more congenial; but not for any of the meretricious reasons whereby Oxford continues to hold so many in its thrall. Michael Wallace-Hadrill's very real sociability is not of the kind that relishes High Table and Common Room living for its own sake, any more than it attracts him to the conference circuit which became a way of life to so many early medievalists in the late 1950s and 1960s. He has been at Spoleto only once ('I don't like flying', was his only comment on his return; 'do you think it is the air hostesses?'), but fortunately in the last year when both Paul Lehmann and F.-L. Ganshof were there to bring much-needed rigour to the notorious *interventi*. It was and is the exchange of ideas with scholars of his own stature, and in the 1960s increasingly with colleagues in Germany (in spite of fundamental differences of approach which were not concealed on a British Council-sponsored tour in 1967) that has most appealed.

That and working in his own room surrounded by his own books. I am struck that, returning to read in the Bodleian Library over many years, I have only once met him there, and on that occasion he was accompanying his younger son on a Christmas Holiday inscription hunt. There may have been some loss here. Michael Wallace-Hardrill's sensitivity to manuscripts and what they (as distinct from the texts they transmit) can tell us is apparent from his review of the Krusch-Levison edition of Gregory of Tours' *Histories*, from his early work on Hincmar of Rheims and above all from his edition of Fredegar. Yet latterly his account of how a few men in each generation influenced the society in which they lived through the written word, or through the spoken word based on writings to which they had access, seems unduly detatched from what I seem to find in many of the books they read: chaos of content, textual inaccuracy and sometimes downright unintelligibility. There has also been clear gain. 'It would be possible to write a big book about Anglo-Saxon kingship, and an even larger one about continental kingship'; and, having been written, it might well be read in its entirety only by reviewers. The 1970 Ford Lectures as delivered and published 'draw attention to some common strands in thought and action that tend to bring English and continental history a little nearer together in one field', and 'endeavour to relate early medieval thinking about kingship to the practices of kings'. This approach and some of its consequences had been adumbrated in a 1949 lecture on 'The Franks and the English in the ninth century'. The economy of scale and language with which two decades of reflective scholarship are presented, a unique vision of what are seen as the central issues, offers the securest guarantee that *Early Germanic Kingship* will be read and re-read so long as the distant past seems important to mature intellects.

More unexpected have been the consequences of Michael Wallace-Hadrill's renewed involvement in college and inter-collegiate teaching, particularly through that uncharacteristic Oxford phenomenon, the graduate seminar, both before and after his elevation (not without reservations on his own part) to the Chichele Chair. He was fortunate, although it is a fortune supported by *virtus*, to encounter a remarkable generation of young historians attracted by his approach to historical enquiry and to the problems of the early Middle Ages. The resultant interaction is well documented: it is reflected in the footnotes and expressions of thanks in several of his later articles; it is the substance of much of the present volume. The shared excitement was and is not confined to those who aspire to a life of scholarship for themselves; it has played a major part in the creation of a television series which has brought the period to the notice of many for whom it would otherwise have been forever Dark. Where we might expect a 'generation gap' we are faced with that rarest of intellectual achievements, a 'generation leap'. His 1974 Inaugural Lecture hints at a whole range of new sympathies which, I am told, have been fully displayed in his obligatory yearly lectures. It would be possible and fitting to add his own name to those seen, at the end of this lecture, as standing out 'in these remote stages of European history . . . against a backdrop of pot and post-hole, fibula and scramasax', had he not then characterized these 'rare inmates' as 'a rum lot'. As it is, we can adapt the lecture's final phrase, without the slightest hint of a *topos*, and recognize his pre-eminence in a succession of historians, 'with this claim to our attention, nobility of mind'.

1

Theodebert I, 'Rex Magnus Francorum'

ROGER COLLINS

When, in the early 580s, Bishop Marius of Avenches was writing his brief continuation of the *Chronicle* of Prosper, he noted in respect of the year 548 that it saw the death of one Frankish king and the succession of another: 'Eo anno Theudebertus rex magnus Francorum obiit, et sedit in regno eius Theudebaldus filius ipsius.'[1] That some historians have though that Marius got the date wrong and that it should be put back by a year is of little consequence;[2] what is striking about this short entry is the application of the epithet *magnus* to the king, a distinction accorded to no other ruler in this work. How and why Theodebert I qualified for this unique description is not explained by the chronicler, and his other references to the king are only two in number. For 539 he records Theodebert's invasion of Italy, devastation of Liguria and Aemilia, and the withdrawal of his army after the outbreak of disease; and for 556, after the king's death, he notes the recovery by the Byzantine imperial army of the Italian lands that had been conquered by the Frankish ruler.[3]

In themselves neither of these entries and the events they describe

[1] *Marii Episcopi Aventicensis Chronica*, ed. T. Mommsen, *MGH, AA* XI, p. 236. Although this and other MS evidence indicates that the spelling of the king's name as Theudebert was probably prevalent by the seventh century and is used elsewhere in this volume, I shall use the form Theodebert , as that is how it is to be found on his coinage, the only source exactly contemporary with his reign, and one officially sanctioned.

[2] The reign of Theodebert lasted from either 533–47 or 534–48; for a discussion, with criticism of Marius, see E. Stein, *Histoire du Bas-Empire* (2 Vols, Paris, 1949), II, excursus N. pp. 816–17; also E. Zöllner, *Geschichte der Franken, bis zur Mitte des sechsten Jahrhunderts* (Munich, 1970), pp. 106–8, who follows Marius.

[3] *Marii Chronica*, pp. 236, 237.

might seem to explain why Marius singled out Theodebert I as being especially deserving of the title of *great* king of the Franks, although the second of them does indicate, contrary to the testimony of the Byzantine historian Procopius, that the Italian conquests were not ephemeral and were retained for the rest of the reign and throughout that of his son Theodebald.[4] Indeed it is impossible to determine from the evidence of Marius's own chronicle whether in the obituary notice he is referring to Theodebert as a king who had achieved greatness, however defined, or is ascribing a formal title to him, perhaps implying a superiority over other kings of the Frankish peoples. Such would in practice have been the position of Clovis in respect of the lesser Frankish kings of his time, some, though not necessarily all, of whom he eliminated during the last years of his reign. Such an interpretation might be supported by Theodebert's own letter to the Emperor Justinian, in which he asserts his authority over all of Francia, however much this may be at odds with the practical realities of the period.[5] Marius's use of *magnus* thus leaves a tantalizing ambiguity that can hardly have been present in his own mind.

A more explicit account of Theodebert has come from the pen of Marius' better-known contemporary Gregory of Tours, who, in writing the third book of his *Histories* in c.584/5, devoted a brief chapter to a statment of that king's virtues.[6] According to Gregory, Theodebert 'magnum se atque in omni bonitate praecipuum reddidit. Erat enim regnum cum justitia regens, sacerdotes venerans, ecclesias munerans, pauperes relevans, et multa multis beneficia pia ac dulcissima accomodans voluntate.' The king is thus again being ascribed with the quality of greatness. This may be held to have been the product of his display of those more precise virtues then listed, but it has been recently suggested that *magnus* represents an additional quality relating to his military achievements, some of which are alluded to elsewhere in this book of the *Histories*.[7]

[4] Procopius, *History of the Wars* VI.xxv.24–xxvi.1, ed. H. B. Dewing (London, 1919–28), pp. IV, 92.

[5] *Epistolae Austrasicae* 20, ed. W. Gundlach, *MGH, Ep.* III, p. 133. The reprint of this edition, incorporating textual corrections suggested by D. Norberg, 'Ad epistulas varias Merovingici aevi adnotationes', *Eranos*, XXXV (1937), pp. 105–15, in *CCSL* CXVII, pp. 407–70, is cited henceforth; see pp. 438–9.

[6] *Gregorii Episcopi Turonensis Historiarum Libri Decem* III.25, ed. B. Krusch and W. Levison, *MGH, SRM* I (2), p. 123.

[7] M. Reydellet, *La Royauté dans la litterature latine de Sidoine Appollinaire à Isidore de Seville* (Rome, 1981), pp. 414–15.

It has been thought that Gregory's assessment of Theodebert is particularly revealing of the bishop's conception of the duties of a king, and that a model ruler is here being described.[8] However, the unusual nature of this short analytical chapter which describes Theodebert's accession and his qualities has not been properly appreciated. In no other case does Gregory give such an explicit statement of an individual king's merits, not even in his presentation of Clovis. It is also noteworthy that, apart from a reference in the same chapter to Theodebert having freed the churches of the Auvergne from their fiscal obligations, and a subsequent story of his conversion of a loan to the citizens of Verdun into a gift, no specific examples are cited in the *Histories* that would explain and give life to the picture of the king here presented.[9] As it was Gregory's way to teach by illustration, and as he was a voracious collector of anecdote and information for inclusion in his work, it is not unreasonable to conclude that he did not know of other such stories concerning Theodebert. His assessment, then, was not based upon his own knowledge, which of both this period and of this king was somewhat slight, but rather upon a statement of the monarch's virtues that must have reached him ready formed.

Thus neither of the two earliest historians writing amongst the Franks really knew much about Theodebert, but on the other hand both expressed surprisingly strong approbation of him. This is in marked contrast to his reputation in contemporary Byzantine historiography. Procopius, writing his *History of the Wars* in the 550s, makes of the king and his people oathbreakers, and their campaign in Italy in 539 a vicious and fruitless fiasco.[10] Procopius' continuator Agathias, working over a decade later, speaks of the king's presumptuous rashness, in particular in conceiving of a grandiose scheme of invading Thrace with the aid of the Lombards and the Gepids, and even threatening Constantinople itself.[11] Some have seen this plan, for which only Agathias can vouch, as little more than a figment of the historian's imagination,[12] something that is almost certainly true of his account of Theodebert's death, in which

---

[8] Reydellet, *Royauté*, pp. 412–16; Wallace-Hadrill, *LHK*, p. 190; O.M. Dalton, *The History of the Franks by Gregory of Tours* (2 Vols, Oxford, 1927), II, p. 511, commenting on III.25. For the reign in general see Zöllner, *Geschichte der Franken*, pp. 86–96.   [9] Gregory, *Historiarum Libri* III.34, pp. 129–30.
[10] Procopius, *History of the Wars* VI.xxv.2., pp.IV,84.
[11] *Agathiae Myrinaei Historiarum Libri Quinque* A.4.1–4, ed. R. Keydell (Berlin, 1967), pp. 13–14.   [12] Wallace-Hadrill, *LHK*, pp. 190–1.

the king, out hunting, was killed when the rotten branch of a tree fell on him when dislodged by the charge of a mortally wounded bull.[13] This contrasts with the explicit statements of both Procopius and Gregory of Tours that he died of disease.[14] Although it is thought that in general Agathias received his information on the Franks from envoys of King Sigibert I of Austrasia, who came to Constantinople in 571, it is possible that this tale was deliberately invented to underline the hubris of a barbarian who sought to threaten the Empire, only to perish in circumstances of such bathos.[15]

Despite both prejudice and the limitations of available information, images of Theodebert were thus clearly formed in both the Frankish and Byzantine historiographical traditions that are quite out of proportion both to his material achievements and to extant contemporary evidence – now little more than a handful of letters and a few score of coins – that relates to him. In particular, his Italian expedition of 539 has generally been seen through hostile Byzantine eyes, hardly sympathetic to the real motives and aims of the undertaking. An approach to the reign through the evidence of its own time, and from a western rather than eastern perspective, is essential. Where this has been sought, modern historians have been struck by such features of his rule as his innovatory coinage and his attitude towards the Emperor, which seem to mark him out from amongst his fellow Frankish and other Germanic rulers, and the roots of his ambitions and the character of his kingship have been sought in the Roman past and in the survival of traditions from the vanished western Roman Empire into his day.[16] Such a view may require modification when it is considered who the king's principal advisors were and what they represented, and what constituted the contemporary realities of Frankish rule in sixth-century Gaul.

Theodebert presented himself to the Emperor Justinian as the ruler over many peoples and regions, including the Visigoths,

[13] *Agathiae Libri Historiarum* A.4.5., p. 14.

[14] Procopius, *History of the Wars* VIII. xxiv.6., p. V, 304; Gregory, *Historiarum Libri* III.36., pp. 131–2.

[15] On the significance of the embassy of 571 as a source for Agathias' knowledge, see A. Cameron, 'Agathias on the early Merovingians', *Annali della Scuola Normale Superiore di Pisa*, serie 2, XXXVII (1968), pp. 95–140; also A. Cameron, *Agathias* (Oxford, 1970), pp. 120–1.

[16] G. Tessier, *Le Baptême de Clovis* (Paris, 1964), pp. 173–6; Wallace-Hadrill, *LHK*, pp. 190–1; K. F. Stroheker, *Der senatorische Adel im spätantiken Gallien* (Darmstadt, 1970), pp. 124–5.

Thuringians, Saxons and the Eucii, the latter probably being the Jutes, and as the master of Francia, Pannonia and the northern seaboard of Italy; an area, as he put it, extending from the Danube and the frontiers of Pannonia to the Ocean.[17] The date of this assertive letter is not clear, but a reference in it to a *profectus Catholicorum* would suggest that it formed part of diplomatic exchanges in the period immediately prior to, or in the early stages of, the attempted imperial reconquest of Italy that began in 535. This and the *profectus communis* of another letter imply a proposal for Frankish participation in the venture, represented as a common undertaking by two powers united in religion against the heretical Arian Ostrogoths.[18] Such a scheme might have been mooted before the despatch of the imperial forces from Africa and their seizure of Sicily, or may have resulted from the difficult position into which they put themselves in 536, when besieged by King Wittigis in Rome.

Theodebert's claims are grandiose, and a reference in Procopius suggests that they may also have extended to authority over Britain. They require some interpretation as, for example, no reference is made to the existence of other powerful Frankish kings, or to an independent Visigothic kingdom in Spain. Theodebert was the ruler over some Visigoths, those living in regions of south-western Gaul that were under his control, including Béziers, which he had captured in 532/3.[19] That the Frankish king was exercising authority over Pannonia and parts of Italy is not otherwise substantiated, but it would be unwise to reject this and other claims out of hand for, as in the case of the Visigoths, however tortuous the logic may seem, a legalistic basis did underlie what otherwise might appear as assertive bombast. Alliances with the Lombards, possibly then already in Pannonia, that were cemented by royal marriages, and the ties of the Lombard dynasty to that of the Gepids might well have been the basis for the statement of his suzerainty in the north-western Balkans, and on the Danube.[20] Rule over the Thuringians, as Gregory of

[17] *Epistolae Austrasicae* 20, pp. 438–9; on the Eucii as Jutes see p. 439 n. 6; also L. Schmidt, *Geschichte der deutschen Stämme bis zum Ausgang der Völkerwanderung; II: Die Westgermanen* (2nd edn, Munich, 1938), I, p. 26.
[18] *Epistolae Austrasicae*, 20; idem 19, pp. 438–9.
[19] Gregory *Historiarum Libri* III.21, p. 121.
[20] For the Lombards in the period prior to their entry into Italy and for their relations with the Gepids and with the Frankish dynasty of Theoderic and Theodebert see J. Werner, *Die Langobarden in Pannonien* (Munich, 1962), chapter 8,

Tours shows, had already been established by Theodebert's father Theoderic I, and his domination over other peoples to the east of the Rhine, the Saxons, Jutes and 'Norsavi', is thus not inherently improbable.[21] The movement of sections of the two former peoples into Britain during the course of the fifth century may underlie the claim to Frankish hegemony there, mentioned by Procopius, and which also emerges in one of the letters of Gregory the Great.[22] These assertions, variable in their foundation in reality, may also be represented in the statement by Agathias that Theodebert resented the Emperor's use of such anachronistic titles as *Francicus* and *Alamannicus*, which implied imperial conquest and subjugation of peoples now ruled by the Frankish king. Such claims, and particularly that of Theodebert's unitary rule over Francia, may represent the aspirations of the circle of Roman and clerical advisors at his court towards a unified kingdom, exercising dominion over subject peoples.[23] Despite the problems involved in interpreting some of the assertions of this letter, it is clear that by an early stage in his reign the king had become, if not heir to the western Roman emperors, than at least to Theoderic the Ostrogoth, as the most powerful ruler in west and central Europe.

Theodebert was not just a conqueror. Indeed, it would be possible to exaggerate this side of his activity. His reputation as a war leader was created during the reign of his father, under whose authority he defeated and killed the Danish king Chlochilaic, and campaigned against the Visigoths.[24] Apart from the Italian expedition, no campaigns are recorded as having taken place during his own period of rule, and the great extension of the territory controlled by his branch of the dynasty was more the result of diplomacy than war; though in view of the limited nature of the surviving sources it would be unwise to be too dogmatic about this.

---

pp. 131–43. also I. Bóna, *Der Anbruch des Mittelalters: Gepiden und Langobarden im Karpatenbecken* (Budapest, 1976).

[21] Gregory, *Historiarum Libri* III.7, pp. 103–5.

[22] Procopius, *History of the Wars* VIII.xx.10., p. V. 24. *Gregorii I Papae Registrum Epistolarum* VI.49., ed. P. Ewald and L. M. Hartmann, *MGH,Ep.* I, pp. 423–4. For discussion see E. A. Thompson, 'Procopius on Brittia and Britannia', *Classical Quarterly* XXX (1980), pp. 498–507; also J. Campbell, *The Anglo-Saxons* (Oxford, 1982), p. 38.

[23] *Agathiae Libri Historiae* A.4.3. p. 13. cf. the claims made for the *bretwaldas*, discussed by Wormald, below pp. 109–11.

[24] Gregory, *Historiarum Libri* III.3, p. 99.

It was, however, clearly his early achievements in war, as well as his being of mature age, that secured him the inheritance of his father's kingdom.

The practice of dividing territories between the male heirs of a former king may have existed amongst the Franks before the time of Clovis, but if so the career of the latter, which vastly increased the size of their territories and the range of influences to which they could be subjected, altered both the scale of the process and its effects.[25] However, as in all of the Germanic kingdoms, both rights and customs in succession could be subordinated to more practical considerations, such as the need for effective war leadership, something that could not be exercised by a child. Where such weakness existed, usurpation and dynastic change might occur or, in the case of the Franks, as one of the benefits of their distinctive system of division, other ruling members of the family might intervene. Thus Childebert I and Chlotar I first delayed the succession of and then murdered their nephews, the sons of Chlodomer.[26] Why, in 533 or 534, they tried to challenge the succession of Theodebert, whose military prowess secured him the support of his father's military following, is not so clear, but may represent an attempt to contest the inheritance of a pre-eminence enjoyed by their half-brother Theoderic.

Military reputation, and the opportunities to obtain it, were the foundation of a king's power in sixth-century Gaul. Since the beginning of the career of Clovis in the 480s, Frankish kings had expanded the limits of the territories under their control with single-mindedness and astonishing success. Continuing expansion had a central role to play in preserving the authority of an individual king and ensuring the stability of his realm. As anecdotes in the work of Gregory of Tours make clear, a ruler's power depended, especially vis à vis his potential dynastic rivals, upon his provision of opportunities for his military following to engage in war and obtain loot. When Theoderic I was reluctant to join his half-brothers in their attack on the Burgundian kingdom in 523, his *Leudes* threatened to desert him in favour of the other kings, but were dissuaded by the promise of easier and more substantial pickings to be obtained from

[25] However, I. N. Wood, 'Kings, kingdoms and consent', in P. H. Sawyer and I. N. Wood (eds), *Early Medieval Kingship* (Leeds, 1977), pp. 6–29, argues strongly that the division of 511 was the first of its kind amongst the Merovingians.

[26] Gregory, *Historiarum Libri* III.18, 33, pp. 117–20, 128–9.

the retributory ravaging of the Auvergne.[27] Likewise, in c.559, Chlotar I, against his own better judgement, was forced into launching a campaign against the Saxons that led to a military disaster.[28]

Successful military undertaking in the form of either raids or conquest also doubtless benefited the kings financially. The considerable resistance, recorded in the pages of Gregory of Tours and elsewhere, to the attempts by successive Merovingian kings to obtain revenue from taxation, must generally have limited their resources to proceeds from fiscal lands, inherited via the Visigoths and Burgundians from the western Emperors, and to revenues from customs tolls.[29] The drain put upon these, perhaps initially considerable, means by the demands of gift giving and the need to reward followers and on occasion to buy loyalty, must have made necessary the acquisition of additional wealth by means of war.[30] During the lives of Clovis and of his sons the continuing expansion of the Frankish kingdoms cannot but have provided extra lands and treasure for these rulers. It is, however, not surprising that when this process was finally checked in the second half of the sixth century and when, under the pressure of Lombard aggression, strengthened Visigothic resistance and the successful revolt of the subject peoples to the east of the Rhine, the Frankish kingdoms began to contract, conflict was turned inwards and, under the guise of a blood feud, a long and bitter internecine war was fought out amongst the Merovingians until only one line of the dynasty survived.[31]

This dependence on war, and the failure of the Frankish kingdoms to develop satisfactory centralized royal government that might parallel even such as existed in the neighbouring Visigothic and Lombard realms, were serious flaws in the Frankish state.

[27] ibid. III.11–12., pp. 107–8. H. Grahn-Hoek, Die fränkische Oberschicht im 6 Jahrhundert (Sigmaringen, 1976), pp. 165–75.

[28] Gregory Historiarum Libri IV.9, pp. 140–1.

[29] ibid. IV.2, V.28, VII.15, IX.30, X.7, pp. 136, 233–4, 336–7, 448–9, 488. See also W. Goffart, 'Old and new in Merovingian taxation', Past and Present, XCVI (1982), pp. 3–21.

[30] Wallace-Hadrill, LHK, p. 67 and n. 5. cf. also J. B. Gillingham, The Kingdom of Germany in the High Middle Ages (London, 1971), pp. 28–9.

[31] J. M. Wallace-Hadrill, 'The bloodfeud of the Franks', in LHK, pp. 121–47. I am by no means convinced that the conflict between rival branches of the Merovingian dynasty that resulted from Chilperic's murder of his Visigothic wife Galsuintha (Gregory, Historiarum Libri IV.28) was motivated by the requirements of bloodfeud: it is not clear that the obligations of feud necessitated the avenging of the blood of a sister-in-law upon a brother.

However, when expansion, with its concomitant benefits for internal order, was possible, whichever branch of the ruling dynasty controlled the Rhineland was especially favourably placed. With the conquest of Gaul completed, limitations imposed by geography made this the natural direction for renewed Frankish growth, or even just raiding. Italy and the Iberian peninsula were not easy of access, especially if the limited routes of ingress were defended. Although the heavily forested lands east of the Rhine presented their own problems of entry, communication and defence, their populations were not as well organized as those of the Mediterranean lands, and the enormous extent of this open eastern frontier gave the Franks the advantage while they remained the aggressors. Control of this vast area from the North Sea to the Alps gave Theodebert, and his father before him, the chance to make themselves far greater kings than the other members of their dynasty, who, after the exclusion of Chlotar I from further part in the conquest of Thuringia, had only the increasingly well-defended Visigothic Septimania and the Pyrenees on which to concentrate their energies.[32]

In the division of the kingdom that followed the death of Clovis, Theoderic I, for whatever reasons, obtained control of the principal Rhineland cities of Cologne, Metz and Trier, as well as other regions of Gaul.[33] It has been customary to entitle the second generation of Merovingian kings by the names of what were held to be their principal royal residences or capitals. Thus Theoderic is often referred to as king of Rheims, or occasionally as king of Metz.[34] This may well be anachronistic, as there is no sure evidence that these, or any other city, provided the main residence for his court, or that the notion of capital as a fixed centre of administration has any meaning in the context of the kingdom of Theoderic and Theodebert, or of the other early Merovingian realms.[35] However, it is clear that this branch of the dynasty did have particular ties to

[32] Gregory, *Historiarum Libri* III.29, pp. 125–6. E. A. Thompson, *The Goths in Spain* (Oxford, 1969), pp. 14–15.

[33] Tessier, *Baptême de Clovis*, pp. 171–3.

[34] E. Ewig, 'Die fränkischen Teilungen und Teilreiche (511–613)', *Abhandlungen der Akademie der Wissenschaften und der Literatur in Mainz* (Wiesbaden, 1952), pp. 651–715, especially pp. 667–75. Dalton, *Gregory's History of the Franks*, I, p. 137, for 'King of Metz'.

[35] E. Ewig, 'Résidence et capitale pendant le Haut Moyen Age', *RH*, CCXXX (1963), pp. 25–72, especially pp. 385–6, argues the case for a 'capital'.

the Rhineland and the cities of north-eastern Gaul under their rule.[36] The site of their royal pantheon is not known, but is likely to have been in this area, probably the scene of their most frequent, though not exclusive, attention, as the evidence for the direction of their interests would indicate.[37]

Possession of this region may have given these rulers certain notional advantages, but these could not be fully exploited at this period. In the fourth century the Rhineland had been a scene of frequent imperial activity, and Trier the residence of several emperors.[38] It was also the administrative centre of the Gallic prefecture. However, despite this former concentration of civilian and military settlements, some of considerable importance, along the Rhine frontier, the available evidence indicates that these went into a serious decline in the course of the fifth century. The residence of the Praetorian Prefect was moved from Trier to Arles by Stilicho, and the former city was sacked in 411. Although certain buildings survived from Late Roman to Merovingian times, it would be unwise to assume that imperial memories did, and to suggest that the associations of the city and region in the fourth century influenced the supposed imperial style of Theodebert in the sixth is also unwise.

Although settlement in both the cities, and in some of the smaller sites, appears to have survived unbroken in a number of cases, the indications are that population declined and the importance of the urban centres plummeted.[39] Archaeological indications of the substantial Frankish resettlement of many parts of the Rhineland in the seventh century suggest that the land was under-occupied in the sixth.[40] Movement of settlement had then been directed westwards, especially in the wake of Clovis' sweeping campaigns of conquest, and even potential new settlers, the Alamanni, pressing on the

[36] Theodebert's daughter Berthoara donated a royal residence in Mainz to the Church, for use as a baptistery; see Venantius Fortunatus, *Carmina* II.11, ed. F. Leo, *MGH,AA* IV.1, pp. 40–1. Ewig, 'Résidence et capitale', p. 385.

[37] A mid-sixth century Merovingian princess's grave has been discovered beneath Cologne Cathedral: J. Werner, 'Frankish royal tombs in the cathedrals of Cologne and Saint Denis', *Antiquity*, XXXVIII (1964), pp. 201–16, summarizing the excavators' reports.

[38] E. M. Wightman, *Roman Trier and the Treveri* (London, 1970), pp. 58–67, with full references.

[39] For Trier: Wightman, *Roman Trier*, pp. 67–70, 122–3, 250–3.

[40] For settlement in the region of Trier: K. Böhner, *Die fränkischen Altertümer des trierer Landes* (Berlin, 1958), esp. Karte 11.

middle and upper Rhine, were deflected by Clovis' victory over them at Tolbiac in 506 towards the south, and were driven into Ostrogothic domination.[41]

The church in the Rhineland, hardly well established before the breaching of the imperial frontier in 406, survived in most parts of the region, but without any significant increase in its hold.[42] Few churches are known to have been erected between the fourth and later sixth century, when a period of major expansion began, and the area was also substantially underdeveloped in respect of monastic foundations.[43] Episcopal continuity across the fifth and early sixth centuries is far from certain, even in the major sees.[44] Obviously in this, as in the other features mentioned, the limitations of evidence – especially the lack of documentary sources relating to the region – make confident assertions unwise, but the general impression to be gained from recent archaeological work all along the former Roman frontier zone from Belgium to Austria is of contraction and decline in the period between the disintegration of imperial rule and the reign of Theoderic I.[45]

Theoderic's rule saw the beginnings of a reversal of this process which, in the course of the next two centuries, was to lead to the transfomation of the region from an extremity into the heart of Francia. The conquests east of the Rhine may have been a start, but their loss in the middle of the sixth century shows how poorly grounded they were. Of greater long-term significance was the appreciation by the house of Theoderic I, very much like their later

[41] Gregory, *Historiarum Libri* II.21, p. 67.

[42] W. Neuss, *Die Anfänge des Christentums im Rheinlande* (Bonn, 1933); also Wightman, *Roman Trier*, pp. 227–37.

[43] H. Atsma, 'Les Monastères urbains du nord de la Gaule', *Revue de l'Histoire de l'Église de France*, LXII (1976), pp. 163–87; only one sixth-century inscription relating to a monastery or to the monastic life has been found in the Rhineland: H. Atsma, 'Die christlichen Inschriften Galliens als Quelle für Klöster und Klösterwohner bis zum Ende 6 Jahrhunderts', *Francia*, IV (1976), pp. 1–57, = inscription no. 8, from Boppard, pp. 7 and 10.

[44] E. Ewig, 'Les Missions dans les pays rhénans', *Revue de l'Histoire de l'Église de France*, LXII (1976), pp. 37–44. See also J. Dubois, 'Les Listes épiscopales témoins de l'organisation ecclésiastique et de la transmission des traditions', *Revue de l'Histoire de l'Église de France*, LXII (1976), pp. 9–23.

[45] H. Vetters, 'Das Problem der Kontinuität von der Antike zum Mittelalter im Österreich', *Gymnasium*, LXXV (1969), pp. 481–515; P. C. Boeren, 'Les Évêques de Tongres-Maestricht', *Revue de l'Histoire de l'Église de France*, LXII (1976), pp. 25–36; J. Werner and E. Ewig (eds), *Von der Spätantike zum frühen Mittelalter* (Sigmaringen, 1979), for studies that treat of this area.

Arnulfing successors, of the need for a revival of the Church, not in their case to help secure the adherence of conquered non-Frankish peoples (although perhaps as a preliminary step to that) but certainly to give new foundations to their rule in an area that had not known stable government for over a century.

Few of the mid-sixth-century Rhineland bishops were indigenous to the region but, like Nicetius of Trier, especially chosen for his office by Theoderic in 527, were imported from other parts of Gaul; in the case of Nicetius from the Limousin.[46] The kings could thus call upon the resources of men and of learning from other, better developed, parts of their extensive domains to begin the task of restoration. Such transfusions of talent were not confined to the ecclesiastical sphere, as the career of Parthenius in civil administration under Theodebert indicates.[47] The period of Nicetius' episcopate (527–66) coincided both with the restoration and development of Trier, Mainz and Strasbourg as centres of the church in the Rhine and Moselle valleys, and also with the beginning of new church building in smaller settlements.[48] This was a period of growth in more than material terms. Eugen Ewig has convincingly argued that Trier under Nicetius became a *Missionsseminar*, where future leaders of the church in the region received their training, some of whom, such as Aredius, were also to serve in the secular administration of the kingdom.[49]

Nicetius and other leading ecclesiastics of the kingdom worked for more than a revival of the Church; they sought for a reformation of the secular power and, on the basis of certain specific late Roman traditions, an education of the ruler to fit into a model of kingship that they were striving to create.[50] What may be the most explicit manifesto of such a programme comes in the form of a letter to King Theodebert from a bishop Aurelian, contained in the collection known as the *Epistolae Austrasicae*.[51] Wilhelm Gundlach, who edited this text for the *Monumenta* series, states that its author was

[46] E. Ewig, 'Der Raum zwischen Selz und Andernach vom 5 bis zum 7 Jahrhundert' in Werner and Ewig, *Von der Spätantike*, pp. 271–96. See Wood, below pp. 43–4, for Theoderic's dealings with the Church in the Auvergne.
[47] For Parthenius see *Prosopography of the Later Roman Empire* (2 vols, Cambridge, 1980), II, pp. 833–4 (= Parthenius 3); also Stroheker, *Senatorische Adel*, p. 199.
[48] Ewig, 'Les missions dans les pays rhénans', pp. 37–44.
[49] E. Ewig, *Trier im Merowingerzeit* (Trier, 1954), p. 293; also 'Der Raum zwischen Selz und Andernach', n. 46.
[50] Cf. Wallace-Hadrill, *EMH*, pp. 181–2.
[51] *Epistolae Austrasicae* 10, pp. 426–8.

Aurelian of Arles (546–51), possibly as he is the only bishop of that name recorded in the *fasti* as a contemporary of the king.[52] This attribution has not been subsequently questioned, and indeed the additional deduction has been drawn that the letter itself is proof that his see of Arles was subject to Theodebert in the brief two-year period from 546 to 547 (or 8) in which his reign and Aurelian's episcopate coincided, having previously formed part of the kingdom of Childebert I.[53]

However, there are serious weaknesses in the original argument. The letter, which makes a reference to the king's accession, starts with the author's apologies for his delay in writing to commemorate that felicitous event, something clearly expected of him.[54] A bishop newly ordained in 546 would hardly refer in such a way to an occurrence of twelve or thirteen years previously, nor at such distance in time would any comment on the king's elevation be required. Moreover, on literary and stylistic grounds this letter is demonstrably not the work of Aurelian of Arles. The latter is known with certainty to have been the author of a *Rule* for monks, intended for use in a monastery founded jointly by himself and Childebert I.[55] Although the style of such a work would be very different to that employed in a formal epistle of the kind addressed to Theodebert, Aurelian of Arles in his *Rule*, and particularly in the preface to it, writes a Latin that is not only simple but also bad, according to the established rules of the grammatical masters and their sixth-century emulators.[56] On the other hand, the letter to Theodebert is composed in a florid and complicated rhetorical style that shows its author to have been a practitioner of that mannered Latin best represented at this time in the works of Ennodius and Cassiodorus. Such a man could not have written with the barbaric simplicity of Aurelian of Arles.

In themselves these are strong arguments, but their force would be vitiated if no alternative bishop Aurelian were to be found. It

[52] W. Gundlach, 'Die Sammlung der *Epistolae Austrasicae*', *Neues Archiv*, XIII (1888), pp. 365–87, especially p. 379. For Bishop Aurelian of Arles (546–51), see L. Duchesne, *Fastes episcopaux de l'ancienne Gaule* (Paris, 1894), I, pp. 251–2.
[53] *Epistolae Austrasicae* 10, pp. 426 n. 10.
[54] *Epistolae Austrasicae* 10, pp. 426–8, ll. 9–18.
[55] *S. Aureliani Regula ad Monachos*, PL LXVIII, cc. 385–98; Gregory I, *Registrum* IX.216, pp. 203–4. I ignore the parallel *Rule for Nuns*, which, like Caesarius' *Rule for Monks*, I believe to be a later adaptation by a different author.
[56] e.g. his use of such a phrase as: 'Quia Deo inspirante, qui . . .', c.385.

must be said that our knowledge of episcopal successions at this period is far from comprehensive. However, another bishop Aurelian does exist, although the identity of his see remains uncertain. This man was a relative of Ennodius of Pavia, and seems to have lived in southern Gaul until driven from his patrimony by what is likely to have been the Frankish defeat of the Visigoths in 507. He subsequently enjoyed the favour of the Ostrogothic king Theoderic, was ordained a priest c.511 and had become a bishop by 515. It has been conjectured that his see was in Ostrogothic Provence, in which case, if still living, he would have passed into Frankish control in 536, although a bishopric in Italy might also be possible.[57] From such a man, correspondent and relative of Ennodius, the tortuous high style of the letter to Theodebert might be expected, and there is no reason why an episcopate commencing in 515 could not have extended until the later 530s or beyond.

As has been recognized by Professor Wallace-Hadrill, the letter itself is of considerable interest.[58] Its author only alludes, although in a complimentary way, to the king's distinction of birth, something that he wishes to minimize as the source of royal authority. He is equally allusive in respect of the monarch's secular power and dominion, whilst again implying that these were substantial.[59] His concern is rather with the moral responsibilities of kingship, and he stresses that it was not Theodebert's birth that made him a good king. A number of desirable regal virtues are listed that include mercy, generosity and constancy. Above all, humility is singled out as the true source of greatness for those in high places.[60] Through the exercise of these virtues the king's temporal felicity and success as a ruler may be assured, and his secular power and achievement as a conqueror is explicitly linked to the quality of his religious life.

---

[57] *Prosopography of the Later Roman Empire* II, p. 200 (= Aurelianus 8); also *Magni Felicis Ennodi Opera* CCLXX, CCCXC, CDLV, ed. F. Vogel, *MGH,AA* VII, pp. 217, 280, 316–17. J. Sundwall, *Abhandlungen zur Geschichte des ausgehenden Römertums* (Helsinki, 1919), p. 95, offers a different dating of the relevant correspondence.

[58] Wallace-Hadrill *LHK*, pp. 191–2.

[59] *Epistolae Austrasicae* 10, p. 427: 'Praetereo generis tui stimma sidereum', 'Dicam igitur, quod ortum moribus transcendisti, quod originalium culminum celsitudines gloriosa, descendens per natalium lineas, praecessisti,' and 'taceo et illud, quod unicus sceptris, multiplex populis, gente varius, dominatione unitus, solidus regno, diffusus imperio.'

[60] *Epistolae Austrasicae* 10, p. 427: 'Didicisti itaque, quam sit arduum excelsa conscendere, et docuisti, quam sit in sublimibus humilitatem servare.'

Through this, Theodebert was told that he could exceed the achievement of previous rulers and, as both restorer and innovator, be an example to those in the future.

Whilst the king was thus being led to expect triumph and dominion as the fruits of his piety, an additional incentive was presented to him in the form of fear of the Day of Judgement, when power, birth, wealth and status would be held as being of no account.[61] That day, which even the angels fear, should be ever present in the king's mind, although bishop Aurelian expected a favourable outcome of it for him, in which he would receive a crown – 'ubi et pro vobis et pro omnium vestrorum profecto accipiatis coronam'; not a symbol of royalty, but the reward of the saints. The *Profectus omnium vestrorum*, with its reminiscences of the *Profectus Catholicorum* and *Profectus communis* of the letters of Theodebert to Justinian, is striking, and with the context of this letter in the later 530s rather than c.546, raises the question of whether that undertaking, or even the Italian expedition of 539, may not have been in the author's mind. Whatever the truth of that, this was the reward promised in the afterlife if Theodebert displayed the qualities of pity, justice, concord, piety, clemency and humility which the letter extols.

This epistle, despite its brevity, is one of the very first explicit considerations of the duties of the Christian ruler, and is a true 'Mirror of Princes'. Although it stands almost at the head of a new genre, some of its roots are not hard to find. The emphasis on the Day of Judgement as an incentive to a line of conduct, and as something to be kept always present in the mind, is a feature of Gallic preaching of the fifth and early sixth centuries, and may be found in sermons of Faustus of Riez and Caesarius of Arles, although the theoretical recommendation of the use of this theme for popular homilies goes back to the *De Catechizandis Rudibus* of Augustine.[62] It was most fully developed in this Gallic tradition,

---

[61] *Epistolae Austrasicae* 10, p. 428: 'Cogita semper, sacratissime praesul, diem iudicii, diem terroris inerrabilis, diem furoris Domini, diem remunerationis iustorum, diem aeternae laetitiae et perpetuae poene, diem ubi damnatio non accipiet terminum, nec iocunditas habet occasum, diem, inquam, illum, ubi omnes angeli, principatus et potestates de expectatione iudicii contremescent, ubi non erit discretio natalium, sed meritorum, ubi non servus et liber, pauper et potens, sed omnia et in omnibus Christus, ubi acceptio personarum non fiet, ubi divitiae non proderunt, nisi praemisse, ubi etiam et cogitationes cordium discutiende sunt.'

[62] *Caesarii Arelatensis Episcopi Sermones* LVI, LVII, LVIII, ed. G. Morin, *CCSL* CIV, pp. 247–58; of these, nos. 56 and 58 are attributed by Caesarius to Faustus.

and in view of the common ties there of the two great preachers, it was quite possibly a distinctive feature of the spirituality of Lérins.

As for the virtues that the ruler is encouraged to exercise, some of these, such as *concordia* and even *pietas*, are deeply embedded in Roman imperial tradition, though still practically desirable for all their venerability. *Mansuetudo* and *misericordia* were formal attributes of Christian emperors of the fourth century, but *humilitas* never was.[63] This last is probably the most striking of the qualities that Aurelian required of Theodebert, and was not generally something that the church had sought or expected of secular rulers.[64] It was, however, something that Ambrose of Milan had especially valued in his dealings with the emperors of his day. In his letter to Gratian he remarked upon the emperor having written to him with his own hand as a sign of 'lofty humility', and he saw it as a way in which God was honoured through the deference shown to His servant the bishop. He returned to this theme in a later letter to Theodosius I.[65]

Ambrose was one of the few Latin Christian authors to treat of the relationship between the secular ruler and the Church during the later Roman period, not least through his personal encounters with emperors in Milan. Although he produced no formal treatise on the subject, his letter collection, especially the epistles to emperors, could serve as a valuable starting point for those in later centuries seeking to define the Church's attitude towards the new Germanic kings and to find how best to mould those rulers' conceptions of their tasks and offices. That Ambrose's ideas were still a living force in the early sixth century is made clear in a letter to Bishop Nicetius

---

'*Eusebius Gallicanus*', Homilia LXI, ed. F. Glorie, *CCSL* CI A, pp. 696–702. Also see the treatment of the subject by Julianus Pomerius: *Juliani Pomerii De Vita Contemplativa* III. 12, ed. J. B. le Brun des Marettes and D. Mangeant, *Sancti Prosperi Aquitani Opera Omnia* (Paris, 1711; repr. Venice, 1782), pp. 42–3. See also R. J. H. Collins, 'Caesarius von Arles', *Theologische Realenzyklopädie*, VII, pp. 531–6; also *idem*, 'Faustus von Reji', *Theologische Realenzyklopädie*, XI, pp. 63–7.

[63] *Epistolae Austrasicae* 10, p. 428: 'Ostendatis ibi opera misericordie, iustitiae, concordiae, pietatis, mansuetudinis, humilitatis . . .' See K. M. Setton, *Christian Attitudes towards the Emperor in the Fourth Century* (New York, 1967), esp. pp. 71, 89, 98, 146, with references.

[64] cf. Bede's story of Aidan's fears for King Oswin of Deira: *HE* III. 14, pp. 156–7.

[65] Ambrose, *Epistolae*, *PL* XVI, cc. 875–9, 1186–8. Ambrose's *De Fide*, addressed to the Emperor Gratian, may also be of interest here, as for example in its stressing of the theme that victory is more to be achieved by faith than by military skill: *Sancti Ambrosii . . . De Fide* I.3., ed. O. Faller, *CSEL* LXXVIII, p. 5.

of Trier from his correspondent Florianus, abbot of the monastery of Romenus in the diocese of Milan. Florianus names his teachers as having been Ennodius, Caesarius of Arles and Theodehad, his predecessor as abbot, to all of whom he links Ambrose 'meum sacratissimum confessorem', whose disciple he says that he seeks to be.[66] Writings of Ennodius also testify to the dominant position in Milan enjoyed by the cult of Ambrose, whose status was overtly equated with that of Peter in Rome.[67]

This Ambrosian tradition, with its emphasis on the moral obligations of the ruler, and with the stories, recorded in the letters and in the *Vita Ambrosii*, may have exercised a direct influence upon the actions and attitudes of Nicetius of Trier. The principal account of Nicetius's life is to be found in the *Vitae Patrum* of Gregory of Tours, who records that his main informant was Aredius, abbot of Limoges, and formerly *Cancellarius* at the court of Theodebert and pupil of Nicetius.[68] Although the treatment is brief, the episodes that Gregory reports of the bishop confronting the king with his adultery, and at a later date, after the death of Theodebald, of his excommunicating Chlotar I – on more than one occasion – for his injustices, are reminiscent of Ambrose's remonstrances to Valentinian II and excommunication of Theodosius I. It is worthy of note that while Theodebert responded well to Nicetius's rebukes, Chlotar had the bishop exiled.[69]

Nicetius's interventions were not confined to the court of his own ruler or just to Gaul. He also wrote to Queen Chlodesinda, granddaughter of Clovis, and wife of the Lombard king Alboin, to seek to counteract the influence of Arians allowed to preach at their court.[70] More striking is his letter to Justinian I, in which, as a consequence of the dispute over the Three Chapters, he rebuked the emperor for a supposed lapse into heresy.[71] A Gallic counterpart to Ambrose did exist in the person of Martin of Tours, whose status

[66] *Epistolae Austrasicae* 5 (7), p. 415.
[67] *Ennodi Opera* CCCXLVI, CCCLXVI, pp. 252–3, 266.
[68] *Gregorii Turonensis Episcopi Liber Vitae Patrum* XVII, ed. W. Arndt and B. Krusch, *MGH,SRM* I, pp. 727–33; on Aredius see also *Gregory, Historiarum Libri* X.29, pp.522–5.
[69] *Gregorii Liber Vitae Patrum* XVII, p. 730.
[70] *Epistolae Austrasicae* 8, pp. 419–23; see also S. C. Fanning, 'Lombard Arianism reconsidered', *Speculum* LVI (1981), pp. 241–58, which argues on the basis of this letter that the Lombards and their king were not Arians at the time, but that Arian missionaries were active at the court.
[71] *Epistolae Austrasicae* 7, pp. 416–18.

was miraculously vindicated when faced with less than respectful treatment by the Emperor Valentinian I.[72] However, important as his cult was coming to be – and Nicetius from the Limousin can hardly have been unaffected by it – his example was not as fully developed as that of Ambrose in respect of the dealings of bishops with secular rulers, and depended more upon divine sanction through miracles than the resolute statement of principles. Behind both lay images and ideas from the Old Testament, notably from the relations of the Prophets with the Kings of Israel, and in Elijah there was a model for both Ambrose and Nicetius.

The strength of the hold on the court of Theodebert by the Bishop of Trier and like-minded reformers is indicated by its having been purged of adulterers and other such flagrant sinners by the king at Nicetius's behest.[73] Likewise, the reception and preservation of the letter of Aurelian is a further pointer to the dominant climate of opinion. However, there were other elements present, notably Parthenius, who by 544 had become Master of the Offices, the head of the royal administrative apparatus. His reputation in clerical circles was severely compromised by his killing of his wife and her supposed lover, but his presence at the court again emphasizes the importance of the southern Gallic and northern Italian connections of Theodebert and his entourage. Parthenius was a member of the leading Roman family of the Auvergne; he was also a secondary dedicatee of the *Historia Apostolica* of his friend the Roman sub-deacon Arator, whom he had met in the course of an embassy to the Ostrogothic Court at Ravenna; this distinction he shared with Nicetius's correspondent, Abbot Florianus of Romenus.[74]

At stake between the bishop and the Master of the Offices was not merely a divergence over moral issues, but also the matter of royal finance. Nicetius is recorded by Gregory as being an opponent of taxation, while Parthenius is said to have been lynched after Theodebert's death because of the burden of tax that he had imposed. That the Franks are named as the particular opponents of Parthenius in this, and the perpetrators of the deed, may suggest

---

[72] *Sulpicii Severi Dialogorum Libri Duo* II.5, ed. C. Halm, *CSEL* I, pp. 186–7; see also Martin's dealings with the Emperor Magnus Maximus: *Sulpicii Severi Vita Martini Turonensis* 20, 1–8, ed. J. Fontaine, *SC* CXXXIII, pp. 294–8.

[73] *Gregorii Liber Vitae Patrum* XVII, pp. 729–30.

[74] For Parthenius see n. 47 above; also Wood, below, pp. 37–8 for details of his family and background in the Auvergne. *Aratori Subdeaconis Romae De Actibus Apostolorum*, ed. A. P. Mc Kinley, *CSEL*, LXXII, pp. 1–2, 150–3.

that fiscal obligations had been placed upon them, perhaps for the first time. The very fact of Parthenius' unfortunate end indicates that he was successful in imposing the unpopular taxation, but it is likely that Nicetius's concern was to obtain clerical exemption, which was certainly granted in the case of the Auvergne.[75]

Lawmaking, like taxation, is an area in which Theodebert's non-Frankish advisers might have been expected to have given a lead. However, after the considerable codifying and legislating of the Visigoths and Burgundians in a relatively short period in the later fifth and early sixth centuries, the very limited character of similar Frankish legal activity is surprising, not least in its formal dissociation from royal initiative. That the various versions of *Lex Salica* were the work of Clovis and some of his successors, although the identity of the latter is not a matter for uniform agreement, does now seem clear; and, more explicitly, regal supplementary edicts are known.[76] However, the fact that royal attributions were not made in the original texts, and did not appear until the compositon of the 'short prologue' in the later sixth century, is still a cause for interested surprise.[77]

For all of the limitations in form and content of the Frankish code in the sixth century, it might have been expected that Theodebert, recognized as the most Romanized of the Merovingians in many respects, would have had at least some part to play in its development. Arguments that seek to give him such a role depend upon the notion of the later confusion or coalescence of identity between him and his father Theoderic in Germanic literary tradition, for to the latter is attributed responsibility for one of the versions, albeit now lost, of *Lex Salica*, whilst the former is never mentioned in any Frankish legal text.[78] However, not even Theoderic I's role in the complex history of the making of *Lex Salica* is assured.

The attribution of a version to this king is not based upon the testimony of the 'short preface', which rather refers to Clovis (by

[75] Gregory, *Historiarum Libri* III.36, pp. 131–2.

[76] *Pactus Legis Salicae*, ed. K. A. Eckhardt, *MGH,Leg.* IV.i, also the collection of Merovingian Capitularies in *Capitularia Regum Francorum* I, ed. A. Boretius, *MGH,Capit.* II; cf. P. Wormald, 'Lex Scripta and Verbum Regis', in *Early Medieval Kingship*, pp. 105–38; Wallace-Hadrill, *LHK*, pp. 179–81.

[77] Short prologue to *Lex Salica*, pp. 2–3, R. Buchner, *Deutschlands Geschichtsquellen im Mittelalter: Die Rechtsquellen* (Weimar, 1953), pp. 15–21.

[78] F. Beyerle, 'Die beiden süddeutschen Stammesrechte', *ZRG*, germanistische Abteilung, LXXIII (1956), pp. 84–140, esp. pp. 125–7.

implication), a king Childebert and his brother Chlotar; instead it is based upon that of the preface to another law-code, the seventh-century *Lex Baiwariorum*, in which, in a parallel trio, Theoderic fulfils the role of Clovis.[79] On such a basis, a Theodorican version of *Lex Salica* has been sought, and although none of the extant MSS of the code offers such a text, an attempted reconstruction has been based upon variants in two of them.[80]

However, it must be recalled that the starting point for the search was a reference in the preface to *Lex Baiwariorum*. This code shows remarkable resemblances to the much earlier Visigothic *Codex Euricanus* of the later fifth century, and indeed has been used to reconstruct the probable content of that now fragmentary text.[81] In the *Code of Euric*, which has lost its preface, the Visigothic king makes occasional references to the laws of his father. This was the Visigothic ruler Theoderic I (419–51), who was possibly named, and his innovatory lawmaking mentioned, in the lost preface to Euric's code. Thus the reference to the origins of *Lex Baiwariorum* in the legal work of the Frankish king Theoderic may, in view of that text's dependence upon the *Codex Euricanus*, have resulted from a confusion between the identically named Visigothic and Frankish kings. Such a conjecture is perhaps reinforced by the reference in the Bavarian code to the legal compilation being made by the king 'cum esset Catalaunis': the Frankish Theoderic is not otherwise recorded with any such connection, but the Visigothic one died in battle against the Huns on the Catalaunian plains.[82]

Thus the responsibility of Theodebert's father for any part of *Lex Salica* seems most doubtful. Even were this not the case, the idea of the confusion of identity between the two and the notion that one or both of them may have been the model for such later heroes of Germanic literature as Hug-Dietrich are now largely discredited.[83]

---

[79] *Lex Baiuuariorum*, ed. E. de Schwind, *MGH,Leg.* V.ii, pp. 201–2; Buchner, *Rechtsquellen*, pp. 26–9.

[80] *Pactus Legis Salicae*, p. ix: Eckhardt's *Texte Classe B*.

[81] *Legum Codicis Euriciani Fragmenta*, ed. K. Zeumer, *MGH,Leg.* I, pp. 3–27; pp. 28–32 for laws reconstructed on the basis of *Lex Baiuuariorum*; also pp. xvi–xviii, and the study by K. Zeumer, 'Geschichte der westgothischen Gesetzgebung', *Neues Archiv*, XXIII (1897), pp. 419–516, XXIV (1898), pp. 39–117 and 571–630, XXVI (1900), pp. 91–149. See also the edition and study of the text in A. d'Ors, *El Codigo de Eurico* (Estudios Visigoticos II: Rome, Madrid, 1960).

[82] Stein, *Histoire du Bas-Empire*, I, p. 335.

[83] For the original conception see G. Kurth, *Histoire Poétique des Mérovingiens* (Paris, 1893), pp. 337–8, 375–8. See now Tessier, *Baptême de Clovis*, pp. 173–4. E.

Such negative conclusons in respect of the lawmaking activity of the line of Theoderic and Theodebert, which was most open to Roman influence, must indicate that contrary to expectation and to what had clearly been a matter of some importance in the preceding Visigothic and Burgundian kingdoms in Gaul, this did not play an important role in the interests and aspirations of these Frankish rulers and their advisors.[84]

On the other hand, the making of ecclesiastical regulations was clearly of great concern, if not to the kings directly then to their bishops. Like his father before him, Theodebert allied with Childebert I against Chlotar, possibly because the latter, who had married a Thuringian princess, had aspirations in the area of new Frankish expansion to the east of the Rhine. Under the aegis of Childebert a series of councils was held, principally at Orléans, also attended by bishops of sees under Theodebert's rule, which represents the only sustained attempt at regular conciliar activity, and the use of it to reform and regulate the church in Gaul, during the Merovingian period.[85]

Whatever the restraints that limited royal initiative in lawmaking, Theodebert and his councellors were not afraid to innovate in respect of coinage, something for which they are justly famed. This king was the first Germanic ruler to infringe what had been an imperial monopoly and put his own name and titles on gold coins

---

Zöllner, *Geschichte der Franken*, p. 86, retains belief in the identification of Theoderic I with *Hugdietrich*.

[84] The same apparent detachment of royal interest and control is equally true of the coinage. Of all the major Germanic kingdoms it is only in that of the Franks that the minting of coins is apparently not a royal monopoly, the Anglo-Saxons imitating them in this, in that the king's name, image and title are not to be found on most extant issues. Much remains controversial in the study of Frankish numismatics; it is possible that the first overtly regal coins are the issues of Theodebert, although J. Lafaurie, 'Monnaies d'or attribuables à Thierry Ier, fils de Clovis', *Bulletin de la Société Nationale des Antiquaires de France* (1968), pp. 30–9, argues for the existence of coins of Theoderic. The single extant coin of Chlotar I is discussed below (p. 30) and as the coins of a king Childebert probably belong rather to Childebert II than to Childebert I (apart from a unique piece linking the king's name with that of Chramn, which is almost certainly a forgery) all of the, admittedly sparse, early Frankish regal issues have ties to the dynasty of Theoderic or to Italy.

[85] *Concilia Galliae*, ed. C. de Clercq, *CCSL* CXLVIII A, pp. 98–161, including the important Council of Clermont of November 535, held in Theodebert's realm. Is it coincidental that this series of councils appears to come to an end after a final gathering in 549?

which in matters of weight, fineness and style otherwise adhered to contemporary Byzantine models.[86] Not even the Ostrogoths and the Vandals, who had previously issued bronze and silver pieces in their rulers' names, had taken this step with gold.[87] The Burgundians seem to have gone as far as putting the monograms or abbreviations of the names of their last kings on the reverses of their otherwise standard pseudo-imperial *solidi*.[88] As is well known, the Frankish move was commented on by Procopius, who suggested (in a reference to the Persian rulers who respected the Byzantine monopoly) that gold coins not bearing the emperor's effigy would be unacceptable in commerical transactions, even amongst barbarians.[89]

Whether or not Theodebert's coins played a substantial role in commerce is uncertain, nor was this necessarily their prime purpose. The coins raise many questions, most of which remain unanswerable due to lack of information. Their places of minting can in most cases not be determined, despite ingenious efforts so to do, nor have sufficient been found in recorded locations to permit any suggestions as to their circulation.[90] It is clear that they were well made, with attention given to quality of design and of gold content; and their reverses bear a wide variety of marks, probably indicative of their places of issue, which are much closer to Ostrogothic monetary practices than anything found previously in Gaul. The mints that made them, and of these there were clearly several, were obviously competently organized and supervised, staffed by moneyers experienced in their craft and able to produce excellent copies of their Byzantine models, altering them in line with changes in the imperial prototypes, and yet able to innovate in respect of new designs and legends when called upon so to do.

Some of the titles and images employed in this coinage are worthy of particular note. The use of *Victor* on the obverse to

[86] M. Prou, *Catalogue des monnaies françaises de la Bibliothèque Nationale: les monnaies mérovingiennes* (Paris, 1982), pp. xxix–xxxv, 9–16.

[87] W. Wroth, *Catalogue of the Coins of the Vandals, Ostrogoths and Lombards in the British Museum* (London, 1911); also F. F. Kraus, *Die Münzen Odovacers und des Ostgotenreiches in Italien* (Halle, 1928).

[88] W. Tomasini, *The Barbaric Tremissis in Spain and Southern France, Anastasius to Leovigild* (New York, 1964), J. M. Merrick and D. M. Metcalf, 'Milliprobe analysis of some problematic Burgundian and other gold coins of the early Middle Ages', *Archaeometry*, XI (1969), pp. 61–6.

[89] Procopius, *History of the Wars* VII.xxxiii.5–6, pp. IV, 438.

[90] J. Lafaurie, 'Les routes commerciales indiquées par les trésors et trouvailles monétaires mérovingiens', *Settimane*, VIII (1961), pp. 231–78, esp. pp. 244–5.

accompany the king's name and more standard epithets of *Rex* or *Dominus Noster* is intersting, and on the analogy of the three-*solidus* triumphal medal of Theoderic the Ostrogoth is likely to signify *Victor Gentium*, a term implying, through the varied meanings of *gentes*, not just a defender of frontiers against the barbarians beyond, but also a protector of orthodoxy.[91] Such an image accords well both with the conceptions of royal duties held by the king's clerical advisors, and with that of the *Profectus Catholicorum*, the proposed Byzantine and Frankish undertaking against the Arian Ostrogoths.

This idea is made more explicit on the reverse of a single extant coin, which bears what was the standard legend on late Roman and early Byzantine coins and also on those of Theodebert, *Victoria Augustorum*, but placed around an original design. This takes the form of the figure of the king striding to the right bearing a great palm of victory over his shoulder, carrying a small image of Victory, and treading a recumbent barbarian under his feet.[92] The design combines late Roman depictions of the emperor, usually mounted, spurning a fallen enemy beneath him, and contemporary Ostrogothic representations, to be found on the reverses of various bronze coins, of their king Theodehad striding to the right bearing a shield and a spear over his shoulder.[93] Theodebert's moneyers replaced the spear with a palm of victory and put the barbarian, likewise from Roman imagery, under the king's feet, thus transforming the pedestrian design of the Ostrogothic coin into a striking image of the *Victor Gentium*. (See Plate I.)

The existence of varying types in the Theodebert gold *solidi* that exactly match changes in the designs of their Byzantine equivalents helps with the dating of his issues. The first imperial type, continuing that which had been standard in Constantinople since the early sixth century, was altered in the Byzantine mints in 538 or 539, when the facing helmeted bust of the emperor with a spear over his right shoulder was replaced by a new design in which a globe surmounted by a cross took the place of the sphere. However, the reverse image of Victory holding a long cross remained unaltered

---

[91] cf. the images displayed in P. Courcelle, *Histoire littéraire des grandes invasions germaniques* (Paris, 3rd edn, 1964), pl. 5. For the medal of Theoderic the Ostrogoth (the reverse legend reads: REX THEODERICUS VICTOR GENTIUM) see Wroth, *Coins of the Vandals, Ostrogoths and Lombards*, frontis. and pp. xxxi, 54.

[92] Prou, *Monnaies Mérovingiennes* 56, p. 15.

[93] Wroth, *Coins of the Vandals, Ostrogoths and Lombards*, pl. IX. 15.

until 545, when the cross was replaced by a *labarum*.[94] As all of these features appear on coins of Theodebert, although his reign ended within two or three years of the initiation of the last of them, it looks as if his moneyers responded remarkably quickly to the alterations in their Byzantine models. That the coin just described, with the novel image of the *Victor Gentium*, has the obverse design of the pre-539 imperial issues, would thus seem to place its minting early in the reign, and indeed it might well be linked to the Italian invasion of 539, to which the message of its reverse would relate it.

Another so far unique coin, which from its obverse design can be dated to the early years of the reign, and which may also be connected with the Italian expedition, has a reverse legend of *Pax et Libertas*.[95] Such a theme, like that of the *Victor Gentium*, would certainly have a meaning in the context of the breakdown of the Ostrogothic order in Italy in the wake of the Byzantine invasion, and might represent a promise of the restoration of those benefits once conferred by the regime of the Ostrogothic king Theoderic, though now in a Catholic guise. It is by no means clear, of course, that these coins were minted in Italy or were intended for Italian circulation, but the nearest parallels to them in the mint organization which they imply, and in their imagery, have to be sought south of the Alps. It is interesting in this context that the only other Frankish precious metal coinage of this period to bear a royal image and title is an issue of silver by Chlotar I, which is very skilfully modelled on a Justinianic prototype from the mint of Ravenna; possibly it was minted after he had succeeded Theodebald and before the expulsion of the Franks from Italy by Narses, i.e. in the years 555 or 556.[96]

Theodebert's Italian venture of 539 is, on Byzantine presentation, seen as a large scale and violent raid, but its purposes may have been more sophisticated, and more in line with what both the connections and the character of his court might lead us to expect. Despite the lack of specific information from the Frankish side, something of this may be glimpsed when the episode is put in context. In 538, with the siege of Rome broken and the collapse of the Ostrogothic realm apparently imminent. Bishop Datius of Milan appealed to

[94] P. Whitting, *Byzantine Coins* (London, 1973), p. 107, pls. 77–9, 102–5.
[95] Prou, *Monnaies Mérovingiennes* 55, pp. 14–15; J. P. Callu, 'Pax et Libertas: une légende monétaire de Théodebert I', *Mélanges de numismatique, d'archéologie et d'histoire offerts à Jean Lafaurie* (Paris, 1980), pp. 189–99. See Plate I.
[96] Prou, *Monnaies Mérovingiennes* 37, p. 9. cf. Whitting, *Byzantine Coins*, pls. 65–6, for the Justinian I issue.

Belisarius for the despatch of a small force which he felt would detach not only the city, but all of Liguria, from Ostrogothic rule. This requested army, some thousand strong, made its way by sea from Rome to Genoa and thence inland to cross the Po west of Pavia, where they defeated the Ostrogothic garrison, and on to occupy Milan without further resistance.[97]

Bishop Datius had been precipitate. King Wittigis sent his nephew Uraias to recover the city, and obtained the aid of an army of Burgundians for so doing. This force, reputedly of 10,000 men, is said by Procopius to have been sent by Theodebert, a statement accepted by modern historians – although the Byzantine author also adds that the Burgundians themselves claimed to be acting of their own free will, something we might be advised to believe. Their efforts, and those of the Ostrogoths, led to the recapture of the city. Procopius' claim that it was then levelled to the ground is clearly nonsensical, as the present survival of pre-sixth-century buildings, and his own statement that the Ostrogoths garrisoned it, would indicate. An imperial relief force meanwhile remained idle on the Po, due to command rivalries between Belisarius and Narses.

This, then, is the context of Theodebert's invasion. It is usually held that he brought his forces across the central Alps by one of the great passes, but there is reason to believe that a different route was employed.[98] The continuator of the sixth-century Latin Byzantine chronicler Count Marcellinus refers to the Franks sacking Genoa, while Procopius records that they crossed the Po prior to setting upon the Ostrogoths, who were expecting them to have come as allies, at Pavia.[99] Such an approach to the city would only make sense if the Frankish army was coming from the west, and the reference to Genoa would substantiate the view that their line of march was from the Mediterranean coast. This thus parallels the route taken by the small army sent by Belisarius to aid Bishop Datius.

That Theodebert attacked both the Byzantines and the Ostrogoths in the vicinity of Pavia has been taken as a sign of the ruthlessness and lack of scruple of the king and his followers, that Procopius

[97] Procopius, *History of the Wars* VI.vii.35–8, VI.xii.26–41, VI.xiii.4, pp. III, 356–8, 392–6, IV, 64.

[98] G. Loehlein, 'Die Alpen und Italienpolitik der Merowinger im VI Jahrhundert', *Erlanger Abhandlungen zur mittleren und neuen Geschichte* (1932), p. 34.

[99] *Marcellini V. C. Comitis Chronicon*, ed. T. Mommsen, *MGH,AA* XI, p. 106 (*s.a.* 539); Procopius, *History of the Wars* VI.xxv.11, pp. IV, 86.

would wish to have us believe in. Such an impression is hardly
concordant with the image of Theodebert in Frankish sources, both
in the way that he wished to present himself in his official correspondence, or indeed in his coinage, and in the way that he was
seen and treated by his Gallo-Roman and Italian advisors. Before
assuming that the episode represents the breaking out of the essential barbarism either of his character or that of the Franks, or that it
was due to the impossibility of controlling such savage elements in
the army as perhaps exemplified by the Alamannic contingent, it is
important to note both the existence of close contacts between some
prominent Milanese and Theodebert's court, and the recent failure
of the Byzantines to save Liguria from a devastating Ostrogothic
attack. Is it not then conceivable that Theodebert and his Franks
were there at the behest of those same provincials, who had in the
previous year appealed to Belisarius with such disastrous consequences? The unprecedented and unrepeated expedition into Italy
might thus have an intelligible explanation, and King Theodebald's
angry response to the Emperor Justinian's denunciation of his father
as an oathbreaker be justified. [100] The events of these years and of the
following decade may also make it easier for us to understand the
reasons for the subsequent success of the Lombards in entrenching
themselves in this same region.

It should not be thought that Theodebert was unique amongst
the Frankish kings of his period in his ability to respond to the
opportunities opened to him by the assimilation of Roman traditions and the close association of the Church. Nor was he alone in
receiving the counsel of his bishops. Remigius of Rheims had told
Clovis to listen to his bishops, and warned him not to forget divine
judgement. Interestingly, this letter formed the second item in the
collection of texts, also including those of bishop Aurelian to
Theodebert and the remains of that monarch's correspondence,
which were put together in a Rhineland centre, probably Metz,
during the reign of Childebert II, and which constitute the *Epistolae
Austrasicae*. [101] Theodebert's uncle, Childebert I, had patronized
church councils, founded monasteries, and was also the recipient of

---

[100] *Epistolae Austrasicae* 18, p. 437. Theodebald calls his father '. . . diversarum
gentium domitorem . . .' (l. 16).
[101] *Epistolae Austrasicae* 2, pp. 408–9. For the collection see Gundlach, 'Die
Sammlung der *Epistolae Austrasicae*', and also the introduction to the original *MGH*
edition (see n. 5 above).

four extant letters from Pope Pelagius I; if not in the pages of Gregory of Tours, then in later Frankish ecclesiastical tradition, his memory was a good one.[102] However, in his power and, more lastingly, in his reputation, Theodebert stood out above the other kings of his day. His achievements were real ones, although some of his territorial gains did not prove long lasting, but perhaps the towering stature that contemporaries and later sixth-century commentators ascribe to him was the product of his regal style.[103] In his far flung concerns, his ability to be more than the war-leader of his people, his capacity to respond to the ideals presented to him by his churchmen and to treat the emperor as an equal, he articulated some of the newly found self-confidence of the Frankish *regnum*. Building on his predecessors' work, he was in a position to take advantage more fully than they of the opportunities made available through the Roman and above all Christian traditions of the Late Empire, and ultimately his greatness was that of his subjects, both Gallo-Roman and Frankish, as they looked upon themselves in the light of a new dawn of optimism and assurance.

---

[102] Papal letters: *Pelagii I Papae Epistulae Quae Supersunt*, ed. P. M. Gassó and C. M. Batlle (Montserrat, 1956) 3, 6, 7, 8, pp. 6–10, 18–19, 20–5, 26–7. For Childebert's later reputation see the exhortatory letter of an unnamed bishop to either Clovis II or Sigebert III, *c*.645; *Epistolae Aevi Merovingici, CCSL* CXVII, p. 493.

[103] In addition, when Childebert II (574–96), under whom the eastern division of Francia, the kingdom of Austrasia, took on much of its distinctive shape, named his two sons Theoderic and Theodebert, his commemoration thereby of his two great predecessors was hardly unintentional: *The Fourth Book of the Chronicle of Fredegar*, 5, 7, ed. J. M. Wallace-Hadrill (London, 1960), p. 6.

2

The Ecclesiastical Politics of Merovingian Clermont

IAN WOOD

The people of Merovingian Gaul were well placed to recognize an ideal bishop. His career was defined by the canons of church councils, his virtues enumerated in many an episcopal epitaph and his power was apparent in numerous hagiographical anecdotes. He was chaste and extremely cautious about the sort of woman who entered the episcopal residence; he was generous, and therefore kept no dogs, in case they restricted access to episcopal hospitality. Above all he was a patron to his city. At the most mundane level this meant that he exercised pastoral care, helping the poor, the widows and the orphans and in times of crisis arranging protection or famine relief. Here, as elsewhere, episcopal virtue was Roman virtue writ large: even eloquence was expected of a bishop. A bishop's position, however, was dependent not only on his virtue but also on the authority inherent in his office, albeit not the full legal authority envisaged originally by Constantine. Once comital power was added, as sometimes happened, we have what the Germans have termed *Bischofsherrschaft*.[1]

Nevertheless, because the evidence for *Bischofsherrschaft* comes primarily from evidence which is concerned to elevate episcopal status, it is instructive to look not at the rhetoric and legislation, but at the ecclesiastical history of a single diocese, the most consistently

[1] Wallace-Hadrill *EMH*, p. 3; M. Heinzelmann, *Bischofsherrschaft in Gallien*, Beihefte der *Francia*, V (Munich, 1976); for the power of bishops: F. Prinz, 'Die bischöfliche Stadtherrschaft im Frankenreich vom 5. bis zum 7. Jahrhundert', *HZ*, CCXVII (1974), pp. 1–35; for legislation on episcopal behaviour see the list in *Concilia Galliae*, ed. C. de Clercq, *CCSL* CXLVIII A, p. 343.

documented of the Merovingian period being that of the *civitas Arvernorum*, the see of the bishops of Clermont. The richness of documentation might seem to imply that Clermont is an exception, but there are no obvious peculiarities about the diocese. Despite the shrine of St Julian (which in any case lies some sixty kilometres to the south of the *civitas* capital), Clermont was no Tours; its saints could not compete with Martin. Nor was it a city frequented by kings; its episcopal history is not unduly influenced by royal interest. That it should be well documented is in fact pure accident. Sidonius Apollinaris' association with the Auvergne began with his marriage; Gregory of Tours' ended with his election to the episcopate; according to Krusch the *Passio Praeiecti* was written by a Lombard living in Burgundy.[2] Unlike Rheims, Clermont had no Flodoard; its source material is not the product of a single interest. The particular feature of the Auvergne which most fascinated post-Roman authors was, in fact, not its ecclesiastical history or its politics, but its scenery. Sidonius described the region as being 'soft to the feet of the traveller, fruitful to the tiller, delightful to the hunter; the ridges of the mountains surround it with pasture, their sides with vineyards, the earthy parts with country houses, the rocky parts with fortresses, the shady woods with coverts, the open parts with cultivation, the hollows with springs and the steep slopes with streams; in short' – and here Sidonius was talking from experience – 'such is the place that, when but once seen, it often induces many visitors to forget their native land.' So great was the fame of the countryside that the author of the *Passio Praeiecti*, who had probably never seen it, waxed eloquent on the subject, and Childebert I exclaimed: 'Fain would I see with my own eyes the Limagne of Auvergne, which men call so bright and so gay.'[3] As often happens, fog obscured the view.

The Limagne is the basin of the Allier, with its rich volcanic soil, stretching from Trezelle in the north to Brioude in the south (see figure 1). On either side this valley is overshadowed by high ranges

[2] *Passio Praeiecti*, ed. B. Krusch, *MGH,SRM* V, p. 219. See also I. N. Wood, 'The *Vita Columbani* and Merovingian hagiography', *Peritia*, I (1982), p. 68. I would now suggest that the author was a monk of St Amarin.

[3] Sidonius Apollinaris, *Poems and Letters*, ep. IV.21., ed. W. B. Anderson (2 vols Loeb, 1963–5), pp. II, 143; *Passio Praeiecti* 14, p. 234; Gregory of Tours, *Gregorii Episcopi Turonensis Historiarum Libri Decem* III. 9, ed. B. Krusch and W. Levison, *MGH, SRM* I (2), p. 106; M. Rouche, *L'Aquitaine des Wisigoths aux Arabes 418–781* (Paris, 1979), pp. 183–4, 395.

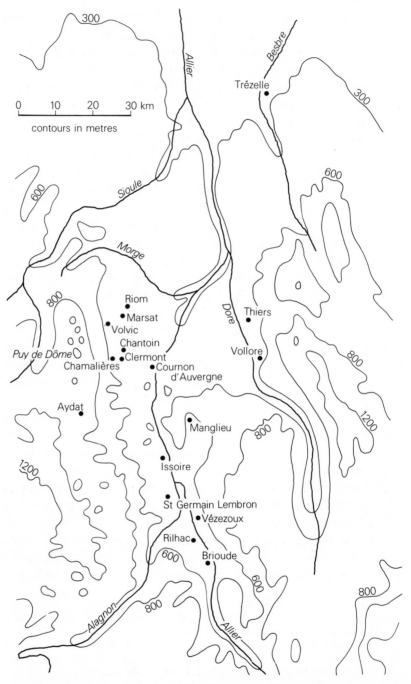

FIGURE 1 *Aristocratic interests in the Limagne d'Auvergne*

of hills, which almost meet at Issoire, dividing the plain into two. The northern section, the Great Limagne, is overlooked by the city of Clermont, situated at the foot of the Puy-de-Dôme. To the south of Issoire is a smaller plain dominated by Brioude and the shrine of St Julian and beyond that lies the boundary with Javols and Rodez. The hills provided good pasture; even Sidonius commented on the presence of shepherds on his estate at Avitacum, and Gregory had stories to tell of the cattle of St Julian pastured in the mountain *saltus*.[4] The real wealth of the Auvergne, however, lay in the corn-fields of the Limagne, Already by the fifth century the plain was densely populated; Gregory of Tours provides an occasional glimpse of village communities with their patrons, alive and dead.[5] One indication of the importance of some of these valley settlements is the presence in them of aristocratic clerics. Epachius, priest in Riom, was notable as a senator and as an alcoholic; perhaps he is to be identified with Eparchius, son of Ruricius of Limoges and cleric in the Auvergne, who is known to have fallen foul of his bishop, Aprunculus.[6]

The recurrence of certain personal names among the clergy whom we meet in the pages of Sidonius, Gregory, the *Passio Praeiecti* and the *Vita Boniti*, might indicate that many of them came from a small group of aristocratic families. Names alone, however, are not enough to prove kinship and it is therefore more rewarding to concentrate on individuals who can be assigned with some certainty to the well-known families of the Aviti and of Gregory of Tours; a third group, the descendents of Hortensius, will concern us later. We may guess that Eparchius, Sidonius' predecessor, was related to the emperor Avitus, who shared his name, but we are on firm ground with Sidonius himself, who was the emperor's son-in-law. Sidonius' own son, Apollinaris, although at first something of a philistine and an adventurer, seems to have experienced a genuine conversion to letters and religion and even attained the episcopate

<hr />

[4] Sidonius, ep.II.2., pp. I, 428, 434; Gregory, *Liber de Virtutibus Sancti Juliani* 17, ed. B. Krusch, *MGH,SRM* I, pp. 571–2.
  [5] G. Fournier, *Le Peuplement rural en Basse Auvergne durant le haut Moyen Age* (Paris, 1962), pp. 85–90; Gregory of Tours, *Liber in Gloria Martyrum* 51, 66, 85–6, ed. B. Krusch, *MGH,SRM* I, pp. 524, 533, 545–6; Gregory, *Liber Vitae Patrum* XIII.3, ed. B. Krusch, *MGH,SRM* I, pp. 716–17.
  [6] Gregory, *Gloria Martyrum* 86, p. 546; Ruricius, *Epistulae* II.56–7, ed. G. Luetjohann, *MGH,AA* VIII, pp. 347–8.

for three or four months in c.515.[7] After the death of Apollinaris the family suffered a series of misfortunes. Alcima, Apollinaris' sister, and Placidina, his wife, angered the long-dead saint Antolianus while building a new church for him; the church was never completed. Perhaps because of the decline in his family's influence, Arcadius, Apollinaris' son, invited Childebert to annex the Auvergne in c.525 and as a result he brought disaster to the *civitas*. Theuderic took his revenge on the district and on Apollinaris' family. Alcima and Placidina were declared exiles and their goods were confiscated; Arcadius fled to Bourges and later became a henchman of Childebert, involving himself in the murder of Chlodomer's sons. [8] Perhaps because of their responsibility for Theuderic's invasion, perhaps also because of their opposition to his hero Quintianus, Gregory did not like the direct descendents of Sidonius. From the *Historiarum Libri Decem* the reader might well conclude that the influence of the Aviti was finished in the Auvergne, although Venantius Fortunatus reveals that Apollinaris' daughter contracted a good marriage to Leontius, later bishop of Bordeaux, and Gregory records the career of Parthenius, grandson of the emperor Avitus, and tax-collector for Theudebert, with some disdain, dismissing him as the murderer of a friend and of his own wife; the historian seems to have regarded his being lynched by a mob at Trier as a just end.[9]

Two later bishops of Clermont, however, were called Avitus and although the case for associating them with the *gens Aviti* depends primarily on their names, there are additional reasons for making this connection. People undoubtedly attached themselves to particular saints; Gregory of Tours was regarded as an *alumnus* of St Julian by Venantius Fortunatus, and as such he went to Vienne to see the tomb of Julian's master Ferreolus.[10] When the possessed at

[7] Sidonius, ep.IX.1, pp. II, 502–4; Ruricius II.26, pp. 332–3; Avitus, *Epistulae* 51, ed. R. Peiper, *MGH,AA* VI.2, pp. 79–81. Gregory, *Historiarum Libri* II.21, III.2, pp. 67, 98; *Gloria Martyrum* 44, p. 518; *Vitae Patrum* IV.1, pp. 674–5.

[8] Gregory, *Historiarum Libri* III.9–13, 18, pp. 106–10, 117–20; despite Arcadius's flight to Bourges, I find it difficult to accept Rouche's hypothesis that he became bishop of Bourges: Rouche, *L'Aquitaine des Wisigoths aux Arabes*, p. 56. For the date, *ibid.* p. 491, n. 13, although Rouche's idea of a second expedition is based on a possible misunderstanding of Gregory. *Virtutes S. Juliani* 23, p. 574, refers not to Gallus's episcopate, but to his *adolescentia*.

[9] K. F. Stroheker, *Der senatorische Adel im spätantiken Gallien* (Tübingen, 1948), no. 307; Gregory *Historiarum Libri* III.36, pp. 131–2.

[10] Venantius Fortunatus, *Opera Poetica* V.3, ed. F. Leo, *MGH,AA* IV.1, p. 106; Gregory, *Virtutes S. Juliani* 2, pp. 564–5.

Brioude cried out that not only was Julian present, but also Martin of Tours, Privatus of Javols, Ferreolus of Vienne, Symphorian of Autun and Saturninus of Toulouse, it is likely that they were giving a precise indication of the religious attachments of the leading members of the congregation.[11] Of course saint cults, particularly major saint cults, became associated with more than one family group; by the time the *Libellus de Ecclesiis Claromontanis* was drawn up in the tenth century, there appears to have been no clear correlation between individual families and particular cults. The religious concerns of Sidonius' decendents and of the two bishops Avitus, however, overlap exactly. The failure of Alcima and Placidina to complete the church of Antolianus seems almost symbolic of the family's decline. Their unfinished church was dangerous, but it was left untouched until Avitus I ordered that it be dismantled; the demolition was miraculous. A century later Avitus II had the bodies of Cassius, Victorinus and Antolianus translated. In fact by this time the cult was widespread and Praeiectus had written a *libellus* on the three saints. Nevertheless the coincidence of personal names and saint cult allows us to see Avitus II and, therefore, his brother Bonitus as members of the same episcopal dynasty as Avitus I and ultimately Eparchius, Sidonius and Apollinaris.[12]

No other Auvergnat family can be shown to have dominated the see so successfully and for so long. Gregory of Tours' great-uncle Inpetratus, however, was a priest in Clermont and his uncle Gallus, became bishop.[13] Gregory's niece married Nicetius, *comes* of the Auvergne and later *dux* in Clermont, Rodez and Uzès,[14] but further episcopal connections are not apparent unless a mid-seventh-century bishop also called Gallus is accepted as being of the same family. Gallus II is said to have translated the body of Amabilis to the church of St Benignus, probably at Riom. Gregory was interested both in the cult of Amabilis and also, more particularly, in that of Benignus, who had been invented by his relative and namesake, Gregory of Langres. Moreover, the historian's mother patronized the cult of Benignus' supposed master, St Polycarp, as celebrated at

[11] *ibid.* 30, pp. 576–7.
[12] Gregory, *Gloria Martyrum* 64, pp. 531–2; *Passio Praeiecti* 9, 17, pp. 230–1, 236; *Vita Boniti* 4, ed. B. Krusch, *MGH,SRM* VI, p. 121.
[13] Gregory, *Vitae Patrum* VI, pp. 681–2; *Virtutes S. Juliani* 23, p. 574.
[14] Gregory, *Historiarum Libri* VIII.18, p. 385.

Riom.[15] Common interest in a particular saint strengthens the case for accepting Gallus as a member of the family of Gregory of Tours.

The interests of these two episcopal families were not confined to the Auvergne. Relations of Sidonius could be found in most of Gaul and in northern Italy and they included bishops of Limoges, Tours, Vienne, Valence and Bordeaux.[16] Gregory's family, apart from providing the majority of his predecessors at Tours, could boast bishops in Lyons and Langres.[17] These two episcopal dynasties were exceptional, but even the disreputable Cautinus, Gallus I's successor at Clermont, was cousin to a bishop of Bourges.[18] Other Auvergnat families held secular office elsewhere; Palladius, son of Britianus, became *comes* in Javols.[19] In the next century Praeiectus' opponent, Hector, a man with landed interests in the Auvergne, was *patricius* in Marseilles, as was Bonitus before he became bishop.[20] The protagonists in the ecclesiastical history of the Auvergne were not members of a backwoods aristocracy.

At the same time, from the little that we can deduce about their landed interests, these families all held estates in a relatively small area in the neighbourhood of Clermont (fig. 1). Eparchius seems to have founded a monstery at Chantoin, although this may have been on ecclesiastical property.[21] Sidonius lived at Aydat, while a contemporary, the *dux* Victorius, built a church at St-Germain Lembron and set up columns at St Julian's, Brioude; he is probably to be associated with the *Castrum Victoriacum*, now identified as Rilhac.[22] Gregory of Tours' family also had close links with Brioude and with Riom, which may have been the nearest centre to the cornfields they held in the Limagne. Gregory's uncle, Gallus, fled as a child to the monastery of Cournon where Palladius, *comes* of

[15] *Acta Sanctorum, Novembris* I, pp. 349–50; Gregory of Tours, *Liber in Gloria Confessorum* 30, ed. B. Krusch *MGH,SRM* I, pp. 766–7; *Historiarum Libri* X.31, p. 535; *Gloria Martyrum* 50, 85, pp. 522–4, 545–6; *Passio Prima Sancti Benigni Martyris* 2, in *Acta Sanctorum, Novembris* I, p. 152.

[16] Stroheker, *Senatorische Adel*, nn. 23, 60, 219, 267, 327.

[17] *ibid.*, nn. 182, 259, 337, 385.

[18] Gregory, *Historiarum Libri* IV.31, p. 166.

[19] *ibid.* IV.39, p. 170.

[20] *Passio Praeiecti* 23, p. 239; *Vita Boniti* 3, pp. 120–1.

[21] Gregory, *Historiarum Libri* II. 21, p. 67, and for earlier ecclesiastical links with the site, I, 44, p. 29.

[22] Sidonius, ep.II.2., pp. I, 416–34; Gregory, *Historiarum Libri* II.20, pp. 65–6; P. Hedde, 'La Famille gallo-romaine des Férreol et le Brivadois', *Almanach de Brioude*, LIX (1979), pp. 73–9.

Javols, was later buried.[23] In the seventh century, bishop Genesius founded a monastery at Manglieu and a namesake, the nunnery at Chamalières.[24] Praeiectus was brought up at Vézezoux and was educated at Issoire, where Cautinus had once been archdeacon. He was martyred at Volvic.[25]

All these places lie between Riom and Brioude and the majority to the north of Issoire. Brioude itself is somewhat out on a limb and, despite the shrine of St Julian, it is surprisingly insignificant in the history of the diocese. Gallus instituted annual pilgrimages to the shrine, but no bishop is known to have been drawn from the clergy of St Julian, whereas both Cautinus and Praeiectus had served the church at Issoire. We may be led to overestimate Brioude because of Gregory. The cult of St Julian was well known and the shrine was well endowed; during the Rogations and on the festival of the saint it was of major importance. Nevertheless, for most of the year it was a backwater.[26] Geographically, however, it has much in common with many of the places associated with the Auvergnat aristocracy, lying at the edge of the plain. Other aristocratic sites are to be found in the immediately adjacent hills, although sometimes at a considerable altitude; Aydat is 825 metres above sea level, almost 500 metres above the Limagne. Doubtless this distribution reflects an economic interest both in the wealth of the plain and the upland pasture.[27] It also indicates that the influential families in the Auvergne lived within easy distance of the *civitas* capital.

Despite the existence of local aristocratic families with strong clerical interests it was possible for outsiders to gain election to the episcopate. Sidonius' successor Aprunculus had been bishop of Langres, but escaped from the Burgundians to Clermont; later Apollinaris' rival and successor, the African Quintianus, fled from

[23] Gregory, *Gloria Martyrum* 47, 83, 85, pp. 520–1, 544–6; *Virtutes S. Juliani* 23–6, 46a, pp. 574–5, 581–2; but see Fournier, *Le Peuplement rural*, p. 210, n. 25; *Vitae Patrum* VI.1, p. 680; *Historiarum Libri* IV.39, p. 171; Gregory may also have a connection with Marsat: *Gloria Martyrum* 8, p. 493.

[24] *Vita Boniti* 16, pp. 127–8: 'coenobium in propria constituit gleba'; *Passio Praeiecti* 15, pp. 234–5.

[25] *ibid.* 2, 29, 39, pp. 227, 242–3, 247; Gregory, *Gloria Confessorum* 29, p. 766; P-F. Fournier, 'Vézezoux, patrie de Saint Priest', *Almanach de Brioude*, LII (1972), pp. 147–56. I am grateful to M. G. Fournier for guidance over material published in the local periodicals of the Auvergne.

[26] Gregory, *Virtutes S. Juliani* is, however, a tribute to the vitality of the cult; see also Flodoard, *Historia Remensis Ecclesiae* II.6., ed. J. Heller and G. Waitz, *MGH,SS* XIII, p. 455.

[27] Rouche, *L'Aquitaine des Wisigoths aux Arabes*, pp. 215–20.

Visigothic Rodez, where he had held episcopal office. Interestingly, he seems to have taken his relatives with him on his travels.[28] The seventh century may have seen other outsiders in episcopal office, almost certainly Bonitus' successor Nordobert was one such,[29] but in general the Merovingian bishops of Clermont seem to have been men with local contacts, even if, like Gallus I and Bonitus, their careers had taken them elsewhere.

The clerical ambitions of the Auvergnat nobility are clearly reflected in their prosopography; the difficulties they faced in achieving those ambitions lead us into the histories of episcopal elections and of subsequent opposition to bishops. The ideal procedure for election is set out, not always clearly, in eight of the Merovingian church councils. All affirmed directly or indirectly the importance of election by the laity and clergy of the *civitas*.[30] The candidates were not to be laymen, nor were they to use simony, lay *patrocinium* or violence to gain the episcopate; they were to be elected on merit.[31] The bishop-elect was to be consecrated in his diocesan centre by the metropolitan, who was occasionally envisaged as having some influence in the election itself, together with his *conprovinciales*.[32] The most significant variation in the description of procedure concerns the role of the king; at Orléans (549) the king's will, the *voluntas regis*, is acknowledged (but not defined), while at Paris (556–73) royal commands are explicitly condemned. In his edict following the council of Paris (614), Chlothar II emphasized the importance of royal consent before consecration and also made provision for the appointment of bishops from the royal household, although the canons do not deal with either of these issues. Some have seen in this legislation evidence of conflict between royal and clerical interest and have consequently interpreted other regulations in this light; the ruling at Clichy (626–7) that only a local should be elected might be taken as an attack on appointments made by

[28] Gregory, *Historiarum Libri* II.23, 36, III.2, pp. 69, 84–5, 98–9; *Vitae Patrum* IV.1, 3, pp. 674–6.
[29] Rouche, *L'Aquitaine des Wisigoths aux Arabes*, p. 104, identifies him as the *comes* of Paris; for his previous career, H. Ebling, *Prosopographie der Amtsträger des Merowingerreiches*, Beihefte der *Francia*, II (Munich, 1974), pp. 196–7.
[30] Clermont (535) 2, Orléans (538) 3, (541) 5, (549) 10, Paris (556–73) 8, (614) 2, Clichy (626–7) 28, Chalon (647–53) 10, in *Concilia Galliae*. On episcopal elections, D. Claude, 'Die Bestellung der Bischöfe im merowingischen Reiche', *ZRG*, kanonistische Abteilung, LXXX (1963).
[31] Clermont (535) 2, Orléans (549) 10–11, Paris (614) 2.
[32] Orléans (541) 5.

the king. Nevertheless there was a precedent for such legislation in a letter of pope Celestine I. In addition, Dalmatius' insistence in his will that no foreigner should be consecrated as his successor may owe less to a resentment of royal power than to memories of hostility between his predecessor, the African Quintianus, and the people of Rodez.[33] There were certainly occasions when kings and bishops were at loggerheads; the outcry raised at the Council of Paris (556–73) was doubtless caused by some specific royal action, just as the concession made to the *voluntas regis* in 549 ought to be seen against the background of the extraordinary number of church councils held during Childebert I's reign (above, p. 27). If bishops wanted to oppose royal intervention in church matters they had precedents for so doing, but if a king made appointments which were generally accepted, the hagiographers could and did invoke divine inspiration as the guiding force in his choice.[34] The canons were ignored if circumstances demanded; each episcopal election requires individual scrutiny.

The elevation of Apollinaris to the episcopate in c.515 is a typically dubious affair. In the *Historiarum Libri Decem* Gregory relates that the people elected Quintianus, but that Alcima and Placidina asked him to step down on the grounds that he had already held episcopal office, allowing the appointment of Apollinaris. The latter was then sent to Theuderic, to whom he offered (presumably customary) gifts, and thus succeeded to the episcopate. When he died a few months later, the king appointed Quintianus in his place. In Gregory's other account of Quintianus' elevation, significantly in his Life of the bishop, he makes no mention of any original election, although it would have enhanced the stature of his subject, but refers only to the royal intervention.[35] It may be that the first version of events is concerned to cast a poor light on Apollinaris and his relatives, but in neither account does Gregory attempt to disguise the uncanonical nature of Quintianus' elevation.

The appointment of Gallus in c.525 reveals rather more about the role of the Auvergnat clergy, but comes no nearer to the Church's

[33] Orléans (549) 10, Paris (556–73) 8 and ep. to Sigebert; Edict of Chlotar II (614) 1, *Concilia Galliae*, p. 283; Clichy (626–7) 28; Celestine, *Cuperemus quidem*, *PL* L, c. 434; Gregory, *Historiarum Libri* III.2, V.46, pp. 98, 256; *Vitae Patrum* IV.1, p. 674; for a secular parallel Wallace-Hadrill *LHK* pp. 214–16. See, however, Rouche, *L'Aquitaine des Wisigoths aux Arabes*, pp. 332–8.
[34] Claude, 'Die Bestellung der Bischöfe', pp. 67–8.
[35] Gregory, *Historiarum Libri* III.2, pp. 98–9; *Vitae Patrum* IV.1, pp. 674–5.

ideal. Gallus spent part of his early career at the court of Theuderic and it seems to have been mere chance that he was in Clermont at the time of Quintianus' death. The local clergy met to elect a successor in the house of Gallus' uncle, Inpetratus, but failed to come to any agreement. The saint, however, divinely inspired, decided that he should become bishop. He was greeted with some scepticism but, on his uncle's recommendation, went to court. Meanwhile the clergy agreed upon a candidate and approached the king with gifts, only to find that Theuderic had already decided upon Gallus' appointment.[36]

The next episcopal vacancy at Clermont, however, coincided with a royal minority, and had all the makings of a canonical election. The bishops who came to bury Gallus in 551 offered to consecrate the priest Cato, apparently the popular choice, and they undertook, to square things with the young Theudebald. Cato, however, regarding himself as canonically elected, declined the bishops' offer and in doing so revealed his own vainglory. Gregory, unfortunately, does not explain why Cato refused immediate consecration; perhaps he had not yet been formally elected by the clergy (Gregory's Latin is ambiguous) or perhaps he wanted royal approval. Once elected, however, he began to act as bishop, although he had not been consecrated, and while doing so foolishly threatened to humiliate the archdeacon Cautinus. The latter fled to Theudebald and was consecrated bishop of Clermont. When the Auvergnat clergy arrived at court to gain approval for Cato's consecration, they and their treasure were promptly handed over to Cautinus. Not surprisingly during the ensuing episcopate there were two clerical factions.[37]

By comparison the election of Cautinus' successor was straightforward. There appear to have been two clear candidates, one of whom, Eufrasius, tried to bribe King Sigebert with money obtained from the Jews. The archdeacon Avitus, on the other hand, relied upon clerical support. Ultimately, after the king had refused Eufrasius' bribe and *comes* Firminus had failed to prevent Avitus visiting the court, the latter was elected by clergy and people and was then consecrated – uncanonically, as it so happens – at Metz. Looking back on events Gregory thought that Eufrasius never had a

[36] *ibid.* VI.3, pp. 681–2.
[37] Gregory, *Historiarum Libri* IV.6–7, pp. 139–40; Rouche, *L'Aquitaine des Wisigoths aux Arabes*, p. 334.

chance of success, since his family had been cursed by Quintianus.[38]

Although the best part of a century elapsed between the election of Avitus and that of Praeiectus, both belong to a recognizably similar society. According to his biographer, Praeiectus had been marked out for greatness by a miracle at his birth. The saint himself did not hesitate to draw attention to this fact when Bishop Felix died. The popular reaction to this information was to ask if he had enough money to buy the bishopric, but Praeiectus refused to commit simony. Moreover he had entered into a pact with the archdeacon Garivald and three other leading churchmen to ensure that their mutual candidate for the bishopric would succeed.[39] This agreement was written down and sealed, but when Garivald heard about Praeiectus' revelations concerning the miraculous circumstances of his birth, he produced the sealed pact, only to discover that the other three clerics involved all supported his rival. Garivald, who had expected to have their suffrage because he was archdeacon, resorted to bribing the laity and thus forcibly obtained the episcopate, only to die ten days later. The majority of people then turned to Genesius, the local *comes*, a man reputed for his piety, and sought royal authorization to have him consecrated. He, however, refused to act in opposition to the canons, with the result that Praeiectus was finally elected and, according to one version, his position was ratified by royal decree.[40]

Almost everything in this story has its parallel in sixth-century Clermont, except the election of Genesius. On the whole laymen were not appointed directly to the episcopate in the early Merovingian period, although there had been earlier instances of this and there were to be many others.[41] At least one and probably two such are recorded in the *Vita Boniti*. Bonitus himself was a secular official when he was elevated to the episcopate in *c*.691 at the request of his predecessor and brother, Avitus II. Later he resigned his see, partly in order to live a more apostolic life and partly because he reckoned it a sin to have received the bishopric as a gift. Despite these qualms, which prefigure the attitudes of the eleventh-century reformers (and Peter Damian was aware of the resignation, or, as he put

---

[38] Gregory, *Historiarum Libri* IV.35, pp. 167–8; Orléans (541) 5.
[39] *Passio Praeiecti* 1, 12–13, pp. 226–7, 232–3; Claude, 'Die Bestellung der Bischöfe', p. 21, n. 84, argues that Garivald was named in the document as the candidate to be supported.
[40] *Passio Praeiecti* 14, pp. 233–4.
[41] e.g. Ambrose. Gregory, *Historiarum Libri* VI.39, VIII.20, 22, pp, 310, 386, 388.

it, deposition of Bonitus), the saint nevertheless arranged that
Nordobert, possibly one-time *comes* of Paris and referendary of
Childebert III, should succeed him.[42]

Genesius, Bonitus and Nordobert suggest a change in the Merovingian Church; all three were probably laymen when offered the
episcopate, although one refused the offer immediately on canonical
grounds and another resigned his see because of the circumstances
of his appointment. Genesius alone was elected by the people of
Clermont, while Bonitus and Nordobert were both appointed by
their predecessors, the former with the clear approval of Theuderic
III and, perhaps more important, of Pippin II. Throughout the sixth
century, by contrast, it is possible to see the local clergy in action at
almost every election; they were involved, albeit on the losing side,
when both Gallus and Cautinus were appointed. A century later
they supported Praeiectus against Garivald, again without success.
They also backed Avitus I against Eufrasius. Moreover, although
Garivald gained the episcopate with lay support, his own claim to
the office rested on the fact that he was already archdeacon, and that
archdeacons naturally became bishops; a reasonable assumption,
granted that the careers of at least four of his predecessors had
followed such a pattern.[43] The laity appear to have been a rather less
regular force in episcopal elections, but Eufrasius' opposition to
Avitus was backed by Jewish money and he seems also to have had
comital support; Garivald owed his eventual success to laymen.

This activity during episcopal elections is all the more curious
when one considers that the appointment of every Merovingian
bishop of Clermont described by Gregory lay ultimately with the
king, even during Theudebald's minority, as Cato found to his
cost. Effectively the first candidate to reach the court was the
successful one, whether or not he had the suffrage of the diocese.
Oddly enough, Gregory offers no comment on this. The uncanonical nature of the elections elicits scarcely a murmur from
him, and the two cases where he does draw attention to the canons
are somewhat surprising. Cato's desire to do everything by the

[42] *Vita Boniti* 3, 5, 9, 15, pp. 120–2, 124, 127, also p. 124 n. 1. Bonitus also describes
himself in a rather Anselmian way as an ox (12, p. 125); it is perhaps alarming that
the earliest MS of this apparently Merovingian *Vita* should be eleventh-century.
[43] Cautinus, Avitus I, Gallus II and Genesius are all known to have been archdeacons; Gregory, *Historiarum Libri* IV.7, 35, pp. 139, 168; *Acta Sanctorum,
Novembris* I, p. 349; *Passio Praeiecti* 4, p. 228. cf. P. Llewellyn, *Rome in the Dark Ages*
(London, 1970), p. 117.

book is seen as an example of vainglory, while the consecration of
Avitus at Metz rather than Clermont is emphasized, but is among
the least of the infringements committed by episcopal candidates
during the century. Moreover, when he records that Cautinus was
consecrated at Metz, Gregory offers not a word of criticism.[44]
Perhaps by emphasizing the one peccadillo in his friend's election he
hoped to draw attention to its comparative probity. On the other
hand Gregory does not appear to have been particularly concerned
about the rights and wrongs of elections. Simony he condemned,
but over royal intervention he did not take the stance adopted by the
bishops present at the Council of Paris (556–73).[45] Gregory did not
see episcopal elections in terms of a conflict between royal and local
power. For him the crucial issue was the merit of the candidate as
revealed by good works, miracles or prophecy. It was enough that
Sidonius had foreseen Aprunculus' election and that Gallus, over-
come by the Holy Spirit, recognized his own worthiness. Nega-
tively the failure of Eufrasius is linked to the curse of Quintianus.[46]
The author of the *Passio Praeiecti* had a similar outlook; like Gallus,
his hero drew attention to his own supernaturally revealed destiny,
and in both cases the claims of fore-ordained greatness were originally rejected. Perhaps this indicates a hagiographical *topos*; alternatively it may illustrate the capacity of sixth- (and seventh-)
century men to look their gift horse firmly in the mouth.[47]

Even after election and consecration a bishop could not depend
on the goodwill of his congregation or his clergy. One joker removed Sidonius' mass book, but the saint knew the office by heart
and may even have composed it. More dangerous, two of his priests
undermined his authority by seizing control of church property
and only the death of one of them prevented the removal of Sidonius
himself from the church. Nevertheless the other lived to appropriate the episcopal estates on the saint's death and behaved like a
bishop himself until he suddenly expired at dinner.[48] Quintianus
faced a similar threat from the priest Proculus, an ex-fiscal agent,
who took over the administration of possessions and almost starved
the bishop; he too died in unfortunate circumstances, on the altar of

---

[44] Gregory, *Historiarum Libri* IV.6, 35, pp. 139, 168.
[45] Gregory, *Vitae Patrum* VI.3, p. 682; *Historiarum Libri* IV.35, VI.39, VIII.22, pp.
168, 310, 388.   [46] *ibid*. II.23, IV.35, pp. 68, 167–8.
[47] P. Brown, *Relics and Social Status in the Age of Gregory of Tours* (Stenton Lecture,
1976), p. 15.   [48] Gregory, *Historiarum Libri* II.22–3, pp. 67–9.

his church at Vollore, during Theuderic's punitive invasion of the
Auvergne.[49] Even Gallus' relations with his clergy were not always
of the best. His claim to divine inspiration offended the cleric
Viventius, although the hostility was quickly and miraculously
ended. Another of his critics, Evodius, only made peace with him
when he went on a tour of the churches of the saints.[50]

Evodius belonged to a family which provided three *comites* for the
civitas Arvernorum during the sixth century. Hortensius, his father,
had the misfortune to arrest Honoratus, a relative of Quintianus and
was consequently cursed, along with his descendants. Evodius
himself was *comes* before becoming a priest and falling foul of
Gallus. Subsequently he was elected bishop of Javols, but was never
consecrated, as a result of local opposition. Of his two sons one,
Salustius, was appointed to comital office by Chramn, the other,
Eufrasius, was Avitus' rival for the episcopate in 571.[51] They were
a powerful family and their failure in ecclesiastical politics required
an explanation, which was to be found, according to Gregory, in
Quintianus' curse. This failure may be the more remarkable if
bishop Eufrasius, Apollinaris' predecessor as bishop, is regarded as
a member of the Hortensii on the strength of his name.[52] The only
family to achieve similar secular success was that of Britianus, who
appears to have succeeded Evodius as *comes*. His son-in-law,
Firminus, probably followed him in office, although he was removed for a while during Chramn's period of rule. Palladius,
Britianus' son, became *comes* of Javols, but fell foul of the bishop and
as a result of ensuing intrigues was driven to suicide.[53] Unlike the
Hortensii, however, the descendants of Britianus did not earn the
hostility of the bishops of Clermont and, once again if names are
anything to go by, they may have produced a bishop themselves in
Praeiectus, whose uncle was called Peladius.[54]

More dangerous than the *comites* were the kings and their hench-
men. Theuderic's raid of *c*.525 was a harsh penalty for Arcadius'
treason, but for Quintianus it was an opportunity to reveal himself
as defender of the city in his negotiations with the king, while abbot

[49] *ibid*. III.13, p. 109; *Vitae Patrum* IV.1–2, p. 675.
[50] *ibid*. VI.3, 4, pp. 682–3.
[51] *ibid*. IV.3, p. 675; *Historiarum Libri* IV.13, 35, pp. 144, 167; *Vita Dalmatii* 9, ed. B.
Krusch, *MGH, SRM* IV, p. 549.
[52] Gregory, *Historiarum Libri* III.2, p. 98.
[53] *ibid*. IV.39, pp. 170–1, although the place of Britianus's birth is not stated.
[54] *Passio Praeiecti* 1, 3, pp. 226–7.

Portianus secured the release of prisoners.[55] Sigivald, however, the man left in charge of the Auvergne by Theuderic, earned the hatred of Gregory by seizing property belonging to St Julian's. It may be that the similar offence of *comes* Becco should be dated to this period, but we know neither when Becco lived, nor where he held comital office. Lytigius, whose insults caused Quintianus to prostrate himself at his feet, was certainly of Sigivald's entourage.[56] Church property also suffered during the rule of Chlothar I's son, Chramn (555–56), and the church of St Julian was violated when, having deprived Firminus of comital office, he had him dragged forcibly from the sanctuary. The prince similarly terrorized the bishop, Cautinus, and encouraged the faction of Cato.[57] More powerful than a count, he was able to challenge the established office holders and provided a focus for the disgruntled members of the Auvergne, who may have been especially numerous as a result of the unusual circumstances surrounding Cautinus' election and his subsequent persecution of the followers of Cato.

Despite such hostility the sixth-century bishops of Clermont survived. None of them were among the handful of early Merovingian bishops who were deposed.[58] Cautinus, who was justly accused before Chlothar of burying alive the priest Anastasius, in an attempt to seize an estate from him, seems to have suffered no penalty.[59] Praeiectus, by contrast, suffered martyrdom. The dispute over property which was at the root of the conflict between him and Hector, *patricius* of Marseilles, does not appear to have been especially noteworthy. Praeiectus insisted that a certain Claudia had left her estate to the Church, while Hector claimed possession through his (violent) marriage to Claudia's daughter. Summoned to the royal court, Praeiectus exploited legal procedure to its full, first refusing to face trial on Easter Saturday and then commending the cause of his church to the queenmother, Imnechildis. At this point a separate conflict involving Wulfoald and bishop Leodegar

---

[55] Gregory, *Vitae Patrum* IV.2, V.2, pp. 675, 678–9.
[56] Gregory, *Historiarum Libri* III.13, 16, pp. 110, 116–17; *Virtutes S. Juliani* 14, 16, pp. 570–1.
[57] Gregory, *Historiarum Libri* IV.11, 13, 16, pp. 142, 144, 147–8; *Gloria Martyrum* 65, pp. 532–3. See the comments of Rouche, *L'Aquitaine des Wisigoths aux Arabes*, p. 62.
[58] Gregory, *Historiarum Libri* IV.26, V.20, 27, VIII.20, X.19, pp. 157–8, 227–8, 233, 386, 510–13.
[59] *ibid.* IV.12, pp. 142–4.

engulfed Hector, who was executed. Praeiectus' murder at Volvic
followed shortly afterwards and although the hagiographer makes
no clear connection between the two events their juxtaposition
seems significant.[60] The conflict between Hector and Praeiectus
does not mark a change in local politics; its outcome was dictated by
the peculiar circumstances of Childeric II's reign over a united
Frankish kingdom (673–75). Nevertheless within the *civitas Arvernorum* itself there is a striking absence of hostility to both Praeiectus
and Bonitus, which may reflect the hagiographers' intentions rather
than any decline in the liveliness of urban society. By contrast with
the Clermont of Gregory of Tours, however, that of the *Passio
Praeiecti* and the *Vita Boniti* is little more than backcloth for clerical
rivalry and good works.

The problems faced by bishops in the sixth and seventh centuries
show that episcopal authority was not taken for granted. The
foundations of *Bischofsherrschaft* were not secure. Chilperic I thought
the wealth of the church excessive, but Gregory did not agree with
him.[61] The recurrent legislation on ecclesiastical land suggests that
the Church, or rather individual dioceses, because there was enormous variety here, could ill afford to lose property.[62] The estates of
the diocese of Clermont were significant enough for clerics to usurp
control over them, but of their extent we know next to nothing.[63]
In addition the bishops themselves, many of whom came from
notable families, would have been able to draw on their own
resources. Their expenditure, however, was probably enormous.
Generosity in almsgiving was expected, but being directed to the
weaker members of the community it was more likely to enhance a
bishop's reputation than to add directly to his power. According to
Gregory, Sidonius distributed his family silver to the poor and
when he died the people lamented the loss of their shepherd, but
none of them are known to have supported their bishop against his
clerical opponents.[64] Aid was more likely to come from the rich.

At the nadir of his career, after the cession of the Auvergne to
Euric, Sidonius, living in exile, set about lobbying those in high

[60] *Passio Praeiecti* 23–6, 29–30, pp. 239–41, 242–3; *Passio Leodegarii* I, 8–12, ed. B.
Krusch, *MGH,SRM* V, pp. 289–95.
[61] Gregory, *Historiarum Libri* VI.46, p. 320; Prinz, 'Die bischöfliche Stadtherrschaft',
pp. 1–2.   [62] *Concilia Galliae*, pp. 341–3.
[63] R. Sève, 'La Seigneurie épiscopale de Clermont des origines à 1359', *Revue
d'Auvergne*, XCIV (1980), pp. 97–9.
[64] Gregory, *Historiarum Libri* II.22–3, pp. 67–9.

places;[65] in times of political crisis at least, a bishop's contacts counted for much. Quintianus' reputation as a martyr for the Frankish case endeared him to Theuderic and may have influenced the king's decision not to plunder the environs of Clermont. Theudebert's remission of taxes to the churches of the Auvergne perhaps owed something to Gallus' early career in Austrasia, or to the fact that the king's finance minister, Parthenius, was of Auvergnat extraction. Unfortunately we know nothing about Childebert II's remarkably similar concession in 590.[66] Eighty years later Praeiectus gained a privilege for his church after a visit to Childeric *pro conditionis ecclesiae*.[67] A bishop might also benefit from his connections with the other leading clergy of the kingdom. Apart from direct family ties, there were formal contacts through *epistolae formatae* and, less regularly, church councils. There were also relations over land held in the Auvergne by churches of other dioceses. Gallus II was involved in a dispute with Anglebert of Rheims and Gyroindus signed the privilege of Emmo of Sens for St Pierre-le-Vif, which may already have been endowed with vast estates in the diocese of Clermont.[68] National contacts must have been influential in a bishop's status in the *Regnum Francorum*, but they were only tangential to his local authority.

Historians, however, have observed in Merovingian Gaul a growth of episcopal power, which they have linked to a usurpation of comital functions, although it has been suggested that these were not usurped but granted by the king in order to facilitate administration. Already in the seventh century Desiderius of Cahors wrote to Caesarius, bishop of Clermont, asking for aid in laying water pipes, and he received a letter from Caesarius' successor, Gallus II, about the closure of main roads to prevent the spread of plague.[69] Later in the century both Avitus II and Nordobert minted coins.[70] Nevertheless

[65] Sidonius, epp. VIII.3, 9, pp. II, 404–12, 440–50.
[66] Gregory, *Historiarum Libri* III.2, 25, X.7, pp. 98–9, 123, 488; *Vitae Patrum* IV.2, p. 675; see Rouche, *L'Aquitaine des Wisigoths aux Arabes*, p. 57.
[67] *Passio Praeiecti* 22, p. 239.
[68] Flodoard II.6, p. 455; J. M. Pardessus, *Diplomata, Chartae, Epistolae, Leges aliaque instrumenta ad res gallo-francicas spectantia* (Paris, 1849), II, pp. 112–14. Rouche, *L'Aquitaine des Wisigoths aux Arabes*, pp. 467–70; Gregory, *Historiarum Libri* II.36, pp. 84–5.
[69] J. Durliat, 'Les Attributions civiles des évêques Merovingiens: l'example de Didier, évêque de Cahors', *Annales du Midi*, XCI (1979); Desiderius, *Epistulae* I.13, II.20, ed. W. Arndt, *MGH,Ep.* III, pp. 200–1, 214.
[70] M. Prou, *Les Monnaies Mérovingiennes* (Paris, 1892), pp. 355, 380.

there was still a count, Genesius, in the days of Praeiectus, and he
was regarded as a suitable candidate for the episcopate by both king
and congregation. Praeiectus himself was a skilful lawyer, to judge
by his defence at court, and Bonitus was taught the Theodosian code
at school.[71] Like him, his successor, Nordobert, may have had a
successful career in royal service before becoming bishop. All these
men were capable of shouldering administrative duties within the
kingdom, and their skills may have helped them in episcopal office.
The situation, however, was different in previous centuries. Law
was a factor in both secular adminstration and pastoral care, but the
legal powers conferred on the church by Constantine were reduced
as early as the fourth century. In the early sixth, Avitus of Vienne
and his correspondents were not always able to enforce ecclesiastical
norms with regard to marriage.[72] Fifty years later Cautinus found it
impossible to sustain a sentence of excommunication when Eulalius,
who was suspected of matricide, insisted on being admitted to
communion because his case had not been properly heard.[73] A
well-respected bishop, however, could use the liturgy as one of the
chief supports of his episcopate.

Sidonius instituted Rogations to raise the morale of the people of
Clermont during the Visigothic siege. To these Rogations Quintianus once added a prayer for rain in response to public demand.
His prayer was instantly successful. Bonitus also ordered fasts and
prayers to end a drought; the result was a flood which had to be
assuaged by additional fasting. In 543 when there was a threat of
plague, Gallus, who had been warned in a dream, instituted a
second set of Rogations, combined with a pilgrimage from Clermont
to Brioude, and the *civitas* was spared. (In similar circumstances
Gallus II and his contemporaries resorted to the use of road blocks.[74])
The power of ceremonies was undoubtedly connected with the
presence of large crowds. In 576, during one of the Easter processions a Jew tipped rancid oil onto the head of an apostate from the
Hebrew faith, who had become a candidate for baptism. The
bishop, Avitus, did not stifle the ensuing sense of outrage, perhaps
deliberately; his predecessor, Cautinus, had earned a bad name for

[71] *Passio Praiecti* 14, 24, pp. 233–4, 239–40; *Vita Boniti* 2, p. 120.
[72] Avitus, epp. 16–18, 55, pp. 48–50, 83–5. For 'episcopalis audientia', Heinzelmann, *Bischofscherrshaft in Gallien*, pp. 179–83.
[73] Gregory, *Historiarum Libri* X.8, p. 489.
[74] Sidonius, epp. V.14, VII.1., pp. II, 216–18, 286–8; Gregory, *Vitae Patrum* IV.4,
VI.6, pp. 676–7, 684–5; *Vita Boniti* 7, pp. 122–3; Desiderius, ep.II.20, p. 214.

himself, at least with Gregory of Tours, over his dealings with Jewish merchants and his rival for the episcopate, Eufrasius, had been backed by Jewish funds. The result was forcible conversion. As Gregory saw it, for a brief moment Clermont had become the new Jerusalem.[75]

The shrines of the saints also drew their crowds. The monastery of St Cirgues put out free wine on its patron's festival and others may have done the same. When Gallus was offended by Evodius, he went on a perambulation of all the churches, which were legion.[76] There were too many for one bishop or one family interest to assimilate. Even Gregory has little to say about St Stremonius, perhaps because the apostle of the Auvergne was culted on the same day as Benignus. Cautinus, however, while still a deacon, fenced off the tomb of the saint, and Praeiectus wrote his lives of Stremonius, Cassius, Victorinus and Antolianus at a similar stage of his career. Bishops did not have a monopoly over saints or shrines; the origins of the *Passio Praeiecti* seem unconnected with the Auvergne and the *Vita Boniti* is monastic.[77] Nevertheless it was as a bishop that Avitus commissioned Gregory's Life of Illidius and set up a shrine to Genesius at Thiers.[78] His namesake investigated the cult of Praeiectus, and both Nordobert and Proculus, with the agreement of the clergy and people of the diocese, negotiated for the return of Bonitus' body from Lyons.[79] When the translation did take place, it was the occasion for public demonstrations of devotion and for miraculous cures. The importance of the saints of Merovingian Clermont is clear from the tenth-century *Libellus de Ecclesiis Claromontanis*: most of the cults listed there were established in the sixth and seventh centuries, although not simply as a result of episcopal activity.

Shrines and processions did not bring automatic authority to a bishop any more than did pastoral responsibility. Again the failure of Cautinus is instructive. Despite the crowds of faithful making the rogation pilgrimage to Brioude, he fled from the procession on

[75] Gregory, *Historiarum Libri* IV.12, 35, V.11., pp. 144, 167, 205–6.
[76] Gregory, *Vitae Patrum* III.1, VI.4, pp. 673, 683; P-F. Fournier, 'Clermont-Ferrand au VIe siècle, recherches sur la topographie de la ville', *Bibliothèque de l'École des Chartes*, CXXVIII (1970), pp. 273–344. *Libellus de Ecclesiis Claromontanis*, ed. W. Levison, *MGH,SRM* VII, pp. 456–67.
[77] Gregory, *Gloria Confessorum* 29, p. 766; *Passio Praeiecti* 9, pp. 230–1; A. Poncelet, 'La plus ancienne vie de S. Austremoine', *Analecta Bollandiana* XIII.
[78] Gregory, *Gloria Martyrum* 66, p. 533; *Vitae Patrum* II.pr., pp. 668–9.
[79] *Passio Praeiecti* 34, pp. 244–5; *Vita Boniti* 32–5, pp. 134–6.

horseback when he thought that Chramn's minions were chasing him.[80] Whereas the anger of Quintianus could spell disaster for a family, Cautinus could not enforce a sentence of excommunication, and whereas Gallus averted the plague by instituting the pilgrimage to St Julian's, Cautinus failed to complete the journey out of fear for his life. Avaricious and alcoholic, he is the opposite of Gregory's heroes. As such he provides an insight into the limitations of episcopal authority in the sixth century. The successful bishops, by contrast, had worked hard to achieve their power; their lives were exemplary and as a result their curses and their prayers were efficacious. Praeiectus and Bonitus also deserved their status. They were generous and ascetic; Praeiectus had his connections with the circle of Luxeuil; Bonitus' *crise de conscience* brought him into contact with the world of reformed monasticism.[81] What distinguishes them from sixth century predecessors is the reduced extent to which they needed to be holy to dominate their congregations. Most of the problems faced by Praeiectus belonged to his early years as a cleric and to the period of his election; the conflict with Hector is an indication of the significance of disputes over property and of the political uncertainty of the reign of Childeric II, but it does not illuminate the position of a bishop in his diocese. Bonitus' major difficulty was his own sense of rectitude. Even his rebuttal of the Novatian heresy, if it was ever more than a literary exercise, belonged to the period after he had resigned office.[82] Both Praeiectus by his martyrdom and Bonitus by his retirement confirmed their sanctity, but in any case the increased administrative demands placed on bishops in the seventh century meant that episcopal authority was stronger than it had been. For one reason or another the *Passio Praeiecti* and the *Vita Boniti* have less to say about difficulties caused by the local clergy and secular administration than has Gregory.

In the sixth century rivals, often of distinguished family, competed for the episcopate both in the city of Clermont and at court, and once elected a bishop had to establish his authority in the diocese and cultivate relations with the king. By the late seventh

---

80 Gregory, *Historiarum Libri* IV.13, p. 144.
[81] *Passio Praeiecti* 15, p. 235; *Vita Boniti* 9, p. 124.
[82] *ibid.* 17, p. 129; cf. Gregory *Historiarum Libri* I.30, p. 22. Praeiectus had already written the *Acta* of Stremonius. See Rouche, *L'Aquitaine des Wisigoths aux Arabes*, p. 400.

century there seems to have been a decline in the local conflict and competition. The Arab invasions of Gaul interrupted any coherent development thereafter. The extent to which this represents the norm for a Merovingian see is difficult to determine because the evidence elsewhere is more fragmentary. The qualities of the individual, the power of the local aristocracy and the nature of the local saint cults would have ensured considerable variety, but the major dioceses of the South, especially Lyons and Vienne (the latter also dominated by a branch of the Aviti) had similar episcopal dynasties,[83] and where anything is known about oppositions to bishops (as at Arles, Langres, Tours and later Noyon) similar anecdotes can be found.[84] In all probability the *civitas Arvernorum* was much like the other sees which lay south of the Loire and outside the immediate purview of the court.

There was an ideal image of the bishop in Merovingian Gaul and it is often found in episcopal epitaphs;[85] there was also an ideal congregation, like the reformed city of Nineveh to which Vienne was compared during the first Rogations[86] or the new Jerusalem imitated by Clermont after the anti-Jewish riots. As Professor Wallace-Hadrill has remarked, 'at this level a Christian community has meaning'.[87] At times, especially during the great festivals, there was a sense of unity under the patronage of the bishop. Such a mood, however, could not be guaranteed. To judge by the evidence of the Auvergne, it was not easy for Merovingian bishops to gain the respect of their congregations and to merit the marmoreal compliments of their epitaphs and hagiographers.

[83] Heinzelmann, *Bischofsherrschaft in Gallien*, pp. 98–179, 220–32.
[84] Gregory *Historiarum Libri* II.23, V.4, 48–9., pp. 69, 198–200, 258–63; *Vita Caesarii* I.21, 29, 36, ed. B. Krusch, *MGH,SRM* III, pp. 465, 467–8, 470–1; *Vita Eligii* II.6, ed. B Krusch, *MGH,SRM* IV, p. 698.
[85] Heinzelmann, *Bischofsherrschaft in Gallien*, passim.
[86] Avitus, homily 6, p. 111.
[87] Wallace-Hadrill, *EMH*, p. 4.

APPENDIX
Episcopal List, Eparchius to Proculus (after L. Duchesne,
Fastes épiscopaux de l'ancienne Gaule, II, Paris, 1899)

Eparchius	name suggests link with Aviti d. *c*.470
Sidonius	Avitus' son-in-law d. *c*.486? (Sidoine Appollinaire, *Poèmes,* ed. A. Loyen, Paris, 1960, p. XXIX)
Aprunculus	from Dijon d. pre-506
Eufrasius	name suggests links with Hortensii d. *c*.515
Apollinaris	Sidonius' son d. *c*.515
Quintianus	African, ex-bishop of Rodez d. *c*.525
Gallus I	uncle of Gregory of Tours d. 551
Cautinus	cousin of Tetradius of Bourges namesake, c. 7 archdeacon, *Vita Boniti*, 15 d. 571
Avitus I	name suggests link with Aviti still alive 592
Desideratus?	
Avolus?	
Justus?	
Caesarius	attends Clichy, 626–27
Gallus II	name suggests relationship with family of Gregory of Tours
Genesius	namesake, *comes, Passio Praeiecti*, 14
Gyroindus	signs privilege of Emmo of Sens, 660
Felix	
Garivaldus	

Praeiectus	name of uncle (Peladius), suggests link with c. 6 *comes* Britianus d. 675
Avitus II	name suggests link with Aviti d. 691
Bonitus	brother of Avitus retires *c.* 700
Nordobert	outsider?
Proculus	namesake, c. 6 priest of Vollore (Gregory, *Historiarum Libri* III.13; *Liber Vitae Patrum*, IV.2)

3

Bureaucratic Shorthand and Merovingian Learning

DAVID GANZ

Jacob Burckhardt recommended the study of early medieval history because of the paucity of evidence: 'In ein Paar Bänden ist Alles beisammen.'[1] More recent historians have produced more volumes, but they continue to exploit the same sources. This paper is concerned with some relatively neglected sources. By exploring some dark corners of the picture of 'literary poverty and cultural decline', which is the standard portrait of Merovingian Gaul, and which Professor Wallace-Hadrill has scrutinized more than once, it seeks to enlarge our view of Merovingian government and scholarship and to illuminate the complexities of the relationship between them.[2]

By the reign of the Emperor Theodosius I, a command of shorthand was the indispensable preliminary to a career in the imperial or local bureaucracy.[3] Church councils were recorded verbatim, sermons, letters and even wills could be dictated.[4] So familiar were these shorthand signs to professional scribes that the annotators of the Bembine Terence used them as *signes de renvoi* for their notes.[5] The earliest surviving shorthand is found in the papyrus documents from Ravenna (c. 540), which preserve late Roman

[1] J. Burckhardt, *Über das Studium der Geschichte*, ed. P. Ganz (Munich, 1982), p. 97.
[2] F. Brunhölzl, *Geschichte der lateinischen Literatur des Mittelalters*, I (Munich, 1975), p. 143; Wallace-Hadrill, *EMH*, pp. 123–6, 139–41, etc.
[3] H. Marrou, *Histoire de l'éducation dans l'Antiquité* (Paris, 1965), pp. 418–50.
[4] E. Tengström, *Die Protokollierung der Collatio Carthaginensis* (Goteborg, 1962); R. Deferrari, 'The presence of *notarii* in the churches to take down sermons when they were being delivered', *American Journal of Philology*, XLIII (1922), pp. 106–10; Paulus in *Digest* XXXVII.1 (6.2), XXIV.1 (40).
[5] S. Prete, *Il Codice di Terenzio Vaticanus Latinus 3226* (*Studi e Testi* CCLXII, 1970), ff. 7r, 12v, 30r, 54r.

chancery usage, but the Munich manuscript of the *Notitia Dignitatum* (Clm 10291) shows shorthand on the scrolls of the *Magister Scriniorum* and of the various *comites*, and a Carolingian copy of the writings of the Roman land surveyors (Vatican Pal.Lat.1564) shows them holding scrolls inscribed with shorthand notes.[6] The most important source for late antique shorthand is the *Commentarium Notarum Tironianum*, a manual of some 13,000 signs for all eventualities, which, most significantly, is preserved in twenty-two Carolingian copies.[7] In its present form, it was assembled in an area where both Greek and Latin were spoken and it must date after *c*. 350, to judge from its list of imperial provinces. It contains terms especially relevant to the needs of an episcopal chancery, and it ends with a list of biblical names.[8]

We know all too little of the status of the *Commentarium* in Merovingian Gaul, and of the extent to which courts at all levels preserved the use of shorthand. But there are two streams of continuity: the shorthand subscriptions to royal and private charters, and the shorthand annotations in surviving manuscripts, some of which can be localized. A comprehensive survey would mean analysing all of these and closely comparing them, a task which has daunted experts. But even a preliminary sketch reveals primary evidence for the study of literary and legal texts, and so provides a context for our understanding of Merovingian education in its public and private aspects. The attitude to the written word which the use of shorthand implies focuses our view of the transition from the classical to the medieval book: it is not an accident that Carolingian Evangelists use it on their gospel scrolls.[9]

[6] J. Tjäder, *Die nichtliterarischen lateinischen Papyri Italiens aus der Zeit 445–700* (Lund, 1954) I, pp. 128–9; *À l'Aube de la France: la Gaule de Constantin à Childéric* (Musée du Luxembourg, 1981), figs 4, 8, 9, for colour plates of Clm 10291; E. Böcking, *Notitia Dignitatum* (Bonn, 1839–55) for engravings showing the Tironian notes. I am grateful to Mildred Budny for drawing my attention to this MS.

[7] W. Schmitz, *Commentarii Notarum Tironianum* (Leipzig, 1893).

[8] C. Zangemeister, 'Zur Geographie des römischen Galliens und Germanias nach den Tironischen Noten', *Neue Heidelberger Jahrbücher*, II (1892), pp. 1–36; A. Mentz, *Die tironischen Noten* (Berlin, 1944), pp. 138–47, 155–6.

[9] The evangelists in the Gundohinus Gospels of 754 (Autun MS 3) hold books inscribed with debased and meaningless Tironian notes. Notes are also found on the evangelists' books or scrolls in Paris BN Lat. MSS 257, 260, 265, 9385, 17968; Paris Bibliothèque de l'Arsenal MS 1171; Stuttgart MS II 4; New York Pierpoint Morgan Lib. MS M 728; Epernay Bibl. Municipale MS I; and on the Apocalypse page (f. 449r) of London BL Add. MS 10546, the Moutiers Grandval Bible. This list is certainly incomplete.

The Merovingian system of Tironian notes was not directly based on the *Commentarium*. Personal names often required an adaptation of the system; it was easiest to simplify it by using a restricted number of signs which frequently recurred, supplementing them with signs for individual syllables which could be combined to form names or other words. Carolingian manuscripts list several syllabic systems, and signs for syllables are found in the *Commentarium*.[10] Though Carolingian in date the various Tironian psalters which use the syllabic system, and often differ in their transcriptions, may show how the system was learned in the Merovingian period.[11] The psalter was the first text studied by clerics, and was an ideal way to memorize symbols.[12] This suggestion is confirmed by pen-trials in shorthand which quote psalter verses; in a royal charter, a verse from Psalm 105 was used as a *recognitio* formula, and psalter verses appear as Tironian pen-trials in Paris BN MS Lat.12097.[13]

Literary references to the study of Tironian notes are sadly sparse. Isidore (*Etymologiae*, I. 22) preserves the teaching of Suetonius, Jerome and Augustine about the origin and function of these notes, 'quas qui didicerunt proprie iam notarii appelantur'.[14] His passage was often quoted, sometimes as a preface to the *Commentarium*. At the end of the Kassel copy (written at St Amand in the late eighth century) is a song to celebrate the Easter holidays, including the lines:

> Multi discentes   placeat parentibus
> Multi discedunt   nobis laudes dicere
> Et nos felices   qui studemus litteras
> Per forum vadunt   dant consilium civibus
> Quocumque vadunt   adorantur omnibus.[15]

---

[10] E. Chatelain, *Introduction à la lecture des notes tironiennes* (Paris, 1900), pp. 145–52, 161–7; P. Legendre, *Un Manuel tironien du Xe siècle* (Paris, 1905).

[11] Chatelain, *Notes tironiennes*, pp. 223–6, pls VII–XI.

[12] *Regula Magistri* LVII, ed. A. De Vogüé, *SC* CVI, p. 268.

[13] M. Tangl, *Archiv für Urkundenforschung*, I (1908), p. 91: a charter of Pippin, dated 8 July 753; Chatelain, *Notes tironiennes*, pp. 136–7.

[14] 'Those who learn them correctly are called notaries.' L. Traube, 'Die Geschichte der tironischen Noten bei Suetonius und Isidore', *Vorlesungen und Abhandlungen* (Munich, 1920), III, pp. 254–72, identifies Isidore's sources.

[15] Roughly translated: 'May it please the parents that many learn. These depart to speak our praises and to say we who study letters are happy. They go through the *forum* and they advise the citizens. Wherever they go they are admired by everyone': Traube, 'Ein altes Schülerlied', *ibid.*, pp. 191–8; *MGH Poet.* IV, xcviii, pp. 657–8.

In a ninth-century copy written at Rheims, the song also contains a
farewell message from the teacher: 'calculum notarium et notas
vestras tenete'.[16] A copy of Marculf's *Formulary* has a preface which
also refers to the learning of *notas*:

> Miror prorsus tam prolixa tempore aut nullum me sermone pagine
> consecutum cuius eloquia vestri velut at verba dictantium polluti,
> mutati ceras afferunt, currunt articula falsitatis; sed ubi venitur ad
> revolvendum, delisse magis quam scribisse.[17]

The mistakes in transcription of a dictated text which are here
referred to seem to result from an ignorance of *notae*, the obvious
tool for the exercise. Charlemagne's *Admonitio Generalis* instructs
bishops and monasteries to teach Tironian notes as well as
grammar, computus and chant: 'Psalmos, notas, cantus, compotum,
grammaticam per singula monasteria vel episcopia.'[18] He thus
institutionalized the systematic clerical takeover of late antique
shorthand. How early can such a change be dated?

Only the completion of *Chartae Latinae Antiquiores* will permit
the comprehensive study of Merovingian original charters.[19] Lauer
and Samaran provide sharp, if sometimes reduced, facsimiles of
royal charters, but for private documents the editions of Pardessus
and the engraved facsimiles of Letronne, Marini and Mabillon are
still essential, if inadequate.[20] The Tironian annotations, which

---

[16] 'Remember the reckoning and use your notes': Traube, 'Die Geschichte', p. 195.

[17] ed. K. Zeumer, 'Uber die ältesten fränkischen Formelsammlungen', *Neues
Archiv*, VI (1881), pp. 21–2. Further evidence of the teaching of Tironian notes in
the Merovingian period is found in the Preface of Paris BN Lat. MS 8779: after
claiming that King David was the first to use them, it speaks of how 'cumque iam
ad hanc artem aliqui convolare se viderint et imitaverit praeceptor quod ars ista sibi
initium sumit AB aliqui contristant eo quod timent alii gaudent eo quod amant. Sed
cum iam ad medietate se conscendere viderint tunc qui prius contristabantur
gaudent sicut dicitur. Non laudatur initium sed finis. Sunt igitur aliqui qui dimittunt ad tertiam partem aliqui tamen ad medietatem et sunt plurimi qui non
dimittunt nisi ubi in fine dicitur PLATEOLA': U. Kopp, *Tachygraphia Veterum*
(Mannheim, 1817), I, pp. 304–9. AB is the first sign in the *Commentarium*,
PLATEOLA the last. The text affirms that the notes were not invented by the men of
Tournai, describes the emotions of students and implies that they learned the
sections of the *Commentarium* one by one.

[18] ed. A. Boretius, *MGH, Capit.* I, p. 60; this interpretation of 'notae' is given by
B. Bischoff. *Paläographie des römischen Altertums und des abendländischen Mittelalters*
(Munich, 1979), p. 104.

[19] *Chartae Latinae Antiquiores*, ed. A. Bruckner and R. Marichal (Zurich, 1954 *et
seq.*); vol. XIII, ed H. Atsma and J. Vezin (1981), begins the French series.

[20] P. Lauer and C. Samaran, *Les Diplômes originaux des Mérovingiens* (Paris, 1908); J.
M. Pardessus, *Diplomata, Chartae, Epistolae, Leges aliaque instrumenta ad res gallo-*

served to validate the document, were written in a *ruche*, criss-crossed by lines, and are consequently difficult to decipher; but this was expertly done by Jusselin, who defended his readings against suggestions by Mentz.[21] When transcribed, they record the names of those who requested or attested the document, often the Mayor of the Palace, who may not otherwise be mentioned in it.

The evidence of these charters has been understood to show that the Merovingian royal chancery was staffed by laymen, though it is more correct to say that virtually nothing is known of the careers of chancery personnel, some of whom were apparently laymen. Other evidence suggests the possibility that some had an ecclesiastical future and conceivably a specifically clerical background. The *Vitae* record how Agrestius, 'qui quondam Theuderici regis notarius fuerat', entered Luxeuil;[22] Dado, who is found as *referendarius* in several authentic charters of Dagobert I, was educated at court and 'anulo regis adeptus';[23] Ansbertus, bishop of Rouen, was 'aulicus scriba doctis conditorque regalium privelegiorum et gerulus annoli regis quo eadem signabatur privelegia';[24] Bonitus, bishop of Clermont, whose career is studied elsewhere in this book (above, pp. 45–6), had been 'grammaticorum imbutus iniciis necnon Theodosii edoctus decretis, caeterosque coetaneos excellens a sophistis probus atque praelatus', and 'anulo ex manu regis accepto, referendarii officium adeptus est';[25] and Desiderius, royal treasurer and bishop of Cahors, 'contubernii regalis aduliscens se indedit dignitatibus hac deinde legum Romanum indagatione

francicas spectantia (Paris, 1849); A. J. Letronne, *Diplomata et chartae merovingicae aetatis in Archivo Franciae asservata* (Paris, 1844–7); G. Marini, *I. Papyri diplomatici* (Rome, 1805); J. Mabillon, *De Re Diplomatica* (Paris, 1681); *Supplementum* (Paris, 1704).
[21] M. Jusselin, 'Notes tironiennes dans les diplômes mérovingiens', *Bibliothèque de l'École des Chartes*, LXVI (1905), pp. 361–89; LXVIII (1907), pp. 481–508; Mentz, *Tironischen Noten*, pp. 166–75.
[22] Jonas, *Vitae Sanctorum* II.9, ed. B. Krusch, *MGH, SRG*, pp. 246–51.
[23] *Vita Audoini*, ed. B. Krusch and W. Levison, *MGH, SRM* IV, p. 555; Dado is found in *MGH, Diplomata Merov.*, ed. K. Pertz, 14, 15, 17, but 17, where the name is no longer legible, is dated to the reign of Clovis II by *Chartae Latinae*, 555.
[24] 'A skilled palace scribe and the writer of royal privileges and the bearer of the king's ring by which those privileges are sealed': *Vita Ansberti*, ed. B. Krusch, *MGH, SRM* V, p. 621.
[25] 'Filled with the rudiments of grammarians and skilled in the decrees of Theodosius excelling others of his age he was approved and preferred by wise men. He received the ring from the king's hand and was appointed to the office of referendary': *Vita Boniti*, ed. B. Krusch, *MGH, SRM* VI, p. 120.

studium dedit'.[26] Moreover, it is significant that, while Desiderius was at court, an abbot, Bertegyselus, wrote to him about the boys under his direction in royal service, and the mandate which appointed him bishop of Cahors describes his virtue in terms which make him look very like a 'clerc': 'et sub habitu saeculari Christi militem gerere ac mores angelicos et sacerdotalem conversationem habere, ut non solum in contiguis set etiam in longinquis regionibus fama eius evulgata crebrescat . . . qui pro nobis vel pro vobis sibique commisis securus ante Christi tribunal Christo preces offeret.'[27] Any such assumption is confirmed by an oft-repeated Merovingian canon: 'Si de palatio eligitur per meritum personae et doctrinae ordinetur.'[28] However often such rules were actually broken (above, pp. 42–6), 'doctrina' must surely imply some clerical training, and the canons show that so much was not too much to expect at court.

Surviving royal original charters form a sequence only from 629–59; then there are groups from 677–89, 691–97, 709–11 and 716. This uneven distribution, and the small number of documents involved, makes the evidence extremely difficult to evaluate. But among the trends, reflected by Tironian notes, which indicate the collapse or erosion of the Merovingian chancery, the increasing frequency of interventions by the Mayor of the Palace is the most striking and important. Two charters of September 677 refer to Ebroin.[29] The first, the deposition of Chramlinus, bishop of Embrun, might appear exceptional, but the second, a grant to Deacon Chaino, seems in no way unusual. A document of 30 October 688 granting the mayor's villa to St Denis bears the Tironian inscription, 'ordinante dono et Berehario maiore domus', and the text records that the grant was made 'ad suggestione precelse regine nostre Chrodochilde seo et inlustri viro Berchario, maiorem domos nostro'.[30] Pippin of Herstal intervenes, reflecting

[26] 'The young man dedicated himself to the dignities of royal majesty and at last he gave himself to the tireless study of Roman law': *Vita Desiderii*, ed. B. Krusch, *MGH, SRM* IV, p. 564.
[27] ed. W. Gundlach, *MGH, Ep.* III, p. 204; *Diplomata*, 13: 'under the mantle of this world he behaved like a soldier of Christ and had the manners of an angel and a priestly mode of life, so that not only nearby but also in distant regions his fame grew.'
[28] *Concilia Galliae*, ed. C. de Clercq, *CCSL*, CXLVIIIA (1963), pp. 44, 105–6, 151, 283.
[29] Lauer and Samaran, *Diplômes originaux* 14, 15; *Chartae Latinae*, 565–6.
[30] Lauer and Samaran, *Diplômes originaux* 17; *Chartae Latinae*, 570.

64   DAVID GANZ

his growing domination of the court of Theuderic III, of Burgundy
and southern Gaul, and of episcopal appointments north of the
Somme,[31] in grants to St Denis and Argenteuil, on 13 December
695 and 3 April 697 respectively, and also in an important group of
private charters listed by Levison.[32] His son, Norbertus, is found in a
note on a grant of immunity to St Maur des Fossés;[33] another son,
Grimoald, whose appointment as mayor (697–701) is recorded in a
charter of 25 February 701, has a claim to half the tolls on foreign
merchants at the St Denis fair in a charter of 13 December 710.[34] By
717, the *maior domus*, Ragenfrid, was performing the referendary's
traditional functions.[35] His interventions in grants to St Denis,
dated 29 February 716, 5 March 716, 16 March 716 and 28 February
717, show not only his influence over his puppet, Chilperic II, but
also his close links with the great abbey;[36] it seems clear, as Semmler
has argued, that it was Ragenfrid who gave the bishop of Paris
control of St Denis in 717.[37] (See Plate II.)

All of this coincides with more or less significant changes of
diplomatic practice: the appearance from 697 of the signatory
formula 'X ad vicem Y', suggesting an erosion of the refenderary's
position; the disappearance of the distinction between 'scripsi' and
'recognovi' after 716; the end of references to a royal assembly in the
documents (cf. Nelson, below, pp. 211–22); the use by the mayor
of the formula 'per annolo', which corresponds to the earlier
'ordinante';[38] and the portentous fact that the last Merovingian
royal charters only confirm privileges whilst those of the

[31] E. Ewig, 'Die fränkischen Teilreiche im 7 Jahrhundert', in his *Spätantikes und Fränkisches Gallien*. I (Munich, 1976), pp. 225–8.
[32] Lauer and Samaran, *Diplômes originaux* 24, 28; W. Levison, 'Zu den Annales Mettenses', in his *Aus rheinischer und fränkischer Frühzeit* (Dusseldorf, 1948), p. 478, n. 4.
[33] Lauer and Samaran, *Diplômes originaux*, 26: the document is dated 695/7 by Ewig, 'Die fränkischen Teilreiche', p. 225, n. 212.
[34] Lauer and Samaran, *Diplômes originaux* 31; Jusselin, 'Notes tironiennes', pp. 503–4; Ewig, 'Die fränkischen Teilreiche', p. 228, n. 226. Grimoald is described as *maior domus* by the *Continuator of Fredegar*, ed. J. M. Wallace-Hadrill, *The Fourth Book of the Chronicle of Fredegar* (London, 1960), 6, p. 86.
[35] *Diplomata*, 87.
[36] Lauer and Samaran, *Diplômes originaux*, 34, 35, 37, 38; but I cannot accept Mentz's reading of the Tironian notes in no. 37, and Ragenfrid was probably not at court in March 716.
[37] J. Semmler, 'Zur pippinidisch-karolingischen Sukzessionskrise, 714–23', *DA*, XXXIII (1977), pp. 14–15.
[38] L. Levillain, 'La Souscription de chancellerie dans les diplômes mérovingiens', *Le Moyen Age*, XXIV (1911), pp. 89–124; Lauer and Samaran, *Diplômes originaux*, 31 (710, adopting Jusselin's reading), 34, 37, (716).

Arnulfings make new grants. If not collapse, we at least have change, hingeing, so far as our evidence goes, around the Mayor of the Palace and the abbey of St Denis.

Professor Wallace-Hadrill suggested that a charter of 629 for St Denis was drafted there, and comparable conclusions might be drawn from effusive references to the monastery and its heavenly and royal patrons in documents of 654 and 688, or from the brief history of the abbey in a confirmation of its privileges, dated 723.[39] It is possible that the especial status of St Denis as patron of the Merovingians, coupled with the accident that so high a proportion of surviving royal originals was preserved in his community, has distorted our image of the Merovingian chancery. The elaborate account of Corbie history in the document confirming the election of Abbot Erembertus may likewise suggest that it was drafted there: the monks engage to pray 'pro nobis et pro stabilitate regni nostri'.[40] The charters for St Bertin and Le Mans, though they lack any such suggestive evidence, may also have been drafted by the beneficiary, and this could explain the curious Le Mans formula, 'Bonitus scripsi et subscripsi'.[41] A charter of St Maur des Fossés is the only original for this abbey, and its script, which is heavy and markedly less cursive than all other original royal charters, led Prou to speculate that it might have been written by a monk of the abbey.[42] By contrast, evidence for lay literacy is often hard to come by. Of the signatories to a charter of June 654, nine, other than bishops, use Tironian notes, twenty-three sign and ten use *signa* (four of them called 'vir inluster'). In one of 673, eleven apparently lay signatories use *signa*, nine write their names and five use Tironian notes as well. Again, it is hard to tell laymen from 'clercs'.[43] The presence of

---

[39] *Diplomata*, Spuria 22; Wallace-Hadrill, *LHK*, p. 210; *Diplomata*, 19, 57; *Chartae Latinae*, 558, 570; *Diplomata*, 93.

[40] *ibid.*, 52.

[41] *ibid.*, 39, 54, 58, 90–2, 96; J. Havet, 'Les Actes des évêques du Mans', *Bibliothèque de l'Ecole des Chartes*, LIV (1893), pp. 597–692, LV (1894), pp. 5–60, 306–36. The formula 'X scripsi et subscripsi' is found in *Diplomata*, Spuria, 78, 81, 85, 89; 78 is a forgery but may draw on a lost original of Theuderic III. *Diplomata*, Spuria 67 ends a witness-list 'Teutsindus clericus explevit, scripsit et subscripsit' but, as in *Diplomata* 41 (663), which ends 'Aidarus presbyter recognovi et subscripsi', this may be the subscription of the cartulary copyist: it is regarded as an addition by W. Bergmann, 'Untersuchungen zu den Gerichtsurkunden der Merovingerzeit', *Archiv für Diplomatik*, XXII (1976), pp. 6, 156–9.

[42] Lauer and Samaran, *Diplômes originaux*, 33.

[43] Pardessus, *Diplomata*, 19; L. Levillain, 'La charte de Clotilde (10 Mars 673)', *Bibliothèque de l'École des Chartes*, CV (1944), pp. 5–63; *Chartae Latinae*, 558, 564.

biblical quotations in the text of five royal charters suggests that they were drafted by clerics, if not by the beneficiary.[44]

Since almost all extant originals are for St Denis, the possibilities of control are slender, but the script of the private charters and of the formulae in a Burgundian manuscript of 727 discussed below (pp. 68–9) makes it clear that bishops, abbots, even lay magnates had a chancery cursive of their own. The charter by which Chrotechilda established her niece as abbess of Bruyères is copied by a scribe, Rigobertus, who used a distinctive 'c' with a loop and a squat 'g', neither of which is found in the royal chancery.[45] He also has four gospel citations in his text. The will of a son of Idda is copied in a script with very few ligatures, an uncial 'n', and 'd' and 'l' with prolonged looped ascenders which slant to the right.[46] The donation charter of Uademir and Ercamberta (with seven *signa* and four autographs) to a group of basilicas and monasteries has distinctive forms of 'l' and 'g', where the descender is extended below the following letters.[47] These chanceries also continued to use papyrus after the royal chancery switched to parchment.[48] All in all, it is quite possible that the character of the Merovingian royal chancery was a good deal more like that of the chancery of Anglo-Saxon kings (below, pp. 109–11, 254–9) than is usually appreciated.

The only attempt to analyse the script of the Merovingian chancery is that of Prou, who described the letter-forms in a charter of 30 June 679.[49] The script of Merovingian royal charters derives from the urban charters of late Antiquity, as Brandi showed.[50] In some cases the *incipit* may be written by a different scribe from the body of the charter, though the script is similar. It is exceptionally stylized, with a pleasure in convolutions of line and a wealth of ligatures. In two cases it is probable that we have two charters copied by the same scribe: documents of 29 February 716 and 16 March 716 were both 'obtained' by Actulius; those of 5 May and 6 June 692 both have the 'recognovit' formula of Aghilius.[51] In

---

[44] R. Falkowski, 'Studien zur Sprache der Merovingerdiplome', *Archiv für Diplomatik*, XVII (1971), p. 93.
[45] See n. 43 above.   [46] *Chartae Latinae*, 569.   [47] *ibid.*, 571.
[48] L. Santifaller, 'Beiträge zur Geschichte der Beschreibstoffe im Mittelalter', *MIÖG, Ergänzungsband*, XV (1953), pp. 66–7; *Chartae Latinae*, 563 (691), 569.
[49] M. Prou, *Manuel de paléographie latine et française* (Paris, 1910), pp. 90–4.
[50] K. Brandi, 'Ein lateinischer Papyrus aus dem Anfang des 6 Jahrhunderts', *Archiv für Urkundenforschung*, V (1914), pp. 269–88.
[51] Lauer and Samaran, *Diplômes originaux* 21, 22, 34, 37.

other cases identity of referendary does not seem to have meant identity of scribe, and the referendary's formula is rarely written by the main scribe of the charter. The distinctive script of the St Maur des Fossés charter may imply that the beneficiary wrote the charter, and the referendary merely checked and approved it: the charter is undated. The small and disciplined script of a *placitum* concerning a *villa* of St Denis also seems different from that of most charters, but *placita*, as Bergman noted, are less well written than diplomas, generally down the length of the parchment, which is often a left-over scrap.[52] The script of the 654 immunity privilege for St Denis is closest to that of the lay signatories, though it is difficult to tell whether Bobo, who 'consinsi et sub' with a *ruche* and Tironian notes in a script very close to the main hand, was a cleric or a layman; the main scribe of this document also seems to have identified the *signa* of magnates who could not write.[53] In general, the Tironian notes in normal charters, especially after the beginnings of 'breakdown', *c.* 695, are very close to the syllabic Tironian notes of Merovingian manuscripts; and chancery cursive must be linked with that of other books.

A cursive with elaborate ligatures is found in a southern French canon law collection, Paris BN MS Lat.12097, and in a copy of the Theodosian Code which was perhaps written at Lyons, Berlin Phillipps MS 1761.[54] In the late seventh century it was used at Corbie for a copy of the first six books of Gregory of Tours' *Histories*, for a Jerome-Gennadius, *De Viris Illustribus* (Paris BN MS Lat.12161), and for parts of Paris BN MS Lat.4403A, an Isidore, *De Legibus* together with the *Breviary of Alaric*, with annotations which establish that it was a working copy.[55] The distinctive ligatures are 'ar', 'b', 'eo', 'ep', 'po', 'ri', 'ro', and 'te'. The sickle-shaped 'u' is also a feature of chancery script. Paris BN MS Nouv. Acq. Lat.1063 is a gospel-book copied in cursive script very close to that of the chancery.[56] At Tours, the chance survival of a group of financial records dating from around 675 shows that the abbey was skilled in a chancery cursive, and in Tironian notes.[57] Surviving

52 Bergmann, 'Untersuchungen', pp. 52–5.
53 Lauer and Samaran, *Diplômes originaux* 6, 6bis; *Chartae Latinae*, 558.
54 Lowe, *CLA*, V, 619–20; VIII, 1064.
55 *ibid.*, V, 671, 624, 556.
56 *ibid.*, V, 679.
57 P. Gasnault and J. Vezin, *Documents comptables de St Martin de Tours à l'époque mérovingienne* (Paris, 1975).

manuscripts from Tours, dating from the 730s and after, incorpo-
rate a wide variety of scripts, revealing a flourishing and well-
staffed *scriptorium*, where Tironian notes were used to collate as well
as annotate manuscripts. The texts copied – Eugippius, Philippus,
Donatus, Pompeius, an abridgement of Orosius, letters and
treatises of Jerome, and a collection of Christian poets – show a
concern for theology and grammar appropriate to a major centre.[58]

As Professor Wallace-Hadrill has observed, 'Calligraphy and
intellectual appetite do not always go hand in hand.'[59] The most
important single witness to later Merovingian intellectual appetite,
a manuscript now divided between Bern and Paris, reveals the
range of interests in a thriving provincial centre, where the bishop
and his entourage were attentive to their responsibilities. There are
no Merovingian parallels to the cathedral *scriptoria* of Verona or
Lucca, and volumes written for bishops still await discovery. But
Bern Burgerbibl. MS 611 + Paris BN MS Lat.10765 (ff.62–9) is a
collection of booklets written in different varieties of cursive script
by several hands, with some uncial and half-uncial sections.[60] It can
be securely dated to 727, and localized in Burgundy, perhaps in the
region of Bourges. Its contents are as follows: two Latin glossaries,
followed by Isidore's Chronicle and his geography (*Etymologiae* IX.
2); the grammer of Asper, the first Latin grammar composed for a
monastic audience; Isidore on Tironian notes; a collection of verse
riddles and a poem on biblical history; Galen on fevers; sections
copied in Tironian notes from Jerome, Augustine and Gregory
concerning clerical ordination, fasting and what it means to be a

---

[58] B. Bischoff, 'Ein wiedergefundener Papyrus und die ältesten Handschriften der
Schule von Tours', in his *Mittelalterliche Studien* (Stuttgart, 1966), I, pp. 6–16.
[59] Wallace-Hadrill, *LHK*, p. 42.
[60] Lowe, *CLA* VII, **604; O. Homburger, *Die illustrierten Handschriften der
Burgerbibliothek Bern* (Bern, 1962), pp. 21–3. Tironian notes in Bern 611 are transcribed by W. Schmitz, in *Deutsche Stenographenzeitung*, III (1888) (which I have not
seen), and in *Commentationes Wolfflinianae* (Leipzig, 1891), pp. 9–13, with plates;
by P. Legendre, *Notes tironiennes* (Paris, 1907), pp. 48–9; and by Mentz, *Tironischen
Noten*, pp. 162–3, with a plate. Notes in Paris 10756 are transcribed by Schmitz in
Mélanges Julien Havet (Paris, 1895), pp. 77–80, and in *Gabelsberger Festschrift*
(Munich, 1890), pp. 116–23; and by Chatelain, *Notes tironiennes*, pp. 226–9. The
notes at the base of ff. 62r–v, 63r in this MS have not yet been transcribed, but
appear to be further theological excerpts. The poem on the ages of the world is ed.
K. Strecker, *MGH, Poet.*, IV, pp. 648–51; the riddles, *ibid.*, pp. 737–59; and the
canonical collection is discussed by H. Mordek, *Kirchenrecht und Reform im
Frankenreich* (Berlin, 1975), pp. 107–9. The formulae are ed. K. Zeumer, *MGH,
Formulae*, pp. 169–70.

true Christian; a Tironian copy of a cento on the End of the World; formulae, now incomplete; a treatise on computus; the oldest version of the *Physiologus*; and a systematic canon law collection dealing with monks, bishops and church land. Lowe characterizes the script of certain sections as 'uncalligraphic', and 'barely distinguishable from charter hands'.

The formulae in this collection refer to bishops, to the *defensor* of the city of Bourges and to the *curia*. Even the riddles reflect this milieu. *De Membrana* (no. 24) ends:

> Manibus me postquam reges et visu mirantur
> Miliaque porto nullo sub pondere multa.[61]

Both script and shorthand are remarkably close to the chancery, especially in the final section, ff. 116–45, where the 'b' with a bow that turns back into itself and a 'g' with a tail that seems to be 'hinged' at the sharply angled base are used: these letters are both rare in book script. The manuscript represents the strongest surviving link between the realms of diplomatic and palaeography: by the first quarter of the eighth century, the production of documents, like the End of the World, was the proper concern of the church. The private charters of St Gall and Wissembourg, copied by the beneficiary, are the natural consequence of the clerical diplomatic which this collection displays. The eclipse of the lay urban chancery and of its *gesta municipalia* is scarcely surprising. A clear account of one of their last moments is found in a document of 675, explaining how the foundation of the abbey of Noirmoutier was recorded at Poitiers by Lupus *amanuensis* and six *curiales*.[62] But north of the Loire nobles and royal officials had recognized that it was the church which offered a permanent hold on property and policy. Classen has shown how the *notarius* became a cleric.

The evidence of charters is minimal and uneven. But it can be supplemented by a survey of the use of Tironian notes in manuscripts. It is clear that this occured in many *scriptoria*, though at this period a *scriptorium* is all too often the precarious inference to be drawn from a manuscript which most probably left the centre at which it had been copied. In such circumstances it is very difficult to

---

[61] Perhaps this may be rendered: 'After kings are admired at the sight of me I carry many thousand things though they have no weight.'
[62] L. Maitre, 'Cunauld, son prieuré et ses archives', *Bibliothèque de l'École des Chartes*, LIX (1898), pp. 239–44.

decide whether any such notes were made to convey information to another reader. Jusselin, interpreting the Tironian list of pericopes in Würzburg MS M p th I a, asserted that they were 'le témoinage d'une étude personelle'.[63] But it seems inconceivable that this applies to the Tironian entries in Bern 611, and at Tours there is evidence of a continuous use of Tironian notes. Paris BN MS Nouv.Acq. Lat.1575, a Eugippius, *Excerpta ex Operibus Sancti Augustini*, was studied by E. K. Rand, who distinguished eight hands writing uncial, three writing half-uncial, and twelve who wrote minuscule; he dated it 725x50.[64] The manuscript has extensive Tironian marginalia, which sometimes summarize the contents, on ff. 13r, 18v, 19r, 45r, 52r, 54v, 55r, 55v, 56r, 77r, 85v, 107r, 108r, 111r, 115v, 116v and 121v. The quire signatures for quires VII to XIV use the Tironian symbol for quaternion. This symbol is also found in Epinal MS 68, dated 744,[65] and Tironian collation symbols occur at the end of quires in Cologne, Dombibl. MS 98, an Isidore, *Quaestiones in Vetus et Novum Testamentum*.[66] Tironian collation and extensive annotation is found in Wolfenbüttel Weiss. MS 86 (Pompeius, Cassiodorus, Julius Severus, Mallius Theodorus and a Greek-Latin glossary), and in Hague Meermano-Westreenianum MS 10 A 1 (Phillipus in Job), which Bischoff dates before 750.[67] All these manuscripts were written by several scribes in what was clearly a well-organized *scriptorium*, and Bischoff suggests that some of these texts may depend on Insular exemplars. The annotations show that they were studied, and that copy was collated with exemplar. The practice of the chancery could be fitted to the needs of the schoolroom.

A second centre where Tironian notes reflect the needs of an episcopal administration is Lyons. In this, the most prestigious

---

[63] P. Salmon, 'Le Système des lections liturgiques dans les notes marginales du MS. M. P. Th Q. 1 a de Wurzbourg', *Revue Bénédictine*, LXI (1951), pp. 38–53. There are plates of the Tironian notes in C. Zangemeister and W. Wattenbach, *Exempla Codicum Latinorum litteris maiusculis scriptorum* (Heidelberg, 1876), pl. LVIII; cf. Lowe, *CLA*, IX, 1429.

[64] E. K. Rand and L. W. Jones, *The Earliest Book of Tours* (Cambridge, Mass., 1934). Rand's list of Tironian notes (p. 49, n. 4), like Lowe's, *CLA*, V, 682, is incorrect; plate XIV shows the notes on f. 55v.

[65] Lowe, *CLA*, VI, 762; plates of the annotations are figs 40–2 in Gasnault and Vezin, *Documents comptables*: they show quire signatures and the notes on f. 115v.

[66] Lowe, *CLA*, VIII, 1157.

[67] *ibid.*, IX, 1394, 1571. All these MSS were magisterially discussed by Bischoff, 'Ein wiedergefundener Papyrus'.

metropolitan see of Gaul, whose bishop might play an international role, are preserved a group of manuscripts which display the highest standards of late antique book production, though the localization at Lyons of the *scriptoria* which copied them is nothing more than a probable inference: one manuscript was repaired by a Visigothic scribe, and others appear to have belonged to a lady. Lowe regarded the script of some marginalia as 'unmistakably French notarial cursive'.[68] The Tironian notes visible on some published facsimiles, some of which may refer to liturgical readings, could not at this stage be studied, but a group of legal manuscripts, which seem to have left Lyons in the Merovingian period, will be considered below (p. 73).

Three manuscripts from Luxeuil have Tironian annotations, and these should be seen in the light of the abbey's influence on the Frankish episcopate. Donatus of Besançon, Chagnoald of Laon, Acharius of Vermandois and Noyon, Ragnachar of Augst, Audomar of Boulogne, Leudoin of Toul, Mummolenus of Noyon and Theodefrid of Amiens were all trained there, and the circle around Desiderius, Dado and Eligius was firmly committed to monasticism on the Luxeuil model. The annotations show further evidence of contact between the court and the abbey. They occur on ff. 9v, 11r, 11v, 38v and 105r of New York Pierpoint Morgan Lib. MS 334 (Augustine, *Homelia in Epistulam Johannis*);[69] here the annotations are syllabic, as in Vatican Reg. Lat. MS 317, the *Missale Gothicum*, where on ff. 75v, 174v, 252r, 252v and 257v they complete prayers and indicate responses.[70] In Valenciennes MS 495, the chronicle of Eusebius-Jerome, they are found on ff. 8v and 10v.[71]

Both Corbie and Chelles, royal foundations linked to Luxeuil by rule and script, produced manuscripts which contain Tironian annotations. Both houses also developed uncial and minuscule scripts derived from those of Luxeuil, and both quickly procured

[68] Lowe, *CLA*, VI, revising his *Codices Lugdunenses Antiquiores* (Lyons, 1924), which must be consulted for additional plates. Lyons MS 604 is inscribed 'Iuliana legit lebrem istum' on f. 86, and Lyons MS 426 is inscribed 'Constantine sum' on ff. 13v–14r. *Notae Tironianae* are found in Lyons MSS 403, 425, 443, 602: Lowe, *CLA*, VI, 771, 772, 774, 782.
[69] Lowe, *CLA*, XI, 1659.
[70] *ibid.*, I, 106; full facsimile, with transcription of the Tironian notes by C. Mohlberg, *Missale Gothicum* (Augsburg, 1929).
[71] Lowe, *CLA*, VI, 841; the notes on f. 10v are shown in E. Chatelain, *Uncialis Scriptura* (Paris, 1901–2), pl. XLIV: Chatelain believed that that notes were copied by an uncomprehending scribe from the exemplar of the MS.

copies of the abridgement of Gregory's *History*.[72] The Chelles Gregory, which, like the Pierpoint Morgan Augustine, belonged to Beauvais cathedral in the Middle Ages, is copied in uncial, though there is a cursive correction on f. 61v; and on f. 86v, originally left blank, are four lines of syllabic Tironian notes which have not been deciphered. Further notes are found on f. 183r of the Chelles copy of the Gelasian Sacramentary, dating 740x50.[73] The prayer for the pope and the bishop has been supplemented by 'et omnibus orthodoxis atque catholici fide cultoribus memento deus rege nostro cum omni populo', which raises the possibility that the volume was used in a royal centre. At Corbie, notes are found in Paris BN Lat. MS 12097, the canonical collection discussed below (p. 000); in Paris BN Lat. MS 12190 (Augustine, *De Consensu Evangeliorum*, reading 'Marcus dixit, quae habent etiam haec verba vel sententia similiter illis');[74] and in Leningrad Lat. MS Q v I 15, syllabic notes on ff. 1v, 6v, 7v and 8r summarize chapters of Isidore, *Proemia in Libris Veteris et Novi Testamenti: de Ortu et Obitu Patrum*; Dr Parkes has shown that this manuscript was in part written by St Boniface, and the notes probably date from the 740s.[75]

Further notes are found in Paris BN Lat. MS 10910, the oldest copy of Fredegar's *Liber Historiarum*, on ff. 34r, 63v, 79r, 132r and 184v, the end leaf. The manuscript is copied in uncial, probably in Burgundy, but Krusch established that the exemplar was written in cursive, the most appropriate script for 'a layman and a man of some standing in the Burgundian court';[76] ff. 20r, 58v, 69r, 83r and 86r have cursive annotations. Another Burgundian manuscript, Leningrad Lat. MS Q v I 2, from the monastery of Réomé (Moutiers St Jean), has extensive notes on ff. 1r, 73r, 79r, 85v, 86v, 89r (dealing with fasting), 89v, 91v, 94v, 103r, 115v, 135v and 210r in the text of Origen's *Homilies*. The flyleaf, though much rubbed, seems to contain several Tironian texts.[77]

[72] Lowe, *CLA*, V, 671; *ibid.*, V, 670, and cf. B. Bischoff, 'Die Kölner Nonnenhandschriften und das Skriptorium von Chelles', in his *Mittelalterliche Studien*, I, pp. 16–34.
[73] Lowe, *CLA*, I, 105; U. Ziegler, 'Das Sakramentum Gelasianum . . . und die Schule von Chelles', *Archiv für Geschichte des Buchwesens*, XVI (1976), pp. 1–95; cf. C. Mohlberg and L. Eizenhöffer, *Liber Sacramentorum Romanae Ecclesiae* (Rome, 1960).　　　[74] Lowe, *CLA*, V, 632. Notes are found on ff. 92v, 98v and 163v.
[75] *ibid.*, XI, 1618; M. Parkes, 'The handwriting of St Boniface', *Beiträge zur Geschichte der deutschen Sprache und Literatur*, XCVIII (1976), pp. 161–79.
[76] Lowe, *CLA*, V, 608; Wallace-Hadrill, *Fredegar*, p. xxii.
[77] Lowe, *CLA*, XI, 1612.

A fragment now in Karlsruhe shows a different use for Tironian notes. It contains portions of a grammatical text commenting on Donatus, copied in cursive script with frequent Tironian abbreviations, in three columns. Column 2 of f. 2 quotes Donatus 377, 13, and the commentary appears to be a re-working of the *Ars Bernensis*.[78] Like the sermons in Bern 611, this is a text designed for exposition, presumably by a teacher who did not expect his pupils to copy the text, but rather to learn its principles. Together with the commentary on Pompeius in the Tours manuscript at Wolfenbüttel (above, p. 70), it marks the entry of Tironian notes into the schoolroom, where Charlemagne wished to see them. (See Plate III.)

But the most important group of annotations are those in manuscripts of civil and canon law. While these manuscripts may be preserved in monastic libraries, they were of particular relevance to bishops. In two cases, there is clear evidence of court connections. Traube noted that Vatican Reg. Lat. MS 886, a copy of the Theodosian Code from Lyons, has notes on f. 122v which read: 'dum deambulare in domo regale vidi hominum per periculum ambolare', followed by a charter *incipit*: 'vir inluster Carlus maiorem domus magnifico fratri ello cometis cognuscatis eo quod'.[79] This is the nearest we have to an original document from the chancery of Charles Martel. On f. 333v is the inscription; 'a terco rigni dmo nuo Theuderige riggi'; it may be no more than the draft of a dating clause, but it may represent the moment of transition from Merovingian royal charters to those of the mayors of the palace. Another charter draft is found in Leningrad Lat. MS F v II 3 (f. 32v), the first part of a canonical collection in uncial and half-uncial script, now divided between Leningrad and Berlin (Phillipps MS 1745).[80] It consists of a *Chrismon*, followed by 'in xpo' in the form of the royal signature. The Leningrad portion also contains marginal summaries, in cursive minuscule, dealing with monks, bishops, ordination and penance. Both these volumes are repositories of canon law used at centres where charters were writ-

---

[78] *ibid.*, VIII, 1128 (Carlsruhe frag. Aug. 133). I know this fragment only through Lowe's photographs, now in the Bodleian; had Dr. B. Barker-Benfield not catalogued these photographs, and those of W. M. Lindsay, and had the library not purchased a set of Père Liebaert's photographs, my task would have been very much harder.
[79] Lowe, *CLA*, I, 110; L. Traube, *Enarratio Tabularum*, in *Theodosiani Libri XVI*, ed. T. Mommsen and P. Meyer (Berlin, 1905), pl. V.
[80] Lowe, *CLA*, VIII, XI, 1061.

ten. Even if the charter fragments are the work of scribes copying the products of the royal chancery, this shows that drafts could be prepared at such centres. Alternatively, the manuscripts may have been used in the royal chancery, or may establish the 'devolution' of the royal chancery into many separate centres of 'royal' power, as perhaps in Anglo-Saxon England (below, pp. 109, 254–8).

Other legal texts contain Tironian annotations. Cologne Dombibl. 212 is a collection dating to 590–604, copied in southern France, and containing many Gallic councils;[81] it had reached Cologne by the eighth century. Its notes on ff. 4v, 9r and 11r, which were read by Schmitz, deal with the judgments of bishops. Munich Clm 22051, a *Breviary of Alaric*, has frequent notes made for a copyist and excerpts from the text; it was studied by Kopp, Ruess and Mentz.[82] Paris BN Lat. MS 12097, the *Collectio Corbiensis* of Gallic and other canons, which was used for the revision of the *Collectio Vetus Gallica*, the first systematic arrangement of canon law, has notes on the flyleaf and on ff. 22r, 23r, 35r, 64v, 147r, 173r, 173v, 178r, 185v, 204r, 207r, 210r and 220r.[83] As in Cologne 212, the notes often summarize the text, though in one case they seem irrelevant to it. Berlin Phillipps MS 1761, another Theodosian code made at Lyons, has Tironian and cursive minuscule notes, which have not been studied.[84]

Whether we look at royal charters, some of which hint at an ecclesiastical origin, or at the books of cathedrals and monasteries, with their administrative concerns and their scribes trained in originally bureaucratic procedures, it is evident that the line between the secular government of the Merovingian palace and the theological and canonical learning of Merovingian bishops and abbots is not so hard and fast as some diplomatic studies have made it seem. The corresponding contrast between Merovingian and Carolingian arrangements can be overdrawn. Both the Merovingians and the Arnulfings needed the church; as is observed elsewhere in this book,

[81] *ibid.*, VIII, 1162. The notes were edited by W. Schmitz, 'Zur Erklärung der tironischen Noten in Handschriften der Kölner Dombibliothek', *Neues Archiv*, XI (1886), p. 118.
[82] Lowe, *CLA*, IX, 1324; U. Kopp, *Palaeographia Critica* (Mannheim, 1817), pp. 333–4; F. Ruess, *Über die Tachygraphie der Römer* (Munich, 1879); A. Mentz, in *Archiv für Urkundenforschung*, XI (1930), pp. 154–7.
[83] Lowe, *CLA*, V, 620; Chatelain, *Notes tironiennes*, pp. 136–8; Mordek, *Kirchenrecht*, pp. 90–4.
[84] Lowe, *CLA*, VIII, 1064.

a 'scholarly personnel' was essential to a ruler's government, and those of the Merovingians were granted increasing privileges. It was these men who supported Columbanus, and compiled collections of Merovingian canons. The Vatican *Theodosian Code*, the Munich *Breviary of Alaric*, the Leningrad and Cologne canon collections, were all studied, annotated and corrected in clerical centres. By *c*.700, the alliance between crown and clergy had channelled chancery skills to the chanceries of cathedrals and monasteries, at just the point when the Arnulfing domination of the royal records becomes evident. If we could localize manuscripts at Metz or St Denis in this period, the Arnulfing strand in the records might emerge more clearly. Until then we must plot the episcopal and monastic dismemberment of the Merovingian realm against a scattered, uneven and inadequate manuscript survival. Amid such shoals and quicksands, Tironian notes are an awkward but indispensable anchor. They grasp onto the late antique legacy of a world where bishops had begun their careers as notaries, and evangelists had known how to take dictation, and they transmit it to a world of kings, courtiers and cloisters, where functions were neither defined nor restricted.

4

Bede's Old Testament Kings

JUDITH McCLURE

One of the most important of recent advances in the study of the *Ecclesiastical History* has been the appreciation that Bede's work as an historian cannot be treated in isolation from his writings on the Scriptures.[1] It has long been clear that most of the judgements implicit in Bede's approach to Anglo-Saxon history must be viewed in the light of his ideal of royal, as well as of religious, behaviour; now it is being realized that his preliminary conception of what that history should be like was formed, in the first instance, by his knowledge of the ancient Israelites. Thus his exegesis of the Old Testament is particularly relevant to the study of his historical writing, because here he was dealing with the people of Israel at various stages of their history, in conditions which he readily perceived were analogous to those determining the development of the Anglo-Saxon kingdoms. Bede had learned from Gregory a view of his own people as a primitive race resembling the Israelites, who had to be led gradually to the fullness of Christian faith, just as God had taught his chosen people with gentleness in the Old Testament.[2] Professor Wallace-Hadrill has pointed the way to the wealth of insights which can be gained from examining Bede's

[1] R. A. Markus, *Bede and the tradition of Ecclesiastical Historiography* (Jarrow Lecture, 1975), pp. 13–14; Roger D. Ray, 'Bede, the exegete, as historian', in *Famulus Christi*, ed. G. Bonner (London, 1976), pp. 125–40; H. M. R. E. Mayr-Harting, *The Venerable Bede, the Rule of St Benedict, and Social Class* (Jarrow Lecture, 1976), pp. 12–22.

[2] See Gregory's letter to Mellitus: *Registrum* XI, 56, ed. P. Ewald and L. Hartmann, *MGH, Ep.* II, p. 331, 11. 18–21: included in *HE* I.30, p. 65. R. A. Markus, 'Gregory the Great and the origins of a papal missionary strategy', *Studies in Church History*, VI (1970), pp. 29–38. For a similar view, also read by Bede, Gregory, *Liber Regulae Pastoralis* III.26, *PL* LXXVII, c. 100.

pictures of the kings of his own day in the light of his commentary on the first Book of Samuel.[3] In the Hebrew, the Book of Samuel was a single work, comprising what the Septuagint and its Latin translations divided into the first two of the four Books of Kingdoms, or later Kings, and it contained various traditions relating to the historical origins of the kingship of Israel.[4] As such, this work is likely to be the one most central to any understanding of the assumptions and perceptions underpinning Bede's historical narrative.

The commentary on I Samuel can be precisely dated to 716: in the preface to the fourth and final book, Bede relates that the brief spell of mental relaxation he had planned, after completing the first three books, had been unduly prolonged by the agitation among his brethren created by Abbot Ceolfrith's unexpected decision to depart for Rome.[5] It was probably his first foray into the immense field of Old Testament exegesis, though he was already an experienced commentator on the New, having completed over the last few years works on the Apocalypse, the Acts of the Apostles, the Catholic Epistles, and the Gospel of Luke.[6] The influence of Gregory had long been paramount in all his writings, so it is not surprising that he should have turned to the Old Testament, on

---

[3] Wallace-Hadrill, *EGK*, pp. 76–8.

[4]

Hebrew Text (before 1448 AD)	Septuagint	Vulgate	Most modern English translations
The Book of Samuel	I Kingdoms	I Kingdoms or Kings	I Samuel
	II Kingdoms	II Kingdoms or Kings	II Samuel
The Book of Kings	III Kingdoms	III Kingdoms or Kings	I Kings
	IV Kingdoms	IV Kingdoms or Kings	II Kings

[5] *In Primam Partem Samuhelis Libri IIII*, CCSL CXIX, ed. D. Hurst, p. 212 (henceforward *In I Sam.*).
[6] C. Jenkins, 'Bede as exegete and theologian', in *Bede: His Life, Times, and Writings*, ed. A. H. Thompson, (Oxford, 1935), pp. 152–200; the evidence for dating is summarized by Plummer, I, pp. cxlvii–cxlix.

which Gregory himself had preached almost exclusively.[7] His choice of the first Book of Samuel for comment is an interesting one. Whether or not he had read the Claudian recension of Gregory's homilies on the first sixteen chapters of that book is a problem not susceptible of easy resolution; what can be certain, however, is that he did not know Gregory to be the author of such a work.[8] He was aiming, therefore, to use the basic methods of his mentor to uncover the many hidden spiritual meanings in a historical work of the Old Testament, which contained as much doctrine and edification as any of the explicitly prophetical books.[9]

As always, Bede declared that he would follow in the footsteps of the Fathers.[10] He must have discovered soon, as Gregory had done before him, that the concerted efforts of the Fathers had done no more than indicate the possibility of a full-scale commentary on Samuel which might find meanings in the whole.[11] In his account of the available exegetical material, Cassiodorus had had to confess himself defeated in the search for a single exposition: he was reduced to compiling for himself a list of homilies, *quaestiones*, letters, and occasional references which had some bearing on various aspects of the text.[12] With the exception of four translated homilies of Origen, only one of which is extant,[13] and Augustine's detailed exposition of the Song of Anna, and comments on other sections of the text relating to his theme of the Two Cities,[14] Latin exegesis had been, for the most part, concerned with various extremely obscure and conjectural problems, adjectives chosen by Cassiodorus, raised by

---

[7] Paul Meyvaert, *Bede and Gregory the Great* (Jarrow Lecture, 1964), pp. 1–26, esp. pp. 13–19.

[8] Bede's editor believes he had read Gregory on Kings: *In I Sam., praefatio* p. V; not so Paul Meyvaert, 'A new edition of Gregory the Great's Commentaries on the Canticle of Canticles and I Kings', *Journal of Theological Studies*, XIX (1968), p. 225.

[9] *In I Sam., Prologus*, p. 9; compare Gregory, *Expositiones in Librum Primum Regum*, ed. P. Verbraken, *CCSL* CXLIV, p. 49.

[10] *In I Sam.*, p. 10: 'patrum vestigia sequens'.

[11] Gregory, *In Librum Primum Regum, Prologus*, 1, pp. 49–50.

[12] *Cassiodori Institutiones* I.ii, 'De Regum': 1–10, ed. R. A. B. Mynors (Oxford, 1937).

[13] R. Devreesse, *Les Anciens commentateurs grecs de l'Octateuque et des Rois* (Paris, 1959), p. 28; the text of the Latin translation of Origen's Homily on I Samuel: *GCS* 33, ed. W. A. Baehrens, pp. 1–25.

[14] *De Civitate Dei* XVII, 4–7, ed. B. Dombart and A. Kalb *CCSL* XLVIII, pp. 554–70.

events or descriptions.[15] The significance of certain actions by David, and the judgment of Solomon, formed the matter of typical *quaestiones*;[16] the two wives of Helchana,[17] the description of Saul as possessed by 'an evil spirit of the Lord' after his earlier reception of the spirit of prophecy,[18] and the divine expression of regret for appointing Saul as king,[19] were all regarded as issues worthy of analysis. It is not surprising, then, that the Book of Samuel, and the Books of Kings in general, should have been generally regarded as productive of difficulties rather than of spiritual guidance; both Origen and Augustine found them natural exemplars of the Pauline veil which covered the Old Testament.[20]

In approaching the Book of Samuel, Bede could draw from Augustine and from Origen the broad typological significance of the main characters and events; from Jerome and Josephus, he discovered the allegorical significance of the many Hebrew names and places in the text.[21] He was evidently aiming to produce a fairly straightforward commentary in which he would occasionally eluci-date the literal meaning, but in general do no more than provide an allegorical exposition of each verse. He did not follow Gregory's generally prolix exegetical methods, involving the provision of three levels wherever possible, and long digressions on the moral lessons that could be drawn from even the slightest indication in the text. It is worth pointing out that Bede's now widely recognized dependence on Gregory,[22] a dependence still fully to be explored, did not inspire him to produce homiletic commentaries on the same scale. Bede knew well enough the limitations of the scholarship and the libraries of his audience, and the general need for works of basic commentary that would be sufficient in themselves to provide the

[15] *Institutiones* I.ii,5, three *quaestiones* of Augustine are called *opinatissimas*; in ii,6, three of Jerome are described as *obscurissimas*.

[16] *ibid.*, I.ii, 3–6, 8; Augustine, *Sermo* X (in reality, a *quaestio*), ed. C. Lambot, *CCSL* XLI, pp. 152–9.

[17] Origen, *Homily on I Samuel*, 3.

[18] Augustine, *De Diversis Quaestionibus ad Simplicianum*, q.1 ed. A. Mutzenbecher, *CCSL* XLIV, pp. 58–74.

[19] *ibid.*, q.2, pp. 75–80.

[20] *ibid.*, Book II, *praefatio*; Origen, *Homily on I Samuel*, 3, p. 5, ll. 8–15.

[21] Bede, *Nomina Locorum ex Beati Hieronimi Presbiteri et Flavi Josephi Collecta Opusculis*, ed. D. Hurst, *CCSL* CXIX, pp. 273–87, *passim*. Bede's editor believes that he had certainly read Origen's homily in Rufinus's translation: *In I Sam.* I.i,32, p. 11.

[22] For Bede's very Gregorian view of the role of *praedicatores* in the church, see Thacker's discussion, below, pp. 130–6.

keys to a fuller allegorical understanding of the Scriptures, in
accordance with the simple rules laid down in Tyconius's handbook.[23] He was certainly prepared to supply more elaborate
interpretations, when these were solicited; thus he replied in detail
to thirty questions on the Books of Kings submitted by Nothelm,
and the *quaestiones*, or 'learned opinions', which resulted were
circulated with the commentary on I Samuel.[24] But his principal
aim is more clearly revealed by the second appendix to the main
commentary, again apparently requested by Nothelm; this was the
Nomina Locorum, a gazetteer of places mentioned in the Books of
Kings, together with a brief description of each, excerpted from the
works of Jerome and Josephus.[25] Bede could not be sure that his
readers possessed even such a fundamental exegetical tool as
Jerome's handbook, the *Liber Locorum*.[26]

In an attempt to determine the extent to which the commentary
on I Samuel can illuminate the study of the *Ecclesiastical History*, it is
important to include a consideration of the two ancillary works, the
Quaestiones in Regum Librum and the *Nomina Locorum*. Not only are
they found with the commentary in the earliest manuscripts, but
with it they represent a related group of Bede's writings on the
Books of Samuel and Kings. He returned to the Old Testament
several times, and to questions of kingship raised by it, but, for
reasons which are not clear, he commented on only the first Book of
Samuel, and thereafter merely wrote on these books to satisfy
Nothelm's precise demands, occasionally as short parts of other
works, and later to comment on the allegorical significance of the
construction of Solomon's Temple.[27]

The limitations of Bede's objectives must also constantly be

[23] Tyconius, *Liber Regularum*, ed. F. C. Burkitt (*Texts and Studies* III.1 1894). Bede
read these rules in Augustine's transcription in *De Doctrina Christiana*, and copied
them into his Commentary on the Apocalypse: Gerald Bonner, *Saint Bede in the
Tradition of Western Apocalyptic Commentary* (Jarrow Lecture, 1966), esp. p. 6. The
influence of these basic rules on Bede's exegesis would be worth investigating.

[24] *In Regum Librum XXX Quaestiones*, ed. D. Hurst, CCSL CXIX, pp. 293–322
(henceforward *In Regum Quaest.*).

[25] Its principal sources are Jerome, *Liber Interpretationis Hebraicorum Nominum*, ed.
P. De Lagarde, *CCSL* LXXII, pp. 57–161; *Liber Locorum*, *PL*. XXIII cc. 869–928;
for Bede's use of Josephus, M. L. W. Laistner, 'The library of the Venerable Bede',
in *Bede: His Life, Times and Writings*, pp. 245–7.

[26] J. N. D. Kelly, *Jerome* (London, 1975), pp. 153–5.

[27] *In Regum Quaest., prologus*, p. 293. I do not include within this group Bede's *De
Templo*, the allegorical commentary on the construction of Solomon's Temple
described in the first Book of Kings. Bede wrote this later in his life, possibly while

borne in mind. His didactic aims, together with the constraints of the patristic framework of interpretation, determined not only the contents, but the nature of his comments on the scriptural text. There are verses of which the modern historian craves to hear his literal interpretation, but in vain; the sack of Jerusalem by Nebuchadnezzar, for instance, is explained to Nothelm purely in allegorical terms, although in them Bede's concern for what he regarded as the spiritual negligence of his own day is manifest.[28] This rigidity of outlook is counterbalanced by the occasions, though few, where Bede was challenged to spend relatively longer on the historical interpretation: a sure indication that the circumstances described bore some contemporary significance for him.[29]

he was completing the *Ecclesiastical History*. The relationship between the two works was suggested by Paul Meyvaert, *Bede and Gregory the Great*, pp. 1, 9–10, and fully developed by H. M. R. E. Mayr-Harting in the appendix to his 1976 Jarrow Lecture (see n. 1 above), pp. 19–22. The idea for this work might well have been suggested by Gregory the Great's homilies on the obscure fortieth chapter of Ezechiel, treating of the prophet's vision of a New Temple: *Homiliae in Hiezechihelem Prophetam*, ed. M. Adriaen, *CCSL* CXLII, pp. 205–398. But it does not belong to this earlier group of writings. Professor Markus has also pointed out, in his *Bede and the Tradition of Ecclesiastical Historiography*, p. 14, that Bede's Commentary on Ezra 'contains a short but unduly neglected treatise on Christian kingship.' In addition, it is worth remarking that the *De Octo Quaestionibus, PL* XCIII, cc. 458–9, contains two opinions concerning King David which are relevant to Bede's view of kingship. It seems almost certain that Bede was the author of the first eight of the *quaestiones*, (recorded in *Clavis* as the *Aliquot Quaestionum Liber*). The spurious later theological *quaestiones* have been separated from Bede's characteristically exegetical comments by P. Lehmann, 'Wert und Echtheit einer Beda abgesprochenen Schrift', *Sitzungsberichte der bayerischen Akademie der Wissenschaften* (Munich, 1919), Heft 4, pp. 8–14. The work thus isolated, the *De Octo Quaestionibus*, was surely not addressed to Nothelm, as Laistner suggests on the grounds of attribution in several manuscripts: the work to which Bede alludes when writing to Nothelm is evidently, as the modern editor maintains, the *Nomina Locorum*: M. L. W. Laistner, *A Handlist of Bede Manuscripts* (Ithaca, 1943) pp. 155–8.

[28] *In Regum Quaest.*, Q.XXX, pp. 320–2. 'Cuius tam defendae historiae quia multum neglegentiae nostri temporis congruit non opinor allegoriam esse reticendam' (p. 320). The Babylonians represented the city of the devil; Jerusalem the city of Christ, the Church. Thus Nebuchadnezzar captured Jerusalem, signifying the occasions when the teachers of the faithful fall into heresy or apostasy (p. 321).

[29] For example, *In I Sam.*, pp. 98–9, commenting on Samuel's speech about kingship, I Sam.,12: 1–25. Here and elsewhere, biblical quotations are taken from the modern Vulgate, in the edition of A. Colunga and L. Turrado (*Biblioteca de Autores Cristianos*, 4th edn., Madrid, 1965). Bede's own text of Samuel was mostly identical with that of the Codex Amiatinus: ed. D. Hurst, *CCSL* CXIX, *praefatio*, p. V.

Nonetheless, the limitations of the exegetical form in providing evidence for the modern historian make it particularly important to remember that Bede may well have been influenced quite simply by the contents of I Samuel, to an extent by no means fully revealed in a commentary written for a precise purpose and audience within a confined literary tradition. So it is necessary to place the *Ecclesiastical History* not only in the light on Bede's commentary, but in that of the text of I Samuel itself.

By the time of the two generations or so which were described in the various traditions contained in I Samuel, the decisive phase of the Israelite migration into Canaan was over.[30] After a long period of piecemeal conquest and gradual infiltration in the thirteenth century BC, the Israelites were able to maintain their power in central Canaan, largely in the hill country which they had wrested from the indigenous inhabitants, by means of a tribal confederacy, prepared to unite in times of emergency under military leaders whose authority extended beyond the territory of their own tribe, misleadingly known as judges. This initial success had been achieved largely as a result of the lack of sophisticated and powerful opposition from Egypt and Mesopotamia. The tribal confederacy could deal with an alliance of Canaanite city states, or with the opposition from the nations of Transjordan: Moabites, Edomites, or Ammonites. In the twelfth and eleventh centuries BC, however, the arrival of the Philistines destabilized the political structure of the whole area, creating a threat to the very existence of the Israelite settlements with which an *ad hoc* confederation of tribes could not effectively deal. By the end of this period, during the lives of Samuel and Saul, the Israelites were working painfully towards a new kind of political leadership, that of kingship, which would enable them to counter the advance of the Philistine empire.

While Bede would not have perceived the history of the Chosen People of God in this way, as he read the first Book of Samuel he would certainly have seen that the Israelites were fighting hard to maintain their settlements in the Promised Land. It is clear that he was interested in the precise conditions under which an invading people struggled to maintain and to extend their conquests in the face of considerable opposition. His search for understanding and for precise knowledge can be traced in his commentary and in the

[30] See the general historical account in M. Noth, *The History of Israel* trans. S. Godman, rev. P. R. Ackroyd (London, 1960), pp. 141–63.

ancillary material he produced to accompany it, and it is to these works we should turn in order to uncover the development of the techniques of investigation which he employed when he came to study the Anglo-Saxon settlement. Bede's historical skills can be seen, in almost every instance, to have been influenced by what he had learned from the Latin tradition of Old Testament exegesis.

In the first place, the Vulgate text of I Samuel is consistent and precise in the vocabulary it uses for geographical descriptions, and in its delineation of the peoples successively holding power over particular areas. This concern for topographical accuracy, and for the position of a particular site within an administrative structure, is reflected in Bede's commentary, and most particularly in his compilation of the *Nomina Locorum*. Mr James Campbell has recently shown how the study of Bede's vocabulary in the *Ecclesiastical History* has a good deal to contribute to the identification of settlements in Anglo-Saxon England and to their functions in royal organization.[31] The establishment of Bede's pattern of linguistic usage, as well as the way in which he understood that settlements were made, and related to one another, can be seen in his much earlier exegetical studies.

Bede's ready appreciation of the importance of geographical factors in his description of the Anglo-Saxon kingdoms needs no documentation. Long before his references to the Humber as a political boundary he had described the similar role of the River Jordan, including additional information from Jerome to indicate its sources, its course, and the derivation of its name.[32] Just as he was interested in the military origins of Fursa's monastery at Burgh Castle, he had earlier noted that the city of Gazer had been built on a naturally fortified site.[33] His concern for precision can be seen in his careful noting of the limits of the region known by a particular name,[34] and by his inclusion on occasion of distances in miles.[35] In general, his interest in these matters is evident from the fact that he did not merely make a compilation from the information in Jerome

[31] 'Bede's words for places', in *Names, Words, and Graves: Early Medieval Settlement*, ed. P. H. Sawyer (Leeds, 1978), pp. 34–54.
[32] *HE* I. 15, p. 31; I.25, p. 45; *Nomina Locorum, s.v. Iordanes*, p. 282.
[33] *HE* III.19, p. 164; *Nomina Locorum, s.v. Gazer*, p. 280. Bede added information here himself, from I Kings 9: 16–18.
[34] *Nomina Locorum, s.v. Moab*, p. 282, *Samaria*, p. 285, *Bezec*, p. 275.
[35] *ibid., s.v. Hebron, Iesimuth*, p. 281.

and Josephus, but supplemented it with material drawn from his own extensive scriptural and exegetical reading.[36]

Bede may well himself have been educated in topographical exactitude by the consistent terminology employed by Jerome and Josephus. The terms *metropolis* and *civitas regalis*, used independently or occasionally together, were restricted to a few royal centres, not necessarily Israelite, which had an undefined authority over a substantial area: in the case of Damascus, over the whole of Syria; in that of Asor, over all the territory of the Philistines.[37] Again, Bede frequently supplied extra information about such sites from his own erudition: whether, for instance, as in the case of Samaria, the surrounding region had taken on its name;[38] what could be known of the foundation and subsequent re-naming of the *metropolis* of Rabbath.[39] He recognized, too, changes in political control, and the decline in status of once great royal cities like Gabaon and Hebron.[40]

Lesser sites were also accurately described. Vague terms, such as *locus*, were reserved for particular spots remembered not as settlements, but because they were associated with an outstanding figure;[41] *regio* was used to denote an area subsequently more precisely described in terms of the settlements it contained.[42] The smallest settlements were known as *villae, vici,* or *viculi;*[43] an *oppidum* was intermediate, and could develop into an *urbs*.[44] The most generally used terms were *civitas* and *urbs*, the former most frequently.[45] The description of Moab seems to suggest that the two could be used interchangeably.[46] *Civitates* were clearly significant settlements, known as such when they possessed strategic and often royal significance; frequently they were fortified.[47] Bede was

[36] *ibid.*, pp. 273–87, *passim.*

[37] *ibid., s.v. Damascus*, 'in omni Syria tenens principatum', p. 277, *Asor*, 'quia metropolis erat omnium regnorum Philisthiim', p. 273, *Saba*, p. 285, *Samaria*, p. 285, *Gabaon*, p. 279, *Hierusalem*, p. 280, *Hebron*, p. 281, *Issachar*, p. 281, *Rabbath*, p. 284, *Tyrus*, p. 286.

[38] *ibid.*, p. 285.   [39] *ibid.*, p. 284.

[40] *ibid.*, pp. 279, 281.

[41] *ibid., s.v. Arama, Athac, Nahioth*, pp. 274, 283.

[42] *ibid., s.v. Chabul*, p. 277.

[43] *ibid., s.v. Bethmacha*, p. 276, *Balsalisa*, p. 276, *Bethel*, p. 275, *Engaddi*, p. 278, *Dan*, p. 277, *Geth*, p. 279.

[44] *ibid., s.v. Bethsan*, p. 276.

[45] *Civitas* is used 43 times, *urbs* 20.

[46] *Nomina Locorum., s.v. Moab*, p. 282.

[47] *ibid., s.v. Abela*, p. 274, *Castra*, pp. 276–7.

interested in their associations, their naming, and in the historical context in which they had flourished; he noted, too, any subsequent decline.[48] There can be little doubt that the terminology of the *Ecclesiastical History* in relation to Anglo-Saxon settlements, together with Bede's interest in tracing their past and their nomenclature, find their roots in his quest for accuracy in studying the first Book of Samuel. It was an interest shared by some at least of his contemporaries; Nothelm in particular had not only solicited the work on the *Nomina Locorum*, but included precise geographical questions to which Bede replied in the *In Regum Quaestiones*, on occasion mobilizing much scriptural and exegetical erudition.[49]

The Vulgate text of I Samuel also influenced Bede's historical perception and methods. Most fundamentally, its account of the judgeship of Samuel, and of the reign of Saul, was set within a loose chronological framework. Usually only vague indications of the sequence of events were given, by the use of such phrases as *in diebus illis, in die illa, quadam die, eo autem tempore, post paucos dies*; occasionally more precision was shown: *cumque pertransissent decem dies*.[50] In particular, the first editors of the different narrative strands which were woven together to form the Hebrew text had made additions to give a more exact notion of regnal years.[51] This had evidently become necessary once the kingship had been securely established and the different traditions concerning its origins were being compiled, both to link together the disparate sources concerning Samuel and Saul, and to anchor them chronologically. One such insertion had been distorted early in transmission, and appeared in the Vulgate text as: *Filius unius anni erat Saul cum regnare coepisset, duobus autem annis regnavit super Israel*.[52] As his commentary reveals, Bede was immediately interested in this passage, which, as Gregory had

---

[48] *ibid., s.v. Aendor*, 'civitas in Iezrahela ubi filii Israhel se ad proelium praeperantes castra posuerunt. Et est hodieque grandis vicus Aendor iuxta montem Thabor ad meridiem in quarto miliario', pp. 273–4; *Sidon*, p. 285.

[49] *In Regum Quaest.*, Q.XV, pp. 307–8; Q.XXI, p. 314; Q.XXII, p. 315.

[50] I Sam.3:2,12; 4:1; 14:1; 17:55; 18:27; 25:38.

[51] The present divisions of the Books of Samuel and Kings must not obscure the separate narrative strands which cut across them, and which have been only loosely, and with obvious breaks, shaped together. The precise nature of the editorial work which produced the Hebrew text of Samuel and Kings is as yet obscure, as there are conflicting conceptions of each stage of the composition of these books. For an introduction to the problems and a full bibliography, O. Eissfeldt, *The Old Testament: An Introduction*, trans. P. R. Ackroyd (Oxford, 1965) pp. 132–43, 241–8, 268–81.   [52] I Sam.13:1.

realized before him, made no literal sense.[53] What is more significant than Bede's attempt to come to terms with a verse that modern
editors simply dismiss, is its relevance to his later efforts to weld the
disparate traditions he had gathered concerning the Anglo-Saxon
kingdoms into an at least apparently sequential narrative.

Bede's interest in chronology long preceded his commentary on I
Samuel, so that he brought to his reading of the text a mind very
alert to the problems of dating, as his detailed comments, and his
answers to a similarly interested Nothelm, reveal.[54] What he had
learned from it, when he came to draft the *Ecclesiastical History*, was
the system of linking his material and making it develop in time by,
wherever possible, precise references to regnal years, sometimes by
means of the kind of summary narrative of the reign of a king, his
demise, and his successor, upon which modern historians naturally
pounce.[55] For Bede, such passages might well have had the level of
importance accorded by the first compilers of the Book of Samuel
to the sentences they added to give structure to their account. Bede,
in the end, did better: his long standing interest in chronology, and
his painstakingly acquired competence in the field, give to his
linking passages the outstanding historical significance that is so
obvious a feature of the *Ecclesiastical History* today. But, like his
Hebrew counterparts, he was content, where chronological precision was impossible, to use vague, and indeed, in Latin translation,
even identical phrases to indicate the passsage of time.[56]

Bede's inclusion of more detailed chronological information cannot be explained solely by his own preoccupations and expertise.
Despite his decision to write a commentary only on I Samuel, he
had naturally read extensively and carefully the scriptural accounts
of the kingship in Israel, and in the first and second Books of Kings
he would have found much more frequent and precise information
about the reigns and families of kings. He would also have seen the

[53] *In I. Sam.*II. xiii, i, pp. 101–2; Gregory, *In Librum Primum Regum* V.45,
pp. 446–7.

[54] *De Temporibus* was written thirteen years before *In I Sam.*, in 703. *In I Sam.* III,
x, 18–19, p. 183, and esp. II, *praefatio*, pp. 68–70, reveal Bede's chronological
concerns; the interest of Nothelm is shown in *In Regum Quaest.*, Q. IV, pp. 298–9;
Q.XXV, pp. 316–7.

[55] For example, *HE* III. 14, p. 154, on the death of Oswald and the succession of
Oswiu.

[56] *ibid.*, III.10, p. 146, 'eodem tempore'; III.18, p. 162, 'his temporibus'; III.22,
p. 171, 'eo tempore'; III.22, p. 173, 'tempore non pauco'; IV.6, p. 218, 'non multo
post haec elapso tempore'.

explicit references to the historical source material used by the editors, in particular to a history of the Acts of Solomon, and to the Royal Annals of the Kings of Israel and of Judah.[57] He could have been in no doubt that the history of the Chosen People, in both spiritual and political terms, depended, under God, on the influence, ability and military strength of its kings. The internal rivalries of the early contenders for power over the Israelites are made very plain in the scriptural text: the dispute between Saul and David, and the attempt to resolve it by marriage alliance;[58] the exile of David in the territories of other kings, and his difficulties there;[59] the final resolution of the conflict in battle, and the subsequent feud between the House of David and the House of Saul.[60] Such material must inevitably have coloured Bede's view, and increased his understanding, of the struggle between the royal families of Bernicia and Deira.[61]

Bede would also have learned from his scriptural reading the overriding significance of the military strength of kings, and their need to serve as effective warleaders in maintaining and extending the position of their own people against the encroachments of surrounding tribes with their own hostile and aggressive kings. Indeed, his understanding of this point is explicit in his commentary, and in his comparison of Aethilfrith of Northumbria, *rex fortissimus et gloriae cupidissimus*, with Saul.[62] So he would have seen the way in which powerful kings like Saul and David extended their territories, and multiplied the peoples under their control;[63] how the authority of a great king like Solomon depended upon the acceptance of his rule over a wide area inhabited by diverse peoples under minor rulers.[64] In the Books of Samuel and Kings, the text is interspersed with brief passages summarizing the military activities of the reigning king, and the development of his power.[65] It was a practice followed by Bede, who in the *Ecclesiastical History* included many such short accounts, now the subject of minute analysis, in

[57] I Kings 11:41; 14:19–20.
[58] I Sam. 18:17–19.
[59] *ibid.*, 27:1–12; 29:1–11.
[60] *ibid.*, 31:1–13; II Sam. 2:1–3:1.
[61] *HE* III.6, pp. 138–9.
[62] *In I Sam.* II.xiv, 52, p. 125. On Aethelfrith, *HE* I.34, p. 71: this passage, and Bede's general view of King Saul, is discussed in Wallace-Hadrill, *EGK*, pp. 76–8.
[63] II Sam.8:1–15.
[64] I Kings 4:1–25.
[65] I Sam.14:47–52, on the wars of Saul.

which he documented the increasing authority of his *Bretwaldas*.[66]
Like the Hebrew editors of the Acts of Solomon, he added to his
description of the peace and prosperity which were the result of
Edwin's victories what he claimed was a current proverb: in his
reign a mother could cross the island unharmed with her baby.[67]
Similar conditions obtained under the powerful king Solomon, heir
to the conquests of David:

> Solomon reigned over all kingdoms from the river to the land of the
> Philistines and the Egyptian border. They brought tribute, and
> served him all his life. . . . For he had dominion over all the region
> between the Euphrates and the Mediterranean, from Tiphsah to
> Gaza, and over all the kings of the area, and he had peace on all his
> frontiers. Judah and Israel lived in security, each man under his vine
> and his fig tree, from Dan to Beersheba, all the days of Solomon.[68]

Bede evidently recognized that the primary cause of a king's
power, and indeed the reason for its acceptance by subject rulers,
was military victory in significant trials of strength with rivals, and,
like his scriptural predecessors, he was prepared to give substantial
space to explaining the causation, course and consequences of
important battles. In his preliminary discussion, his analysis of the
strength of the rival forces and their leaders and of the attitudes of
prominent war commanders who preferred to wait on the side
lines, his realization of the importance of geographical factors, and
his description of the battle itself and its outcome, Bede had gained
much from the Books of Samuel and Kings. An analysis of his
famous account of the Battle of the Winwaed in AD655, in the third
book of the *Ecclesiastical History*, will serve to illustrate the way in
which he had learned to ask the pertinent questions about significant military encounters in the history of his own people.

Long-standing conflict between the Northumbrians and the
Mercians came to a head, according to Bede, because Penda, who
had killed Oswiu's brother Oswald in battle, had carried out a series
of raids into Northumbrian territory; similarly, David decided to
do battle with the Philistines, the old enemies of the Israelites, when
he heard they had attacked Keilah and were plundering the area.[69]

---

[66] *HE* II.9, p. 97, on the power of Edwin.
[67] *ibid.*, II.16, p. 118.
[68] I Kings 4: 21, 24–5.
[69] The Battle of the Winwaed: *HE* III.24, pp. 177–8. David and the Philistine
raid: I Sam.23:1–6.

Oswiu, unprepared for battle, offered Penda substantial tribute, just as Ahab, king of Israel, offered silver and gold to Benhadad, king of Aram, who was laying siege to Samaria.[70] Penda is described as a heathen; Goliath, the Philistine who fought David in single combat, was uncircumcised.[71] Oswiu, forced to do battle, offered gifts to the God of his people; David prayed to the God who drove nations and gods out before the Israelites.[72] When Penda drew up his army, it included the forces of thirty royal commanders, while Benhadad of Aram brought thirty-two kings with him against Israel.[73] Oswiu's nephew Ethelwald ought to have supported him against Penda, in Bede's view; instead, he waited in a safe place while the battle was fought, until its outcome was clear.[74] Similarly, in one of Saul's battles against the Philistines, many Israelites hid in the highlands of Ephraim, only joining Saul when they heard that the Philistines were on the run.[75]

The Battle of the Winwaed itself was described in terms all to be found in the Vulgate text of Samuel and Kings. The introductory ablative absolute, *inito . . . certamine*, was used of a battle between Saul and the Philistines: it evidently remained in Bede's mind, for he used it again himself, before he wrote the *Ecclesiastical History*, in his answers to Nothelm. He was dealing with the defeat of Benhadad of Syria, in terms which strongly suggest that the scriptural account of the aggressive behaviour of that king, and the eventual crushing of his proud boasts, formed the view of Penda in the *Ecclesiastical History*: 'battle was joined, and Benhadad returned home, not triumphing over conquered enemies, but in flight, with his army cut to pieces'.[76] The vocabulary of the battle is, not surprisingly, that of Jerome's Late Latin, with the use of *fugare, caedere, pugnare, interficere*.[77] The inclusion of geographical factors is, however, perhaps more directly influenced by the Scriptures: the battle between Penda and Oswiu was fought near a river, which had flooded its banks; Saul met the Philistines once between Socoh and Azekah, with the Valley of the Terebinth lying between the armies assembled on the hills.[78] In the defeat of Penda's army which was

[70] I Kings 20: 1–6. [71] I Sam.17:26.
[72] II Sam.7:18–29. [73] I Kings 20:1.
[74] *HE* III.24, p. 178. [75] I Sam. 14:22.
[76] *ibid.*, 4:2, *In Regum Quaest.*, Q.XVII, p. 311: '. . . inito certamine Benadab non victis adversariis triumphans sed caeso suo exercitu fugiens domum rediit.'
[77] For descriptions of battle, I Sam. 4:1–2, 10–11; 14:20–22; 31:1.
[78] *ibid.*, 17:1–3.

the outcome of the Battle of the Winwaed, many more Mercians and their allies were drowned than were killed by the sword.[79] In the terrible battle which saw the death of Absalom, of the rebels against David 'the forest claimed more victims that day than were devoured by the sword'.[80]

Thus in his descriptions of what might seem to be the objective reality of Anglo-Saxon kingship, particularly in his brief accounts of the acquisition and increase of power by kings, Bede evidently had received much guidance in the recording of the information at his disposal, and in his precise assessments of the relative strength of individual kings, from his Old Testament reading. His perception of the behaviour of the rulers of his own day must also have been sharpened by the accounts in the Books of Samuel and Kings of the political use of marriage alliances, of public displays of military power and ruthlessness, and of the treatment of rivals for royal authority.[81] Bede's understanding of the clashes between Oswiu and Oswin, and of the exile of Edwin, must have been developed by the detailed account of Saul's jealousy of David, even to his ploys when his rival sought refuge among the Philistines.[82] Much more significant for Bede than such incidental insights was the fundamental presupposition familiar immediately to the reader of the Ecclesiastical History, which he had seen exemplified and discussed at length in the various traditions preserved in the Scriptures relating to the emergence of kingship among the Israelites: that each king had a special place in the divine plan, and that moral judgements could and must be passed on all his actions.

The first Book of Samuel contains two very different accounts of the recognition of Saul as first king of the Israelites. In one he was a successful military leader, who managed to unite the tribes when they were most threatened by external enemies. Secretly anointed by Samuel, he proved himself in battle and was subsequently acclaimed by the people.[83] In the second source, however, Samuel's

[79] HE III.24, p. 178: 'contigit, ut multo plures aqua fugientes, quam bellantes perderet ensis.'
[80] II Sam.18:8: 'multo plures erant quos saltus consumpserat de populo, quam hi quos voraverat gladius in die illa.'
[81] Bede's understanding of the need for ruthless displays of power by conquering kings is revealed by his comment on I Sam. 17:54, which described David's taking of Goliath's head to Jerusalem: In I Sam.III. xvii, 54, p. 162.
[82] HE III.14, pp. 154–5; II.12, pp. 107–10; I. Sam.18:6–16; 19:1–24; 22:1–5; 27:1–12; 29:1–11.   [83] I Sam.9; 10:1–16; 11.

attitude was hostile: pressed by the Israelites to set up a monarchy, he tried to dissuade them by the threat of God's disapproval, and by warning them of the tyranny which would ensue.[84] Once he had become king, Saul proved himself an active and successful military leader, until he disobeyed a divine command which he had received through Samuel. Thereafter he was rejected by God, and sank into morose and self-defeating suspicion of his vivid young protégé, David.[85] At the end of I Samuel he was defeated in battle by the Philistines, and took his own life after he had heard of the deaths of his three sons.[86]

The Vulgate text of I Samuel thus contains many events, and many passages, both descriptive and analytical, upon which Bede's comments on the literal meaning, had he made them, would have been extremely illuminating for the student of the *Ecclesiastical History*. In particular, the speeches of Samuel both in praise and in criticism of the institution of monarchy would be precisely relevant to Bede's treatment of Anglo-Saxon kingship, as would the scenes of confrontation between Samuel and Saul, and the anointing of Saul.[87] Nowhere is the historian more frustrated by the constraints imposed by the Latin exegetical tradition, and by Bede's own sense of the needs of his audience. Indeed, he was not even much concerned with some of the fundamental problems which had exercised earlier exegetes, such as the texts relating to the divine choice and subsequent rejection of Saul.[88] In general, he adhered to the basic task he had set himself of providing a useful allegorical interpretation. It can certainly be said from his few direct literal comments that he appreciated the universal significance of Samuel's great speech on kingship to the Israelites, in which the prophet emphasized that the king's good deeds would bring success to his people. Bede pointed out that this text had a general application.[89]

The limitations of Bede's interpretation should not conceal the fact that he saw quite clearly in I Samuel both the central role of kings in assuring the temporal welfare of their people, and the

[84] *ibid.*, 7; 8; 10:17–24; 12.
[85] *ibid.*, 15; 28:3–25.
[86] *ibid.*, 31:1–13.
[87] *ibid.*, 12:1–25; 15:10–35; 10:1; 16:1–13.
[88] Augustine, *De Diversis Quaestionibus ad Simplicianum*, Q.2, pp. 75–80; Eucherius, *Libri Instructionum*, ed. K. Wotke, CSEL XXXI, Book I, 'De Regum', I–III, pp. 82–3.
[89] *In I Sam.* II. xii,1, p. 98; Wallace-Hadrill, *EGK*, p. 76.

function of prophets to guide their every action in the light of God's will, and to determine the needs of the kingdom and its people.[90] Bede noted in the text comments discussing the personal qualities desirable in kings, especially humility.[91] The decrees of God's law, he explained to Nothelm, laid down the manner in which a king ought to live.[92] The career of Saul showed quite clearly the success in battle which attended a king who followed God's commands, as well as the ignominious failure and defeat, and divine rejection, consequent upon disobeying the word of a prophet.[93] Where else, then, when Bede came to draft the *Ecclesiastical History*, with its message for the kings, and their advisers, of his own day, would he find the right approach to royal activity and its true ends and successes, but in the Books of Samuel and Kings, upon which he had expended so much thought?

It ought to be borne in mind that Bede was known as an expert on the kings of the Old Testament long before he came to write about his own people. It is usually assumed that, as the foremost scholar of his day, he was the obvious choice as historian of the coming of Christianity to the Anglo-Saxons. But it is possible to be more precise. We cannot know exactly what Abbot Albinus envisaged when he first approached Bede. It may have been no more than the preservation in suitable literary form of the Canterbury traditions relating to the Gregorian mission, defined by Gregory himself as sent to the *gens Anglorum*.[94] What must be almost certain is that Nothelm, the London priest and future archbishop of Canterbury, who visited Rome and Wearmouth-Jarrow, and thus played such a significant part in Bede's preliminary research, had some role also in the early discussions.[95] He had had an early contact with Bede if, as seems likely, he wrote to him fairly soon after the Commentary on I Samuel was published around 716. The learned correspondence which followed, to be glimpsed now only in the *Quaestiones in Regum Librum* and the *Nomina Locorum*, reveals, as we have seen,

---

[90] *In I Sam*. II. xii,15, p. 101.

[91] *ibid.*, II.xiii, 1, p. 102; II.xv, 20, pp. 132–3.

[92] *In Regum Quaest.*, Q.XVIIII, on II Kings 11:12, pp. 313–14.

[93] Bede commented again on the causal relationship between Saul's sin and his defeat in battle in the *De Octo Quaestionibus*: '. . . quasi rex impius, et pro suo scelere interemptus ab hostibus . . .' *PL* XCIII, c. 458.

[94] *HE* I.32, pp. 67–8; Gregory, *Registrum* VI.49, I, p. 423, where Gregory regrets the lack of interest shown by the British bishops in the conversion of the Angles.   [95] *HE praefatio*, p. 6.

that Nothelm was well aware of, and himself shared, Bede's precise interest in textual, chronological and geographical problems arising from the Books of Samuel and Kings.[96] As a man competent to do research in the papal archives, Nothelm would surely have recognized from Bede's work on the Books of Samuel and Kings that he could be even more than a distinguished chronographer, exegete and hagiographer. It is not surprising that Nothelm should come second to Albinus, and in close relationship with him, in Bede's introductory acknowledgement of scholarly debts.

Our ignorance of the terms of reference suggested by Albinus, and of the crucial phase of early correspondence and of meetings with Nothelm, makes it impossible to state conclusively that the conception and compass of the final work were Bede's alone. In the end, of course, it was entitled *Historia Ecclesiastica Gentis Anglorum*, and much energy has been devoted to working out the significance of those four words. Professor Markus has shown that, for Bede, the only work of ecclesiastical history before his own was that of Eusebius, which he knew in the Latin adaptation of Rufinus.[97] There are clear signs of the influence of Eusebius upon Bede, beyond the explicit indication of the title of his work: he found in Rufinus's version the triumphs following Constantine's conversion, precise accounts of the succession of bishops to important sees, the verbatim quoting of important texts, the confounding of heretics, the use of martyr acts, and even a description of synods summoned to discuss the Paschal Controversy.[98] Taken together, the items are impressive, but the differences between the work of Eusebius and that of Bede remain vast, as the most cursory perusal of Rufinus reveals. Eusebius was writing in an entirely different historical context, in a form which related little of secular affairs beyond the inclusion of imperial regnal years to provide a chronological framework;[99] the writing of history itself was an independent literary form still flourishing in the fourth century. The contrast with Bede is obvious. Nor was Eusebius writing hagiography, a genre which had yet to develop. Bede, however,

[96] For Nothelm's awareness of textual problems, *In Regum Quaest.*, Q.III, p. 298.

[97] Markus, *Bede and the Tradition of Ecclesiastical Historiography*, p. 3.

[98] On the succession of bishops, L. W. Barnard, 'Bede and Eusebius as Church historians', in *Famulus Christi*, p. 107. Eusebius/Rufinus, *HE* V.23–4, GCS 9 (1), ed. T. Mommsen, pp. 489–97, deals with a Paschal Controversy.

[99] Markus, *Bede and the Tradition of Ecclesiastical Historiography*, pp. 8–9.

included in his *Ecclesiastical History* much material that can only be described as hagiographical.[100]

The problem of Bede's literary antecedents has been variously resolved, most usually in the form of some kind of symbiotic relationship between the literary traditions of ecclesiastical history and of hagiography. While such an analysis can sometimes be extremely helpful, and results in the observation of exact points of contact, it leaves far too many questions unanswered, many of them relating to the most distinctive features of Bede's work. A more useful approach might be to take seriously, as Nothelm did, Bede's earlier exegetical studies, and in particular his commentary and ancillary studies of the first Book of Samuel. It was here that he found an historical situation analogous to that of the early genera-tions of Anglo-Saxon settlement and, as we have seen, its influence is everywhere to be seen in the *Ecclesiastical History*. Bede no doubt saw in Eusebius a literary predecessor; in practice, however, he was much closer in aims and techniques to the unknown editors of the history of the Israelites, who produced the historical account of the emergence of the kingship by assembling and interpreting the ancient traditions at their disposal to teach a religious lesson to their contemporaries.[101]

Like the editors of I Samuel, Bede was concerned with a people and their religion. Just as the Philistines, or the Amalekites, or the Ammonites, enter into the biblical account only when they come into contact with the Israelites, so Bede was not directly concerned with the British Kingdoms, or the Picts. Like his biblical predeces-sors, he recognized that the history of God's dealings with his people was inextricably linked with the history of its kings, and of the holy men who guided them. So when he came to accumulate his source material, he sought to gather as much precise information about Anglo-Saxon kings as possible, including, again like the editors of I Samuel, regnal lists and genealogies, and to relate it as carefully as he could to the traditions preserved about the bishops, priests and monks who had led them to Christianity.[102] All this he

[100] James Campbell, 'Bede', *Latin Historians*, ed. T. A. Dorey, (London, 1966), pp. 159–90.
[101] There seems to be no doubt that a redaction of the material we now describe as the Books of Samuel and Kings was carried out, possibly as part of a larger whole, in the mid-sixth century BC. The precise nature of the work involved is still controversial. See Eissfeldt, *The Old Testament: An Introduction*, pp. 241–8, 268–81.
[102] D. P. Kirby, 'Bede's sources', *Bulletin of the John Rylands Library*, XLVIII (1966), pp. 341–71.

sought to locate geographically, by trying to secure the kind of detail he had compiled for Israelite sites in the *Nomina Locorum*: the names by which each settlement was known, in which language and with what etymology, the nature of the site, and its political significance.[103] To clarify his account he even preceded it with a geographical and historical background to the settlement in many ways similar to that which he would have read in the Book of Joshua, which described the geography of Canaan and the parcelling out of its land among the tribes of Israel.[104]

When Bede came to construct his work, he decided to set it, as the first Book of Samuel was set, within a loose chronological framework based on the reigns and wars of Saul and David, with the material relating to prophetic activity interspersed and sometimes mingling with it. So far as his kings were concerned, he looked for the kind of information contained in the biblical account: their families, dates, successors, wars, and above all their dealings with the prophets who led them away from the paganism of the neighbouring peoples towards their own God. When he gathered material about holy men, he sought precise details, where possible, of their lives and backgrounds, together with the edifying material preserved by their followers. In putting all these diverse traditions together, Bede decided to make clear the nature of his sources, as he had learned from Gregory the Great to do;[105] having done that, he assembled his material, all of which was in his mind relevant to the history of the *gens Anglorum*, a people who, like the Israelites, were

---

[103] *HE* III. 6, p. 138: Bamborough 'in urbe regia, quae a regina quondam vocabulo Bebba cognominatur'; III. 22, p. 173: 'in civitate, quae lingua Saxonum Ythancaestir appellatur, sed et in illa, quae Tilaburg cognominatur; quorum prior locus est in ripa Pentae amnis, secundus in ripa Tamensis.' Compare *Nomina Locorum, s.v. Azotus* 'quae Hebraice dicitur Asdod' (p. 273); *Tyrus* 'quae Hebraice Sor appellatur' (p. 286); *HE* IV.17, p. 246: 'Est autem Elge in provincia Orientalium Anglorum regio familiarum circiter sexcentarum, in similitudinem insulae vel paludibus, ut diximus, circumdata vel aquis; unde et a copia anguillarum, quae in eisdem paludibus capiuntur, nomen accepit.' Compare *Nomina Locorum s.v. Dan* (p. 277): 'viculus in quarto a Paneade miliario euntibus Tyrum qui usque hodie sic vocatur terminus Iudaeae provinciae contra septemtrionem de quo et Iordanes flumen erumpens a loco sortitus est nomen . . .'
[104] Joshua 13:1–21:43.
[105] Gregory the Great, *Dialogorum Libri Quatuor* I, *prologus*, 10, ed. A. de Vogüé, SC CCLX, p. 16: 'Sed ut dubitationis occasionem legentibus subtraham, per singula quae describo, quibus mihi haec auctoribus sint conperta manifesto.' Compare *HE, praefatio*, p. 6: 'Ut autem in his, quae scripsi, vel tibi, vel ceteris auditoribus sive lectoribus huius historiae occasionem dubitandi subtraham, quibus haec maxime auctoribus didicerim, breviter intimare curabo.'

internally divided, but were being guided towards the true God in the land they had invaded. Just as in the biblical narrative, he included accounts of miracles worked by prophets, together with stories connected with their early lives and court traditions describing their confrontations with, or praise of, various kings.[106] Direct speech, and even poetry, similarly had their place.[107]

In some instances Bede did not follow the example of his biblical predecessors. The Books of Samuel and Kings, for example, contain many stories of atrocities committed by the Israelites or their enemies; frequently too, they included the numbers of those slain in particular battles.[108] There is also some account of the paganism of the peoples who surrounded the Israelites, with references to the names of their gods and the nature of their worship.[109] In some cases it could be said that Bede was lacking evidence, especially of numbers; in others, he may well have decided to omit facts which might have weakened his spiritual message. His references to the victories of Cadwallon in Northumbria, for instance, and to the dismembering of Oswald's body, make it clear that he knew something of the likely treatment of defeated enemies by victorious kings, whether pagan or Christian; likewise, it is hard to imagine that he knew so little of Anglo-Saxon heathenism.[110] But, since the fourth century, Latin exegetes had realized that not everything in the Old Testament was edifying in its literal sense: the behaviour of the Israelites in war, no less than the marriage customs of their kings, might be better ignored when dealing with a people in similar need of divine education.[111]

Care must also be taken in assessing the influence of the Vulgate text on Bede's Latin. Some recent judgements have come dangerously close to asserting that the distinctive prose style of the *Ecclesiastical History* is in some sense founded upon the re-working

[106] I Sam. 1–3, the early life of Samuel; II Sam. 7:1–17, Nathan prophesies to David; 12:1–12, Nathan confronts David.
[107] Bede was fully conscious of his borrowing here: *HE* IV.18, p. 247: 'et imitari morem sacrae scripturae, cuius historiae carmina plurima indita, et haec metro ac versibus constat esse conposita.' Noted by Ray, 'Bede, the exegete, as historian', p. 127.   [108] I Sam. 11:8; 13:5; 31:9–13; II Sam. 4:12.
[109] I Sam. 5:2; 7:3–5.   [110] *HE* III.1, p. 128; III.12, p. 151.
[111] The frequently repugnant contents of the Old Testament, as they appeared to fourth-century Christians, are described by Augustine, *Confessiones* III.iv–v, ed. M. Skutella (Leipzig, 1934), and also the view, which eventually triumphed through the spread of Origenist ideas, that the conduct of the patriarchs had an allegorical meaning, but historically represented an early stage in God's education of his people: III.vii.

by Jerome of the *Vetus Latina*.[112] While undoubtedly biblical echoes can be found in Bede's language, many of his constructions have no Vulgate counterpart, and in general his Latin betrays a conscious sophistication unknown to the first literal translators of the Septuagint and deliberately eschewed by Jerome. It would be unwise to develop this argument before a detailed study of Bede's Latin has been undertaken,[113] but it is worth pointing out that the present underestimation of Bede as a skilled stylist, backed only by vague allusions to the Vulgate and to the *sermo humilis*, can lead to misleading historical assumptions. The passage in the *Ecclesiastical History* Book II, for instance, in which the extended power of seven Anglo-Saxon kings is described, has led to the isolation of the word *imperium* and the belief that it possessed, for Bede, a special meaning, implying that certain kings held a distinctive authority over other kingdoms and peoples.[114] This depends on two assumptions about Bede's Latin, both demonstrably untrue: the first is that his vocabulary of royal power was limited, precisely defined, and mutually exclusive; the second, that the word *imperium* in particular was used only in this specialized sense. However, it is evident that Bede was a stylist who looked for variety of language, especially when describing occurrences frequently to be repeated in his history. Thus he used many forms to narrate deaths, or baptisms;[115] similarly, he had several ways of summarizing periods of royal rule.[116] In his Roman sources he would have found the words *imperium* and *regnum* used interchangeably, meaning no more than 'rule': such was the usage of Late Latin, and Bede copied it literally in his extracts from Eutropius and Orosius.[117] When he came to

[112] Ray, 'Bede, the exegete, as historian', p. 134: 'The very language and style of the *Historia* bear a profound biblical stamp.'
[113] There is only the limited but useful study of D. R. Druhan, *The Syntax in Bede's Historia Ecclesiastica* (Washington DC, 1938).
[114] But see now the full study by Wormald, below pp. 107–9.
[115] *Deaths: HE* III.7, p. 140: 'Defuncto autem et rege'; III.8, p. 142: 'Eadbald rex Cantuariorum transiens ex hac vita'; III.14, p. 154: 'Translato ergo ad caelestia regna Osvaldo'; *ibid.*: 'transivit ad Dominum'; III.14, p. 157: 'de saeculo ablatus'; III.17, p. 159: 'Hunc cum dies mortis egredi e corpore cogeret' (six consecutive examples, excluding death in battle, from less than twenty of Plummer's pages). *Baptisms:* III.1, p. 127: 'fidei erat sacramentis inbutus', 'baptismatis sunt gratia recreati'; III.7, p. 139: 'fonte baptismi cum sua gente ablueretur'; III.21, p. 169: 'fidem et sacramenta veritatis perceperunt.'
[116] *ibid.*, III.6, p. 138: 'quo regni culmine sublimatus'; III.7, p. 140, 'successit in regnum'; III.8, p. 142: 'Earconbercto filio regni gubernacula reliquit'; III.14, p. 154: 'suscepit regni terrestris sedem.'
[117] *ibid.*, I.3, p. 15; I.4, p. 16; I.5, p. 16; I.9, p. 23; I.11, p. 24.

paraphrase his sources, he used both: Constantine, Arcadius, Theodosius II, Marcian undertook *regnum*, Maurice *imperium*.[118] The use of *Ecclesiastical History* II.5 is not, therefore, a distinctive one; *imperium* means there, as elsewhere, no more than 'rule'. Certainly it could be used to describe the authority of especially powerful kings like Aethelbert and Edwin,[119] but it could apply, equally, to the rule of Caedwalla of the West Saxons, or even to the accession of Osred of Northumbria, aged about eight.[120] A recognition of the biblical models which influenced Bede must not overshadow his great sophistication as a writer and as an historian.

No less than the editors of the first Book of Samuel, all of Bede's historical and editorial research was in the end subordinated to his religious aim. When the early traditions of the kingship of Israel were being sifted and interpreted, the Israelites were in the process of being driven from their land; they were intended to gain comfort and strength to face the future from the account of God's dealings with them in the past. When Bede wrote, he was equally anxious about the political situation of his people, and about the progress and depth of their Christianity; they too were meant to cast off slothfulness by recognizing the lessons of their past.[121] The history of Israel had showed Bede that the past was inevitably complex, and that God could deal harshly with his people. But, just as everything in the Scriptures was written to instruct the reader, so the history of the Angles was full of spiritual messages, elucidated by the holy men who peopled its pages. Like Gregory, Bede recognized that the Vulgate's first Book of Kings was more properly the first Book of Samuel, because it was the prophet who by his words and deeds shed light on the meaning of events.[122] It was he, and men like him, who showed kings and people how to live. Bede approached the history of the Anglo-Saxons with precisely this outlook, and with the expertise he had acquired in his exegetical studies. If we wish to understand the ways in which he perceived and described the rulers of the Anglo-Saxon kingdoms, we must first enquire about his knowledge of the world of the kings of the Old Testament.

[118] *ibid.*, I.8, p. 22; I.10, p. 23; I.13, p. 28; I.15, p. 30; I.23, p. 42.
[119] *ibid.*, II.5, p. 89; I.25, p. 45; II.16, p. 118.
[120] *ibid.*, V.7, p. 292; V.18, p. 320; V.19, p. 321. See Wormald, below, pp. 107–8.
[121] See Thacker, below, pp. 132–3.
[122] Gregory, *In Librum Primum Regum, prologus*, 4, p. 52; Bede even changed the title of the book to *In primam partem Samuhelis: HE* V.24, p. 357.

5

Bede, the *Bretwaldas* and the Origins of the *Gens Anglorum*

PATRICK WORMALD

When King Alfred asked the archbishop of Rheims for help in restoring ecclesiastical order to his kingdom, Fulk thought it symbolic that he had applied to the see of the Apostle of the Franks:

> Just as once the *gens Francorum* deserved to be freed by the same blessed Remigius from manifold error and to know the worship of the One True God, so the *gens Anglorum* may beg to receive such a man from his see and teaching . . .

For the work of Augustine, 'the first bishop of your *gens*, sent to you by your Apostle, the blessed Gregory', was necessarily incomplete.[1] The late ninth-century bishops of Rheims were among the first to draw parallels between the histories of the Franks and the English, the historical method which has been so distinctive and rewarding a feature of Professor Wallace-Hadrill's scholarship and teaching. The purpose of this paper is to ask how the equation was possible. How did it come about that, by the later ninth century, one could speak of a 'gens Francorum' and a 'gens Anglorum' in almost the same breath, when the political history of sub-Roman Britain was ostensibly so different from that of Gaul that such continental scholars as Wenskus and Wolfram omitted the English from their surveys of the emergence of the European Kingdoms?[2]

[1] *BCS* 556, trans. *EHD*, p. 884; cf. Hincmar, as quoted by J. L. Nelson, 'The Church's military service in the ninth century', *SCH*, XIX (1983). I wish to thank Dr Nicholas Brooks, Dr Simon Keynes, Mr James Campbell and my pupil, Heather Edwards, for reading this paper, and Dr Jenny Wormald for her customary encouragement, assistance and indeed patience.
[2] R. Wenskus, *Stammesbildung und Verfassung* (Cologne-Graz, 1961), p. 574; H. Wolfram, 'The shaping of the early medieval kingdom', *Viator*, I (1970), p. 1.

The contrasts were real enough. The kingdoms which emerged quite rapidly in post-Roman Gaul, Spain and Italy had perhaps two main ingredients. One was the Germanic *Heerkönig*, the leader of an extended retinue of warriors and their kin, recruited from various tribes of which one was usually dominant and gave its name to the rest; such 'tribes in the making' focused their common identity on a king, who may thereby have acquired 'sacral' status.[3] The second was the indigenous educated class of the province in question, which christianized and to variable extents romanized the new-comers, and which, in search of an at least relatively ordered regime, helped to promote a single royal authority within the boundaries of that province; King Theudebert's circle is a case in point (above, pp. 23–5).[4] In the special case of Ireland, it was the vernacular learned tradition of the *filid* and *brithemain* that fostered a sense of cultural Irish community, and the ideal, if not the reality, of Irish political unity.[5]

These key ingredients are not very evident in Anglo-Saxon Britain. Bede's most notorious passage categorizes the invaders as Angles, Saxons and Jutes; he says nothing of tribal mergers or unified leadership. The vast archaeological debate which he inspired is now simmering down into a consensus that, while Anglian and Saxon cultures tended to merge along their common border, in England as on the continent, they remain distinct at their geo-graphical poles in each area; and the Jutes were something else again.[6] Chadwick believed that the Anglo-Saxon invaders must have been 'large and organized forces', like the Vikings and the Normans. He therefore postulated that the Anglians already dominated the Saxons in the continental homeland, and that the invasion was, in effect, led by an Anglian *Heerkönig*. A relic of this united enterprise was the *imperium* over the southern English which Bede ascribed to seven kings between the late fifth and the later seventh century, and to which one text of the *Anglo-Saxon Chronicle* seems to give the title *Bretwalda*. The political and dialectal divisions

[3] Wallace-Hadrill *EGK*, pp. 2–16; Wolfram, 'Shaping of the early medieval kingdom', pp. 4–9.

[4] *ibid.*, pp. 9–18; P. Wormald, '*Lex Scripta* and *Verbum Regis*', in P. H. Sawyer and I. N. Wood (eds), *Early Medieval Kingship* (Leeds, 1977), pp. 125–8. Cf. also Ganz, above, pp. 62–3.

[5] D. Ó'Corráin, 'Nationality and kingship in pre-Norman Ireland', in T. M. Moody (ed.), *Historical Studies, XI* (Belfast, 1978), pp. 5–8.

[6] *HE* I.15, p. 31; for an excellent recent summary of the archaeological position, D. Brown, *Anglo-Saxon England* (London, 1979), pp. 25–8.

evident in our earliest sources come *later*, like the 'early medieval principality' on the continent.[7] This characteristically brilliant and seemingly modern reconstruction does at least explain what Chadwick rightly called the 'inexplicable fact' that even Saxons came to call themselves 'English'. But it was effectively challenged by Hoops, and its recent archaeological resurrection seems unlikely to command faith.[8] Such courageous attempts to conjure an Anglian Clovis out of the mists of the fifth and sixth centuries have to confront more than the multiplicity of seventh-century kingdoms, to which the familiar 'Heptarchy' hardly does justice, or the survival of at least four to be mopped up piece-meal by the Vikings.[9] Whereas continental barbarians and even the Irish equipped themselves with a unitary legend, it is modern scholars, not the Anglo-Saxons, who fabricate the links between the invaders of Britain.[10]

It has also been suggested that the Anglo-Saxons inherited the unity of *Britannia* in much the same sense as did the Franks that of *Gallia* or the Visigoths that of *Hispania*. The word *Bretwalda*, meaning 'Britain-ruler', could express the idea of an Empire of Britain, transmitted and promoted by the Britons themselves, and Bede's seven overlords correspond significantly with the seven 'imperatores a Romanis in Britannia' listed in the *Historia Brittonum* of 'Nennius'.[11] But, though scholars have more faith than they used to in 'continuity' from Roman Britain to Anglo-Saxon England, the emphatically German culture and resolutely pagan faith of the Anglo-Saxons in 597 are decisive evidence of discontinuity at the level of the educated class, and it was this class that mattered when it came to political horizons.[12] A possibly archaic Welsh poem envis-

[7] H. M. Chadwick, *Origins of the English Nation* (Cambridge, 1907), pp. 12–14, 182–4; H. Wolfram, 'The shaping of the early medieval principality', *Viator*, II (1971), pp. 33–51.

[8] Chadwick, *Origins*, p. 86; J. Hoops, 'Angeln', in *Reallexikon der germanischen Altertumskunde* (1911–13), I, pp. 86–95; G. Osten, 'Die Frühgeschichte der Langobarden und die Bildung eines Grosstammes der Angeln', *Niedersächsisches Jahrbuch für Landesgeschichte*, LI (1979), pp. 77–136.

[9] J. Campbell, *Bede's 'Reges' and 'Principes'* (Jarrow Lecture, 1979).

[10] e.g. V. I. Evison, *The Fifth-Century Invasions south of the Thames* (London, 1965).

[11] *Nennius*, ed. and trans. J. Morris (London, 1980), p. 64; cf. C. Erdmann, 'Die nichtrömische Kaiseridee', in his *Forschungen zur politischen Ideenwelt des Frühmittelalters* (Berlin, 1951), pp. 9–10.

[12] P. H. Sawyer, *From Roman Britain to Norman England* (London, 1978), pp. 86–91.

ages Cadwallon of Gwynedd and Edwin of Northumbria compet-
ing for the rule of Britain; but this competitive hostility is by no
means the same thing as the collaboration of continental *Romani*
with Germanic hegemonies.[13] The numerical coincidence between
Bede and 'Nennius' is scarcely as persuasive now as it seemed when
the latter was thought to pre-date the former;[14] indeed, given that
'Nennius' admits an alternative tradition that there were *nine* such
emperors, and that its list is a tissue of historical confusions, it seems
more likely that Bede influenced 'Nennius' than *vice versa*. Finally,
Britannia as the Romano-Britons saw it was not the same place as the
Bretwalda's sphere of operations. The *Bretwalda* was essentially a
southumbrian overlord, though some are described as supreme
over virtually the whole island (pp. 105–7). Nothing in the
administrative geography of Roman Britain really explains why
Britannia should have come to be bounded by the Humber rather
than the Wall.[15] The 'Orbis Britanniae' in a wider sense was not a
Roman political unit, like Isidore's *Spania*, but a geographical and
literary expression. Some Anglo-Saxon kings aspired to rule it all,
just as King Authari of the Lombards could touch a column on the
very toe of Italy with his spear and declare that it marked the
boundaries of the Lombards; but the ambition need owe nothing to
the ideals or assistance of the Britons.[16]

If the Anglo-Saxons had no 'Romani' to nourish their coherence,
their own poets and law-speakers hardly compared with the *filid*
and *brithemain*. Germanic learned classes left few traces from
Caesar's day onwards, except perhaps in Scandinavia.[17] The legislation of Aethelbert and Ine is professedly Kentish or West Saxon, not
allegedly national like the early Irish law-tracts. As Chadwick
pointed out, early Anglo-Saxon poets drew their heroes from the
Germanic world as a whole, as did the authors of the royal

---

[13] I. Foster, 'The emergence of Wales', in I. Foster and G. Daniel (eds), *Prehistoric
and Early Wales* (London, 1965), p. 231; a Welsh edition of this poem by R. Geraint
Gruffydd is in R. Bromwich and R. Brindley Jones (eds), *Studies in Old Welsh Poetry*
(Cardiff, 1978); I thank Dr Thomas Charles-Edwards for this reference.

[14] See now D. Dumville, 'Nennius and the *Historia Brittonum*', *Studia Celtica*,
X–XI (1975–6), pp. 78–95; and his 'On the North British section of the *Historia
Brittonum*', *Welsh History Review*, VIII (1977), pp. 345–54.

[15] P. Salway, *Roman Britain* (Oxford, 1981), map VII.

[16] Paul the Deacon, *Historia Langobardorum*, ed. G. Waitz, *MGH,SRL*, III.32,
p. 112; Isidore, *De Laude Spaniae*, ed. T. Mommsen, *MGH,AA* XI, p. 267.

[17] C. Stancliffe, 'Kings and conversion', *Frühmittelalterliche Studien*, XIV (1980),
pp. 75–6.

genealogies;[18] theirs was a cosmopolitan rather than national vision. The use of the vernacular was better and earlier developed in England than anywhere else in north-western Europe except Ireland; but its earliest products did very little to establish a sense of 'Englishness'.

Yet, by *Maldon* and the laws of Cnut, such a sense had developed.[19] In the tenth century England was permanently united, politically and administratively: much earlier than France, let alone Spain, Italy or Germany.[20] It is of course smaller than France or Germany, less geographically intractable than Spain or Italy; but the Anglo-Saxons began so much further back on the road to unity than the Franks or Visigoths. One might argue that English unification was only possible because the Vikings cleared the political ground, and was only maintained because the Normans abolished the great earldoms, which do resemble incipient territorial principalities; but the important point is that the makers of England could exploit what German historians of the theme would call an English *Zusammengehörigkeitsgefühl* that was evident by the later-ninth century, at least in more exalted circles:

> So completely had learning decayed in England [*Angelkynn*] that there were very few on this side of the Humber who could apprehend their services in English [*Englisc*] . . . and I think that there were not many beyond the Humber . . . I cannot recollect a single one south of the Thames when I succeeded to the kingdom.[21]

The most interesting thing about Alfred's famous observations is not their much-discussed accuracy, but the fact that, though himself a *Saxon*, and though acknowledging the basic frontiers of Anglo-Saxon politics, the Humber and the Thames, he yet called

[18] H. M. Chadwick, *The Heroic Age* (Cambridge, 1912), p. 34; K. Sisam, 'Anglo-Saxon royal genealogies', *Proceedings of the British Academy*, XXXIX (1953), pp. 287–346. It is becoming unfashionable to see *Beowulf* as even pre-Viking: see most (not all) papers in C. Chase (ed.), *The Dating of Beowulf* (Toronto, 1981). In deference to critics of my paper, 'Bede, *Beowulf* and the conversion of the Anglo-Saxon aristocracy', in R. T. Farrell (ed.), *Bede and Anglo-Saxon England* (BAR, XLVI, 1978), pp. 32–95, I would point out that I did not 'assume an eighth-century date for the poem', committing myself only to the dating range 675–875 (pp. 94–5); Chadwick's arguments, scarcely considered in the Toronto volume, are one reason why I am still reluctant to widen it.

[19] *Gesetze*, I. pp. 318–19, 344–5, 350–1.

[20] J. Campbell, *The Anglo-Saxons* (Oxford, 1982), p. 240ff.

[21] *EHD*, p. 888; text: *King Alfred's West Saxon version of Gregory's Pastoral Care*, ed. H. Sweet (Oxford, 1871–2), pp. 2–3.

the whole area 'Angelkynn' and its language 'Englisc'. If there are hints of propaganda in his claim, when treating with Guthrum, to be spokesman of 'ealles Angelcynnes witan', propaganda is wasted on a hostile or uncomprehending audience.[22] Gregory of Tours did not, unlike modern scholars, entitle his work the History of the Franks, but Bede did call his the Ecclesiastical History of the English. People in all parts of what is now England considered themselves English long before many of their neighbours considered themselves French.[23]

This was extraordinary; just how extraordinary, in European terms, few modern English historians have realized. For most, the process of English unification has seemed almost organic, its yeast, once again, the southern *imperium* whose leader was the *Bretwalda*. Conceived in the very dawn of Anglo-Saxon historical studies as a 'species of Agamemnon', the *Bretwalda's* role was definitively expounded by Stenton. *Bretwalda* was 'not a formal style accurately expressing the position of its bearer', but belonged 'to the sphere of encomiastic poetry', its origin to be 'sought in the halls of some early king whose victories entitled him, in that uncritical atmosphere, to be regarded as lord of Britain'. This military leadership 'gradually assumes a political character'; by the end of the seventh century, overlords treated subordinate kings like members of their own hereditary nobility, confirming or annulling their charters, taking their tribute, leading them to war. Offa of Mercia, who claimed to be 'rex Anglorum', deprived many lesser kings of royal status itself. Thus, a 'primitive confederacy' paved the way for 'the ultimate unity of England'.[24]

But it may be noted that until Chadwick revived them in 1907, the *Bretwalda's* historiographical fortunes were mixed. Kemble dismissed the *imperium* as 'a mere fluctuating superiority such as we may find in Hawaii, Tahiti or New Zealand, due to success in war, and lost in turn by defeat'. As a result of his scathing critique, Stubbs was cautious about *Bretwaldas*, and, in an important judgement which Plummer endorsed, observed: 'The Archbishop of Canterbury stood constantly, as the *Bretwalda* never stood, at the

[22] *Gesetze*, I, pp. 126–7.
[23] For Bede's title(s) see n. 94. W. Kienast, *Studien über die französischen Volksstämme des Frühmittelalters* (Stuttgart, 1968); K. Werner, 'Les Nations et le sentiment national dans l'Europe mediévale', *RH*, CCXLIV (1970), pp. 285–304.
[24] Stenton, *ASE*, pp. 33–6, 202, 206–12. For the views of the earliest scholars see Kemble's passage in next note.

head of an organized and symmetrical system.'[25] Controversy has raged in German historical scholarship on the closely related question of the imperial terminology of 'insular' writers and its contribution to the coronation of Charlemagne on Christmas Day 800.[26] Even Stenton found the issue 'an enigma', defying 'full solution', no easier to make sense of today than it must have been in the ninth century.[27] And while Eric John's sparkling essay on the 'Orbis Britanniae' brought the historiographical wheel full circle back to Palgrave's pre-Kemble 'Empire of Britain', the most recent writers, English and German, have begun to show some of Stubbs's caution.[28] Can an institution which has caused historians such difficulties really have been the key factor in English unification? In this paper, I shall first argue that in fact it was not, and then that the unity of the *gens Anglorum*, an ideal long before it was a reality, can be traced to an altogether different source.[29]

One must admit at the outset that the hard evidence for the status of *Bretwalda* amounts to just three items. The first is Bede's passage on the death of Aethelbert of Kent:

> He was the third English king to rule over all the southern kingdoms which are divided from the north by the river Humber; but he was the first to enter the kingdom of heaven. The first king to hold the

[25] J. M. Kemble, *The Saxons in England* (2 vols, London, 1849), II, pp. 8–22; W. Stubbs, *Constitutional History of England* (3 vols, Oxford, 1873–8), I, pp. 162–3; Plummer, II, pp. 200, 205.

[26] Erdmann, 'Nichtrömische Kaiseridee'; E. Stengel, 'Kaisertitel und Suveranitätsidee', and 'Imperator und Imperium bei den Angelsachsen', *DA*, III (1939), pp. 1–56, XVI (1960), pp. 1–65; R. Drögereit, 'Kaiseridee und Kaisertitel bei den Angelsachsen', *ZRG*, germanistische Abt., LXIX (1952), pp. 24–73. Cf. also H. Löwe, *Die karolingische Reichsgründung und der Südosten* (Stuttgart, 1937), p. 131ff.; K. Werner, 'Das hochmittelalterliche Imperium', *HZ*, CC (1965), pp. 1–60.

[27] 'The supremacy of the Mercian kings' (1918), cited from Stenton, *CP*, p. 48; Stenton, *ASE*, p. 35.

[28] E. John, ' "Orbis Britanniae" and the Anglo-Saxon kings' in his *Orbis Britanniae and other Studies* (Leicester, 1966), pp. 1–26; cf. F. Palgrave, *The Rise and Progress of the English Commonwealth* (2 vols, London, 1832), I, p. 562ff. H. Vollrath-Reichelt, *Königsgedanke und Königtum bei den Angelsachsen* (Köln-Graz, 1971); B. Yorke, 'The vocabulary of Anglo-Saxon overlordship', *Anglo-Saxon Studies in Archaeology and History*, II (BAR, XCII, 1981), pp. 171–200.

[29] In what follows, I obviously differ in some respects from all scholars so far cited, just as I have been guided by them in others. I have not generally indicated areas of agreement or disagreement, for reasons of space and taste; but I should acknowledge here the debt I owe to Stenton's mighty scholarship, and also a more personal debt to Dr Vollrath-Reichelt, whose gift of her book first set me thinking along these lines.

like sovereignty was Aelle, king of the South Saxons; the second was
Caelin, king of the West Saxons, known in their own language as
Ceawlin; the third was Aethelbert . . . the fourth was Redwald, king
of the East Angles, who, while Aethelbert yet lived, conceded to
him the leadership of his own people; the fifth was Edwin, king of
the Northumbrians . . . (who) had still greater power and ruled over
all the inhabitants of Britain, English and Britons alike, except for
Kent only . . . The sixth to rule within the same bounds was Oswald,
the most Christian king of the Northumbrians, while the seventh
was his brother Oswiu who for a time held almost the same territory, and also overwhelmed and made tributary the peoples of the
Picts and the Scots.

Bede says similar things about Aethelbert, Edwin, Oswald and
Oswiu elsewhere; and, at the very end of his book, he seems to add
Aethelbald of Mercia to the roll.[30] The second piece of evidence is
the *Anglo-Saxon Chronicle's* annal for 827 (*recte* 829):

And that year King Egbert conquered the kingdom of the Mercians,
and everything south of the Humber; and he was the eighth king
who was 'Bretwalda' [*sic* MS A; other MSS, 'Brytenwalda' etc.].

After listing the other seven, from Bede, the annal continues that
Egbert attacked Northumbria and was offered 'submission and
peace'.[31] Finally, there is the Ismere Diploma, an 'original' charter

---

[30] *HE* II.5, p. 89: 'Tertius quidem in regibus gentis Anglorum cunctis australibus
eorum provinciis, quae Humbrae fluvio . . . sequestrantur a borealibus, imperavit;
sed primus omnium caeli regna conscendit. Nam primus imperium huiusmodi
Aelli rex Australium Saxonum; secundus Caelin rex Occidentalium Saxonum, qui
lingua ipsorum Ceaulin vocabatur; tertius, ut diximus, Aedilberct. . . . quartus
Reduald rex Orientalium Anglorum, qui etiam vivente Aedilbercto eidem suae
genti ducatum praebebat, obtinuit; quintus Aeduini rex Nordanhymbrorum
gentis . . . maiore potentia cunctis, qui Brittaniam incolunt, Anglorum pariter et
Brettonum populis praefuit, praeter Cantuariis tantum . . . sextus Osuald, et ipse
Nordanhymbrorum rex Christianissimus, hisdem finibus regnum tenuit;
septimus Osuiu frater eius, aequalibus pene terminis regnum nonnullo tempore
cohercens, Pictorum quoque et Scottorum gentes . . . maxima ex parte perdomuit,
ac tributarias fecit.' My translation is based on that of B. Colgrave and
R. A. B. Mynors (eds), *Bede's Ecclesiastical History* (Oxford, 1969), pp. 149–51.
But Vollrath-Reichelt, *Königsgedanke und Königstum*, pp. 80–8, points out that
'praebebat' must mean that Redwald was 'offering', not 'gaining', the *ducatus*. I
owe to Dr Brooks the suggestion (which he will defend elsewhere) that Bede
means to say that in Aethelbert's lifetime Redwald continued to concede lordship
of the East Anglians to him: it fits with *HE* II.15, p. 116. For Bede's other
references to the power of these kings and Aethelbald, see *HE* I.25, II.3, 9, 16, III.6,
24, IV.3, V.23, pp. 44–6, 85, 97, 118, 137–8, 180, 206, 350.
[31] *ASC, s.a.* 827.

of 736, where Aethelbald of Mercia is styled, in the *dispositio*, 'king not only of the Mercians but also of all the kingdoms that are known by the general name *Sutangli*', and in the witness-list, 'rex Britanniae'. The charter thus confirms Bede's hint that Aethelbald should be added to his list, and it supports the *Chronicle's* implication that the southern overlord was known as 'ruler of Britain'.[32]

The Anglo-Saxon historian is used to inadequate evidence, but in a case as important as this the failure of the dog to let out more than the odd yelp is curious: there are many other charters and many other annals. It deserves emphasis that the word *Bretwalda* itself is attested by one text of one annal; many scholars prefer *Brytenwalda* (wide-ruler?) as the original form.[33] Moreover, there is an ambiguity throughout this evidence. Bede's *Bretwaldas*, the Northumbrians apart, were overlords south of the Humber, as was Aethelbald; and it is after his southern conquests but before his Northumbrian campaign that the *Chronicle* claims the status for Egbert. Yet it is possible to call such an overlord 'ruler of Britain'. It was presumably these contradictory elements in the title that led Stenton to suggest that it was coined in an 'uncritical atmosphere'. The evidence establishes that southern overlordship was once a live political concept, and it may well, as has been suggested, have originated in an anti-British confederation under a *dux*.[34] But in order to give it an abiding significance and to include among its holders kings that the lists omit, such as the Mercians, Penda, Wulfhere and above all Offa, historians have recourse to more controversial evidence.

In the first place, did the use of *imperium* and its cognates by Bede and others reflect a coherent and uniquely 'insular' imperial ideology, hegemonial rather than universal in character, which Alcuin then exported to influence what happened to Charlemagne on

[32] *S* 89. This is the only charter to combine 'South English' with 'British' rule; for other titles with the former element, see *S* 94, *S* 101, *S* 103, *S* 287, *S* 291; for *Britannia* etc., see the (generally dubious) *S* 52, *S* 233, *S* 93, *S* 1410.

[33] John, *Orbis Britanniae*, pp. 7–8, following Erdmann. It is difficult to decide this issue: the agreement of five *Chronicle* MSS on 'Brytenwalda' could possibly arise from a foible of their common archetype. The 736 charter shows that by then 'rule of Britain' was uppermost, but the vernacular translation of a charter of Aethelstan, *S* 427, seems to use 'Brytenwalda' in this sense! I retain *Bretwalda* here because it is common usage, and because that it what 'rex Britanniae' seems to convey. See now C. Hart, 'The B text of the *Anglo-Saxon Chronicle*', *Journal of Medieval History*, VIII (1982), pp. 272–3.

[34] cf. E. A. Thomson, *The Early Germans* (Oxford, 1965), pp. 13–14, 40, and *The Visigoths in the time of Ulfila* (Oxford, 1966), p. 44; H. Wolfram, 'Athanaric the Visigoth', *Journal of Medieval History*, I (1975), pp. 257–78.

Christmas Day 800? Dr McClure is not alone in doubting whether Bede's language can be pressed so far (pp. 97–8). Bede uses imperial vocabulary for Egfrith and Osred of Northumbria, Caedwalla and Ine of Wessex, and Wulfhere and Aethelred of Mercia, few of whom feature even in modern lists of *Bretwaldas*, but never of his special hero Oswald.[35] All one can say is that, if one excludes regnal formulae like 'anno imperii . . .', and also cases where 'imperium Anglorum' means simply 'English rule', Bede tends to reserve such terminology for more powerful kings. Adomnan's assertion that, after his defeat of Cadwallon, Oswald 'was ordained by God the emperor of the whole of Britain' must now be seen in the light that 'such high-flown language testifies to ambition rather than achievement' when used by Adomnan and the Iona annalists of their Uí Néill kinsmen in Ireland, powerful though these were.[36] When Boniface denounces the laicization of monasteries, 'whether by emperor or king or anyone endowed with the secular power of prefects or counts', he seems to be asserting a general principle rather than referring specifically to Aethelbald as emperor; the phrase 'imperator vel rex' recurs in the Good Friday liturgy of the *Gelasianum*.[37] Likewise, when addressing Aethelbald as 'inclita Anglorum imperii sceptra gubernanti', he is clearly echoing Aldhelm's address to the Northumbrian King Aldfrith, though he obviously expects much of Aethelbald's power.[38] Finally, Alcuin himself used imperial vocabulary in much the same way as Bede. When the men of Kent, a 'regnum imperiale', are told: 'From you the first power of empire proceeded, and the origin of the Catholic Faith sprang up', the reference may well be to Bede's account of the power and salvation of Aethelbert.[39] Its connection with Alcuin's

[35] *HE* IV.12, p. 228 (cf. Plummer, I, pp. 368, 390); V.18, 19, pp. 320–1; IV.12, V.18, pp. 228, 320; V.7, p. 294; V.24, p. 354. Aldhelm's usage is similar: compare the address to Aldfrith, 'Aquilonalis imperii sceptra gubernanti' with that to Geraint, 'Occidentalis regni sceptra gubernanti', *Aldhelmi Opera*, ed. R. Ehwald, *MGH,AA* XV,pp. 61, 480–1; and cf. *ibid.*, pp. 14–16, 65, 77, 135, 302, 305, 311, 491, etc.

[36] Adomnan, *Life of Columba*, ed. and trans. A. O. and M. O. Anderson (London, 1961), I.1, pp. 200–1; F. J. Byrne, *Irish Kings and High Kings* (London, 1973), p. 255.

[37] *Die Briefe der heiligen Bonifatius und Lullus*, ed. M. Tangl, *MGH, Ep. Sel., I* (1916), p. 169; *The Gelasian Sacramentary*, ed. H. Wilson (Oxford, 1894), p. 76.

[38] *Briefe Bonifatius*, p. 146; cf. n. 35.

[39] Alcuin, *Epistolae*, ed. E. Dümmler, *MGH,Ep.* IV, pp. 191–2; cf. Alcuin, *Carmina*, ed. E. Dümmler, *MGH,Poet.* I, p. 172; Alcuin, *Vita Willibrordi*, ed. W. Levison, *MGH, SRM* VII, pp. 127, 133.

now notorious vision of an *imperium Christianum*, an empire of the Faith entrusted to Charlemagne rather than a hegemony over kings won by the sword, is tenuous.[40]

'Insular' imperial terminology suggests that some kings were more powerful than others and that some of them liked to be flattered. It does not necessarily reflect a constitutional principle that could be transmitted from one people to another. English and continental writers had Isidore to tell them that an *imperator* was more than a *rex*, and was the title of the greatest rulers of all; powerful Biblical kings are sometimes described in imperial terms.[41] In the circumstances, it is less surprising that such language was occasionally applied to great contemporary kings than that it was not used more often. We can show that Bede was no Humpty-Dumpty in his use of words like *imperium* only if we can also show that he was describing real and systematically organized power. That remains to be seen.

The same goes for the royal titles in Anglo-Saxon charters, which, though still at this stage written in the most prominent local *scriptorium*, may be considered in some sense 'official', because bishops and abbots were regularly at court.[42] Apart from the styles in the Ismere Diploma, there are three other significant categories of title. First, kingship of the Mercians and surrounding peoples is attributed to Aethelbald at the end of his reign and, in a not wholly reputable series, to Offa; but as the peoples are not named, these do not take us much further.[43] Second, an apparent 'original' of 798 calls Cenwulf of Mercia 'rector et imperator Merciorum regni'; this charter, like some others of this king, is dated by his 'imperial'

[40] Alcuin, *Epistolae*, pp. 241, 292, 310, 331, 336, 379, 397, 402, with pp. 177, 288. For a more convincing interpretation of Alcuin's imperial ideal, see W. Ullmann, *The Carolingian Renaissance and the Idea of Kingship* (London, 1969), p. 135ff.; and for overdue perspective on the whole issue, Professor Bullough's forthcoming study of Alcuin.

[41] Isidore, *Etymologiae*, ed. W. M. Lindsay (Oxford, 1911), IX.iii.2–3, 14. Cf., e.g., I Samuel, 2:10; I Chronicles, 18:3; Judith, 1:1, 2:3; Esther, 1:3, 20; Daniel, 6:26, 9:1; Luke, 3:1; and McClure, above, p. 88.

[42] P. Chaplais, 'The origin and authenticity of the royal Anglo-Saxon diploma', *Journal of the Society of Archivists*, III (1965–9), pp. 48–61; N. P. Brooks, 'The Early Charters of Christ Church Canterbury' (Oxford, unpubl. D. Phil. thesis, 1969), pp. 128–92. Cf. H. Wolfram, *Intitulatio, I, MIÖG, Ergänzungsband*, XXI (1967), pp. 18, 20–1; and John, *Orbis Britanniae*, pp. 2–4. Yorke, 'Vocabulary', has a useful table of the relevant titles.

[43] *S* 96; *S* 116–18; *S* 121; *S* 127.

year.[44] This puzzlingly tentative title is perhaps best explained by
Alcuin's 'imperial' letter to the Kentishmen: the style is confined to
charters that were probably written at Canterbury, and there are
other Alcunian traces in this charter and in one of the next year.[45] In
any case, it shows, like the vast majority of Cenwulf's charters, that
what mattered to him was the *regnum Merciorum*, which included
Kent and much else besides.

Third and most important, there are charters claiming kingship
of 'the English'. Many are transparent forgeries.[46] Stenton argued
in 1918 that three charters of Offa for Christ Church Canterbury,
which style him 'rex Anglorum' (774), 'rex totius Anglorum
patriae' (774) and again 'rex Anglorum' (?795) were 'originals', but
he was most uncharacteristically mistaken. All three belong to that
most instantly suspect of all categories of Anglo-Saxon records, the
single-sheet in much later script than the date of the purported
transaction. The third is certainly a tenth-century forgery; although
those of '774' are probably not complete fabrications, the scribe
of the first also penned the deeply suspect grant of Pagham by
Caedwalla to Wilfrid and ultimately Canterbury.[47] Offa has this
title in charters from Selsey and Worcester as well as Christ
Church.[48] One is tempted to think that it occurs so often that it must
be a genuine feature in even the most dubious text. But 'rex
Anglorum' was the title used in many tenth- and eleventh-century
charters. Offa's greatness was well known by then, and a forger
might well have used it: it appears in only one of the surviving
versions of two authentic Worcester charters.[49] In genuinely 'origi-

---

[44] *S* 153; *S* 155; *S* 157; *S* 1264; *S* 168. Two of the forgeries with this style were
produced in early ninth-century Kent, as Dr Brooks's forthcoming study shows:
S 22; *S* 90.

[45] Compare the 798 charter with Alcuin, *Epistolae*, p. 181 (to King Cenwulf,
797): 'illum semper habeas in mente qui te regnum exaltavit super principes populi
sui rectorem'; and *S* 155 – 'Offa rex et decus Brittaniae' – with Alcuin, *Epistolae*,
p. 107 (to Offa): 'vos estis decus Brittaniae . . .'

[46] e.g. *S* 93; *S* 320; and see n. 48.

[47] *S* 110–11; *S* 132; *S* 230; Stenton, 'Supremacy', pp. 60, 62, 64. See *Facsimiles of
Ancient Charters in the British Museum*, ed. E. A. Bond (4 vols, London, 1873–8), IV
4, IV 2, III 4; and *Facsimiles of Anglo-Saxon Manuscripts*, ed, W. B. Sanders (3 vols,
Southampton, Ordnance Survey, 1878–84), I 3. Cf. W. H. Stevenson, 'Trinoda
Necessitas', *EHR*, XXIX (1914), p. 692, n. 18.

[48] *S* 108; *S* 104; *S* 109; *S* 145; *S* 121; *S* 1178; *S* 54; *S* 146; some of these are certainly
forged, and others show signs of interpolation.

[49] cf. the table accompanying H. Kleinschmidt, *Untersuchungen über das englische
Königtum im 10 Jahrundert* (Göttingen, 1979); and for a hint of Offa's resurrected

nal' Kentish diplomas of the last part of his reign he is 'rex Merciorum'; those who accept that he was 'rex Anglorum' in the 770s must explain why he ceased to be.[50]

One reason for Stenton's belief that the titles of the *Bretwalda* period were 'sober statements of fact . . . clearly intended to be understood in their literal meaning' was that they were so much less inflated than the grandiloquent claims of charters from Aethelstan's time onwards (pp. 250, 257).[51] But at least the latter are consistent, and reveal consistency of ambition. Like the literary sources, charters before the tenth century speak mostly of kingship, and with reference to the king's own people. Nor does simple language in itself prove good faith. It is hard to see that Aethelbald's kingship of Britain was a statement of fact, sober or otherwise, or that Offa was literally king of the English. Charters written in ecclesiastical *scriptoria* may after all be 'official', but by the same token they were the work of courtiers. Without proof of power, their claims remain claims, howsoever couched.

Because we lack the sort of systematic description that is found in the Irish law-tracts, the only proof of a *Bretwalda*'s rightful powers is what he did in fact. But three things must be borne in mind when considering this evidence. In the first place, there is room for more complexity in the world of early Anglo-Saxon politics than the fashionable obsession with overlordship allows. It may have been because he was overlord that Aethelbert prompted the conversion of King Saebert of Essex, though Saebert was also his nephew.[52] But this cannot be true of Oswiu's part in the conversion of Saebert's successor, Sigebert, which happened when Penda of Mercia's power was at its height; still less when he persuaded his

---

reputation, *The Chronicle of Aethelweard*, ed. and trans. A. Campbell (London, 1962), p. 24. Patrick Young's transcript of the original of S 109, BL Cotton MS Vitellius C ix, f. 129, is burnt at the crucial point, but the visible descender of the first letter of the word after 'rex' makes it look like an 's', and 'seniorum' follows 'Anglorum' in the cartulary texts. Both texts of S 146 are perhaps suspect in the light of the 'original' S 139, and the only text to give 'Anglorum' is the generally unreliable BL Cotton MS Nero E i: N. R. Ker, 'Hemming's Cartulary', in R. W. Hunt *et al., Studies in Medieval History presented to F. M. Powicke* (Oxford, 1948), pp. 65–7.

[50] Yorke, 'Vocabulary', pp. 181–3. It is possible, but *not* certain, that a legend on one of Offa's coins can be extended as 'Rex Anglorum': N. P. Brooks, *The Early History of the Church of Canterbury* (Leicester, 1983), ch. 6, n. 37.

[51] Stenton, 'Supremacy', p. 54.

[52] *HE* II.3, p. 85.

son-in-law and Penda's own son to become Christian.[53] These were surely diplomatic transactions, alliances against a common enemy or treaties designed to bring an interval of peace. Thus, when Oswald married the daughter of Cynegils of Wessex, sponsored his baptism and co-founded Dorchester, this may be an instance of overlordship; equally, it may be a marriage-alliance, such as two of Oswald's nephews also made with Wessex, and Oswald may have attested Cynegils's grant simply because he was there.[54] Again, Beorhtric of Wessex married Offa's daughter, but there is no charter evidence of his subordination, whereas he did attest a grant which his brother-in-law made at Bath in his presence.[55]

It is generally believed that Mercian overlords operated a smooth and regular system whereby lesser kings were first demoted in status from *rex* to *subregulus* or *dux* and then consigned to oblivion. This is strictly true only of Sussex kings.[56] Not all local rulers were subordinated natives. Berhtwald 'rex' or 'subregulus', who gave land to Malmesbury in 685, was described by Eddius as a 'praefectus' and Aethelred of Mercia's nephew; Frithuwold 'provinciae Surrianorum subregulus', who made an early grant to Chertsey, was probably not a scion of an otherwise unknown Surrey dynasty but a relative of the Frithuric who attested his charter and himself disposed of huge Middle Anglian estates.[57] Even the princes of the Hwicce, who claimed to be local by the eighth century, may have been descended from a Bernician prince installed by Penda of Mercia when he conquered the area in 628; the notoriously disputed Frankish or Bavarian origin of the Agilolfing Dukes show how completely even imposed rulers could 'go

[53] *HE* III.21–2, pp. 169–72.

[54] *HE* III.7, p. 139; Eddius, *Life of Wilfrid*, ed. and trans. B. Colgrave (Cambridge, 1927), 40, pp. 80–1; *ASC, s.a.* 718.

[55] *ASC, s.a.* 789, 792 (D,E); *S* 148, and cf. *S* 149. What are often taken as instances of an overlord's military leadership may also be alliances: one cannot logically cite Aethelbald's campaign, *ASC, s.a.* 743, without citing Ine's, *ibid.*, 710. The same goes for cases of two or more kings in a witness-list: the papal legates' account of their 786 encounter with Offa and Cynewulf of Wessex hardly suggests the latter's inferiority: Alcuin, *Epistolae*, p. 20. Anglo-Saxon equivalents to the Irish *rígdál* may not have been unknown: J. Bannerman, *Studies in the History of Dal Riata* (Edinburgh, 1974), pp. 162–70.   [56] *S* 108; *S* 1184; *S* 1178; *S* 1183.

[57] *S* 1169, with Eddius, *Wilfrid*, 40, pp. 80–1; *S* 1165, with F. M. Stenton, 'Medeshamstede and its colonies', in Stenton, *CP*, pp. 181–2. As against Stenton's view that the princes of the Magonsaete were not, as later tradition alleged, descendants of Penda, Stenton, *ASE*, p. 47, see Sawyer, *Roman Britain to Norman England*, p. 39.

native'.[58] Of the arguably native dynasties, that of Kent was not downgraded but displaced, after a stout fight. First, in 764, Offa replaced one Kentish king and reissued one of his grants as the associate, not the superior, of the other; by the following year, there were again two native kings. In 774, if we may thus far trust the 'rex Anglorum' charters, Offa was sole king of Kent, but the presumably indigenous King Egbert was back in charge in 778–9. Finally, from 785 at the latest, Offa was undisputed master, and native kings had vanished. He was the rival, not the overlord, of Kentish kings.[59] Like the Carolingians, it seems, Mercian overlords preferred to intrude their own kin or followers rather than rely on the loyalty of local dynasties; unlike the Ottonians, they could.[60]

Offa's Kentish experiences highlight the second point about the *Bretwalda's* 'powers', which is that we seldom know how long they lasted. Oswiu dominated Mercia for three years after his defeat of Penda; but the power over all southern England which he may have had at this stage was scarcely possible before 655 or after the revolt of Wulfhere in 658.[61] His is the one case in Bede's list where we have detailed information. Likewise, we know that in 829 Egbert also took direct control of Mercia. But the *Chronicle* admits that Wiglaf recovered his throne next year; for six years thereafter, there is no good evidence that Egbert's supremacy was acknowledged anywhere, and some that Wiglaf retrieved his predecessors' position.[62]

[58] *S* 99; *S* 55; *S* 57; H. P. R. Finberg, *The Early Charters of the West Midlands* (Leicester, 1961), pp. 167–80; E. Zöllner, 'Die Herkunft der Agilolfinger', *MIÖG*, LIX (1951), pp. 245–64.

[59] Sawyer, *Roman Britain to Norman England*, pp. 101–2. Note that Aethelbald's remissions of toll for Kentish churches (listed in Campbell, *Anglo-Saxons*, p. 252) show that he was the patron, not necessarily the lord, of Kent. Of the other dynasties: the (probable) king of the East Saxons was still 'rex' in *S* 168 (811); in *S* 1791, though Sigeric, *minister* of King Wiglaf of Mercia, receives the grant, Sigeric, *king* of the East Saxons attests it. In his sole appearance on the stage of history, a king of Lindsey is still 'rex' in *c*.791: F. M. Stenton, 'Lindsey and its kings', in Stenton, *CP*, pp. 129–31. To judge from coins, there were no East Anglian kings between the execution of Aethelbert and the death of Ludeca: *ASC, s.a.* 794, 827; C. Blunt *et al.* 'The coinage of southern England, 796–840', *British Numismatic Journal*, XXXII (1963), pp. 25–30.

[60] K. Leyser, *Rule and Conflict in an Early Medieval Society* (London, 1979), pp. 110–111. [61] *HE* III.24, p. 180.

[62] Blunt, 'Coinage of southern England', p. 34; D. Dumville, 'Kingship, genealogies and regnal lists', in Sawyer and Wood, *Early Medieval Kingship*, p. 100: *ASC, s.a.* 830. *S* 270 (?833) is highly suspicious in the light of *S* 23; *S* 279 (836) is the first Kentish charter of Egbert after 830 that commands respect. On the other hand, cf. *S* 188, *S* 190, for Wiglaf, and the coinage evidence: Blunt, 'Coinage of southern England', pp. 15–25, 30–4.

Can a title based on such transitory achievements have been an office in any real sense? Can it have helped to unify England?

If effective hegemony was often brief, this may explain why there is just one contemporary record of one early Anglo-Saxon king taking tribute from another, though one would think this a normal function of overlordship (the king who attempted it, Wulfhere, is not in the ancient lists, and the king who succeeded, Egfrith, is rarely in the modern.)[63] From this lone cactus in the desert of evidence historians often fall back on the oasis, or mirage, of the *Tribal Hidage*. The main reason why a list of hidages for all the southern English, headed by the Mercians, is considered the tribute-list of the Mercian empire is, very reasonably, that it looks like that. To quote Corbett, its first important student: 'Primitive peoples do not undertake statistical enquiries out of mere curiosity.'[64] Even if this is true – and some modern scholars prefer a more 'literary' interpretation of the document, like the scribe of the earliest extant manuscript, who immediately proceeded to list such other well-known national characteristics as 'victory of the Egyptians', 'stupidity of the Anglo-Saxons' and 'lust of the Irish' – the *Tribal Hidage* might still represent what one great Mercian king hoped to collect on one occasion. It does not prove that *Bretwaldas* took tribute everywhere, regularly and as of right.[65]

Which brings one to a third and final consideration. Some Anglo-Saxon kings were so powerful that they could impose their wills on other kings; but this was not necessarily a matter of accepted political manners rather than naked political force. Historians have suggested that Aethelbert's 'assistance', when Augustine met the British bishops somewhere in the province of the Hwicce, reflected his status as *Bretwalda*: did he actually do more than supply a powerful escort which then ringed the meeting-place?[66] Mercian kings seized London from the East Saxons and Berkshire (perhaps more besides) from Wessex; the West Saxon kings are usually

[63] Eddius, *Wilfrid*, 20, pp. 42–3.

[64] For the text, BCS 297–297B. The literature ranges from W. J. Corbett, 'The Tribal Hidage', *TRHS*, n.s. XIV (1900), pp. 187–230, to W. Davies and H. Vierck, 'The contexts of Tribal Hidage', *Frühmittelalterliche Studien*, VIII (1974), pp. 223–93. See now Campbell, *Anglo-Saxons*, pp. 59–61.

[65] Sawyer, *Roman Britain to Norman England*, pp. 110–13; R. H. Hodgkin, *A History of the Anglo-Saxons* (2 vols, Oxford, 3rd edn, 1952), II, p. 389; N. R. Ker, *Catalogue of Manuscripts containing Anglo-Saxon* (Oxford, 1957), no. 239.

[66] *HE* II.2, p. 81: 'adiutorio usus Aedilbercti regis'.

thought to have resisted prolonged Mercian dominance, and perhaps Essex did too.[67] The most fundamental and discussed of the *Bretwalda's* 'prerogatives' was the right to confirm a subordinate's charters, and here one must distinguish between two types of intervention: advance permission, specified in the *dispositio*, which shows potential control of the transaction; and ratification, recorded in the witness-list, which could, sometimes visibly did, occur long after it. There are no known cases of a presumptively native king himself acknowledging an overlord's prior consent.[68] The rulers who do this are sub-kings or kings under external patronage, like one of the 'reges dubii vel externi' who disturbed Kent in the later seventh century, the rulers of the Hwicce, and eventually those of Sussex.[69] This is logical enough: whether a *subregulus/dux* was locally deposed or externally imposed, his overlord would wish to control the royal demesne, and we can see that Mercian kings were disposing of Hwiccian property as early as the local rulers.[70] But it proves nothing about an overlord's rights vis à vis other kings.

The nodal evidence of the necessity of advance permission is the famous 'Aldhun affair'. In 799, Cenwulf restored three estates to Christ Church. Two had been given to the community by King Egbert of Kent; the third he gave to his *minister* Aldhun, who himself gave it to Christ Church:

> But afterwards Offa, king and glory of Britain, transferred the possession of these lands, and distributed them to his thegns, saying that it was wrong that his thegn should have presumed to give land allotted to him by his lord into the power of another without his permission.

Stenton took this to mean that Offa regarded Egbert as his thegn and denied his right to dispose of royal property; it was thus the *locus classicus* of an overlord's rights in this respect. Others have understood that, in Offa's view, it was Aldhun who should have had Egbert's consent. The scribe's command of Latin is such as to

[67] *HE* III.7, p. 141; F. M. Stenton, *The Early History of the Abbey of Abingdon* (Oxford, 1913), pp. 21–9; H. P. R. Finberg, *The Early Charters of Wessex* (Leicester, 1964), p. 218; Sawyer, *Roman Britain to Norman England*, p. 100. cf. also *S* 1679, *S* 1692, *S* 152.

[68] *S* 65 is no exception: 'cum licentia Aedelredi regis' refers to the status of Paeogthath 'comis', not that of 'Sueabraed rex Eastsaxanorum'.

[69] *HE* IV.26, p. 268; *S* 12; *S* 52; *S* 58; *S* 1183.

[70] e.g. *S* 75; *S* 89; *S* 113.

support neither side decisively.[71] In any case, there is another equally instructive instance of Offa's aggressive attitude to church lands. In 781, the Worcester community were told 'that we were wrongly holding in our power without hereditary right the inheritance of his kinsman, King Aethelbald'. But in the case of at least one estate this was demonstrably untrue; for Aethelbald's 'rex Britanniae' diploma had granted Ismere to a retainer, and his son had passed it to Worcester with Offa's own express permission![72] In other words, Offa sometimes had no respect for even his predecessor's charters and was prepared to use highly dubious arguments (he probably got what he really wanted out of it, though not Ismere). Perhaps then, we should view the Aldhun affair as essentially a question of power rather than principle. In practice, it was because Offa had replaced the kings of Kent that he claimed control of their fisc and reserved the right to revoke their grants.[73] It is a fair bet that he and others did so often; after all, the extant records concern only church property that was ultimately restored.[74]

It was thus 'common sense' for a charter's beneficiary, anyway responsible for drafting it in the case of the greater churches, to seek the consent of a threatening neighbour, either at the time or when the threat materialized. The bishop of Rochester did so in or after

[71] S 155: 'sed harum post modum possessiones terrarum Offa rex et decus Brittaniae inmutavit suisque distribuit ministris dicens iniustum fuisse quod minister eius praesumsisset terram sibi a domino distributam absque eius testimonio in alterius potestatem dare'; trans. EHD, p. 511; cf. Stenton, ASE, p. 36, and Vollrath-Reichelt, Königsgedanke und Königtum, pp. 163–71. 'Harum . . . possessiones terrarum' (plural) favours Stenton's interpretation, in that the phrase seems to refer to all of Egbert's gifts as well as Aldhun's; but 'terram . . . distributam' supports the opposition, because it is hard to see how Offa can have thought that he had endowed Egbert. A later charter, saying that Offa behaved 'quasi non liceret Ecgberhto agros hereditario iure scribere' may reinforce Stenton's case, but it also shows that Canterbury denied Offa's rights: S 1264, and cf. S 1259.

[72] S 1257: 'Aiebat enim nos sine iure hereditario propinqui eius Aethelbaldi scilicet regis hereditatem sub dominio iniusto habere'; trans. EHD, p. 506. cf. S 89, S 1411.

[73] Offa's treatment of Rochester property is instructive: S 32–3 are grants by Sigired, 'rex dimidiae partis provinciae Cantuariorum', and presumably another 'outsider' (cf. n. 69); in S 105, Offa, replacing Sigired as Heahbert's associate, renews one of these grants immediately, but he did not renew the other until 789: S 131. Similarly, S 130 ultimately renews two grants by Egbert (S 35–6). What Offa could re-grant in his own good time he could also keep.

[74] Other examples of Offa's behaviour: S 149; S 1258; S 1435. Egbert of Wessex seems to have been equally ruthless: S 1438.

765.[75] Offa's consent to all Sussex charters either evidently was, or else may well have been, retrospective.[76] In the only known West Saxon case, a charter of Cynewulf for Bath, it comes right at the end of the witness-list, and Offa controlled the abbey from 781.[77] There is little evidence in all this of constitutional principle. Interventions by one king in the grants of another are sufficiently explained either by social and diplomatic relations between rulers or by power and the fear of power; and if such power could be fiercely real it could not necessarily be sustained. In a nutshell, a king with great power might be hailed as *Bretwalda*; but a *Bretwalda* may not, as such, have had powers.

In tracing the remorseless growth of English unity, it is easy to forget that overlords were resented and indeed resisted. Oswiu and Egbert were soon expelled from Mercia. The native dynasty was restored in Kent and probably East Anglia as soon as Offa was dead; it took Cenwulf two years to crush the Kentish rebels, who expelled the Mercian archbishop and may have sacked the cathedral archives.[78] Even Oswald's remains were shut out of Bardney in Lindsey; 'because he belonged to another kingdom and had once conquered them, they pursued him even when dead with their former hatred.'[79] As in *Beowulf*, so in the world of its 'audience', the struggle for power could cause bitter feuds between kings and noblemen. Bede thought the death of Aelfwine, brother of the vanquished king and brother-in-law of the victor, at the Battle of

[75] Hodgkin, *History of the Anglo-Saxons*, p. 402 – a perceptive and neglected passage; *S* 34: Offa's Peterborough confirmation could have come at any date up to 772, when the next bishop of Rochester attested *S* 108. cf. earlier Kentish ratifications: *S* 10; *S* 233.

[76] *S* 46; *S* 50; *S* 49; *S* 1184; *S* 1183: later confirmation is either explicit or implied by its position on the witness-list. Exceptions: *S* 108, a grant in the Domesday rape of Hastings a year after Offa had overrun the 'gens Haestingorum' (*HR, s.a.* 771); and *S* 1178, when the native dynasty were already 'dukes'.

[77] *S* 265; *S* 1257. Of the East Saxon charters, *S* 1785 shows only that kings of Mercia and Essex each consented to a grant (cf. n. 55); and *S* 65, though in early script, is not 'original', because the consent of successive Mercian kings is recorded in the same hand: the order of witnesses could have been rearranged, and Mercian recognition might be retrospective.

[78] *ASC, s.a.* 798; *HR, s.a.* 798; Alcuin, *Epistolae*, pp. 188–92; Blunt, 'Coinage of southern England', p. 26. For the loss of the archives, see Brooks, thesis (as n. 42), pp. 4–26.

[79] *HE* III.11, p. 148; the different atmosphere in Sussex, *HE* IV.14, pp. 233–5, is explained by the commitment of its apostle, Wilfrid, to Oswald's cult: D. P. Kirby, 'Bede's native sources', *Bulletin of the John Rylands Library*, XLVIII (1966), p. 350.

the Trent was 'grounds for sharper war and longer enmity between the kings and their fierce peoples'. Theodore made peace by securing compensation for the vengeful Egfrith; but, as in Beowulf's famous account of how hostilities between Dane and Heathobard would break out at the very wedding-feast designed to bring peace, more than royal feelings were involved in 679. A Northumbrian warrior would have been killed by his Mercian captor had his rank been detected at once: ' "Now you deserve to die because all my brothers and relatives were killed in that battle".'[80] This was no basis for cosy political consensus between the Anglo-Saxon kingdoms.

But it may explain what has puzzled historians since Kemble about the extant lists of *Bretwaldas*: the omission of the great Mercian kings from Penda to Cenwulf, though their power is better documented than most.[81] Stenton's first suggestion was that the *Chronicle's* gap was 'quite possibly nothing more subtle than the mistake of an unintelligent annalist'. Later, though readier to countenance the *Chronicle's* 'prejudice', he thought that Bede closed his list where he did because he 'wished to avoid the anti-climax of carrying it beyond the great name of Oswiu'.[82] One might reply that the *Chronicle's* ability to omit at least three, perhaps six, of the Mercian kings with claims to the status betrayed a degree of carelessness bordering on the wilful; and Bede's reluctance to include Wulfhere suggests that Northumbrian pride had influenced his stylistic taste (he shows that Wulfhere's religious achievement was no less than Oswiu's). Much the simplest solution is that, like the Irish kingship of Tara, the *Bretwalda* was less an objectively realized office than a subjectively perceived status. Just as Adomnan and the Iona annals claimed for the Uí Néill (and Munster sources for Munster kings) what would not be achieved before Brian Boru and could not then be sustained by his successors and their rivals; so great English kings claimed, or were flattered by, the title, and one acknowledged such claims in one's own kings, or those who left one alone, but not in one's enemies.[83] Alfredian or not, the *Chronicle*

[80] *HE* IV.21–2, pp. 249–51; *Beowulf*, ed. F. Klaeber (London, 3rd edn, 1950), ll. 2009–69 (and also ll. 2999–3027).
[81] Hence one of the attractions of the 'Nennius' hypothesis' (above, pp. 101–2). Vollrath-Reichelt's solution relies, for Egbert, on unacceptable charters (pp. 187–91), and her evidence on other kings is as well explained by the solution adopted here.   [82] Stenton, 'Supremacy', pp. 48–9; Stenton, *ASE*, p. 34.
[83] Byrne, *Irish Kings*, pp. 254–9.

was written in Wessex, and we know from Asser that neither Offa nor his daughter were fondly remembered there.[84] Aethelbald's stirring titles were probably composed at Worcester, whose patron he was, just as Cenwulf's imperial style may arise from his *rapprochement* with Canterbury after 798.[85] Bede's own list is patriotically Northumbrian, but also shows traces of Kentish influence: it is quoted in the context of material about Aethelbert, and rule over Kent is either delayed or excluded for his successors.[86] The reason why Stenton had to discover 'The Supremacy of the Mercian Kings' is a basic fact of Anglo-Saxon history. There are Northumbrian and West Saxon sources, with Kentish traditions embodied in both, but only charters are *committed* to Mercian greatness.

So the debate returns to the three items of evidence where it began. There was an ideal of southumbrian supremacy and a strangely related ideal of the kingship of Britain. We can only guess how the former originated and was linked to the latter, and we may not be able to give the combination any constitutional significance. We know that the much more trumpeted power of tenth- and eleventh-century kings over Britain as a whole was occasional and sometimes resisted; it certainly did nothing for the unification of Britain. We can hardly claim more for their pre-Viking counterparts even in England itself: it seems that attempts to realize power stirred up political currents that have muddied our view of who was *Bretwalda* and who was not.[87] Such 'progress' as there was towards unity was a matter of larger kingdoms swallowing smaller. It had a long way to go when the Vikings transformed the situation: neither Offa at Benson nor Egbert at Wroughton won a 'World's Decisive Battle' like Clovis at Vouillé.

---

[84] Asser, *Life of Alfred*, ed. W. H. Stevenson (Oxford, repr. 1959), 14–15, pp. 12–14.

[85] Above, nn. 32, 44.

[86] Above, n. 30. *HE* pr., pp. 6–7, can be read as implying what one would anyway expect, that most of Bede's information on episcopal successions came from Canterbury; thus the news of Aethelbald's power, which he records in such a context, may also have come from Albinus and Nothelm (cf. McClure, above, pp. 92–3). Yorke, 'Vocabulary', pp. 195–6, also argues that Bede's list was second hand; and cf. Thacker, below, pp. 146–8.

[87] Cf. Leyser, *Rule and Conflict*, pp. 28–31, for a most interesting anthropological insight into how a struggle for supremacy within a political system contributes to the system's coherence; but Leyser brings out the fragility of such a structure: above, n. 60.

It is hard to resist the feeling that early English historiography has been as determined by the extraordinary success story that the making of England ultimately was, as that of Germany has been by its own prolonged 'failure'.[88] English unification was not taken for granted, but the hard-won triumphs of the tenth (and nineteenth) century were 'read back' in quest of their natural roots. The *Bretwalda* filled a need. But the Anglo-Saxons were not spared the sort of pressures that undermined or obstructed unification elsewhere. If *Beowulf* is indeed a window on the thought-world of the Anglo-Saxon aristocracy, their minds dwelt on local grievance and international glory.[89] In the strictly political sphere, Alfred the Great was no better off than Otto the Great. The paradox is that there *is* evidence of a remarkably precocious sense of common 'Englishness', and not just in politically interested circles; it was memorably expressed by what may have been a Northumbrian source in the *Chronicles* for Edward the Confessor's reign.[90] But it was much older. Such a sense must help to explain the making and sheer persistence of England. But its source was not the almost unchartable White Nile of early Germanic politics.

What we have to explain is not only the sense of community which Anglo-Saxons acquired against the political odds, but also the fact that they all came to be called English. Alfred knew that he was a Saxon: when he took control of south-west Mercia in the 880s, his new title was 'rex Anglorum [et] Saxonum' or 'rex Angulsaxonum'.[91] But he also wrote of 'Angelkynn' and 'Englisc'. His nostalgia for the learning and glory that 'England' had lost was undoubtedly inspired by Bede. From his earliest works, Bede stressed the common destiny of all his fellow barbarians in Britain: 'Anglorum gens in Brittaniam venit . . . Saxones in Britannia fidem

---

[88] J. B. Gillingham, *The Kingdom of Germany in the High Middle Ages* (London, Historical Association, 1971), p. 3.

[89] Above, n. 18. For 'individualist' exiles and adventurers among the early Anglo-Saxons, see now Campbell, *Anglo-Saxons*, pp. 54–6. Bede envisaged Northumbrian warriors seeking better rewards 'trans mare', Plummer, I, p. 415.

[90] *ASC, s.a.* 1051–2, and Whitelock's introduction to her 1961 edn, pp. xiv–xvi. H. Loyn, 'The king and the structure of society in later Anglo-Saxon England', *History*, XLII (1957), pp. 87–100.

[91] D. Whitelock, 'Some charters in the name of King Alfred', in M. King and W. Stevens (eds), *Saints, Scholars and Heroes: Studies in honor of C. W. Jones* (Collegeville, Minn., 1979), pp. 77–98. The famous and unique Alfredian coin whose legend is normally expanded as 'Rex Anglorum' could also have included a 'Saxon' element: R. H. M. Dolley (ed.), *Anglo-Saxon Coins* (London, 1961), p. 81.

Christi suscipiunt.'[92] And such hesitation about their proper name was later rare; in the early Apocalypse commentary, he wrote of the 'laziness of our English people', who had recently received the Faith from Gregory, and in one of his last works he pointed out that, because the Greek for darkness was singular, his 'English' readers need not bow to Latin authority by making it plural in their own language![93] His was an 'Ecclesiastical History of our island and people', but the 'gens Anglorum' is well to the fore. Except when founding one of the most flourishing of archaeological industries by describing the continental origins of Britain's invaders, Bede only used 'Saxon' when it was in his foreign source, when it was accurate (as for the East, West or South Saxons) or when referring to the vernacular.[94] These English were as much a singular 'gens' or 'natio' as the 'populi' and 'regna' that went to make them up, and they have their singular church: Theodore was the first archbishop obeyed by 'omnis Anglorum ecclesia'.[95] The island's Celtic inhabitants give the story its context and play their part in it. But the main theme is the growth and expansion of the Christian Faith of the English people, from Gregory the pope to Egbert the pilgrim; it is the story of their Covenant (cf. above pp. 92–6).

Bede was to some extent a visionary (and also, it must be said, an Angle). If he inspired Alfred's English consciousness, neither was necessarily typical. Yet there are indications that a sense of English-ness was spreading in the ninth century. Alcuin wrote to Offa of 'regnum tuum immo Anglorum omnium' and denied infidelity to 'King Offa and the English people'; to the men of Kent he strikingly described 'divisio . . . inter populos et gentes Anglorum' as a 'regnum in se divisum'.[96] Like Bede, he was patriotically North-umbrian, but many of his letters home express what one might call

---

[92] *De Temporibus*, ed. T. Mommsen, *MGH,AA* XIII, pp. 304, 309.

[93] *Explicatio Apocalypsis, PL* XCIII, c. 134; *Retractatio in Actus Apostolorum*, ed. M. Laistner (Cambridge, Mass., 1939), p. 100.

[94] *HE* pr. (Albinus), pr. (Ceolwulf), V.24, pp. 3, 5, 356–7, 359; I.14, 15, 20, 22, III.7, 22, IV.14, V.9, pp. 30, 31, 38, 42, 140, 173, 233, 296, and cf. below, n. 105. In *HE* III.19, p. 167, Bede neatly substitutes 'Angles' for the 'Saxons' of the continental original: *Vita Fursei*, ed. B. Krusch, *MGH,SRM* IV, p. 437.

[95] *HE* IV.2, p. 204.

[96] Alcuin, *Epistolae*, pp. 147, 125, 192. It is possible that the circulation of Alcuin's letters to Offa inspired the 'rex Anglorum' titles perhaps subsequently attributed to him (above, n. 49). But I should not regard Alcuin's usage as evidence that Offa himself used the title: 'rex Anglorum' could mean, in effect, 'English king', as Sawyer points out, *Roman Britain to Norman England*, p. 107.

a sense of English national destiny: 'Britannia' was the 'patria'
which English ancestors won because of the sins of the Britons, and
which was now imperilled by Viking assault because of the sins of
the English themselves. At a humbler – and often non-Anglian –
level, charters from the later eighth century frequently use some
such phrase as 'quamdiu fides Catholica in gente Anglorum
perseveret', and in 816 'English bishops' were told to emancipate
'Englishmen'.[97] Charters also refer to a common vernacular,
though this is usually, as in Bede, described as 'Saxon' (and
'Saxonia', never 'Anglia', is the preferred geographical term).[98]
Moreover, as Fulk's letter shows, the habit caught on abroad. Like
the Celts (to this day), seventh- and eighth-century continentals
always called the Germanic inhabitants of Britain 'Saxones'; the
term 'Anglo-Saxon' may have been coined to avoid the confusion
this created with the 'Old' Saxons.[99] But whereas for Einhard
Alcuin was 'de Britanniae Saxonici generis', Notker simply says
that he was 'de natione Anglorum'.[100]

Much more important, Bede no more invented the 'gens
Anglorum' than did Alfred. Long before he heard of the 'candela
ecclesiae' in the North, Boniface had acquired a sense not of national
destiny but of national shame. He repeatedly observed how badly
the 'English' were shown up by their propensity to sodomy,
adultery and drunkenness, not to mention the forced labour of
monks. He could appeal to 'all God-fearing *Englishmen*' for help
in converting continental *Saxons*, who were of the same 'blood
and bone'.[101] For Eddius, 'gens nostra' meant Sussex as well as
Northumbria, and Wilfrid was spared from execution at Lyons
when identified as 'transmarinus de Anglorum gente ex Britannia'.[102]
For the author of the Whitby *Life of Gregory*, it meant both

[97] S 153, cf. N. Brooks, 'England in the ninth century', *TRHS*, 5th ser., XXIX
(1979), p. 13, n. 52; A. W. Haddan and W. Stubbs (eds), *Councils and Ecclesiastical
Documents* (3 vols, Oxford, 1869–78), III, pp. 579, 583.
[98] S 148; S 190; S 287; S 1436; Haddan and Stubbs, *Councils*, III, p. 52.
[99] We should not know from *Liber Historiae Francorum* that Balthildis was an
insular 'Saxon', but for what is said in her own *Vita*: ed. B. Krusch, *MGH, SRM* II
(1888), pp. 315, 483. For 'Anglo-Saxon' cf. W. Levison, *England and the Continent
in the Eighth Century* (Oxford, 1946), pp. 92–3, and *Artemis Lexikon des Mittelalters*,
I (1981), *s.v.* 'Angelsachsen'.
[100] Einhard, *Vita Karoli*, ed. O. Holder-Egger, *MGH,SRG*, 25, p. 30; Notker, *De
Gestis Karoli Magni*, ed. H. Haefele, *MGH,SRG*, 2, p. 3.
[101] *Briefe Bonifatius*, pp. 74–5, 150–1, 156, 169, 171.
[102] Eddius, *Wilfrid*, 6, 11, 41, pp. 14–15, 22–3, 82–3.

Northumbria and the English as a whole, and 'noster Gregorius' would lead the 'gentem Anglorum' before the Judgement Seat.[103] Of the earliest English writers, only Aldhelm, it seems, had never heard of the 'Angli'; he described himself and his kings as 'Saxon', and he probably meant 'West Saxon'. But even Aldhelm could see the 'citizens whom fertile Britain holds in its lap' as pupils of Gregory, and he claimed to the Northumbrian King Aldfrith that no one before him 'nostrae stirpis prosapia genitum et Germanicae gentis cunabulis confotum' had attempted such an exercise as his *De metris*; his contemporary, King Ine, already called his West Saxon subjects 'English', if we may trust the extant text of his code.[104]

National sentiments in learned or official sources are no more proof of political realities than imperial terminology. But the remarkable thing, in the political circumstances, is that they existed at all. Equally remarkable is the associated victory of 'Angle' over 'Saxon'. At first, these terms were to some extent interchangeable: 'Saxonia' (like 'Germania') may have been borrowed from neighbours, and the foreign pedagogues who first taught the Anglo-Saxons Latin probably described their 'lingua' as 'Saxonica'.[105] Given the exclusively 'Saxon' terminology of all external sources before Charlemagne's day, it is perhaps surprising that it did not prevail internally. Instead, Saxons like Boniface and Alfred spoke of 'the English'. Those who have even seen a problem here either, like Chadwick, invoke the dim possibilities of the invasion period, or else point to Anglian political and cultural dominance in the seventh and eighth centuries. But why should Alfred and his predecessors have wished to acknowledge Mercian dominance in this way? Why should Boniface, with his debt to Aldhelm and his ignorance of Bede until the last decade of his long life, have thought Anglian culture superior?[106]

There is another possible way of explaining why the unity of the 'gens Anglorum' was at least an ideal as soon as we have written

[103] *The Earliest Life of Gregory the Great*, ed. and trans. B. Colgrave (Lawrence, Kan., 1968), 6, 12, pp. 82–3, 94–5.

[104] *Aldhelmi Opera*, pp. 14–16, 498, 390, 202; *Gesetze*, I, pp. 100–1, 110–11, 114–15, 120–1: Alfred probably did not change the text of Ine's code, but it may well have been adjusted between Ine's time and his.

[105] *HE* IV.17, p. 239, and V.8, pp. 295–6, may each reflect Theodore's usage; cf. W. M. Lindsay, *The Corpus, Epinal, Erfurt and Leyden Glosses* (Oxford, 1921), pp. 81–2.

[106] *Briefe Bonifatius*, p. 158; M. Lapidge and M. Herren, *Aldhelm, the Prose Works* (Ipswich, 1979), pp. 2, 179 n. 9.

sources, but it is so obvious as to seem almost banal. The *Stammsagen* of the Franks and the Lombards began with puns, respectively by a Roman Emperor and a Germanic God. Bede's story begins, in effect, with a pun by a future pope. Bede had his doubts about this famous episode, and modern historians have more. But one of its circumstantial elements is that the pagan slave-boys who so impressed Gregory genuinely were Anglians: they came from the Deiran kingdom of Aelle.[107] And this helps to explain an otherwise very strange thing. The Germanic invaders of Britain were known throughout the West as 'Saxons' until long after Gregory's day; even Procopius, who had probably seen an Angle, knew that the Angles were not the only barbarians in Britain.[108] But Gregory's copious correspondence *never* describes the targets of his mission as other than 'Angli'. For his tidy Roman mind, the 'gens Anglorum' were as much the barbarian masters of Britain as were the Franks of Gaul, the Goths of Spain, or the Lombards of much of Italy. Aethelbert was 'rex Anglorum' as the descendants of Brunechildis were 'reges Francorum'. The 'Anglorum ecclesia', the 'Anglorum animae' were entrusted to Augustine, 'episcopo Anglorum', together (and this is also important) with 'omnes Brittaniae sacerdotes', 'Britannorum omnes episcopos'.[109] Gregory was of course wrong about many aspects of conditions in Britain; very probably, he was wrong to apply an 'English' label to Aethelbert and all other barbarians in Britain, and he may well have exaggerated Aethelbert's power. But the point about his vision of a single 'ecclesia' for a single 'gens Anglorum', however it arose, was that this powerful image soon acquired a reality of its own.[110]

[107] *Liber Historiae Francorum*, 2, pp. 242–3; Paul the Deacon, *Historia Langobardorum* I.8, p. 52; *HE* II.1, pp. 79–80; *Life of Gregory*, 9, pp. 90–1.

[108] Procopius, *History of the Wars*, ed. and tr. H. B. Dewing (Loeb series, 1928), VIII.20, pp. V, 252–5: he associates the Angles with the Frisians – perhaps, as Chadwick suggested, confusing the latter with Saxons.

[109] *Gregorii Registrum*, ed. P. Ewald and L. Hartmann, *MGH,Ep*. I, II, pp. I,389, 423, II,30–1, 199, 304, 305–6, 308–10, 312, 315, 319–20, 331, 333, 334, 336, 338; and the pope's epitaph, p. 470, and notice in the *Liber Pontificalis*, ed. L. Duchesne (2 vols, Paris, 1886–92), I, p. 312.

[110] One cannot say much about the usage of Gregory's successors, for want of badly needed research on *Papsturkunden* in pre-Conquest England. To judge from reliable sources, Rome continued to think of 'Britannia' and the 'gens Anglorum': *HE* II.10, 17, pp. 100, 119; *Liber Pontificalis*, pp. I,376, II,53, 161–2. Where they did not, this was either strictly accurate (*HE*, V.7, p. 293), or, one suspects, because 'Saxon' long remained continental usage (*HE*. III.29, p. 196; *Liber Pontificalis*, p. I,391).

Above all it did so at Canterbury. Canterbury never produced its own historian (unless it was Bede), and its notorious post-conquest forgeries are no substitute for the archives probably destroyed in 796–8.[111] We can still see that, in spite of its precarious start, Canterbury took the rights and responsibilities bequeathed by Gregory very seriously indeed. The 679 Council of Hatfield styled Theodore 'archiepiscopus Britanniae', and he was 'archbishop of the English' in the epilogue to his *Penitential*. His successor, Berhtwald, was 'Bretone heahbiscop' in Wihtred's law-code, and was addressed by the bishop of London as 'totius Brettaniae gubernacula regenti'.[112] When the final creation of the archbishopric of York restricted its official sphere to the area south of the Humber, Canterbury fought off Offa's scheme for a Lichfield archbishopric as the heir of Augustine and Gregory, apostles of the 'gens Anglorum'. In 814–16, the bishop of Lichfield acknowledged Canterbury as 'caput totius gentis Anglorum'; and when Archbishop Wulfred clashed violently with Cenwulf, a Christ Church charter complained that 'tota gens Anglorum' was deprived of his ministry for almost six years.[113] Canterbury had no doubt about the unity of its flock, the 'gens Anglorum' (and Canterbury sources inevitably speak of 'Angli' rather than 'Saxones').

What this meant was that, from Theodore's arrival at the latest, all Anglo-Saxons were exposed to a view of themselves as a single people before God – a people who, though they lived in 'Britannia' or 'Saxonia' and though they called themselves Saxons as well as Angles, were known in Heaven as the 'gens Anglorum'. The humblest grave-digger could trace his authority back to the 'Apostles of the English' at Canterbury. Though manuscripts do not survive, it is a good guess that the 'gens Anglorum' received the same sort of liturgical boost as the 'gens Francorum'. A significant canon of the 746–47 Council of Clovesho enjoined the celebration of the feasts of Gregory and Augustine, 'genti Anglorum missus a praefato Papa et patre nostro'; when the 'Second' English Corona-

---

[111] Most recently, M. Gibson, *Lanfranc of Bec* (Oxford, 1978), pp. 231–7. The last word has yet to be said: Brooks, thesis, (as n. 42), pp. 96–102, 315–16.

[112] *HE* IV.17, p. 239; Haddan and Stubbs, *Councils*, III, p. 203; *Gesetze*, I, p. 12; *BCS* 115.

[113] Haddan and Stubbs, *Councils*, III, p. 552; *BCS* 310; M. Richter (ed.), *Canterbury Professions* (London, Canterbury and York Society, LXVII, 1972–3), 9, p. 9; *S* 1436.

tion *Ordo* was drawn up in the early tenth century, the reference was to the 'regnum Anglorum vel Saxonum' at the politically sensitive moment of consecration, but where Hincmar's prayer of benediction invoked the Virgin and All Saints, the English *Ordo* has the Virgin, St Peter and 'St Gregory Apostle of the English'.[114] Aldhelm, Eddius and the author of the Whitby *Life* were all exposed in different ways to Canterbury's view of things.[115] So, above all, was Bede, whose founder-abbot had once ruled Augustine's own abbey, who explicitly acknowledged the inspiration of Biscop's successor-but-one there, and whose concentration on the 'gens Anglorum' within a wider British context exactly corresponds with the brief that Gregory gave Augustine.[116] It is hard to imagine a more effective way of imparting a sense of unity to diverse and feuding peoples than reminding them that they were all, as Englishmen, represented in Heaven by the same saints.

Archbishops of Canterbury had the same sort of interest in political cohesion within their sphere of authority as had sub-Roman aristocracies in the unity of their old 'province'. Too powerful an overlord could threaten the independence not only of Kent but also of the see itself, as Offa and Cenwulf showed. Nevertheless, overlords provided a necessary political context for the archiepiscopal shepherd. There is no good seventh-century evidence of a royal president for a council of the whole 'ecclesia Anglorum': Whitby was a synod of the Northumbrian Church and Hertford and Hatfield were chaired by Theodore.[117] But Aethelbald

114 Haddan and Stubbs, *Councils*, III, p. 368. For the Coronation *Ordo*'s lively history see C. Hohler, 'Some service books of the later Saxon Church', in D. Parsons (ed.), *Tenth Century Studies* (London, 1975), pp. 67–9. Hincmar's prayer is *MGH, Capit.* II, p. 456, and the English version is ed. P. Ward, *EHR*, LVII (1942), p. 356. I was guided through this minefield by Dr Janet Nelson, and a forthcoming article by her and Dr Pauline Stafford should solve many remaining problems.
115 Aldhelm studied there: *Opera*, pp. 478, 492–3; Eddius came from Kent: *HE* IV.2, p. 205; Whitby preserved Canterbury traditions: *Life of Gregory*, pp. 37, 53. Most of this was perceived by Wallace-Hadrill, *EMH*, pp. 115–16.
116 We may thus account for the British element in *HE*, rightly stressed by J. Stephens, 'Bede's Ecclesiastical History', *History*, LXII (1977), pp. 1–14, without supposing that it is anything less than an '*Ecclesiastical* History of the *English*'; McClure, above, p. 93.
117 *HE* III.25, IV.5, 17, pp. 183, 214–15, 239. Whitby was not an all-English affair, called by Oswiu in his capacity as *Bretwalda*; bishop Agilbert of the West Saxons was an exile, bishop Cedd of the East Saxons was a member of the Northumbrian Church, and, even if we accept that there were vacancies at Canterbury and in Mercia at this point, we must still explain the absence of bishop Boniface of the East Angles: *HE* III.7, 20, 21–3, IV.5, pp. 140, 169, 170–7, 217. Wulfhere, if anyone,

did preside at the 746–7 council, and from 781 began a series of regular meetings between the archbishop and bishops of the southern ecclesiastical province and the Mercian king and court, which are a neglected feature of the Age of Offa and Cenwulf. Most such meetings are known only from the charters issued at them; but others besides Clovesho (803) and Chelsea (816) may have produced ecclesiastical, even secular, legislation.[118] These councils showed what the archbishops had to gain from the political unity of the 'gens Anglorum', and their regularity must itself have fostered at least a sense of spiritual community among Anglo-Saxons. Sir Richard Southern suggested that 'Canterbury [under Lanfranc] inherited the pretensions of the Anglo-Saxon kings to quasi-imperial authority over Britain and the adjacent islands'; we know that Lanfranc himself thought the political and ecclesiastical unity of the English indissoluble.[119] But it may also be that powerful kings in the seventh and eighth centuries were heirs to the spiritual ambitions of Canterbury and that, though Canterbury did not invent the *Bretwalda*, it preserved, even influenced, the idea. Bede twice refers to overlords amidst information that must have come from Canterbury, and his list is curiously sensitive about Kentish freedom. Alcuin described Kent as a 'regnum imperiale'. Above all, the 'double meaning' of *Bretwalda*, at once southumbrian and pan-British, makes little sense in terms of Roman Britain, but closely corresponds with the at once wide and narrow authority which

---

was *Bretwalda* by this time (above, n. 61); and the same difficulty arises with the more widely accepted view that Oswiu helped to choose the archbishop of Canterbury after 664, despite *HE* III.29, p. 196. See an important note by J. Campbell, 'Bede', in T. A. Dorey (ed.), *Latin Historians* (London, 1966), p. 187, n. 30.

[118] The following charters are attested by an approximate complement of southern bishops: *S* 1257 (781); *S* 123 (785); *S* 125 (786); *S* 129 (788); *S* 136 (793 – a rank forgery, but the episcopal element in the witness-list seems sound); *S* 137 (794); *S* 153 (798); *S* 155 (799); *S* 106 + 158 (801); *S* 1260 + 1431 (803); *S* 161 (805); *S* 180 (816); *S* 1433–4 (824); *S* 1435–7 (825); *S* 190 (836). *S* 1438 (838–9) implies full episcopal attendance on the West Saxon kings, but the witness-lists contradict this; West Saxon ascendancy ended the system that served Canterbury so well. Legislation is extant for the councils of 803 (*BCS* 310, 312) and 816 (Haddan and Stubbs, *Councils*, III, pp. 579–85); also, if the meetings are the same, for that of 786: Alcuin, *Epistolae*, pp. 19–29.

[119] R. W. Southern, *Saint Anselm and his Biographer* (Cambridge, 1961), pp. 128–9; Hugh the Chanter, *History of the Church of York*, ed. C. Johnson (London, 1961), p. 3.

Gregory gave Canterbury, and whose ambivalence underlay the trauma that Augustine's church experienced after 1070.

The point reminds us that nations are made not just by conquest and political manoeuvre but by shared ideals. Whatever obstacles were still be to surmounted by tenth- and twelfth-century kings of the English, they inherited a sense of Englishness that was established in ruling circles and arguably at least residual elsewhere. Bede was probably right to focus not, like other historians of early medieval *gentes*, on migration and conquest under *Heerkönige*, but on the evangelical initiative of a pope as the key to English *Stammesbildung*. If the Anglo-Saxons had no 'Romani' to further their political coherence in their own interest, and no 'men of art' to carry ideals of common identity across political frontiers, they had a Church which played both roles. Canterbury was Apostolic to an extent that even Fulk's Rheims was not. What the *Reichskirche* allegedly did to restrain the centrifugal forces of Otto the Great's kingdom, Canterbury did in fulfilment of its own *raison d'être*.

'The beginnings of nations, those excepted of whom Sacred Books have spok'n, is to this day unknown'; thus John Milton, among the first to publish a printed history of pre-Conquest Britain, and perhaps the last to see it as a warning of God's wrath.[120] England, like all European nations, was founded in a 'Dark Age'; we shall never quite understand how. The main objection to belief in the inevitability of English unification is that it is all too easy. It is virtually incredible that what did not happen until long afterwards in countries that *were* initially subjected to a single political authority should have happened automatically in a country that was not. Moreover, in investing the *Bretwalda*, a status that probably did exist, and possibly under that name, with functions and rights that are frankly anachronistic, we have overlooked something more remarkable: with few of their neighbours' initial assets, the Anglo-Saxons developed a sense of communal identity which inspired one of the world's great histories, and which drew its strength from spiritual ideals rather than political realities. Indeed, it is arguable that it was because 'Englishness' was first an ideal that the enterprise launched by Alfred, his children and his grandchildren was so astoundingly successful. English communal identity may have

---

[120] John Milton, *The History of Britain before the Norman Conquest* (London, 1671), repr. *The Complete Prose Works of John Milton, V* (Yale, 1971), p. 1.

begun with the dangers posed by whatever King Arthur later came to represent; but its persistence when the danger passed was probably due to Canterbury's papally inspired vision of their unity before God. To that extent, the long-forgotten views of Kemble and Stubbs were right. Symbolically at least, Napoleon's nation of shopkeepers began in Gregory's market-place at Rome.

6

Bede's Ideal of Reform

ALAN THACKER

Unlike the other great early medieval scholars Bede lived a life comparatively remote from the practical world of royal and ecclesiastical government. He has convincingly been presented as an idealist, interested above all in the workings of divine grace.[1] Yet he was also concerned about the world in which he lived, and in this paper it will be argued that his later writings were permeated with a vision of reform in church and society which was to leave its mark on more than his own generation. That vision is a key to the understanding of all Bede's later works, not only the commentaries and homilies, but the hagiography and histories as well. Indeed, it emerges with especial vividness in the latter and it is on them that much of what follows will be focused.

Throughout his active life as a teacher, but especially in his later writings, Bede was much preoccupied with the role of those whom he variously called the *spirituales magistri*, the *sancti praedicatores*, the *rectores* or *doctores ecclesiae*. In particular, he favoured the expressions *doctor* and *praedicator*. For him preaching had a pre-eminent, even a sacramental, significance; it was not envisaged as confined to a narrowly liturgical context, but as embracing a whole range of doings concerned with converting the heathen or promoting the moral well-being or theological understanding of the faithful. Bede's teachers and preachers were the spiritual leaders and guides of the people of God, the successors of the prophets and apostles, to whose *ordo* they belonged and whose role they fulfilled in the contemporary Church.[2]

[1] e.g. P. Wormald, 'Bede and Benedict Biscop', in G. Bonner (ed.), *Famulus Christi* (London, 1976), p. 155; above, pp. 76, 98.

[2] e.g. Bede, *De Tabernaculo*, ed. D. Hurst, *CCSL* CXIX A, pp. 26–30; *De Templo, ibid.*, pp. 200–3; *In Ezram et Neemiam, ibid.*, pp. 343–4, 354–5; *Super*

Bede saw these men as charged with the transmission of the Church's intellectual heritage; they were to be faithful interpreters of the Scriptures and a bulwark against heresy.[3] Equally important, they were *custodes animarum*, guardians of souls, who were to exhort and instruct the faithful and convert the heathen.[4] Such men had of necessity to be of superior education and intellect, initiates into the higher mysteries of the faith which the common crowd of ordinary believers could not understand. They were the 'eyes' of the Church who penetrated the *superficies litterae* of Holy Writ to the heavenly *arcana* beneath.[5] Above all (and this was a theme to which Bede constantly returned), they were to set a holy example, to show in deed what they taught by word.[6] In short, they were to be an intellectual and moral elite.

Bede was thus concerned with a group whose qualifications were not primarily institutional, and indeed he deliberately refrained from identifying his *doctores* and *praedicatores* with the ordained hierarchy of bishops, priests, and deacons. In a sermon he argued that spiritual pastors ordained to preach the mysteries of the word included not only those in major orders but also the rulers of monasteries and even the heads of secular households, however small. Elsewhere he claimed that in the Scriptures the term *sacerdos* was mystically to be understood as comprehending not only the ministers of the altar but all who excelled in right living and healthful doctrine. He even envisaged women preachers.[7] For him the traditional hierarchy and the *ordo* of teachers and preachers overlapped but were not identical; there was a distinction between *sacerdotes*, *episcopi*, and *presbyteri*, who were ordained, and *doctores* and *praedicatores*, who were instituted.[8]

Parabolas Salomonis, PL XCI, c. 991; *In Cantica Canticorum, PL* XCL, cc. 1130–99; *In Marcum*, ed. D. Hurst, *CCSL* CXX, pp. 469–74; *Opera Homiletica*, ed. D. Hurst, *CCSL* CXXII, p. 281.
[3] Bede, *Super Par.*, cc. 970, 997; *De Templo*, p. 162; *Homilies*, p. 49; *In Primam Partem Samuhelis*, ed. D. Hurst, *CCSL* CXIX, pp. 261, 263; *In Librum Beati Patris Tobiae, PL* XCI, cc. 928, 933; *In Cantica Cant.*, c. 1125.
[4] Bede, *In Librum Tobiae*, cc. 927–8; *Super Par.*, c. 1001; *De Tab.*, pp. 80–1, 83; *De Templo*, pp. 217–8; *In Ezram*, pp. 250, 324, 354–5.
[5] Bede, *In Cantica Cant.*, cc. 1129, 1130.
[6] e.g. Bede, *De Tab.*, p. 106; *De Templo*, pp. 186–7, 203; *In Ezram*, pp. 323, 354–5.
[7] Bede, *Homilies*, p. 49; *De Templo*, p. 194; *In Ezram*, p. 257.
[8] Plummer I, p. 410; cf. *In Ezram*, pp. 277, 379–80; *De Tab.*, pp. 101–2.

These views are essentially those of a monk in an age when religious communities included priests and increasingly felt themselves part of the clerical elite, even though ordination was still far from the norm. Bede's emphasis was peculiarly adapted to such a group, associated with yet not identical to the established hierarchy of the major orders.[9] His conception of the relationship between the faithful and their spiritual leaders was essentially monastic; the faithful had a duty to listen to their pastors, they were *subjecti* or *discipuli*, bound to obey their spiritual *rectores* or *magistri*, the administrators and custodians of the *disciplina regularis*.[10] A chance remark in the letter to Egbert indicates that he hoped that the laity would be brought to some understanding of the monastic life, if not by experience then by hearsay, and in a sermon he recommended that the active virtues be pursued by the *populus* as they were *in coenubio*.[11]

Bede's commendation of a monastic pastorate and the imposition of monastic discipline on the faithful reflects a primary conviction running through all his work, namely that the ideal *conversatio* involved a balancing of the contemplative and active lives; on the one hand, the preacher and teacher could only fulfil his role successfully if he essayed the monastic skills of withdrawal and contemplation, on the other, the monk could only achieve the contemplative ideal after long practice in virtuous living, in *bona actio*. In his homily on St John the Evangelist, Bede presented his subject as typifying both the contemplative and the *praedicator*; by Christ's express command John entered into that *speculativa felicitas* which anticipated the eternal joys of heaven, while remaining throughout his long life an active teacher and preacher and foe of heresy. Though Bede undoubtedly believed that the contemplative life was superior to the active, he regarded both as essential to sanctity.[12]

These preoccupations have to be seen in the context of Bede's growing anxiety about the state of Church and society in his day. As early as 716, in his commentary on I Samuel, he condemned

---

[9] P. Schmitz, *Histoire de l'ordre de S. Benoît* (Maredsous, 1948), I, p. 287; H. M. R. E. Mayr-Harting, *The Venerable Bede, The Rule of St. Benedict, and Social Class* (Jarrow Lecture, 1976), pp. 14–18.
[10] Bede, *Homilies*, pp. 46, 345; *In Lucam*, ed. D. Hurst, CCSL CXX, pp. 260–1; *Super Par.*, c. 980.
[11] Plummer I, p. 416: *Homilies*, p. 65.
[12] M. T. A. Carroll, *The Venerable Bede and his Spiritual Teachings* (Washington, 1946), pp. 198–215; Bede, *In Cantica Cant.*, c. 1154; *In Lucam*, pp. 64–5, 225–6; *De Templo*, p. 151; *Homilies*, pp. 64–5.

those *magistri inertes* whose inadequacies allowed compromise with heathen practice. Thereafter he increasingly deplored the lack of the necessary intellect and virtue, the avarice, venality, and indolence of contemporary *doctores* and *sacerdotes*, whose failings left their flocks uncorrected and unsupervised. Even in the monasteries he detected unsatisfactory teachers.[13] His fears were given definitive expression in 734, in the letter to Egbert, in which he criticized certain bishops for setting bad examples, drew attention to pastoral failures in remote places, condemned many monasteries as bogus, and lamented the decline of spiritual standards among the laity.

Bede, however, had remedies. He wanted to see more priests ordained, more *doctores* instituted, and, in accordance with the Gregorian plan, more sees created. This reform of the diocesan system was to be accompanied where necessary by a redeployment of monastic resources; the new bishops were to be based in existing monasteries which were to be enriched if necessary by endowments taken from false communities. Bede, in fact, wished to see the monasteries fully integrated into the diocesan system and hoped to beget thereby reform in Church and society. As episcopal *familiae* the monasteries would be able to assist bishops in maintaining standards; under their supervision there could be a revival in the pastoral care of the laity, implemented by suitable *doctores*.[14]

Such ideas, of course, were not original. Much emphasis had already been laid on the office of preaching by Caesarius of Arles, who in his sermons often reminded his hearers of their duties towards their *doctores* and *praedicatores* and towards the *magistri* whose *subditi* they were.[15] Bede, like Caesarius, was impressed by rural resistance to Christian teaching, and made in many ways a similar response, couched in similar terminology. Yet there were important differences (not least Caesarius's emphasis on a teaching ministry based on parish rather than monastery), and there is no evidence that Bede had any first-hand knowledge of Caesarius's works.[16] Ultimately we must look elsewhere for the source of his ideas: to the writings of Gregory the Great. Gregory's treatment of

[13] Bede, *In Sam.*, pp. 122–3; *De Tab.*, pp. 95–6, 115; *De Templo*, pp. 206–7; *In Ezram*, pp. 303, 324, 360.
[14] Plummer I, pp. 407–19.
[15] Caesarius of Arles, *Sermones*, ed. G. Morin, *CCSL* CIII–CIV, pp. 2, 7, 359, 422, 467, 480–1, 483, 606, 862, 867–8.
[16] e.g. Caesarius, *Sermones*, pp. 8, 10.

the pastorate is strikingly similar to Bede's. His works are studded
with allusions to teaching and preaching, seen as the principal
function of his *pastores* and *rectores*.[17] For him as for Bede the pastors
were the eyes of the Church with a duty to perform in deed what
they expounded in word.[18] Above all he emphasized that preaching
– in the broad sense of the doctrinal and moral supervision of the
faithful – should be performed by those who had received a firm
grounding in the ascetic life, that it required both active and contemplative virtues.[19] Like Bede, Gregory was concerned with an
elite order of preachers who were to teach and more particularly
embody the holy life, but were not necessarily to hold specific office
in the hierarchy.[20]

Bede valued Gregory's writings very highly,[21] and his reliance on
them in crucial sections of his own commentaries shows how much
they influenced him. In the *De Tabernaculo*, for example, he borrowed passages from the *Cura Pastoralis* which interpreted portions
of the book of Exodus as figuring the virtues of spiritual rulers and
the right balancing of the active and contemplative lives.[22] These
and many other such borrowings[23] indicate that Bede's own spiritual
rulers were to be understood as fulfilling the Gregorian ideal.
Gregory, moreover, used the homily to express his disquiet about
the conduct of the ecclesiastical leaders of his day. Preaching, he
believed, was inadequate; avarice was rife; silent pastors continued
to receive the offerings of the faithful and even sold the spiritual
grace it was their duty to bestow. In his letter to Egbert Bede

[17] e.g. Gregory the Great, *Liber Regulae Pastoralis*, PL LXXVII, cc. 13–128;
Homiliae in Ezechielem, ed. M. Adriaen, CCSL CXLII, pp. 29, 139, 361; *Homiliae in
Evangelia*, PL LXXVI, cc. 1138–49; *Moralia in Job*, PL LXXV, cc. 515–1162,
LXXVI, cc. 13–782.
[18] Gregory, *Reg. Past.*, cc. 15–16, 28–30, 124; *Moralia* LXXVI, cc. 597–8.
[19] Gregory, *Reg. Past.*, cc. 19, 20–1, 30–2, 33, 38–42, 49, 96–8; *Moralia* LXXV,
cc. 760–1, LXXVI, c. 630; C. Dagens, *Grégoire le Grand* (Paris, 1977), pp. 133–63.
[20] e.g. Gregory, *Moralia* LXXV, cc. 760–5, 938–9, LXXVI cc. 126, 467, 549–51,
597–8, 629–30; *Hom. in Ez.*, pp. 29, 34–8, 61–4, 71–3, 137, 145–9, 164–5, 170–3,
355–77, 390; Dagens, *Grégoire le Grand*, pp. 311–44; K. Hallinger, *Papst Gregor der
Grosse und der hl. Benedikt* (*Studia Anselmiana*, Rome, 1957), pp. 269–77. I am much
indebted to Dr J. McClure's discussion of the *Moralia* in a paper delivered to a
seminar in Late Roman Studies at Manchester University on 25 February 1976.
[21] P. Meyvaert, *Bede and Gregory the Great* (Jarrow Lecture, 1964); McClure,
above, pp. 77–8.
[22] Exodus 25:12–15; 28:6–8; Gregory, *Reg. Past.*, cc. 29–30, 31, 49, 50; Bede,
De Tab., pp. 15–16, 97–9, 111.
[23] e.g. Bede, *In Lucam*, p. 119; *De Templo*, pp. 190, 214–7; Gregory, *Hom. in Ev.*,
cc. 1144–5; *Hom. in Ez.*, pp. 235–6, 243–4, 363–4, 373–4, 391–4.

commended the 'words of the most holy Pope Gregory . . . on the life and vices of rulers'. Clearly his condemnation of contemporary evils in the Church was given shape by Gregory's treatment of earlier ecclesiastical abuses.[24]

But Gregory was not merely the author of abstruse works of exegesis; he also illustrated his dominant ideas with the vivid *exempla* of the *Dialogues*, a book which Professor Wallace-Hadrill has recently characterized as full of grim warnings for the Italian clergy.[25] In these stories of Italian saints and churchmen, which Bede knew well, the pope laid great emphasis on the monastic contribution to the work of teaching and preaching. Abbot Equitius of Valeria, for example, though not in holy orders, preached widely in the area surrounding his monastery, 'in churches, towns, villages, and the homes of each one of the faithful'. As his authority for these activities he alleged a personal vocation, and when he was condemned as an unlicensed preacher his claims were miraculously vindicated. Equitius's exemplary life accorded with his teaching: he fulfilled his monastic duties on his expeditions, dressing humbly and riding a poor beast. His story, one of the longest in the *Dialogues*, illustrates admirably Gregory's (and Bede's) attitude towards the monk's personal role and provides a foretaste of the much fuller treatment of these themes in the *Life* of Benedict, where Gregory celebrates his ideal preacher, ascetic, and monastic teacher and reformer. Benedict, of course, surpassed Equitius in that he implemented his teaching in a rule which Gregory held up for especial commendation. His was the portrait which was to exercise the most profound influence over Bede.[26]

Bede, then, was thoroughly conversant with the whole range of Gregory's writings and must have appreciated the relationship between his commentaries and his hagiography. That relationship provided him with a model (if one were needed) for his own approach to history and saints' lives. Certainly, in the preface to the *Ecclesiastical History* he alluded to his sources in phrases borrowed

[24] Gregory, *Hom. in Ez.*, cc. 1139–40, 1141–2, 1145; Plummer I, p. 406; Dagens, *Grégoire le Grand*, pp. 328–31.
[25] Gregory, *Dialogues* I prologue, ed. A. de Vogüé, *SC* CCLX, p. 16, also editor's introduction, p. 3; review by J. M. Wallace-Hadrill, *Journal of Theological Studies*, XXXI (1980), pp. 224–6.
[26] Gregory, *Dialogues* I.4, II, pp. 38–54, 126–248. Though Gregory did not use the Rule of Benedict, he certainly knew it: Hallinger, *Papst Gregor der Grosse*, pp. 231–319; Meyvaert, *Bede and Gregory*, p. 19.

from the *Dialogues*, a clear acknowledgement that the latter were in his mind when he was working on his masterpiece.[27]

Perhaps the most revealing example of Bede's hagiographical technique is his treatment of Cuthbert, partly because he himself produced three accounts of the saint, but even more because there was also an earlier anonymous *Life*.[28] The survival of all this material provides a unique opportunity to examine various stages in Bede's reshaping of a legend. Cuthbert, who died in 687, had been successively prior of Melrose and prior and bishop of Lindisfarne. He was enshrined at Lindisfarne, his body having been elevated in a wooden chest in 698, at which time it was found to be uncorrupted. The cult was undoubtedly an important one; it became widely known and miracle stories about the saint were preserved in several communities, including (besides Lindisfarne itself) Melrose, Jarrow, Ripon, Whitby and Carlisle. Its status can be gauged by the scale of the operations undertaken at Lindisfarne in the decades immediately following the elevation, above all in the production of a sumptuous gospel-book probably intended for display by the tomb-chest itself. The anonymous first *Life* of the saint also belongs to this early phase of activity, and seems to have been written by a monk of the community about AD 700, very soon after the enshrinement.[29] The work is a lively one and incorporates eye-witness accounts of events in Cuthbert's life, but it is clear too that the author shaped his material in accordance with certain celebrated literary models. One of these is Evagrius's Latin translation of Athanasius's *Life* of St Anthony, which he quotes on several occasions and which inspired his description of Cuthbert's life as a hermit on Farne.[30] Another, even more influential, was Sulpicius Severus's account of St Martin, which supplied two lengthy passages, including the important *topos* of the saint maintaining his monastic and ascetic way of life without neglecting his episcopal office. Like Martin, Cuthbert is depicted as an enthusiastic evangelist, visiting remote rural communities and

[27] *HE*, pr., p. 5; Gregory, *Dialogues* I pr., p. 16.
[28] *Vita S. Cuthberti Auctore Anonymo* and *Bedae Vita S. Cuthberti Prosaica*, ed. B. Colgrave (Cambridge, 1940), pp. 60–138; *Vita S. Cuthberti Metrica*, ed. W. Jaager, *Palaestra*, CXCVIII (1935); *HE* IV.27–32, pp. 274–80.
[29] B. Colgrave, *Two Lives of St. Cuthbert*, pp. 3–10, 13, and 'St. Cuthbert and his times', in C. F. Battiscombe (ed.), *The Relics of St. Cuthbert* (Oxford, 1956), pp. 115–43; R. Cramp, *The Background to St. Cuthbert's life* (Durham Cathedral Lecture, 1980).
[30] *V. Cuth. Anon.* I.1, II.1, III.7, pp. 62, 74, 104–6.

converting and baptizing their heathen or heretical inhabitants; that the parallel was conscious and deliberate is clear from a number of verbal and structural similarities between these episodes and comparable ones in the Sulpician *oeuvre*.[31]

There is a strong Irish background to all this. It has been argued persuasively that the Lindisfarne author's adoption of the Antonian and Martinian models was a product of his community's connection with Iona, where undoubtedly they left a strong imprint on Adomnan's *Life* of Columba. But it is worth remembering that similar use was made of them in Irish-influenced milieux in Gaul, with which Lindisfarne was also in contact. Martinian idealism was widespread on the continent as in Britain.[32]

Though such parallels were employed extensively in the Lindisfarne *Life*, they were largely implicit; Cuthbert is never expressly compared with other saints. The anonymous was not didactic, and did not emphasize his subject's moral relevance for his contemporaries. He was primarily interested in his hero as a miracle-worker, and such references as he makes to his pastoral activities are mostly incidental and merely to provide a context for the wonders. Such a *Life* was well-adapted to serve a cult, which required the advertisement of the saint as a figure of power, able by his intercession to manipulate divine grace on behalf of his clients; it was not, however, suited to the inculcation of wider ethical teaching.

Bede's approach was different. Though in his earlier metrical *Life*, produced between 705 and 716, he departed little from his source (except to include an additional miracle), in the prose *Life*, completed by 721, he made considerable modifications.[33] The later work was commissioned by the Lindisfarne monks, and as a result of their co-operation and Bede's assiduity in collecting fresh material it offers a more coherent account of the saint than the anonymous.

---

[31] *V. Cuth. Anon.* I.2, II.5–6, IV.1, 3–7, pp. 62, 84–8, 110, 116–22; H. M. R. E. Mayr-Harting, *The Coming of Christianity to Anglo-Saxon England* (London, 1972), p. 162; A. T. Thacker, 'The Social and Continental Background to Early Anglo-Saxon Hagiography' (unpublished Oxford D. Phil. thesis, 1977), pp. 87–92; Wallace-Hadrill, *EMH*, p. 91.

[32] D. A. Bullough, 'Columba, Adomnan and the achievement of Iona', *Scottish Historical Review*, XLIII (1964), pp. 110–30, XLIV (1965), pp. 17–33; for related Gallo-Irish work see Jonas, *Vita S. Columbani*, ed. B. Krusch, *MGH,SRM* IV, pp. 61–108; *Vita S. Amandi*, ed. B. Krusch, *ibid.* V, pp. 428–9.

[33] Bede, *V. Cuth. Met.*, pr., 3, pp. 65–7. For the dates of the two versions see M. Manitius, *Geschichte der lateinischen Literatur des Mittelalters*, I (1911), pp. 84–5.

Indeed, it has often been criticized for its diffuseness. Plummer, for example, felt that Bede had amplified his source 'with rhetorical matter which can only be called padding', and more recently it has been pointed out that modern taste is unsympathetic to the prose *Life's* 'elegant morals'.[34] But Bede's additions have a very definite purpose. He sought to interpret the Lindisfarne author's simple descriptions of Cuthbert's acts, to bring into focus the figure of the saint himself, as prior, hermit, and bishop. This was attempted primarily in the chapters which describe Cuthbert's mode of life at the various stages of his career, passages which have no obvious counterparts in the Lindisfarne *Life*.[35] Scattered too throughout the work are shorter comments setting the miracles within the context of Cuthbert's exemplary pastorate. Indeed, from the very beginning Bede stresses the saint's diverse roles as active monk, contemplative, and *magister*, and he carefully structures the *Life* to show the unfolding of each in turn.

In constructing this portrait, Bede relied partly on the models which dominated the Lindisfarne *Life*. But he shifted the emphasis. Though he expressly draws attention to the Antonian parallel, the Martinian one is treated with caution and the saint never mentioned. That reserve did not stem from ignorance; though Bede, strangely, does not seem to have known the writings of Sulpicius himself, he was familiar with the later metrical *Lives* of Fortunatus and Paulinus of Périgueux, and there are signs that he recognized and occasionally sharpened the Martinian imagery of the Lindisfarne author.[36] There can be no doubt, moreover, that he was in sympathy with the principal ideals of the cult of Tours, with its emphasis on Martin's ascetic episcopate and his combination of humility and missionary zeal. But it was not, perhaps, the Martinian associations of these ideals with which he was primarily concerned; rather they seem to have been seen as having a Gregorian resonance. Gregory himself had been impressed by the figure of Martin, and the Sulpician writings had a considerable influence on the *Dialogues*, especially the portrait of Benedict. It is these Gregorian exemplars that Bede had particularly in mind when he was writing the prose *Life*.[37]

[34] Plummer I, p. xlvi; Mayr-Harting, *Coming of Christianity*, p. 165.
[35] See esp. Bede, *V. Cuth Pros.*, 6, 9, 16, 22, 26, pp. 172–4, 184–6, 206–12, 228–30, 240–2.
[36] Thacker, 'Social and Continental Background', pp. 117–21.
[37] M. Mähler, 'Évocations bibliques et hagiographiques dans la vie de S. Benoît par S. Grégoire', *Revue Bénédictine*, LXXXIII (1973), pp. 398–429; and see especi-

The first section of the work deals with Cuthbert's entry into the monastic life and his emergence as a model preacher. In a chapter devoted to his training at Melrose, Cuthbert is presented as the favoured disciple of prior Boisil, and as an exemplary monk more diligent than his fellows in the conventional monastic duties. His diet in particular is singled out for commendation: he abstained, we are told, from all alcoholic stimulants, yet ate sufficient to enable him to continue necessary work. Though such observances cannot conclusively be associated with any specific rule, it is clear that they are very much in accord with Benedict's. For Benedict viewed abstinence from alcohol as a spiritual gift, while nevertheless stressing the need for temperance rather than extreme asceticism, and mitigating the rules of fasting for those working in the field.[38] It looks then as if Cuthbert is meant to be seen as conforming to Benedict's most demanding standards. At the same time his relations with Boisil show him receiving instruction and a prophetic confirmation of his vocation as a spiritual ruler from another great monastic teacher. Eventually he succeeds Boisil as both prior and *praedicator*, and is shown making frequent journeys to bring word and sacraments to the neighbouring *vulgus*. Bede goes into considerable detail about these journeys: he mentions Cuthbert's mode of travel, sometimes on horseback, sometimes on foot, perhaps to show that, while properly humble, he never let personal asceticism interfere with the work of God;[39] he also emphasizes the saint's efforts to visit remote *viculi*, whose inaccessibility and poverty kept other teachers away. Above all, he stresses Cuthbert's skill in teaching, in particular his ability to secure repentance and conversion both by his eloquence and his saintly life.[40]

Here then is a portrait of an active and prayerful preacher, the very type of the pastor Bede was to recommend to archbishop Egbert some fifteen years later. It is followed by several stories taken from the Lindisfarne *Life*, illustrating the wonders wrought

---

ally Sulpicius Severus, *Dialogues* II.4., ed. C. Halm, *CSEL* I, pp. 184–5; Gregory, *Dialogues*, II.32, pp. 226–30; *V. Cuth. Anon.* IV.6, pp. 118–20.
[38] Bede, *V. Cuth. Pros.* 6, pp. 172–4; Benedict, *Rule* 40–1, ed. A. de Vogüé, *SC* CLXXXI–CLXXXII, pp. 578–82, Columbanus expressed rather similar views: *Regula Monachorum* 3, ed. G. S. M. Walker, *Sancti Columbani Opera* (Dublin, 1970), pp. 124–6.
[39] Unlike Chad, who had to be forced to ride by archbishop Theodore: *HE* IV.3, p. 206.   [40] Bede, *V. Cuth. Pros.* 9, pp. 184–6.

by Cuthbert on his travels. Significantly, two of these were expressly compared by Bede (though not by the anonymous) with miracles performed by two heroes of the Gregorian *Dialogues* – bishop Marcellinus of Ancona and Benedict himself.[41] Bede, it is clear, wanted Cuthbert to be seen as the ideal monk and pastor, both as depicted by Gregory in his portrait of Benedict and as demanded by the rule which the pope especially admired. Other revisions of the anonymous's material confirm this. Bede's version of the story of Cuthbert's journey into Pictland transformed a *peregrinatio* of uncertain length into a temporary expedition on specific monastic business; he discreetly omitted the Lindisfarne author's revelation that Cuthbert eventually sailed away to a secret retreat and had to be constrained to return to monastic life, probably because he was conscious that such behaviour consorted ill with the Benedictine virtue of *stabilitas*.[42]

In the section devoted to Cuthbert at Lindisfarne Bede concentrates on rather different aspects of his hero's career. Though the saint's activities among the surrounding rustics are briefly noticed, he is now viewed primarily as a monastic teacher and reformer. Cuthbert's revision of the Lindisfarne rule and his technique in overcoming resistance to that revision are dealt with at length. 'Very often', Bede tells us, 'during debates in the chapter of the brethren concerning the rule, when he was assailed by the bitter insults of his opponents, he would rise up suddenly and with calm mind and countenance (*placido vultu*) would go out, thus dissolving the chapter; but none the less on the following day, as if he had suffered no rebuke he would give the same instruction as before to the same audience until . . . he gradually converted them to the things that he desired.' The passage is an interesting one; here again Cuthbert's actions, though not based on any specific precept, conform to the general tenor of the Benedictine *Rule*, in which the abbot is instructed to act with prudent moderation in administering correction and not to overdrive his flock. Significantly too, Bede's remarks recall an episode in Gregory's account of Benedict, in which the saint confronts a community who had rebelled against the Rule he had sought to impose and tried to poison him. Benedict miraculously foils the attempted murder and is described as rising

---

[41] *ibid*. 10–14, pp. 188–202; Gregory, *Dialogues* I.6, pp. 62–4.
[42] Bede, *V. Cuth. Pros.* 11, pp. 192–4; Benedict, *Rule* 4, 58, 60–1, pp. 464, 628–30, 636, 638.

and leaving with a calm countenance (the phrase used is *placidus vultus* as in the *Life* of Cuthbert). So Cuthbert is to be seen as a Northumbrian Benedict, a reformer who successfully faced danger and calumny in his attempts to prohibit deviations from approved monastic custom. The passage concludes with a description of Cuthbert's own diligent and exemplary observance. Again moderation is the keynote: Cuthbert wore clothing notable neither for elegance nor slovenliness, very much as was prescribed in the Benedictine *Rule*. The saint's constant supervision of the brethren and his sharing in their manual labour and communal sleeping arrangements represent Bede's considered ideal of abbatial behaviour and closely resemble his portrait of abbot Eosterwine of Wearmouth in the *Historia Abbatum*.[43]

Having shown Cuthbert as monastic preacher and reformer, Bede moves on to a depiction of Cuthbert's life as contemplative. Like that of the Lindisfarne author, the portrait is much influenced by the Evagrian *Life* of St Anthony, and indeed goes further in including a direct comparison between Cuthbert and the Egyptian saint. But it is also skilfully tailored to Gregorian and Benedictine ideals. In particular, Bede, while stressing Cuthbert's achievement as an ascetic contemplative, is very careful not to depreciate the monastic life. The hermit's solitude is viewed as the crowning accomplishment of the monk: from the long *perfectio* of the active life Cuthbert rose to the ultimate *otium* of divine contemplation. Bede expressly states that Cuthbert entered his hermitage with the *gratia* of his abbot and brethren, and depicts the saint as remaining in close contact with his community. Above all he makes Cuthbert say that the *vita coenobitarum*, the life of monks, was to be admired for its own sake and to be regarded as a perfectly sufficient route to holiness.[44]

Finally, Bede presents Cuthbert the bishop. Here he had as a model the Lindisfarne author's portrait, with its quotation from the *Life* of St Martin, but, significantly, he rewrote the passage in such a way that it reads like a summary of the qualities later to be recommended in the letter to Egbert. Cuthbert was a perfect *doctor*, who preserved the rigours of the monastic life amid the thronging crowds,

[43] Bede, *V. Cuth. Pros.* 16, pp. 206–12; Gregory, *Dialogues* II.3, p. 142; Benedict, *Rule* 64, pp. 648–52; Plummer I, pp. 371–2.
[44] Bede, *V. Cuth. Pros.* 17–22, pp. 214–30, esp. 17, 22, pp. 214, 228–30; Benedict, *Rule* 1, pp. 436–8.

followed apostolic exemplars, and protected the people committed
to him with assiduous prayers and wholesome admonitions.[45] This
account is supplemented by numerous wonder stories which Bede
took from the Lindisfarne author and to each of which he added a
few significant sentences calling attention to Cuthbert's diligent
performance of all the duties required of a bishop. The saint is
presented as ordaining, conferring the veil on a royal postulant,
visiting the scattered villages of his diocese, and ministering to areas
stricken by the plague. His last act as bishop was a long pastoral
journey visiting his flock and others of the faithful.[46]

   To sum up: Cuthbert is presented as an exemplary monk, ascetic,
and bishop, fulfilling in these roles all the requirements of a Bedan
rector, doctor, and *praedicator.* He is seen as the Northumbrian
equivalent of the great holy men of the Christian past, and as the
ideal Gregorian, who acts in the spirit of the Benedictine Rule and
closely resembles Benedict himself and (to a lesser extent) other
heroes of the *Dialogues.* Quite a lot of this is implicit in the
Lindisfarne *Vita,* which refers, for example, to Cuthbert as 'following the contemplative amid the active life',[47] but the anonymous's
portrait is much less didactic and Gregorian in tone. Bede's re-
modelling reinterpreted the saint's spirituality and his views won
the day: in the early ninth century the author of the *Vita Alcuini,*
surely inspired by Alcuin himself, alluded to Cuthbert as standing
in the tradition of Gregory and Benedict.[48]

   The *Life* of Cuthbert provided a vivid illustration of Bede's
ideals, and perhaps a vehicle for publishing them beyond the
monastic elite who formed the audience of his commentaries. But
Bede's most ambitious attempt to inspire enthusiasm for his views
was the *Ecclesiastical History,* a work addressed to *auditores* as well as
lectores, and dedicated to a king. Bede's masterpiece was in part at
least 'a gallery of good examples', a collection of models of right
living and teaching which demonstrated the way reform could be
achieved.[49] Bede, following Gregory, interpreted his people's past

[45] Bede, *V. Cuth. Pros.* 26, pp. 240–2; *V. Cuth. Anon* IV.1–2, pp. 110–12.
[46] Bede, *V. Cuth. Pros.* 27–35, pp. 242–66.
[47] *V. Cuth. Anon.* III.1, p. 94.
[48] *Vita Alcuini, PL* C, c. 93; D. A. Bullough, 'The Missions to the English and
Picts, and their heritage', in H. Löwe (ed.), *Die Iren und Europa im früheren
Mittelalter* (Speyer, 1982), p. 96.
[49] *HE* pr., p. 5; J. Campbell, 'Bede', in T. A. Dorey (ed.), *Latin Historians* (London,
1966), pp. 168–76, 182.

in Old Testament terms. He saw the English as a chosen nation, a *populus dei*, who like the children of Israel in the desert had fallen away from their divine mission.[50] In the central books of the *Historia Ecclesiastica* he presented a golden age, the story of the calling of the English and their responding to that call in the period between the coming of Augustine and the death of King Egfrith at Nechtansmere, after which he expressly says 'the hopes and strength of the English kingdom began to ebb and fall away'.[51] Bede's depiction of that period and the great preachers and holy communities which adorned it was designed to recall his degenerate contemporaries to that path of righteousness from which he believed they had so seriously erred. It was above all a record of monastic achievement, of an ascetic pastorate which, in contrast to the luxurious and avaricious ecclesiastics condemned in the letter to Egbert, rejected worldly possessions, rich gifts, and ostentatious modes of travel, and was zealous in preaching, converting the pagan, and defeating the heretic. All exhibited to a greater or lesser degree the characteristics most completely presented in the portrait of Cuthbert. One or two examples must suffice.

Gregory and the Roman missionaries form an obvious starting point. The pope's own career is summed up in a chapter of great prominence – at the beginning of Book II, inaugurating Bede's account of the golden age.[52] Gregory's monastic vocation is described at length. He was a true ascetic and *doctor*, able to pass in contemplation beyond the barriers of the flesh and to unfold the mysteries of a book as difficult as Job. Yet at the same time he gave priority to his pastoral responsibilities. He would have become a preacher himself and come to England, but the Romans would not allow it and when pope he was obliged to content himself with sending missionaries in his stead. Bede was anxious to stress that this union of the active and contemplative lives was successful. Gregory's own admission that his pastoral responsibilities interfered with his contemplative life is dismissed, as springing from humility: 'We need not believe that he lost any of his monastic perfection by reason of his pastoral cares'.

---

[50] R. W. Hanning, *Vision of History in Early Britain* (New York, 1966), pp. 63–90; C. P. Wormald, review in *Durham University Journal*, LXVII (1975), pp. 232–3. cf. McClure, above, pp. 82–96.
[51] *HE* IV.26, p. 267.
[52] Meyvaert, *Bede and Gregory*, pp. 2–3; Wallace-Hadrill, *EMH*, p. 91.

Complementing the portrait of Gregory are those of the evangelists whom he sent to the English. Emphasis is laid on the fact that they are both monks and preachers, who lived according to the doctrine they taught and won converts through their life and doctrine; the monastic element is central to Bede's account of the Roman mission.[53]

Bede's treatment of Aidan and the Lindisfarne community, while it is often thought to be more affectionate, is in fact very similar, if more detailed and personal by virtue of the extra resources which he had at hand in his native Northumbria. Aidan's life is explicitly contrasted with the *segnitia* which Bede discerned in his own time, and he is presented as a learned monastic ascetic and an exemplary and active preacher. His community is similarly praised. In the great tribute to the brethren on the eve of their departure for *Scottia* in 664, they appear primarily as pastors and teachers to the surrounding *rustici*.[54] Indeed, Bede was anxious to set Lindisfarne in a Gregorian context. In an important passage which appears both in the *Life* of Cuthbert and the *Ecclesiastical History*, he draws attention to the arrangements instituted by Aidan, under which the island was *episcopi . . . et abbatis et monachorum locus*, gliding over the fact that the bishop, although in control of his diocese, was subject to the abbot within the monastery, an arrangement which though not uncommon in Ireland would certainly have been viewed as irregular in Rome; and he emphasizes that the episcopal *familia* at Lindisfarne, composed as it was entirely of monks, stood in worthy succession to the establishment ordained by pope Gregory for Augustine and his brethren in Canterbury.[55]

Cuthbert too is given his due place in the *History*, in the concluding chapters of Book IV.[56] These were clearly intended to be read in conjunction with Bede's earlier writings on the saint, to which they several times refer. The material in the *History* was thus consciously a selection, and its contents are significant. The passages describing Cuthbert's life at Melrose and Lindisfarne are all in substance included, together with several important miracle stories, two of which had only just come to Bede's notice. Cuthbert, in short, with his place at the conclusion of the three central books devoted to what Bede regarded as the greatest period of his people's

[53] *HE* I.26, pp. 46–7.
[54] *HE* III.3, 5, 26, pp. 131–2, 135–6, 190–1.
[55] *HE* IV.27, pp. 270–1; *V. Cuth. Pros.* 16, p. 208.
[56] *HE* IV.27–32, pp. 274–80.

history, was meant to represent the finest fruit of the conversion initiated by Gregory the Great. He is the most perfect exponent of a pastoral ideal which Bede saw exemplified by such forerunners as Augustine, Aidan, Cedd and Chad, and such later figures as John of Beverley.

Bede's account of Aidan and his community is often regarded as a description of normal Celtic practice, and his Cuthbert as primarily a Celtic figure.[57] But in this context it is instructive to examine his treatment of another Celtic *peregrinus*: Fursa. Bede relied on a Gallo-Irish *Vita*, which still survives and which he followed fairly faithfully. Nevertheless, he contrived to add a number of characteristic touches, presenting the saint as a learned monk-preacher who set an example of virtue in accordance with his teaching and who instituted the *regularis disciplina* in his monastery. Equally significant is the treatment of Fursa's vision. Bede omits the more grotesque elements and concentrates on the miraculous burns sustained by the saint in the course of his vision; he emphasizes that Fursa continued to preach by word and example, and adds a description of the saint sweating, either from terror or ecstasy, at the recollection of what he had seen. All this has a very Gregorian flavour, and recalls stories of visions in the fourth book of the *Dialogues*, especially that of a Spanish monk who is said to have been inspired to such feats of penitence by the horrors he had seen that even if he had kept silence the manner of his life would have borne witness to his experiences. That this episode undoubtedly made an impression on Bede is clear from his direct allusion to it in his description of another vision, very similar to Fursa's. Bede followed Gregory in believing that reports of such occurrences could intensify the spiritual life of those disposed to repent. Both Fursa and his vision were placed in a securely Gregorian context.[58]

Bede, then, was not a simple admirer of Celtic monachism. His portraits were coloured by his reforming idealism, and are the

[57] e.g. Colgrave, *Two Lives,* p. 5; G. W. O. Addleshaw, *Pastoral Structure of the Celtic Church in Northern Britain* (Borthwick Papers 43, 1973), pp. 14–19; R. A. Markus, *Bede and the Tradition of Ecclesiastical Historiography* (Jarrow Lecture, 1975), pp. 7–12.

[58] *Vita S. Fursei,* ed. B. Krusch, *MGH,SRM* IV, pp. 434–40; *Visio Fursei, Acta Sanctorum, Januarii* II, pp. 36–41; *HE* III 19, V.12, pp. 163–8, 303–10. Gregory, *Dialogues* IV *passim,* esp. 37, *SC* CCLXV, pp. 127–8. Gregory's 'etiam si tacerit lingua, conversatio quippe loqueretur', p. 128, is echoed by Bede's 'etiamsi lingua sileret, vita loqueretur', p. 304.

product of an intelligent and cultivated mind, informed by high moral purpose, reacting upon material of very varying quality about men who had generally died long before. Bede was probably less conscious of the distinction between Celt and Roman than some have suggested. While he admired Irish saints such as Aidan and Fursa, he did not see them as the embodiment of some peculiarly Celtic mode of goodness; rather they were models of orthodox holiness, practitioners of virtues inculcated by the Fathers, above all Gregory the Great. In assimilating the practice of Lindisfarne to that recommended by Gregory to Augustine, Bede made his intentions clear: Irish monasticism provided him with an important exemplar in so far as it accorded with, or could be shown to accord with, the teaching and observance of the most respected authorities.

It is time now to turn to the secular implications of Bede's ideas about reform. Bede was not unaware of political realities. He knew that kings mattered in the life of the Church, and the *Ecclesiastical History*, as has often been noticed, is much concerned with kings. In that work Bede depicted rulers who had felt the impress of monastic ideals, such as Oswin of Deira, and even some, such as Sigebert of East Anglia, who abandoned their kingdoms altogether and entered monasteries. But above all he held up for admiration those who, although they submitted to the teachings of the Church, retained their power and prospered. Such were the warrior kings Edwin and Oswald, who fought to extend the boundaries of English Christendom, who protected the Church and ultimately died for it and reaped a heavenly reward.[59] Significantly, the *Ecclesiastical History* is dedicated to a king, Ceolwulf, the then ruler of Northumbria, and Bede in his preface states that he hoped that he would learn from it and 'in his zeal for the spiritural well-being of us all' would publish it more widely. Bede, indeed, had high hopes of Ceolwulf; in the letter to Egbert he told the archbishop that he would find the king a very ready helper, and advised him to obtain royal co-operation in the work of reform.[60]

Bede was a patriotic Northumbrian, whose pride in Northumbrian achievements in the seventh century is unmistakable. The *Ecclesiastical History* was not simply a history of the conversion of the English as a whole, it also showed the central part which the author's own

[59] Wallace-Hadrill, *EGK*, pp. 72–97; Campbell, 'Bede', pp. 168–72; Stancliffe, below, p. 158; McClure, above, pp. 90–2.
[60] *HE* pr., p. 5; Plummer I, p. 412.

people had played in that process. Bede regarded Egfrith's defeat at the hands of the Picts as a disaster, and was concerned for the temporal as well as the spiritual well-being of the Northumbrian state; in the letter to Egbert he condemned false monasteries not only because they failed in their proper service to God, but also because they were socially useless, depriving the kingdom of land which could otherwise be employed in supporting the warriors necessary to its defence.[61] Above all, he evinces anxiety about the internal stability of the *regnum*, formed from a fragile union of two originally separate *provinciae*, Bernicia and Deira. Although the Bernician dynasty had with difficulty emerged as victors after the disintegration in 633 and between 642 and 655, the survival of strong Deiran loyalties is shown by the continuing need for a Deiran *subregulus* in the late seventh century, and by the affection given to the native dynasty in a *Life* produced in the early eighth century at the monastery of Whitby, the mausoleum of the Deiran royal family.[62] The *Ecclesiastical History* makes evident this chronic instability, but it was not something on which its author chose to dwell. Unlike the Whitby writer, who refers to the *Humbrenses* (i.e. to those dwelling on either side of the Humber), Bede alludes only to the *tota Nordanhymbrorum progenies* or *Transhumbranan gens*.[63] The re-emergence of division in 633 was clearly regarded as disastrous, marked by evil kings, whose names were to be expunged from the regnal lists. Their successor Oswald's *industria* in accomplishing the reunion of the two kingdoms was considered a great achievement, and its impermanence acknowledged only with reluctance. The collapse after Oswald's death in 642 was glossed over, and the Deiran Oswin referred to as Oswiu's *consors* in the royal dignity of the *Transhumbrana gens*. Oswin was a well-loved king and an exemplary Christian, but significantly, although his murder was condemned, its perpetrator, Oswiu, almost entirely escaped censure, for it was only through Oswin's removal that the two kingdoms could again be united.[64]

[61] *HE* IV.26, p. 267; Plummer I, pp. 414–15. cf. Wormald, above, p. 118.
[62] *HE* II.9, 12, III.1, 14, 24, pp. 97–100, 106–11, 127–8, 154–6, 177–80; P. H. Blair, 'The Bernicians and their northern frontier', in N. K. Chadwick (ed.), *Studies in Early British History* (Cambridge, 1954), pp. 152–3; Thacker, 'Social and Continental Background', pp. 49–50; *Earliest Life of Gregory the Great* 12–19, ed. B. Colgrave (Lawrence, Kan., 1968), pp. 94–104.
[63] P. H. Blair, 'The Northumbrians and their southern frontier', *Archaeologia Aeliana*, 4th ser., XXVI (1948), pp. 98–126; *Life of Gregory* 12, p. 94.
[64] *HE* III.1, 6, 14, 24, pp. 127–8, 138–9, 154–7, 177–9.

It will be clear from this that Bede's sympathies were with his
own native dynasty, the Bernician house of Ida. That is especially
obvious in his account of the holy kings Edwin and Oswald.
Edwin, the man who received Paulinus and established the Gregorian
mission in Northumbria, demanded most favourable treatment,
yet he is never presented as a saint. Bede suppressed all reference to
Edwin's cult, although he probably knew the Whitby *Life* which
records it and was certainly in close touch with the Whitby community. Full cultic honours were reserved for Oswald, whose
miracles and *inventio* receive much prominence in the *Ecclesiastical
History*; he was *rex christianissimus*, the greatest of Northumbrian
rulers, who held all the nations and *provinciae* of Britain under his
sway.[65]

The ecclesiastical counterpart of Oswald is Cuthbert. His community of Lindisfarne had always been closely associated with the
Bernician royal house, and he himself was a royal *amicus*, the
favoured holy man of Egfrith and other members of his family, and
the recipient of numerous royal grants.[66] Such circumstances made
it especially likely that Cuthbert's cult would achieve particular
importance, and there are hints of this even in the Lindisfarne *Life*.
The parallels with Martin of Tours, for example, suggest, that
Cuthbert was already being promoted as the Northumbrian equivalent of the Gaulish *Reichsheiliger*.[67] Bede developed the theme much
more strongly. He omits many of the local references provided by
his predecessor and emphasizes that on Farne Cuthbert's visitors
included many from remote parts of Britain. In his version of
Egfrith's defeat and death at Nechtansmere the saint is wholly
identified with the Northumbrian cause; he grieves deeply over the
disaster and attempts to prepare his people for the news. Cuthbert's
episcopal ministrations are expressly said to have extended beyond
his diocese, and before his withdrawal to Farne the saint is depicted
making a progress through the country. Significantly, stress is laid
on the connection with Whitby, whose royal abbess Aelfflaed, the

[65] *HE* II.9–20, III.1–3, 6, 9–13, IV.14, pp. 97–126, 128–31, 137–9, 144–54, 232–6,
Wallace-Hadrill, *EGK*, pp. 83–4.
[66] *HE* III.3, 12, pp. 131–2, 151–2; *V. Cuth. Pros.* 24, 27, pp. 234–8, 242–8;
E. Craster, 'The patrimony of St. Cuthbert', *EHR*, LXIX (1954), pp. 177–99.
[67] Thacker, 'Social and continental background', pp. 124–7; C. A. Bernoulli, *Die
Heiliger der Merowinger* (Tübingen, 1900), pp. 222–7; Wallace-Hadrill, *EMH*, p. 91.

custodian of her grandfather Edwin's cult, was portrayed as Cuthbert's friend and admirer.[68]

In the death scenes Bede presents Cuthbert as fully aware that he would become the focus of a great cult. 'Unworthy as I am' (he is made to say) 'reports about me as a servant of God have gone forth.' The saint is depicted accepting that his enshrined body would become a celebrated place of sanctuary, and concerned lest the influx of fugitives should disturb the Lindisfarne brethren. Indeed, desire to emphasize Cuthbert's supremacy led Bede to show his relics as effective where those of other saints had failed, a kind of miracle he elsewhere conspicuously avoids.[69] Cuthbert, in short, is presented as the selfconscious patron of the whole of Northumbria, a role which complemented his function as model monk and pastor: exemplified by the *Reichsheiliger*, Bede's pastoral ideas were certain to reach a wide and influential audience.

Bede's later years were dominated by his preoccupation with what he regarded as the interdependent problems of the spiritual and temporal decline of his people. The principal works of this period were all concerned with a general reform of Church and society, the instruments of which were to be an instructed king and aristocracy, a rejuvenated episcopate and, above all, a reformed monasticism. The commentaries were intended to educate pastors, and in particular to recall an elite of monastic teachers and preachers to duties which Bede believed their predecessors had performed more successfully. The *Lives* and *Histories* illustrated these themes. In the prose *Life* of Cuthbert Bede described an ideal pastor; in the *Historia Ecclesiastica* he turned from individuals to communities. That great work contained portraits of model monasteries as well as model teachers, and was intended to inculcate in the minds of as wide an audience as possible the story of a people's progress to salvation. What Bede discerned as he looked back, he hoped to see in being again – a united Northumbrian nation, under exemplary kings and pastors, adorned with a host of holy communities, marching with the other English *gentes* along the road to redemption.

It remains to consider how far Bede's reforming ideals were translated into reality. In one area at least it is clear that they were not without effect: the attempt to make Cuthbert the patron of a

[68] Bede, *V. Cuth. Pros.* 22–3, 26–7, 29–30, 32–4, pp. 228–34, 240–8, 252–4, 256–64.
[69] *ibid.* 37, 41, pp. 278, 288–90.

united Northumbria in some measure succeeded. Significantly, King Ceolwulf, the dedicatee of the *Ecclesiastical History*, showed especial affection for Lindisfarne and its saint and helped to diffuse the cult. When in 737 he resigned the kingdom and received the tonsure he chose Lindisfarne as his place of retreat and on his death in 764 he was buried near the saint. His gifts to the community included Warkworth where he is said to have built a church dedicated to Cuthbert.[70] Though the evidence is sparse, it looks too as if the cult was fostered in Deira. Not only was Cuthbert remembered at Whitby (whose interest is perhaps reflected in the number of churches bearing his dedication in the eastern North Riding), but he was also venerated at Crayke, another early royal gift to Lindisfarne; Crayke was the site of a hermitage in the mid-eighth century and a resting-place of the saint in the ninth.[71] By the early eighth century Cuthbert's mass was probably circulating on the continent along with Oswald's, and by the end of it Alcuin could allude to the saint as venerated throughout Britain and regard him as worthy of extended treatment in his poem on York, despite his limited associations with the city.[72]

In the matter of ecclesisatical reform – the subject, after all, which concerned Bede most deeply – the effect of his ideas is more questionable. The eighth century was not entirely deaf to his teaching; it saw the growth of the school of York, where his writings were much admired, and, in the reign of Eadbert (737–58), co-operation between king and archbishop as recommended in the letter to Egbert.[73] Ideas similar to Bede's on the subject of preaching and ecclesiastical reform can also be found in the canons of the 747 Council of Clofesho, though here his influence is much less certain;[74]

---

[70] Plummer I. pp. 360–1, II. p. 340; Craster, 'Patrimony', p. 185.
[71] *Victoria History of the County of Yorkshire, North Riding*, ed. W. Page (2 vols, London, 1914–23); Craster, 'Patrimony', pp. 182–3; Symeon of Durham, *Historia Dunelmensis Ecclesiae* II.13, ed. T. Arnold (2 vols, RS, 1882), I, pp. 68–9.
[72] C. Hohler, 'The Durham Services in honour of St. Cuthbert', in Battiscombe, *Relics*, pp. 157–8; *Sankt-Bonifatius Gedenkgabe* (Fulda, 1954), p. 92; Alcuin, *Carmina*, ed. E. Dümmler, *MGH, Poet.* I, pp. 184–6, 233; for doubts see D. A. Bullough, 'Hagiography as patriotism: Alcuin's "York Poem" and the Early Northumbrian *Vitae Sanctorum*', in *Hagiographie, Cultures et Sociétés* (Paris, 1981), pp. 344–8.
[73] P. H. Blair, 'From Bede to Alcuin', in *Famulus Christi*, pp. 239–60; D. A. Bullough, 'Alcuino e la tradizione culturale insulare', *Settimane*, XX (1973), pp. 582–3; Alcuin, *Carmina*, p. 197.
[74] A. W. Haddan and W. Stubbs (eds), *Councils and Ecclesiastical Documents* (3 vols, Oxford, 1869–78), III, pp. 360–76. The parallels with the letter to Egbert were noticed long ago by Plummer, II, pp. 378, 380, 383, 385.

they probably owe more to Boniface, who saw his own role as bishop and pastor in terms borrowed directly from Gregory the Great and was only just getting to know Bede's works in the 740s.[75]

Boniface, however, quickly became aware that Bede's writings could be useful to the preacher, and he and his successor, Lull, were responsible for their diffusion on the continent. In 764 Lull sent gifts to honour Bede's relics, and in return asked for (and received) the prose and verse *Lives* of St Cuthbert. Later he wrote to the archbishop of York to ask for the commentaries on Samuel, Ezra and Nehemiah, and Mark, and to the abbot of Wearmouth-Jarrow for the *De Templo*.[76] Indeed it has recently been suggested that demand for Bede's works was so great in the later eighth century that attempts to meet it imposed a severe strain on the *scriptorium* at Wearmouth-Jarrow.[77]

But perhaps the most notable evidence of the persistence of Bede's ideals comes, as might be expected, from a Northumbrian author: Alcuin. That Alcuin greatly admired Bede is clear from his letters, his poem on York, and certain other works. He followed Bede in his reverence for Gregory the Great (*noster Gregorius*), and almost certainly shared Bede's perception of Cuthbert as a Gregorian.[78] His commentaries, derivative as they are, include selections from Bede's writings which show a clear understanding of the latter's priorities. Alcuin's exposition of the Song of Songs, for example, anthologizes Bede's work on the same subject, and has much to say about the role of *doctores* and *praedicatores*.[79] The commentary on John, perhaps the most ambitious of his exegetical writings, is similarly coloured by Bede's teaching on the office of preaching and the mixed *conversatio*. It opens and concludes with excerpts from Bede's homily on St John, presenting the evangelist as a great exponent of both the active and contemplative lives;[80] elsewhere it includes passages which exalt the office of preaching

---

[75] Boniface and Lull, *Epistolae*, ed. M. Tangl, *MGH,Ep.Sel.* I, pp. 156–9, 166–9, 213.

[76] *ibid.*, pp. 206–7, 250–2, 263, 264–5.

[77] M. Parkes, *The Scriptorium of Monkwearmouth and Jarrow* (Jarrow Lecture, 1982).

[78] Alcuin, *Epistolae*, ed. E. Dümmler, *MGH,Ep.* IV, pp. 55, 132, 360, 443; *Carmina*, pp. 184, 198, 294; Bullough, 'Alcuino', pp. 583–4.

[79] Bede, *In Cantica Cant.*, cc. 1065–1236; Alcuin, *Compendium in Cantica Canticorum*, *PL* C. cc. 639–64.

[80] Alcuin, *Commentaria in S. Joannis Evangelium*, *PL* C, cc. 741–2, 1005–7; Bede, *Homilies*, pp. 64–6.

and lay stress on the *arcana divinorum eloquiorum* hidden from the *vulgus* or understood by them only when expounded by *doctores*.[81]

Alcuin's other writings show that these borrowings were not casual but stemmed from a fundamental sympathy with Bede's ideas. One example of this is his emphasis in several letters on the importance of preachers, who might include not only bishops and priests but also *boni laici*.[82] Another is his thinking on kingship. The Christian king was *doctor* and *praedicator* as well as military and political leader, with a duty to guide his people to salvation.[83] Bede, of course, did not refer to kings in quite such exalted terms. Though he clearly saw that they had an important role in the spiritual instruction of their people, he tended to view it as an assisting one; thus Oswald acted as bishop Aidan's interpreter when he was preaching and Ceolwulf was to be Egbert's *promtissimus adiutor* in reform.[84] Nevertheless, it is easy to see how Bede's category of teachers and preachers was a convenient one for Alcuin in his attempt to interpret Charlemagne's authority in the Church; in the *Admonitio Generalis*, for example, it was announced in the preface that Charlemagne would follow the example of King Josiah, who went round his kingdom correcting, advising, and recalling his people to the worship of the true God, an analogy reminiscent of the reference to King Osred as a new Josiah in the metrical *Life* of Cuthbert.[85]

Alcuin's influence on Charlemagne's ecclesiastical legislation makes his debt to Bede of especial interest. It looks as if we find here one of the roots of that emphasis on teaching and preaching so characteristic of the Carolingian capitularies. As early as 789 in the *Admonitio Generalis* Charlemagne was recommending his bishops to watch over monasteries, to ensure that the faith was preached throughout their dioceses, and to send out priests who were to preach and teach the Creed, the Lord's Prayer, and the proper singing of psalms.[86] Later capitularies echo these decrees, and in-

[81] Alcuin, *Comm. in Joannis*, cc. 761, 765; Bede, *Homiliœ*, pp. 125–6.
[82] Alcuin, *Epistolae*, pp. 156–62, 208–10.
[83] *ibid.*, pp. 84, 294–6, 414–16; Wallace-Hadrill, *EGK*, pp. 101–2; L. Wallach, *Alcuin and Charlemagne* (New York, 1959), pp. 12–22.
[84] *HE* III.3, p. 132; Plummer I, p. 412.
[85] Bede, *V. Cuth. Met.* 21, pp. 99–100; Wallace-Hadrill, *EGK*, p. 94. Alcuin's involvement in the *Admonitio Generalis* has been defended by Professor Bullough in his Ford Lectures of 1980.
[86] *MGH,Capit.* I, pp. 52–62; R. McKitterick, *The Frankish Church and the Carolingian Reforms* (London, 1977), pp. 5–8, 80–114; M. Gatch, *Preaching and Theology in*

sistently add that the preacher should embody the truths that he taught.[87]

Such themes also appear in the late eighth century in a famous text closely associated with Alcuin, the *De Litteris Colendis*.[88] The document, which was probably a mandate sent to leading bishops and abbots, survives in the copy addressed to abbot Baugulf of Fulda and his community, *fideles* and *oratores* of the Frankish king. It is concerned with the inculcation of learning in the episcopal and monastic schools and is couched in terms which Bede would have found familiar. In particular, the author expresses the view that Christians should receive instruction according to their capacity and that those who sought to please God by right living should not neglect right speaking; the recipients, therefore, were urged to continue their study of letters, 'that they might more easily and correctly penetrate the mysteries of Holy Writ.' The whole text reads rather like Bede's addresses to the learned elite at Wearmouth-Jarrow, and indeed seems to have been intended for a similar audience: the *oratores* of the *inscriptio* are probably to be understood as teachers and preachers.[89]

Clearly others besides Bede could read Gregory, and Bede was not the only nor even the most important exponent of his ideas to the Carolingians. Nevertheless, through the activities of the Anglo-Saxon missionaries Bede's works became widely available among the Franks, and helped to shape their religious thought-world as Professor Wallace-Hadrill has stressed;[90] to an early ninth-century Carolingian poet he was *nostri didascalus aevi*, 'the teacher of our age'.[91] Above all, Bede's influence on Alcuin, who acknowledged him his favourite master, ensured that his ideal of reform left its mark on Carolingian capitularies and synodical decrees, and thus made a lasting contribution to the history of Latin Christianity.

Anglo-Saxon England (Toronto, 1977), pp. 30–9; C. W. Jones, 'Bede's place in medieval schools', in *Famulus Christi*, pp. 261–85.
[87] *MGH,Capit.* I, pp. 93, 153–4, 170, 178–9; *MGH,Conc.* II.1, pp. 250–2, 255, 268, 276, 287; Theodulf of Orléans, *Statuta* I, *PL* CV, c. 192.
[88] Wallach, *Alcuin and Charlemagne*, pp. 198–226.
[89] *ibid.*, pp. 202–4, 214.
[90] At Murbach in Upper Alsace a mid–ninth-century list shows that the library contained many of Bede's works: W. Milde, *Der Bibliothekskatalog des Klosters Murbach aus dem 9 Jh.* (Beih. zum Euphorion, 4; Heidelberg, 1968), esp. pp. 42–4. cf. Jones, 'Medieval schools', pp. 270–1, 275; Wallace-Hadrill, *EMH*, p. 182.
[91] *MGH,Poet.* II, p. 665.

7

Kings who Opted Out

CLARE STANCLIFFE

Kings hold the stage in Anglo-Saxon England. But what can one say of those who laid aside their kingship to adopt the religious life? By attempting in a literal fashion to translate into reality the Gospel precept, 'Seek ye first the kingdom of God', these kings have opted out of the fortunes of this world which is the historian's normal concern. And yet, the sheer number of Anglo-Saxon kings taking this decision in the seventh and eighth centuries should interest historians. Indeed, the negative decision to abandon their rule may even reflect some light back onto the kingship which they laid aside.

The first to opt out was Sigebert, king of the East Angles from *c*.631. He had previously been converted while an exile in Gaul, and when he became king he fostered Christianity among his people. Then, afire for the heavenly kingdom, he abdicated and entered a monastery. Here he remained until his people, threatened by a Mercian army, dragged him out to encourage their forces. But he, conscious of his monastic profession, refused to carry any weapon but a stick. He was killed, and his army slain or scattered.[1]

Centwine, king of the West Saxons *c*.676/8–685, is not even mentioned by Bede, who was poorly informed about Wessex;[2] but his victorious warfare followed by his conversion to the religious life is noted in a poem written by Aldhelm between 689 and 709. Aldhelm is quite explicit: Centwine 'reached out to seek the consecrated life, while he left his own kingdom for the sake of Christ's

---

[1] *HE* II.15, III.18, pp. 116–17, 162–3. Was Sigebert inspired by St Martin's boast? Sulpicius Severus, *Vita Martini* 4, 5, ed. J. Fontaine, *SC* CXXXIII, p. 260. I would like to thank T. M. Charles-Edwards for commenting on this paper.

[2] Stenton, *ASE*, pp. 68–9; Plummer, II, pp. 220–1; D. Kirby, 'Problems of early West Saxon history', *EHR*, LXXX (1965), pp. 10–29.

name.' Earlier, he had been a successful warleader and had ruled happily, 'until, once converted, he transferred to a kindly cell.'[3] Aldhelm's wording rules out the possibility that he is referring to Centwine's death when he talks of his translation from his kingdom into *sacratam vitam*, and *in almam cellam*. Nor is it likely that Centwine was compelled to enter a monastery by his successor, Caedwalla, for in that case some of Aldhelm's language, considering the poem was addressed to Centwine's daughter, would have been in bad taste, while the *Anglo-Saxon Chronicle* confirms his picture of Centwine as a successful warleader.[4] Centwine probably responded to the same call as Sigebert, who had also been a *dux strenuissimus*.

So too with Aethelred, king of Mercia from 675, who was remembered in Kent for his devastation of churches and monasteries. In 704, however, he entered Bardney monstery where he soon became abbot. Surprisingly, Bede mentions this event only *en passant* and in his chronological summary: he has no word of commendation for the Mercian king.[5] Sebbi, king of the East Saxons *c.*664–94, is cast in a different mould. He was a devout man who would gladly have exchanged his kingdom for the monastic life long since if only his wife had allowed it. In his final illness, however, she gave way, and Sebbi died as a monk in London.[6]

After Bede's narrative ends the annalists take up the tale. Although laconic, they do not gloss over unpleasant happenings as Bede can. They record that Ceolwulf, the Northumbrian king to whom Bede dedicated his *History*, was 'captured, tonsured, and restored to his kingdom' in 731. Six years later he was tonsured of his own volition and withdrew to Lindisfarne, leaving his kingdom to his cousin Eadbert. His death is recorded in 764.[7] Meanwhile his successor had

---

[3] *Aldhelmi Opera*, ed. R. Ehwald, *MGH.AA* XV, pp. 14–15; cf. K. H. Krüger, 'Königskonversionen im 8 Jahrhundert', *Frühmittelalterliche Studien*, VII (1973), p. 179.

[4] *ASC, s.a.* 682.

[5] *HE* IV.12, V.19, 24, pp. 228, 329, 355–6; cf. Eddius, *Life of Wilfrid*, ed. and trans. B. Colgrave (Cambridge, 1927), 57, pp. 124–5. Besides Aethelred's devastation of Kentish churches, Bede probably thought that he passed too swiftly from secular power to an abbacy; cf. Plummer, I, pp. 416–17. He was already abbot on Wilfrid's return in 705.

[6] *HE* IV.11, p. 225; cf. III.30, p. 199; Plummer, II, pp. 176–7. Note that Bede's source for Sebbi was hagiographical: *HE* IV.7–11, pp. 219–27.

[7] 'Baedae Continuatio', *s.a.*, in Plummer, I, p. 360; *HR, s.a.* 732, 737, 764. Although Bede is silent about the practice, often encountered in Gaul, of compulsorily tonsuring political leaders, it definitely occurred in Northumbria under Osred: Aethelwulf, *De Abbatibus*, ed. and trans. A. Campbell (Oxford, 1967), p. 7.

followed suit. After a long and apparently successful reign, Eadbert also resigned (758) and became a canon at York, where his brother, Egbert, was archbishop. He died at York in 768.[8] Thereafter the Northumbrian scene grows murky, with rival families contending for the kingship. Some kings were tonsured, but unwillingly. Even Osbald, king for one month in 796, does not fall within our purview, for he did not voluntarily abandon the throne to become a monk; rather he was expelled, and then made the decision.[9] I omit all such cases.

Alongside our six kings who opted into a monastery we should consider five more who resigned to go to Rome on lifelong pilgrimage, together with two others who intended the journey. The first Anglo-Saxon king to plan a journey to Rome was Alchfrith, son of Oswiu, and sub-king of Deira. About 664 Alchfrith, doubtless infected by Benedict Biscop's (and Wilfrid's) enthusiasm, hoped to accompany Biscop 'to venerate the threshold of the apostles'. However, Oswiu forbade him – perhaps because Biscop apparently planned to remain there permanently.[10] Seven years later Oswiu himself, in his final illness, purposed if he recovered to go to Rome and end his days there; but death prevented him.[11]

The first English king to reach Rome was Centwine's successor in Wessex, Caedwalla. Previously, when he had been a landless exile, he had been helped by Wilfrid, whom he much respected. After winning control of Wessex Caedwalla subjugated Sussex and then turned to the Isle of Wight, intending to exterminate all its inhabitants. Though still unbaptized he vowed that, if successful, he would give a quarter of the island to God – all of which suggests that he saw the God of the Christians as a powerful God of battles, along the lines of Woden (though much in the Old Testament also lends itself to this interpretation).[12] Caedwalla was victorious and kept his vow, though he was wounded in the fighting. After a

[8] Plummer, I. p. 363; *HR*, *s.a.* 758, 768.
[9] *HR*, *s.a.* 796, 799; Alcuin, *Epistolae*, ed. E. Dümmler, *MGH,Ep.* IV (1895), p. 156.
[10] Bede, *Historia Abbatum*, Plummer I, p. 365. For Biscop's plans for permanent *peregrinatio*, Irish style, Bede, *Homeliae* I.13, ed. D. Hurst, *CCSL* CXXII, p. 91.
[11] *HE* IV.5, p. 214; on the date, Plummer II, p. 211.
[12] Eddius, *Wilfrid*, 42, pp. 84–5; *HE* IV.15–16, pp. 236–8; Paul the Deacon, *Historia Langobardorum*, II.27, ed. G. Waitz, *MGH,SRL* (1878), p. 87, (on which see Wallace-Hadrill, *EMH*, p. 22). From the Old Testament see e.g. Deuteronomy, 20:16, 32:39–42.

two-year reign he resolved to go and seek baptism in Rome, where he died shortly after (689).[13]

Caedwalla's pilgrimage to Rome set a new ideal before Anglo-Saxon kings. In 709 his example was followed by the joint pilgrimage of Cenred of Mercia and Offa of the East Saxons: both nephews of monk-kings (viz. of Aethelred and Sebbi). Cenred was a God-fearing king, who had urged repentance on one of his ill-living thegns. But in vain: evil spirits produced a large book detailing the man's sins, then pierced him hand and foot with knives. These were working their way through his body, and when they met, he would die and be dragged down to hell. William of Malmesbury attributed Cenred's decision to abandon his kingdom and become a pilgrim to the effect of this incident.[14] That it affected Cenred deeply is likely enough, though Bede does not link the events.

Bede approved of Cenred's decision: though he had reigned 'very nobly', he renounced his kingdom 'with still greater nobility'. As for Offa, a promising young man who as yet may have been but a sub-king, Bede gives us a glimpse of the disappointment his renunciation aroused amongst his people without revealing his own feelings.[15] The *Liber pontificalis* notes the arrival of Cenred and Offa in Rome, with a great following, and says that they died not long after.[16] In contrast to Caedwalla, Cenred and Offa, Ine ruled the West Saxons for thirty-seven years before handing over his kingdom (726). He then went to Rome to *peregrinari* a while at the saints' tombs so that they might welcome him more warmly to heaven.[17] Ine is the last royal pilgrim recorded by Bede, but the *Anglo-Saxon Chronicle* notes that in 798, Si[ge]ric, king of the East Saxons, went to Rome.[18] If he returned, he marks the beginning of a new type of pilgrimage, there and back again, which falls outside the scope of this study. Otherwise he represents the last example of lifelong royal *peregrinatio*.

What should we make of these kings who resigned for the sake of the religious life? From one angle, they are but typical of their fellow

[13] *HE* V.7, pp. 292–4.
[14] *HE* V.19, V.13, pp. 321–2, 311–13; W. J. Moore, *The Saxon Pilgrims to Rome ASE*, pp. 71–3.
[15] The text of *HE* V.19 does not expressly call Offa a king, but the list of chapter contents does: Plummer II, pp. 314–15; in *S* 1784, Offa grants land as a king.
[16] ed. L. Duchesne (2 vols, Paris, 1886–92), I, p. 391.
[17] *HE* V.7, p. 294. Bede says little of Ine: Wallace-Hadrill *EGK*, p. 90; Stenton *ASE*, pp. 71–3.   [18] *ASC* (F), *s.a.*; Moore, *Saxon Pilgrims*, p. 79.

countrymen at this time. The conversion of England was accompanied by the mushrooming of monasteries and convents, while from the late seventh century pilgrimage to Rome also became popular.[19] And just as Benedict Biscop, a thegn of King Oswiu, or as Owine, head of the household of Queen Aethelthryth, could abandon their secular positions for the sake of journeys to Rome or the monastic life, so too with kings and their families.[20] There was no suggestion that their office barred them from adopting the religious life themselves. The trend seems to have been encouraged by churchmen. Even Bede, who in his letter to Egbert shows a surprising degree of realism about the importance of retaining a sufficient number of warriors to defend Northumbria, can apparently commend the decision of a king who was ruling well (*viz.* Cenred) to abandon his kingdom for pilgrimage to Rome.[21] Of course, since the Church was always proclaiming that earthly power and possessions were to be despised for the sake of the heavenly kingdom, kings might seem an obvious target; why should we expect churchmen to have treated kings as a special case?

However, we have but to glance across the English Channel to perceive the oddity of the Anglo-Saxon monk-kings. When Columbanus audaciously suggested that a Merovingian king should exchange his kingdom for the Church, the bystanders laughed: 'they had never heard of a Merovingian who had been raised over a kingdom becoming a cleric of his own free will!'[22] Well might they gasp, for in Merovingian circles the tonsuring of a prince or king and his confinement within a monastery was simply a political act, designed to remove a rival king. Widowed queens and princesses are indeed found entering convents; but not kings. Further, this went not only for the Franks, but also for the Goths and Lombards. Amongst all the Germanic peoples of the barbarian west, kings voluntarily abandoning their rule for the sake of the religious life are found only in England.[23]

There are two exceptions, and these prove the rule. The first is

[19] Monasteries: J. Campbell, 'The first century of Christianity in England', *Ampleforth Journal*, LXXVI (1971), pp. 14–15; pilgrimage to Rome: *HE*, V.7, p. 294; Moore, *Saxon Pilgrims*; but cf. P. Sims-Williams in *ASE*, V (1976), pp. 14–15.
[20] Plummer, I, pp. 364ff; *HE* IV.3, pp. 207–8.
[21] Plummer, I, p. 415; *HE* V.23, p. 351. See McClure, above, pp. 90–2 and Thacker, above, p. 146.
[22] Jonas, *Vita Columbani* I.28, ed. B. Krusch, *MGH,SRG*, pp. 217–18.
[23] I omit kings whose adoption of the monastic life was supposedly voluntary, but where in reality circumstances gave them little choice. This probably applies to

Carloman, son of Charles Martel, who, though not a king in name, as Mayor of the Palace shared effective power over Gaul with his brother Pippin after his father's death in 741. In 747 Carloman, inspired with religious fervour, resigned his kingdom and went to Rome, where he was tonsured. Initially he settled in the monastery of St Silvester on Monte Soracte, transferring to Monte Cassino in 748–9. Although we know little about Carloman's motivation, the indirect evidence points strongly to Anglo-Saxon influence – probably from Boniface. For Boniface, who himself had visited Rome many times, was in direct touch with Carloman; he can be seen giving hard Christian counsel to King Aethelbald of Mercia, which indicates the sort of line he would have taken with the Frankish rulers; he would have known from his West Saxon background about the careers of Centwine, Caedwalla and Ine; and he had encouraged his disciple Sturm to visit monasteries in Italy, including Monte Cassino itself.[24] In resolving to exchange his kingdom for the cloister Carloman may therefore be seen as following in the wake of earlier Anglo-Saxon kings.

This knock-on effect probably extended to our only other continental king to opt into a monastery. In 749 Ratchis, king of the Lombards, was dissuaded by the pope from attacking Perugia, and shortly afterwards received the tonsure from the pope in Rome, becoming in his turn a monk at Monte Cassino. The *Liber Pontificalis*, our principle source, ascribes the key role to pope Zacharias, who preached to the king and influenced him by his spiritual zeal. But anecdotes in Paul's *History of the Lombards* suggest that Ratchis was already of a biddable disposition, and he could previously have come under the influence of monks from Bobbio or Farfa, or, more significantly, of pilgrims to Rome. Indeed, Carloman may well have stayed with him on his journey south two years previously.[25]

---

three Spanish monk-kings: Vermudo I of the Asturias (788–91), Fortun Garces of Pamplona (c.880/90–905), and Alfonso IV of Leon (925–30): see R. Collins, *Early Medieval Spain: Unity in Diversity, 400–1000* (London, forthcoming).
[24] *Annales Regni Francorum*, ed. F. Kurze, *MGH,SRG*, pp. 6–7; *Continuation of Fredegar*, ed. J. M. Wallace-Hadrill (London, 1960), pp. 100–1; *Liber Pontificalis* I, p. 433; Krüger, 'Königskonversionen', pp. 183–202.
[25] *Liber pontificalis* I, pp. 433–4, and cf. p. 439; Krüger, 'Königskonversionen', pp. 212–17, and cf. pp. 171–3, 218–22, suggesting that the Italian designation of Ratchis as 'dudum rex, tunc autem Christi famulus' derives from 'quondam rex tunc autem abbas', *HE* V.19, p. 329. English pilgrims did go to Rome in large numbers, and some visited the Lombard court *en route*: W. Levison, *England and the Continent in the Eighth Century* (Oxford, 1946), p. 14.

In any case, it is virtually certain that Ratchis would have known of Carloman's abdication and adoption of the religious life; and it is likely that pope Zacharias held up Carloman to Ratchis as an exemplary Christian ruler. Although it must remain conjectural, I would regard the fact that Ratchis took the same course as Carloman only two years later, especially when set against a continental background where such behaviour was otherwise unknown, as too remarkable to be set down to pure coincidence.

Apart from these two exceptions, England is the only Germanic country where monk-kings are found. Of course, England was also the only one to have been evangelized by monks, and we might expect such missionaries to proclaim and foster the spiritual ideals which inspired them. However, Augustine's mission, under the direction of pope Gregory, is unlikely to have deliberately encouraged kings to adopt the monastic life. Gregory's letter to King Aethelbert exhorts the king to take an active part in christianizing his people, revealing the positive role which Gregory envisaged for Christian kings.[26] Aethelbert is invited to follow the example of the emperor Constantine, to use his position as king to overthrow paganism, to set his subjects a good example, and even to teach his people. The pope envisages a partnership between Aethelbert and Augustine, with Aethelbert himself making a significant contribution. The king could scarcely do all this if he abdicated. We might recall that in his *Pastoral Care*, Gregory condemned the (otherwise) exemplary Christian who refused to accept the office of bishop, selfishly keeping his gifts to himself. Gregory thought that such a man should be ready to lead and teach, so that he might benefit others; and, of course, Gregory himself showed his willingness to do just than when he accepted the papacy.[27]

Even more pertinent is a passage where Gregory recalls the biblical summons to leave all for the sake of eternity, yet immediately adds: 'but these things are given to few.' Gregory, recognizing that most people cannot leave worldly affairs entirely, instead stresses inner renunciation as the crucial goal which is attainable by all. Those who cannot literally abandon everything can still free themselves from all possessiveness vis à vis worldly goods and outward power; they can carry on in the world although their true concerns lie wholly with eternity. Gregory then holds up count Theophanius as

[26] HE I.32, pp. 67–70.
[27] *PL* LXXVII, cc. 18–19; C. Dagens, *Saint Grégoire le Grand* (Paris, 1977), pp. 284–99.

an example. He had continued in secular office, but displayed great hospitality and mercy, and his death was marked by miracles. Gregory deliberately cited his case to show that it was possible for some 'to wear secular dress, while not having a secular mind. For necessity binds men like this in the world . . .'[28]

The Roman missionaries, then, are unlikely to have encouraged kings to abdicate and enter monasteries. Such ideas more probably stem from the Irish, or conceivably even the British churches. Remarkably enough, one of the first kings known to have renounced his kingdom for the cloister is none other than Gildas' *bête noire*, Maelgwn of Gwynedd. Not that he stayed there; but his action is still interesting. Perhaps, as Gildas suggests, he was motivated by remorse for the bloody manner in which he had cut his way through to the throne.[29]

Considerably more evidence for kings entering monasteries comes from Ireland, though here our sources can be difficult to interpret. The saints' lives are, with few exceptions, late – at least in their present form. But for what it is worth, they show us Cormac son of Diarmait, a king in southern Leinster, abandoning his kingdom as an old man to end his days in Comgall's monastery of Bangor; and there being afflicted with a profound longing for his homeland, which was laid to rest only when, by Comgall's prayers, he fell asleep and dreamed that he was walking around his beloved Leinster, with its castles and its flowery meads, and that he was king again, sitting surrounded by his nobles. Then, continues the *Life*, when he awoke he conceived a hatred for all he had seen and was content to remain in Bangor for the rest of his days.[30] This dream may be apocryphal; but it brilliantly evokes the traumatic change facing a king who put himself as a monk under another's authority.

More historical are the Irish annal entries to the effect that such and such a king took the *bachall*, or died *in clericatu*.[31] But even here

[28] *XL Homiliae in Evangelia* II.36, *PL* LXXVI, cc. 1272–4; Krüger, 'Königskonversionen', p. 176. cf. also Dagens, *S. Grégoire*, pp. 393–4.
[29] Gildas, *Ruin of Britain*, ed. M. Winterbottom (London, 1978), p. 102.
[30] *Vita S. Comgalli*, 42, and cf. *Vita S. Fintani*, 17, ed. C. Plummer, *Vitae Sanctorum Hiberniae* (2 vols, Oxford, 1910), II, pp. 16–17, 102–3. cf. F. J. Byrne, *Irish Kings and High Kings* (London, 1973), pp. 136–7.
[31] 'Bachall' is a staff or crozier: 'Gabaid bachail' could mean 'he takes holy orders', as well as 'he takes the pilgrim's staff' (*Dictionary of the Irish Language*, Dublin, Royal Irish Academy, 1913–76, *s.v.*). However, the annal entries are customarily taken in the latter sense, which is confirmed by its use in saints' lives: see *Vita S. Cainnechi*, ed. W. W. Heist, *Vitae Sanctorum Hiberniae* (Brussels, 1965), pp. 188,

there are considerable problems of interpretation, and the picture is further confused by the fact that the line between monks and those remaining in the world is more blurred than elsewhere. Laymen who had committed serious sins would do a spell of penance attached to a monastery, normally returning to the world once their penance was completed.[32] Or laymen might go to a monastery and stay there 'on pilgrimage' for an extended length of time, without themselves taking monastic vows and so becoming actual monks.[33] Sometimes they undertook this for a limited period such as a year; but at other times they regarded it as a permanent step. So, for instance, Artgal, king of Connacht, took up his pilgrim's staff in 782 and went on pilgrimage to Iona the following year; but his death on Iona is recorded only in 791.[34] We may assume the same practice with those kings who are reported to have died 'in pilgrimage at Clonmacnois': Aed, king of the Airthir (roughly Co. Armagh), c.610, and Indrechtach, king of Connacht, in 723. Alongside these we should also class Bécc of Bairche, king of the Ulaid, who assumed the pilgrim's staff in 707 and apparently remained a pilgrim till his death in 718; Niall Frossach, king of Tara, who according to late sources died in pilgrimage on Iona in 778; and Dúnchad, king of the Uí Maine (in south Connacht), who assumed the pilgrim's staff in 784 and died the following year.[35]

A different slant on this practice appears in a story told by Adomnan. An abbot brought an Irish prince, Aed the Black, back to his Tiree monastery 'in clerical garb', so that he might be a pilgrim there for some years, and he had him ordained priest. Aed,

---

193; and cf. the MS variants from 'M' and 'R' in Plummer, *Vitae Sanctorum Hiberniae, I*, p. 165. I am grateful to Dr R. Sharpe for these references.
[32] C. Stancliffe, 'Red, white and blue martyrdom', in D. Whitelock, R. McKitterick and D. Dumville (eds), *Ireland in Early Medieval Europe: Studies in memory of Kathleen Hughes* (Cambridge, 1982), p. 40ff.
[33] Well illustrated by Adomnan, *Life of Columba* I.32, ed. A. O. and M. O. Anderson (London, 1961), pp. 270–2.
[34] *AU, s.a.* 781, 790.
[35] Aed: 'The Annals of Tigernach', ed. W. Stokes, *Revue Celtique*, XVII (1896), p. 168; *Chronicon Scotorum*, ed. and trans. W. M. Hennessy (RS, 1866), p. 72. Indrechtach: 'Tigernach', p. 231; *AU, s.a.* 722. Bécc: *AU, s.a.* 706; cf. Hennessy's note, p. 155, n. 13, and G. MacNiocaill, *Ireland before the Vikings* (Dublin, 1972), pp. 114–15. Niall: *AU, s.a.* 777; Hennessy's notes, pp. 248–9; Byrne, *Irish Kings*, p. 156. Dúnchad, *AU, s.a.* 783, 784. Further, according to MacNiocaill, *Ireland before the Vikings*, p. 135, Fergus, son of Cellach, king of Connacht (742–56) died on pilgrimage in 756.

who belonged to the royal family of one of the Ulster peoples (the Cruithni), had already taken an active part in Irish power struggles, having killed the southern Uí Néill overking in 565. Later he left the monastery and became king of his own people, and even overking of Ulster, before being slain in 588.[36] Here, then is a case reminiscent of Maelgwn's, with a poweful noble of royal blood who became a cleric and a pilgrim, but who nonetheless returned to the political arena. The story of the East Anglian Sigebert, dragged out of his monastery to lead his people against Penda, warns us against interpreting every instance of a monk-king returning to political life as evidence of a force or insincere commitment to monasticism; but in the absence of any fuller information than the annals afford, I shall set aside the entry into clerical or monastic life of Fínsnechta Fledach, king of the southern Uí Néill, in 688, and of Selbach, king of Dál Riata, in 723. Both these appear to have re-emerged from their monasteries to play an active political role once more. Nechtan, king of the Picts, also belongs to this category.[37]

Even more confusion arises from the fact that, at least by the ninth century, the same man might be both king and abbot simultaneously.[38] This development may have already begun in the eighth century, with Ólchobar son of Flann (died 796); and we may question whether it reaches further back to the time of Domnall son of Murchad, king of Meath, whose career displays both vigorous kingly activity and two entries *in clericatum*.[39] But the latter may have been only of a temporary nature.

Leaving aside these kings who mingled political activity with the religious life, let us turn to those who resigned for good to become clerics and/or enter monasteries. The earliest possibility is Domangart, king of Dál Riata. Under the year 506 (*recte* 507) the *Annals of Ulster* have: 'Domhangart mac Nisse reti secessit anno

---

[36] Adomnan I.36, pp. 278–82; cf. the Andersons' introduction, p. 75, and MacNiocaill, *Ireland before the Vikings*, pp. 75, 88.

[37] Fínsnechta: *AU, s.a.* 687, 688, 694; 'Tigernach', pp. 210, 213–14; MacNiocaill, *Ireland before the Vikings* pp. 107–10. Selbach: *AU, s.a.* 722, 726, 729; 'Tigernach', p. 231; Anderson edn of Adomnan, pp. 56–7; M. O. Anderson, *Kings and Kingship in Early Scotland* (Edinburgh, 1973), pp. 181–2. Nechtan: 'Tigernach', pp. 231–2, 234, 236; Anderson, *Kings and Kingship*, pp. 176–8.

[38] K. Hughes, *The Church in Early Irish Society* (London, 1966), pp. 211–14, 221–2.

[39] Ólchobar: *AU, s.a.* 795 call him king of Munster; *Annals of Inisfallen*, ed. S. Mac Airt (Dublin, 1951), *s.a.* 797, abbot of Inis Cathaig. See Hughes, *Church*, p. 212; MacNiocaill, *Ireland before the Vikings*, pp. 132–3. Domnall, *AU, s.a.* 739, 742–3, 752, 755, 762; MacNiocaill, *Ireland before the Vikings*, p. 126.

xxxv' (*withdrew in his 35th year*). The *secessit* here, coupled with the
fact that the *Annals of Inisfallen* record (*s.a.*503) the 'quies Domongairt
Cind Tire', so using a word for his death which is reserved for
churchmen's *obits*, implies that Domangart withdrew from his
kingdom to enter a monastery.[40]

Disregarding two unconvincing cases,[41] we now move on to 705
when the annals record the death of Cellach son of Ragallach, king
of Connacht, after his entry into religion. He had become king only
in 702, when he was already in his fifties (or more). As he was
fighting his enemies as late as 704, he cannot have been a monk for
long before he died. His adoption of the religious life may be seen as
the retirement of an old man who realized that his days were
numbered.[42]

Flaithbertach son of Loingsech is one of three mid-eighth-century
kings of Tara who exchanged their kingdom for the religious life.
Flaithbertach himself may have been not so much opting in to the
religious life as stepping down because his position had become
untenable. He had been king of Tara since 728, but in 732, 733 and
734 he and his people had been attacked and defeated by a rival
branch of the northern Uí Néill under his distant cousin, Aed
Allán; and when he retired in 734 it was Aed who succeeded him as
king of Tara. Flaithbertach himself lived on for over twenty years,
dying at Armagh in 765.[43]

Little is known of the other eighth-century kings who ended their
days *in clericatu*: Domnall son of Ceiternach, king of the Uí Garrchon
(in the Wicklow area), whose *obit* is recorded in 783; Gormgal son
of Eladhach, king of Knowth (i.e. north Brega), in 789; and
Cummascach son of Fogartach, king of south Brega, in 797.[44]

[40] So Anderson edn of Adomnan, pp. 36–7; J. Bannerman, *Studies in the History of
Dalriada* (Edinburgh, 1974), pp. 75–6, is more sceptical. 507 is of course two
generations before contemporary annal-writing begins; but the early form 'Reti' (I
assume 'moccu' or 'Dáil' has dropped out, and prefer this explanation to Mac Airt,
Annals, p. 70, n.a.) does suggest a very early stratum; and king-lists and genealogies pre-date annals.
[41] On Aedán son of Gabrán of Dál Riada, see Anderson edn of Adomnan, p. 45, and
Bannerman, *Dalriada*, p. 87; Aed Dub, abbot of Kildare (d. 639) was never king,
despite 'Tigernach', p. 185: K. Meyer, 'Aed Dub mac Colmáin', *Zeitschrift für
celtische Philologie*, IX (1913), pp. 458–9.
[42] *AU, s.a.* 702, 704; the death of Cellach's father is recorded, *AU, s.a.* 648 (= 649).
MacNiocaill, *Ireland before the Vikings* p. 118; Byrne, *Irish Kings*, pp. 247–8.
[43] *AU, s.a.* 731, 732, 733, 764; cf. Hennessy's notes, pp. 189, 231. Byrne thinks that
he was compelled to abdicate: *Irish Kings*, p. 247; MacNiocaill, that he simply
opted out: *Ireland before the Vikings*, p. 124.   [44] *AU, s.a.* 782, 788, 796.

Let us now draw together the results of our investigation into Irish monk-kings up to c.800.[45] Chronologically, the movement starts in a small way in the sixth and seventh centuries and increases dramatically after c.700, becoming a veritable flood in the last quarter of the eighth century, with five cases within twelve years. However, this patterning probably derives at least in part from the incidence of the records that were kept.[46] Up to c.740 we depend largely, if not exclusively, on annals that were originally compiled on Iona. Naturally, then, they note the entry into religion of a Dál Riata king (507), an Airthir king (610), and an Ulaid king (707), while overkings of Connacht and Tara were sufficiently important to be included in any case (705, 723, 781, and 765, 778). Domnall of the Uí Garrchon, whose death is recorded in 783, is the first monk-king from Leinster to be mentioned; he is also the first who is neither a provincial king nor a king in north-east Ireland. This, and the references in 789 and 797 to kings of Brega, tally interestingly with Alfred Smyth's conclusion that there was no annalistic centre regularly covering events in Leinster until Clonard began keeping contemporary annals from c.775, but that thereafter events in north Leinster and under the southern Uí Néill are considerably better documented.[47] Conversely, the absence of any monk-king from Munster, and from Connacht with the exception of the important provincial kings and the relatively important Uí Maine king in 784, probably reflects nothing more than the paucity of our annalistic records for Munster and Connacht up to 800.[48] Similarly I would regard Cormac as a genuine sixth-century monk-king from Leinster despite his omission from the annals. We may conclude that kings opting into the religious life are found in Ireland before, during, and indeed after the incidence of such monk-kings in England. The gaps in our evidence for Ireland should prevent us from assuming that such a practice was necessarily rare in Ireland until the eighth century, and that it first became common in England; it would be wiser to keep an open mind. But certainly some Irish kings took this

[45] Irish – and indeed Welsh – monk-kings continued after 800, but the later ones are not relevant to a study of Anglo-Saxon monk-kings.
[46] A. P. Smyth, 'The earliest Irish annals', *Proceedings of the Royal Irish Academy*, LXXII C (1972), pp. 1–48.
[47] *ibid.*, p. 28; cf. also K. Hughes, *Early Christian Ireland: Introduction to the Sources* (London, 1972), pp. 124–6.
[48] Smyth, 'Earliest annals', pp. 31–2, though cf. Hughes, *Sources*, pp. 105–7, 110–13.

step before Sigebert, our earliest Anglo-Saxon example: as, indeed, we might have guessed from Columbanus' forthright recommendation to King Theudebert.

Let us keep these Irish analogues in mind as we return to the motives of the Anglo-Saxon monk-kings. Those like Aethelred or Ine who resigned after long reigns seem easier to understand. A king had to be ready to fight to defend his borders, and when old age had 'robbed him of the joys of strength', he obviously stood as a disadvantage beside a younger man.[49] More subtly, as he sensed that his physical journey on earth was nearing its end, so he might find his thoughts tending more to the inner journey. As Bede put it on his death bed:

> Before the journey that awaits us all,
> No man becomes so wise that he has not
> Need to think out, before his going hence,
> What judgment will be given to his soul
> After his death, of evil or of good.[50]

In Ireland, certainly, such thoughts put men in mind of penance, of attaching themselves to a monastery, or of going on pilgrimage:

> Only two years
> Are lacking of my three score; –
> It were time
> To remain in some place under one rule.[51]

Some English kings were similarly motivated. There is Oswiu; and even Sebbi's queen gave way when her husband was struck down by his final illness.

However, other kings resigned in their prime: Caedwalla and Offa, certainly; probably also Sigebert, Centwine and Cenred. Nor is there any hint that these men were 'monkish' by disposition, and unsuited for the role of king (as, arguably, Sebbi was). On the contrary, Caedwalla, Centwine and Sigebert were proven warriors, and Bede particularly mentions that all the East Saxons were longing

---

[49] *Beowulf*, ed. F. Klaeber (Lexington, 3rd edn, 1950), ll. 1885–7 and 1769–78. E. Peters, *The Shadow King* (New Haven, 1970), pp. 97–100.

[50] ed. and trans. R. Hamer, *A Choice of Anglo-Saxon Verse* (London, 1970), pp. 126–7; Plummer, I, p. clxi.

[51] ed. and trans. P. L. Henry, *The Early English and Celtic Lyric* (London, 1966), pp. 64–5 (cf. also pp. 50–63). Another angle on the same practice comes from the remarkable 'Lament of the Old Woman of Beare', of *c*.800, ed. and trans. G. Murphy, *Early Irish Lyrics* (Oxford, repr. 1962), no. 34.

to have Offa as their king.[52] Here, then, conversion to the religious life was a more dramatic step: a rejection of the cup that was brimming full.

Fortunately Felix's *Life of St Guthlac* may throw some light here. True, Guthlac was never a king; but he was a potential king, a man of royal blood who gathered a warband about him and lived by pillage, much as Caedwalla had done before he seized power in Wessex. For nine years Guthlac immersed himself in 'the glorious overthrow of his adversaries . . . by frequent blows and devastations.' Then one night he saw his life differently.

> For when, with wakeful mind, he contemplated the wretched deaths and the shameful ends of the ancient kings of his race in the course of the past ages, and also the fleeting riches of this world and the contemptible glory of this temporal life, then in imagination the form of his own death revealed itself to him. [Forthwith] he vowed that, if he lived until the next day, he himself would become a servant of Christ.[53]

Guthlac was then twenty-four.

Guthlac's train of thought is mirrored in some of the greatest Old English poetry, notably in *The Wanderer* and *The Seafarer*, where the poet broods over the transience of former heroes:

> Where is the horse now, where the here gone. . . .
> Where are all the joys of hall?
> Alas for the bright cup, the armoured warrior,
> The glory of the prince. That time is over,
> Passed into night as it had never been.

The fleeting nature of riches and of man himself lays bare the contrast with God and Heaven, which stand for ever: that is man's true home, and he should give thought to how he may get thither.[54]

Although these poems may be later in date, the themes they express occur elsewhere in Old English poetry; they stand for a whole cast of mind that was then widespread. This can be traced back through Latin Christian authors to its biblical roots; but what is significant is that the Anglo-Saxons seized on these particular themes to develop, and that they did so in vernacular verse which

[52] *HE* V.19, p. 322.
[53] Felix, *Life of Guthlac*, ed. B. Colgrave (Cambridge, 1956), 16–18, pp. 80–3.
[54] *Wanderer*, ll. 92–6, 114–15, using Hamer's translation (see n. 50), pp. 180–1; *Seafarer*, ed. I. L. Gordon (London, 1960), ll. 64ff., 106, 117–22. cf. *HE* II. 13, p. 112.

might have been sung in the great halls of kings.[55] This meant that English kings could have been reminded of mortal man's fate and the need to turn to God not simply by what they heard in church, but by the forceful rendering of such ideas in vernacular poetry. This would have struck them far more powerfully than anything that was available to their Merovingian contemporaries in Gaul, where the scope for expressing Christian concepts in the vernacular seems to have been inadequately realized before the advent of the Anglo-Saxon missionaries.[56]

Interestingly enough, the contrast between the transience of earthly kings and the eternity of God's kingdom recurs in vernacular poetry from Ireland (though the mood of the poetry differs markedly).[57] And, of course, Irish penitential practices, indeed Irish spirituality *tout simple*, deeply influenced the Anglo-Saxons.[58] All this suggests that the practice of kings opting into the religious life, which occurred in both countries, stems from the same ascetic Christian habits of thought.

This likelihood is further strengthened by the recurrence of the pilgrimage theme. Both Irish and Anglo-Saxon kings frequently opted for a life of pilgrimage rather than becoming a monk in their local monastery. Now Irish *peregrinatio* differs from the normal Christian pilgrimage in being conceived as a long-lasting exile endured for the sake of God: it was not a journey to a particular holy place from which one speedily returned to one's home and one's normal life.[59] The Anglo-Saxons adopted this *peregrinatio* ideal, but gave it their own particular twist: whereas for the Irish, one could be a pilgrim to another part of Ireland, for the English, *peregrinatio* necessarily involved journeying abroad.[60] Secondly, the Anglo-Saxon

[55] See even *Beowulf*, ll. 2249–66, 183–8; and note too the emphasis on Doomsday in OE poems and homilies.
[56] Such is the implication of a revealing story in Liudger's *Life of Gregory of Utrecht*: see F. Delbono, 'La letteratura catechetica di lingua tedesca', *Settimane*, XIV (1967), pp. 727–8.
[57] Henry, *Lyric*, pp. 228–34.
[58] Hughes, *Sources*, pp. 88–9; K. Hughes, 'Aspects of Irish influence', *Studia Celtica*, V (1970), pp. 48–61; P. Sims-Williams, 'Thought, word and deed', *Ériu*, XXIX (1978), pp. 78–111.
[59] Irish ascetics did not create their *peregrinatio* ideal, but they were its chief practitioners: H. von Campenhausen, *Tradition and Life in the Church* (London, 1968), pp. 231–51. In its most demanding form, Irish *peregrinatio* amounted to life-long exile from Ireland, but see above, n. 33 and below, n. 60.
[60] T. M. Charles-Edwards, 'The social background to Irish *peregrinatio*', *Celtica*, XI (1976), pp. 43–59.

kings all chose Rome as the place to spend the rest of their lives – in this, as in their adoption of the monastic life in England, sharing in a widespread English phenomenon. Here, they were clearly motivated by their particular veneration for St Peter, the influential doorkeeper of Heaven, and by the special link between England and Rome which had been established by Gregory the Great whom they regarded as their true apostle. Thus the pilgrimages of English kings resembled those of Irish kings in comprising a lifelong sojourn in a holy place, not a journey there and back again; but while the Irish kings opted for an Irish monastery such as Clonmacnois or Iona, all the Anglo-Saxon ones chose Rome.

As regards the individual circumstances that prompted each decision, we can pick out at least some relevant factors. Sigebert, the first Anglo-Saxon monk-king, drew his Christian inspiration from Gaul, where he had been baptized as an exile, and whence came his bishop, Felix; and from Ireland, whence he welcomed the *peregrinus*, Fursa. He may also have been influenced by the fusion between Irish and Gallic Christianity that had already been effected as a result of Columbanus' sojourn in Gaul; for Felix's Burgundian origins, coupled with his missionary impulse, suggest that he came from the Hiberno-Frankish circle of Luxeuil.[61] Indeed, Sigebert might have known some of the leaders of this circle himself, at first hand. Such conjectures are relevant when we recall not merely Columbanus' advice to king Theudebert, but also the interesting observation that whereas Austrasian saints' lives concern themselves with improvements in man's condition in this world, the lives of Irish and Hiberno-Frankish saints emphasize rather man's citizenship of the kingdom of Heaven.[62] As for the possiblity of Fursa's influence, we might note that Fursa could tell, from his own vision experience, how searching were the questions raised before any man was allowed to proceed to Heaven; and he had been specifically charged to go and preach penitence to all, which he did with no respect of persons. The vividness of his experiences communicated itself to at least one

[61] *HE* II.15, III.18–19, pp. 116–17, 162–3; Campbell 'The first century', pp. 19–22. On the Hiberno-Frankish movement, see F. Prinz, *Frühes Mönchtum im Frankenreich* (Munich, 1965), ch. 4; and *idem*, in H. B. Clarke and M. Brennan (eds), *Columbanus and Merovingian Monasticism* (BAR, Int., CXIII, 1981), pp. 77–82. The indigenous monasticism of Burgundy had no such missionary zeal (I. Wood, *ibid.*, p. 19), which makes a Hiberno-Frankish background for Felix likely.
[62] Riché, *ibid.*, pp. 69–70, citing the unpublished thesis of J. C. Dérouet. cf. *HE* III.18, p. 162.

listener. Though Bede gives no hint that Fursa, or for that matter Felix or anyone else, influenced Sigebert in his decision, this is likely – at least in an indirect manner.[63]

We know too little to say who or what prompted Centwine of Wessex to enter a monastery. Haedde was his bishop. But Aldhelm, abbot of Malmesbury and a passionate advocate of celibacy, was a more commanding figure, and it was he who wrote the poem for Centwine's daughter cited earlier.[64] His influence is a strong possibility.

We can, however, point to the chief inspirer of royal *peregrinatio* to Rome: Wilfrid – with Benedict Biscop as a further possibility in the first instance. Wilfrid was seemingly the first Englishman to conceive the desire, while he was at Lindisfarne, to go to Rome on pilgrimage (*c*.652); he left the next year with Benedict Biscop. Wilfrid did not stay indefinitely in Rome; but on his third visit he expressed the desire to do so. He was now (704) about seventy, and hoped 'to crucify the world to himself in his old age and finish his life there'. Although at the pope's behest he returned to England, he never abandoned his intention, though he was unable to fulfil it.[65]

The first Anglo-Saxon king to plan a pilgrimage to Rome was Alchfrith, *c*.664: precisely when he was a close friend and admirer of Wilfrid's. Of course, Alchfrith's enthusiasm for Rome may have derived equally from Benedict Biscop; but elsewhere it is Wilfrid's name that comes up, both with Oswiu and with Caedwalla. Eddi shows Wilfrid materially assisting the exiled Caedwalla after an agreement that Wilfrid should help him as a father, while Caedwalla, as a son, would learn from Wilfrid and be obedient to him. Once Caedwalla became king he summoned Wilfrid and 'made him

[63] *Vita S. Fursei*, ed. W. W. Heist, *Vitae Sanctorum Hiberniae* (Brussels, 1965), 9–13, 21–2, 26, pp. 40–3, 47–8; *HE* III.19, p. 163ff.; the *Vita*, 29, p. 49, has King Anna and his people appealing in a crisis to Fursa, 'tamquam altioris ingenii', for advice.
[64] Above, n. 3. On Aldhelm see H. R. M. E. Mayr-Harting, *The Coming of Christianity to Anglo-Saxon England* (London, 1972), pp. 192–9; *Aldhelm, the Prose Works*, tr. M. Lapidge and M. Herren (Ipswich, 1979), pp. 1–10, 146–7. For possible British influence on West Saxon Christianity, see Mayr-Harting, *Coming of Christianity*, pp. 118–20.
[65] Eddius, *Wilfrid*, 3, 4, 55, 63, pp. 8, 10, 120, 136–8; Mayr-Harting, *Coming of Christianity*, pp. 142–3; Plummer, II, pp. 316–20. Bede was mistaken in implying that Wilfrid was simply concerned to inform himself about Roman ecclesiastical practices: *HE* V.19, p. 323.

supreme counsellor over the whole kingdom'.[66] Shortly afterwards Wilfrid was recalled to Northumbria, and in 688 Caedwalla set out for Rome. Perhaps the wounds he had received when capturing the Isle of Wight had set him thinking along lines similar to Guthlac's; but we can also guess that his veneration for St Peter's body and his desire to go to Rome for baptism owed much to Wilfrid's teaching.[67]

Besides his links with Northumbria, Sussex and Wessex, Wilfrid also exercised influence among the Mercian royal family, which might have played a part in prompting Cenred to take the road to Rome. But by this date (709), we need not look for specific advisers who could have put the idea into a king's head, for the example of earlier monk-kings was already at hand. The potency of such examples is indicated by the patterning of conversions. Sigebert in the 630s was an outlier. The phenomenon of kings adopting the religious life gathers momentum only in the latter part of the seventh century, peaking in the years 685–710 when no fewer than six kings took this decision. This pattern of conversions, especially as it involved three consecutive kings of Wessex and two of Mercia, coupled with the joint pilgrimage of Cenred and Offa, implies that once the movement had begun in earnest, the example of other monk-kings exerted a powerful influence. Maybe Bede's collection of so many examples influenced King Ceolwulf to do likewise.[68] Further, we have already seen that Anglo-Saxon influence and example in all probability prompted Carloman's decision to adopt the religious life, and that this in turn had a similar influence on the Lombard king, Ratchis. For a time the monk-king looked set to become a European, not just an Insular, phenomenon: Charlemagne apparently considered retiring into a monastery in his old age, as did his son, Louis the Pious, while still in his prime.[69]

However, this was not to be. Charlemagne and Louis remained in the world, and in the ninth century the phenomenon of the monk-king died out even in England. True, Burgred of Mercia fled

---

[66] Above, n. 10; *HE* IV.5, p. 214; Eddius, *Wilfrid*, 7, 8, 9, 42, pp. 14–16, 16–18, 18, 84; Wilfrid's relations with Caedwalla are confirmed by *S* 235, *S* 1248, and cf. *HE* IV.16, p. 237, and Plummer, II, p. 229.

[67] cf. D. Farmer, 'Saint Wilfrid', in D. Kirby (ed.), *Saint Wilfrid at Hexham* (Newcastle, 1974), p. 51.

[68] Wallace-Hadrill, *EGK*, p. 91.

[69] Charlemagne's will gave directions in the event of his death or 'voluntariam saecularium rerum carentiam': Einhard, *Vita Caroli* 33, ed. O. Holder-Egger, *MGH,SRG*, p. 39. On Louis, see below.

to Rome in 874 and stayed there; but this was forced upon him by the Vikings. A sign of the changing times is the fact that Aethelwulf, king of Wessex, went on a pilgrimage to Rome in 855, but then returned to resume his rule.[70] Cnut did the same in 1027; and it is equally significant that Edward the Confessor, who, like Sebbi, seemed better suited to religious than kingly office, remained king to the end.

What lies behind this changing pattern? Obviously we could link the attraction of monasticism for kings with its attraction for the nobility. The monk-kings of the seventh and eighth centuries co-incided with a monastic 'craze', which swept up both kings and their thegns. Conversely, by the ninth century monasticism had lost its impetus. Asser writes that although monasteries were still standing, the regular monastic life had lapsed because no noble or free-born man would opt for such a life; and so Alfred had to look abroad for monks for Aethelney.[71] If no English noble would opt for the religious life, then we should not expect kings to do so. Further, in the ninth century the Vikings provided a new *raison d'être* for Christian kings, who were now needed as defenders of Christendom. Kings show their awareness of this in their insistence, on occasion, that the Vikings must accept Christianity.[72]

All this is true enough. But, while it might account for why kings stopped opting into the religious life in the ninth century, it does nothing to explain why monk-kings are found only in the British Isles in the early Middle Ages, and not (saving Carloman and Ratchis) in the other Germanic kingdoms which succeeded to Rome. What follows is an attempt to make sense of this fact.

Where there was continuity from the western Roman Empire, and where the barbarians were converted by the indigenous clergy, the latter viewed Christian kingship in a positive light. Although Latin churchmen were never as fulsome as Eusebius about Christian emperors, they still thought that these had a valuable role to play in promoting Christianity. The same outlook came naturally to the bishops of Gaul and Spain in their dealings with Frankish and Visigothic kings, and it appears in Gregory I's letter to Aethelbert, cited above. There, I linked Gregory's positive role for the king

[70] *ASC, s.a.* 874, Asser, *Life of Alfred*, ed. W. H. Stevenson (Oxford, repr. 1959), 46, p. 35; *ASC, s.a.* 855, but (more truthfully), Asser, 11–13, pp. 9–11, 194.
[71] Asser, 92–3, pp. 79–81.
[72] Wallace-Hadrill, *EMH*, pp. 203–4, 207–8, 226–7; Wallace-Hadrill, *EGK*, pp. 140–1.

with his teaching elsewhere that a ruler must be prepared to use his gifts for others, and therefore might not be free to undertake the monastic life himself.

It is striking that this is precisely the line taken later on the continent à propos of rulers desiring the monastic life. When Louis the Pious was afire to imitate his great-uncle Carloman, he was prevented by 'the opposition of his father, or rather by the command of the divine will, which did not wish a man of such piety to lie hid in caring only for his own salvation, but rather to increase the salvation of many through him'.[73] So Louis remained king, and fostered a widespread monastic renewal in Aquitaine. Again, a century later bishop Gausbert dissuaded Gerald, count of Aurillac, from entering a monastery out of consideration 'for the general welfare of the provincials'; and precisely the same points recurred in the eleventh century when Gregory VII protested against Cluny admitting Duke Hugh of Burgundy, and when Cluny refused to receive King Alfonso VI as a monk on the grounds that it was better for him to remain in the world.[74]

On the continent, this affirmative attitude to kingship was rooted in the positive evaluation of political activity which passed from the Greek *polis* to the Romans. But Ireland had a different past, devoid of Greco-Roman intellectual influence; and its best-known missionary, Patrick, took his ideas from the Bible, not classical tradition, and showed more concern for his converts as a group than for the role of the Christian ruler.[75] Further, the circumstances in which Christians found themselves in fifth- and sixth-century Ireland, as a believing minority amid a largely pagan society, gave them more in common with the continental Church of pre-Constantinian days, with its ambivalent attitude towards the government, than with the post-Constantinian Church.[76] Naturally much changed once

[73] *Vita Hludovici Imperatoris* 19, ed. G. H. Pertz, *MGH,SS* II, p. 616.
[74] Odo, *Life of Gerald* II.2, *PL* CXXXIII, c.670; D. Baker, '*Vir Dei*: secular sanctity in the early tenth century', *SCH*, VIII (1972), p. 45; H. Cowdrey, *The Cluniacs and the Gregorian Reform* (Oxford, 1970), pp. 144–7. But for the no less dramatic direction which the ideology of kingship took in this period, see John, below, pp. 309, 312–13.
[75] C. Stancliffe, 'Kings and conversion', *Frühmittelalterliche Studien*, XIV (1980), pp. 65–6. The Old Testament could sharpen awareness of the crucial role of kings (McClure, above, pp. 87–90); but Patrick was primarily influenced by Paul and the New Testament.
[76] Hughes, *Church*, p. 45; Charles-Edwards, 'Irish *peregrinatio*', pp. 55–6. cf. the interesting remarks of R. A. Markus, *Saeculum* (Cambridge, 1970), pp. 73–5.

Christianity became accepted throughout Irish society, around the later sixth century; thereafter the Church rapidly acquired wealth and power. Also, while from the moment of its conversion Ireland was potentially open to Christian influences from Britain and the continent, by the seventh century such influences were beginning to make themselves felt in the activities of the 'Roman' party in Ireland; and the dating of Easter was not the only point on which these churchmen sought to follow continental example.[77]

Against this background of change, and of diversity within the Church, it is dangerous to generalize. Broadly speaking, however, we may say that Irish churchmen between the fifth and seventh centuries did not expect kings to play such an active part – if any part – in promoting Christianity as did churchmen abroad.[78] Conversely, Irish ascetics at this early period seemingly preached the same Christian message to kings as to nobles or peasants; they did not adjust it to render it more amenable to those who were not private individuals, but the holders of political power and warriors by profession.[79] So much, at least, I would deduce from the results of Irish missionary work abroad. For it was the Irish-instructed king Oswin of Deira whom Aidan regarded as so wonderfully humble a king that he could not be expected to survive long; it was the Irish *peregrinus* Columbanus who upbraided King Theuderic for his concubines and refused to bless his bastards, disregarding the fact that the Merovingians had long practised polygamy; he also refused to pray for the victory of one Merovingian king over another, reminding his disciple that Jesus had taught us to pray for our enemies, and that the important thing was for God's will to be done. The same Irish influence was also operative on King Sigebert of Essex, who was murdered by his kinsmen 'because he was too ready to pardon his enemies', his crime being 'that he had devoutly observed

---

[77] Hughes, *Church*, pp. 10–12, for an introductory sketch.

[78] Byrne, *Irish Kings* pp. 34–5. The C7th Irish *De XII Abusivis Saeculi* (ed. S. Hellmann, *Texte und Untersuchungen*, XXXIV, 1910, esp. pp. 51–2) exhorts the king to act in a Christian manner in the political and personal spheres (punishing adultery, defending widows and churches, being regular in prayer, etc.); but it does not envisage him leading his people to the true faith, or having any role as *praedicator*. Contrast Gregory's exhortation to Aethelbert, *HE* I.32, pp. 67–70.

[79] Note the conditional nature of *Penitential of Cummean* IX.11, ed. and trans. L. Bieler, *Irish Penitentials* (Dublin, 1963), p. 126; it reproduces that of Gildas, 23, *ibid.*, p. 62, but was omitted by Archbishop Theodore, as is pointed out by Wallace-Hadrill, *EGK*, p. 69.

the gospel precepts'.[80] If the Irish and their Anglo-Saxon disciples could be as idealistically indifferent as this to the needs and traditions of successful warrior kingship, we need feel no surprise that their ascetic teaching should lead kings to adopt the religious life; they would have seen nothing untoward about this.[81]

Conversely, we might link the cessation of kings opting into the religious life in England not simply with the general decline of monastic vocations, but also with a more positive attitude to kingship eventually making itelf felt. Ironically, Bede, while collecting examples of monk-kings, himself did much to promote Gregory's view of kingship entailing particular responsibilities. Bede may well have contributed to Carolingian thinking on kingship, and Carolingian theory and practice in turn had a considerable impact on England. For these new developments, we need but recall Offa's claim to be *rex a rege regum constitutus*, the visit of the papal legates to England in his reign and their decrees on kingship, and the anointing of his son Egfrith.[82] These are indications that English kings now saw their role as Christian leaders in a way that was very close to their Carolingian contemporaries. Small wonder, then, that Alfred – a perfect candidate for a monk-king – remained at the helm, having taken to heart the teaching of Gregory: a Christian king had a function *qua* king and should not opt out.[83] The climax of this positive Christian attitude to kingship would come in the tenth century, with the Ottos in Germany and Edgar in England, both countries emphasizing the analogy between the anointed king (*rex christus*) and Christ the King. And, surely, it is not irrelevant that the late tenth and eleventh centuries also saw the first kings to achieve sanctity by their life – not by death as a 'martyr', or by opting out of kingship into the religious life.[84]

[80] *HE* III.14, 22, pp. 156–7, 173; Jonas, *Vita Columbani* I.18–19, 28, pp. 186–93, 217–19. cf. Campbell, 'The First Century', pp. 23–4; Mayr-Harting, *Coming of Christianity*, pp. 100–1. Some Gallic churchmen also took a strong line, as Collins's Nicetius, above, p. 23; but most did not.
[81] For an astonishing rebuke to a warleader for fighting his people's enemies, followed by his conversion to asceticism, see *Vita S. Endei* 2, ed. Plummer, *Vitae Sanctorum Hiberniae*, II, pp. 60–1. Note also R. Sharpe, 'Hiberno-Latin *laicus*', *Ériu*, XXX (1979), esp. pp. 91–2 and n. 83. Contrast Bede, above, n. 21, and the willingness of Frankish and Visigothic Churches to bless preparations for war: Wallace-Hadrill, *EGK*, p. 99; J. N. Hillgarth, *The Conversion of W. Europe* (Englewood Cliffs, NJ, 1969), pp. 90–2.
[82] Wallace-Hadrill, *EMH*, pp. 156–61; Wallace-Hadrill, *EGK*, *passim*. See also Thacker, above, pp. 146–8.   [83] Wallace-Hadrill, *EGK*, pp. 143–8.
[84] F. Graus, *Volk, Herrscher und Heiliger im Reich der Merowinger* (Prague, 1965), pp.

We should recognize that the contrast outlined above between Roman and Irish attitudes to kingship, and its relationship to hindering or encouraging kings to become monks, is somewhat speculative. Problems remain. Should we really see Wilfrid, usually associated with Rome, as a purveyor of (modified) Irish attitudes vis à vis *peregrinatio* and its appropriateness for kings? This is not so odd if we separate Wilfrid's actual attitude to the Irish from the anti-Irish stance ascribed to him by Eddi; and if we recall that it was at Lindisfarne that Wilfrid first conceived his desire to go on pilgrimage to Rome, that the monks there encouraged him, and that some Irish churchmen were already in direct contact with Rome.[85] Perhaps Bede himself presents more of a problem. He was a fulsome admirer of Pope Gregory, and his account of Cuthbert clearly reflects Gregory's view that Christian leaders should sacrifice their own yearning for quietude in order to guide others.[86] Bede also believed that kings had a duty to promote Christianity among their people. How could he, then, have approved of so many kings resigning for the sake of the religious life? Possibly his *History*, guarded as it is, does not reveal all that he thought about these monk-kings. Or perhaps, for all his readiness to acknowledge his debts to Gregory and Rome, while passing lightly over those to the Irish, his Northumbrian spirituality owed more to the Irish than we realize.[87] However, it might be unwise to adopt a rigid kind of determinism which would 'explain' such conversions solely in terms of concepts of a king's role, leaving nothing to individual choice. In the final analysis, it was they who took the decision to opt out. Or perhaps, taking a less anachronistic view, we might say rather that they opted in *ad visionem apostolorum in caelis*.[88]

425–8, 431–3; J. L. Nelson, 'Royal saints and early medieval kingship', *SCH*, X (1973), esp. pp. 42–3; for some resulting complexities, John, below, pp. 312–14.
[85] Eddius, *Wilfrid*, 3, p. 8; *HE* V.19, p. 323. See Farmer, *Wilfrid* (see n. 67) p. 39; Mayr-Harting, *Coming of Christianity*, pp. 142–4; E. John 'Social and political problems of the early English Church', in J. Thirsk (ed.), *Land and People: Studies presented to H. P. R. Finberg, Agricultural History Review*, XVIII, Suppl. (1970), pp. 60–1. On seventh-century Irish and Hiberno-Frankish contacts with Rome, see Hughes, *Church*, p. 105, n. 5, and Riché in *Columbanus* (see n. 62), pp. 65–6.
[86] *HE* IV.27–8, pp. 269–70, 272–3. See R. W. Hanning, *The Vision of History in Early Britain* (New York, 1966), pp. 85–7; and Thacker, above, pp. 144–5.
[87] Note the cautionary tales in *HE* V.13–14, pp. 311–15, urging the very Irish concern of penance; V.13, p. 312 includes the Irish motif of 'thought, word and deed' (cf. n. 58 above).
[88] *HE* V.19, p. 322.

8

Burial, Community and Belief in the Early Medieval West

DONALD BULLOUGH

Sometime in 795/6, Alcuin wrote to 'the brethren of the church of York' recalling the past and looking to the future, where only death was certain. The 'most beloved brothers and fathers', he tells them, come first in his prayers wherever he might be in the *iter instabilitatis* which was currently taking him to various 'holy places of the martyrs and confessors of Christ'; and he asks for their prayers in return.

> I will be yours whether in life or death. Perhaps God will pity me, so that he whom you raised in childhood you will bury in old age. And if another place is assigned to my body, yet – wherever that is to be – I believe that my soul will through your prayers by God's grace be granted rest together with you. For as we learnt from our boy Seneca's vision, we have reason to believe that the souls of our brotherhood are to be re-united in the same place of gladness: and though diversity of merits will make one more blessed with joy than another, yet all equally will be living happily in Eternity.[1]

Alcuin's faith in a future beyond the grave, the manner in which it is to be secured and the language in which these are expressed are firmly rooted in the earliest Christian traditions. The structure of thought and language, however, reflect the shift in emphasis – very evident in eighth-century liturgical and para-liturgical prayers with which he may be assumed to have been familiar – from an earlier *requies* of the body, released from the travails of earthly life and the

---

[1] *Ep*. 42, ed. E. Dümmler, *MGH,Ep*. IV, p. 86.

assaults of demonic powers, to a 'rest' of the soul purged of sin in an intermediate place awaiting the general Ressurection; and at the same time a greater concern with the physical location of the pre-Resurrection body.[2]

The extensive and technically accomplished excavations at York have failed to reveal anything that might have been the graveyard where Alcuin would have liked to have been buried among his former brethren. Indeed, they have failed to reveal any evidence of the eighth-century cathedral, even though this seems to have been, like so many of its counterparts on the continent at this time, a complex of churches rather than a single church. It is even possible that the 'cathedral cemetery' was outside the walls of the city, although this is not very likely: a fragment of a sepulchural cross dated on palaeographical grounds to the later eighth century is among the earlier stone work incorporated in the foundation-raft of the Norman minster; the late Saxon burials under the south transept of that building, evidently part of a larger cemetery, are on the same alignment as the buildings and streets of the Roman city; and the church of St Stephen, for which Alcuin's letters seem to be the only source, could well be connected with the burial area.[3] By contrast, there is steadily accumulating archaeological evidence for pre-

---

[2] For Alcuin's language, cf. A. B. Kuypers (ed.), *The Prayer Book of Aedeluald the Bishop commonly called 'the Book of Cerne'* (Cambridge, 1902), p. 84, ll. 11–17, and the fifth of the *Orationes ad defunctum* in the 'Frankish [*al.* eighth-century] Gelasian' sacramentary in Berlin MS Phillipps 1667, published and commented on by D. Sicard, *La Liturgie de la Mort dans l'église latine des origines à la réforme carolingienne* (Münster Westfalen, 1978), pp. 353–354. For the changing understanding of *requies* see, in addition to Sicard, *Liturgie de la Mort, passim,* J. Ntedika, *Évocation de l'au-delà dans la Prière pour les Morts. Études de patristique et de liturgie latines. IVe_VIIIe s.* (Louvain, 1971); and more generally Philippe Ariès, *L'Homme devant la Mort* (Paris, 1977), esp. chapter 4. Alcuin's mature conception of the Soul will be found in J. J. M. Curry (ed.), *De Ratione animae* (Cornell University Ph.D. thesis, 1966; University Microfilms Inc., Ann Arbor, 1979), a considerable improvement on Migne, *PL* CI, cc.639–50.

[3] B. Hope-Taylor, *Under York Minster: Archaeological Discoveries 1966–71* (York, 1971); E. Okasha, *Hand-List of Anglo-Saxon Non-runic Inscriptions* (Cambridge, 1971), p. 133 no. 150, and the forthcoming fuller account of the sculptured stones by J. T. Lang (Durham); K. Harrison, 'The pre-Conquest churches of York', *Yorkshire Archaeological Journal,* XL (1960), pp. 232–49, where pp. 241–3 discuss the church of *Alma Sophia* (a unique dedication for an English church), for which the only evidence is Alcuin's poem 'On the Saints of York', new edn by P. Godman (Oxford Medieval Texts, 1982), ll. 1507–20; Alcuin, *Ep.* 209, p. 347. Compare the dedications of the churches forming the cathedral complex at Metz, on which now C. Heitz and F. Heber-Suffrin, *Églises de Metz dans le haut moyen-age* (Paris, 1982).

I Two unique gold solidi of Theodebert I (Prou, nos. 55, 56). See pp. 29–30. The style of the obverses would put their date of minting into the peroid 533–*c*.540. The mint marks have not yet been satis-factorily identified, but the issues may be associated with the king's Italian interests. (*Courtesy: Bibliothèque Nationale, Paris*)

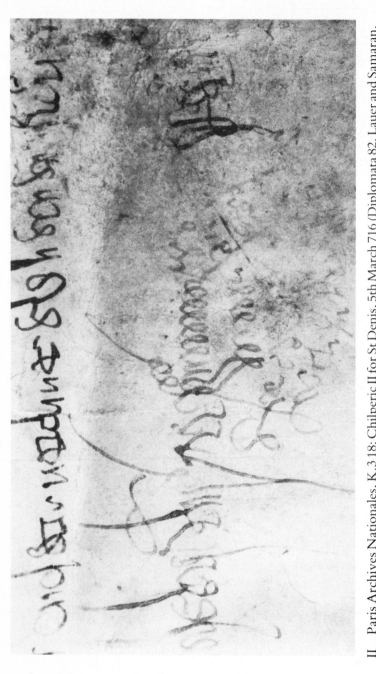

II Paris Archives Nationales, K.3 18: Chilperic II for St Denis, 5th March 716 (Diplomata 82, Lauer and Samaran, 35). See p. 64. The last line reads: 'Chrodobertus recognovit. [In Tironian notes:] *Ch-ro-do-(bertus) decretante Ra-gan-fri-do maiore domus*'. Only the notes reveal the role of Ragenfrid as protector of St Denis. (*Courtesy: Archives Nationales, Paris; photograph by Genevra Kornbluth*)

III Karlsruhe Frag. Aug. 133, f.2 (205 × 167 mm) (*CLA* 1128). See p. 73. Commentary on Donatus, copied in Merovingian cursive and Tironian notes, with frequent ligatures. The text is linked to the Ars Bernensis (ed. H. Hagen, *Anecdota Helvetica Grammatici Latini, VIII* (Leipzig, 1880), pp. 100, 121, 139) and to the Ars Ambianensis. On the composite nature of these two insular grammars see V. Law, *The Insular Latin Grammarians* (Studies in Celtic History, III, Woodbridge, 1982), pp. 67–77. (*Courtesy: Badische Landesbibliothek, Karlsruhe*)

IV Last Judgement (or Christ in Majesty) from the 'Aethelstan Psalter', B. L. Cotton Galba A xviii, f.2v (128 × 88 mm). This miniature, by an Anglo-Saxon hand, was inserted before 939 into a ninth-century Carolingian Psalter which apparently belonged to Aethelstan. It shows Christ surrounded by the instruments of his passion. See pp. 267–8 and E. Temple, *Anglo-Saxon Manuscripts, 900–1066* (London, 1976), no. 5. (*Courtesy: British Library*)

V Christ in Majesty from the 'Aethelstan Psalter' (see plate IV), f.21r.
By a different though contemporary hand from plate IV, it shows the
wound in Christ's side, a most unusual iconographical feature for this
period. Note also the Carolingian acanthus on the frame, foreshadow-
ing the 'Winchester' style of the later tenth century. (*Courtesy: British
Library*)

VI Frontispiece from Corpus Christi College Cambridge MS 183, prose
and verse *Lives* of St Cuthbert, plus Anglo-Saxon royal genealogies,
regnal and episcopal lists, showing King Aethelstan presenting the
book to St Cuthbert (293 × 191 mm) (Temple, *Anglo-Saxon Manuscripts*, no. 6). The earliest presentation picture in English art, its
Carolingian features include an architectural setting in semi-perspective.
See plate VII and pp. 268–9. (*Courtesy: the Master and Fellows of Corpus
Christi, Cambridge*)

VII   Charles the Bald kneeling (before a crucifix on the opposite page) from the 'Gebetbuch Karls des Kahlen', Munich, Schatzkammer Residenz, f.38v (135 × 110 mm). The king's crown and costume is in various ways reminiscent of Aethelstan's, and in the (destroyed) presentation scene from B. L. Cotton Otho B ix Aethelstan was apparently shown kneeling. See p. 269. (*Courtesy: Schatzkammer Residenz, Munich*)

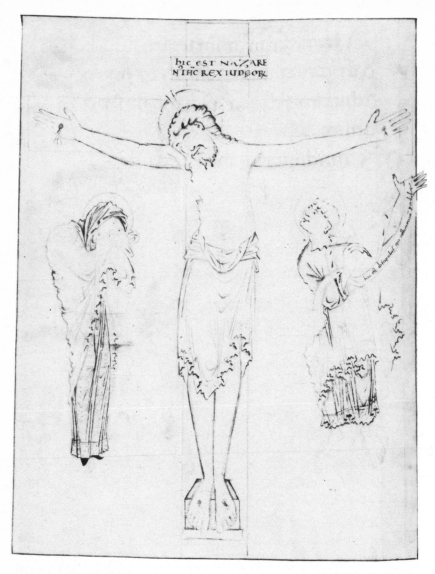

VIII Crucifixion from the Harley Psalter, B. L. Harley MS 2904, f.3v (285 × 242 mm), showing Christ dead on the cross, flanked by the Virgin and St John. The artist responsible for this miniature (probably at Winchester in the last quarter of the tenth century) also did drawings of personified constellations in a Fleury MS containing works of Abbo, reinforcing the connection between Abbo, the school of Aethelwold and the theology here reflected. See pp. 306, 310 and Temple, *Anglo-Saxon Manuscripts*, nos. 41, 42. (*Courtesy: British Library*)

eleventh-century cemeteries associated with other intra-mural, 'parish', churches, the earliest possibly of Alcuin's lifetime.[4]

At Tours, where Alcuin became abbot of St Martin's shortly after writing the letter to the York brethren, he would quickly have been aware of a more complex relationship between cemetery and community. The city's first Christians would normally have been buried, like their contemporaries throughout the Roman Empire, amongst their pagan fellow-citizens in one of the established sepulchral areas beyond the limits of habitation: although (if bishop Gregory is to be trusted on the matter) there was already a cemetery with specifically Christian associations before the 'peace of the Church'.[5] The burial place chosen for the second bishop, Litorius (*ob.* 371?) and the erection of a church over his tomb gave a pre-eminence to a cemetery on the city's western edge which was to endure for some seven centuries, during which time the southern cemetery which provided the epithet for S. Petrus *ad coemeterium* had come into and passed out of use. The burial of Martin in what had previously been an inhabited part of a city now sharply retracted was to have momentous consequences. Bishops after Martin usually chose to be buried in 'his' church where, as the late-fifth-century tomb inscription declared: 'Here he is fully present, made plain in miracles of every kind.' The privilege of burial *ad sanctos* was eagerly sought in the fifth and sixth centuries, prompting for a time adverse comment from the *doctores* but eventually accepted and even encouraged by the hierarchy, subject only to canonical restraint on access to the church itself and 'privatization' of what should be public. At St Martin's by the late sixth century an unknown number of clergy and laity – but surely only a privileged few – had their tombs around or close to the apse of the several times rebuilt church.[6] Bishop Gregory, in the first

[4] Namely, St Mary Bishophill Junior, the provenance of Okasha, *Hand-List*, no. 148 (*ex. inf.* Mr Dominic Tweddle, Assistant Director, York Archaeological Trust), where the text is wrongly described as a pentameter: it is in fact a (bad) hexameter, with a word order that Alcuin would never have used.

[5] Gregory of Tours, *Historiarum Libri Decem* X.31, ed. B. Krusch and W. Levison, *MGH, SRM* I (2), p. 526.

[6] *ibid.* X.31, pp. 526–7, VI.10, pp. 279–80; C. Lelong, 'Evolution de la topographie religieuse de Tours du IVème au VIème siècle', *Bulletin de la Société Archéologique de Touraine*, XXXIV (1965), pp. 169–86; L. Pietri, 'Bâtiments et sanctuaires annexes de la basilique Saint-Martin de Tours à la fin du VIème siècle', *Revue d'Histoire de l'Église de France*, LXXII (1976), pp. 223–34; P. R. L. Brown, 'Relics and Social Status in the Age of Gregory of Tours' (Stenton Lecture; Reading, 1977), repr. in Brown, *Society and the Holy in Late Antiquity* (London, 1982), pp. 222–50.

year of his episcopacy (573/4), introduced relics of a number of saints into the oratory he had founded in his official residence (*domum ecclesiasticam urbis Toronicae*): it is only very much later that there is evidence of burials in the cathedral or in proximity to it, and of a 'cathedral cemetery' there is no trace. Possibly in Gregory's lifetime a monastery was founded in the once inhabited area between St Martin's and the river, on a site occupied in later medieval centuries by the collegiate (parish) church of Saint-Pierre-le-Puellier which inherited its dedication. In the early decades of the tenth century part of the old cemetery of Saint-Lidoire, which until recently had received new burials, was built over in the interests of St Martin's. But later in the same century a small cemetery was established to the north of St Pierre, first fenced, then walled, and then considerably extended in the course of the eleventh century – apparently the earliest 'urban parish' burial ground at Tours.[7]

The change in western Europe from (Roman) suburban to (medieval) intra-mural burial – sudden and dramatic in some instances, as when a saint's relics were publicly translated to a church inside the city; slow and almost imperceptible in others – has been amply documented and commented on in the past thirty years. Historians of architecture, of urban topography and of ecclesiastical organization are now prepared, in spite of the almost infinite number of local variations, to make general statements about causes, character and consequences.[8] By contrast, contemporary or comparable changes in Europe's rural areas, where the mass of the

[7] Gregory, *Liber Vitae Patrum*, II.3: ed. B. Krusch, *MGH,SRM* I, p. 670, cf. *Liber in Gloria Confessorum*, 20: *ibid.*, p. 759; H. Galinié, 'Fouilles archéologiques sur le site de Saint-Pierre-le-Puellier à Tours', *Bulletin de la Société Archéologique de Touraine*, XXXVIII (1976), pp. 155–72; *idem*, 'Archéologie et topographie historique de Tours, IVème – XIème siècle', *Zeitschrift für Archäologie des Mittelalters*, VI (1978), pp. 33–56, esp. pp. 38, 42–3, 48–9.

[8] E. Dyggve, 'L'origine del cimitero entro la cinta della città', *Atti dello VIII Congresso internazionale di Studi Bizantini, 1951*, II (Rome, 1953), pp. 137–41, and R. Krautheimer's review of A. Grabar's *Martyrium* in *Art Bulletin*, XXXV (1953), 57–61, provided the impetus and the guide-lines. Particularly helpful among subsequent studies (all with good references to other literature) are C. Violante and C. D. Fonseca, 'Ubicazione e dedicazione delle Cattedrali delle origini al periodo romanico nelle città dell'Italia centro-settentrionale', *Atti del I° Convegno Internazionale di Studi medioevali di Storia e d'Arte, Pistoia 1964* (Pistoia, s.d.), pp. 303–46; C. N. L. Brooke, 'The ecclesiastical geography of medieval towns', *Miscellanea Historiae Ecclesiasticae V* (Louvain, 1974), pp. 15–31; M. W. Barley (ed.), *European Towns: their Archaeology and Early History* (London, 1977), pt 4, pp. 459–509.

population was born, lived – usually miserably – and died have attracted much less attention. Their end product in this world, the provision for the burial of the ordinary country-dweller – dying with the hope but hardly the expectation of salvation – and the relationship between priest and community that followed from it, are not in doubt. By the end of the eleventh century, if not earlier, most of the inhabitants of the lowland or arable areas of western Europe could expect to be laid to rest in the graveyard of the village church where they had been baptized and had attended mass in their lifetime, or exceptionally in the graveyard of a field-church or chapel subordinate to the parish church in a distant village.[9] The rural cemetery of the earliest Christian-era centuries is visible to the historian in various guises, usually through the evidence of excavation or material evidence (epigraphic or other) surviving above ground and only exceptionally in the written record. Every *Carte Archéologique*, every 'calendar of recent excavations' for any part of the Roman Empire before the Germanic invasions provides at least minimal indications of several sites away from a town or military settlement where the inhabitants of one or more communities have been buried through several generations.[10] In the post-fifth-century western Mediterranean region and in western and northern (Celtic) Britain, their counterparts are more spasmodically and uncertainly recorded: for without distinctive man-made objects in direct association with the dead it is only occasionally possible to establish a date or dates, and almost always impossible to define satisfactorily the social or political context. Over-generous use of ethnic labels is probably the least helpful approach to a fuller understanding. There

---

[9] See, for England, F. Barlow, *The English Church 1000–1066* (2nd edn, London, 1979), pp. 183–208, esp. 195–9, 208, and (for an archaeologist's view) L. Butler, 'The churchyard in eastern England, AD 900–1100', in P. Rahtz, T. Dickinson and L. Watts (eds), *Anglo-Saxon Cemeteries 1979* (BAR British Series LXXXII, 1980), pp. 383–9. The chapter 'The origins of churchyard burial' (in R. Morris's *The Church in British Archaeology* (CBA Research Report 47, 1983), was generously made available to me in manuscript when my own paper was nearly complete: although our approach is somewhat different, the areas of agreement are considerably greater than the areas of disagreement. Compare, for Italy, L. Nanni, *La parrochia studiata nei documenti lucchesi dei secoli VIII–XIII* (Rome, 1948), who however assumes that *plebes baptismales* would invariably have had their own cemetery as early as the eighth/ninth century, when the (extensive) contemporary record is conspicuously silent on the point.

[10] An excellent recent example is in *Britannia*, XII(1980), pp. 177–252 [Leech], cf. pp. 314–68 *passim* [Grew].

is no good reason for attributing the cemeteries of 'head-niche sarcophagi' on the hillsides of northern Lazio (Italy) – at Corviano, Palazzolo (Bomarzo) and elsewhere – to Moors brought in during the Gothic Wars, except on the assumption that the native population (partly, it seems, inhabiting rock-cut villages!) would not have been buried in that way; and there is not much more for attributing the eighty-tomb cemetery at Grancia on the Ombrone (two kilometres from Grosseto) to the Lombards.[11] Peter Brown's characterization of Cimitile, formed around the shrine of Saint Felix, as 'the meeting point of a loose confederacy of hill villages whose importance had grown' at the expense of urban Nola, if not entirely supported by the texts he cites, may have a wider relevance. The extraordinary cemeteries of the Vienne valley (eastern Poitou) and notably Civaux – where the *locus* of holiness was seemingly the imported relics of SS. Gervasius and Protasius – with 10,000 or more burials and Saint-Pierre-les-Églises with well over 5,000 are difficult to account for except on the assumption that they drew to themselves the inhabitants of a wide area of the adjacent uplands. The real puzzle is the economic or social basis of large-scale burial in stone sarcophagi in the seventh century and possibly even later.[12] Their closest, if more modest, counterparts on the other side of the Channel are the very large rural cemeteries of south-west Britain, such as Cannington (Somerset) which has over 1,000 graves extending in time from the second/third to the eighth centuries, and the bigger 'long cist' cemeteries of northern England and southern Scotland. At Cannington the excavator, Professor Rahtz, has detected two foci – the later, the tomb of a young girl covered by a mound marked with a setting of imported stone – and has suggested an original link with a neighbouring hill-fort. The wider context is plausibly the predominantly pastoral economy of both regions in

[11] J. Raspi Serra, 'Una necropoli altomedioevale a Corviano (Bomarzo) ed il problema delle sepolture a "logette" . . . ', *Bolletino d'Arte*, 1976, nos. 1–2 (Jan.–June), pp. 144–69: similar sarcophagi found in two different levels under the cathedral of Santiago di Compostella are characterized by E. Kirschbaum (*Römische Quartalschrift*, LVI, 1961, pp. 234–52) respectively as 'late-Roman' and 'Suebian' (fifth century?); Otto von Hessen, *Primo Contributo alla Archeologia Longobarda in Toscana: le Necropoli* (Florence, 1971), pp. 53–67, 69–79.
[12] P. Brown, *The Cult of the Saints: its Rise and Function in Latin Christianity* (Chicago and London, 1981), p. 43 and n. 98; E. James, *The Merovingian Archaeology of South-West Gaul I* (BAR International Series XXV, 1977), pp. 174–6, *idem*, in Rahtz *et al.*, *Anglo-Saxon Cemeteries*, pp. 48–51.

the late Roman and post-Roman centuries, with a corresponding minimal social differentiation.[13]

Fifth/sixth century Germanic migration into north-west Europe had as one of its consequences the introduction of a new kind of rural or 'field' cemetery (germ. *Feldfriedhof*), often of considerable size and occasionally extending to several thousand graves. Burials are predominantly individually in trenches, less commonly in coffins or stone-lined graves. Some at least of the men were buried with one or more weapons and with other objects, as well as with articles of dress, women with brooches, hairpins, girdles etc. On the European mainland from *c*.500 the larger cemeteries were commonly laid out in more or less regular rows (hence 'row-grave cemeteries'). This regularity seems largely absent from the major English cemeteries, a difference that can no longer be accounted for by unsatisfactory excavation and inadequate recording.[14] A development apparently peculiar to southern England in the late-sixth/early-seventh century is the cemetery 'where most interments are placed beneath small individual mounds'; more or less contemporaneously, and over a much wider area, individual burials began to be made in much larger isolated 'barrows' or in one of a small group of such barrows – most famously, of course, at Sutton Hoo, about the interpretation of which Professor Wallace-Hadrill entered his famous caveats more than twenty years ago.[15] In general,

[13] C. Thomas, *The Early Christian Archaeology of North Britain* (Glasgow, 1971), chapter 3; P. Rahtz, 'Late Roman cemeteries and beyond', in R. Reece (ed.), *Burial in the Roman World* (London, 1977), pp. 53–64; B. Hope-Taylor, *Yeavering: an Anglo-British centre of early Northumbria* (D.O.E. Archaeological Reports, 7; London, 1977), pp. 252–8. For south-western pastoralism see, e.g. W. G. Hoskins, *The Westward Expansion of Wessex* (Leicester, 1960), pp. 4–7. But note that Hope-Taylor *contrasts* the area between Tweed and Forth in which most 'long cist' cemeteries have been found with the more obviously pastoral region to the south (cf. his pp. 10, 16–23) and explains the cemeteries in other social/cultural terms.

[14] E. James, 'Cemeteries and the problem of Frankish settlement in Gaul', in P. H. Sawyer (ed.), *Names, Words and Graves: Early Medieval Settlement* (Leeds, 1979), pp. 55–89: an exceptionally lucid and independent account of seemingly intractable material; Rahtz *et al.*, *Anglo-Saxon Cemeteries*; and the recent descriptions of the Finglesham (Kent) cemetery (n. 39 below).

[15] J. Shephard, 'The social identity of the individual in isolated barrows and barrow cemeteries in Anglo-Saxon England', in B. C. Burham and J. Kingsbury (eds), *Space, Hierarchy and Society* (BAR International Series LIX, 1979), pp. 47–79, the extraordinary opacity of whose language and the somewhat naïve 'correlation' with Kentish documentary evidence does not detract from the interest and importance of his material and of his interpretative techniques; J. M. Wallace-Hadrill,

English cemeteries whose beginnings are datable to the sixth or early seventh centuries are not merely more numerous but smaller than those beginning earlier; and there is some evidence for a comparable, if not precisely simultaneous, development in parts of Francia.[16] Many, perhaps most, of the early English burial places are on an elevated site and often on or near what is later documented as an estate- or parish-boundary. (The inference that these boundaries were therefore one of pre-existing estates is not one that seems self-evident to the mere historian: and latterly a more pragmatic, economic, 'model' has been favoured by some archaeologists, namely, the location of cemeteries on relatively poor land, marginal to an arable settlement.) In the Benelux and northern French regions of Merovingian Francia, 'row-grave' and other cemeteries seem similarly often to have been on high ground away from the settlements they served, and particularly on the south-facing river slopes.[17] The later (seventh/eighth century) 'field' cemeteries, where datable, are generally more poorly furnished than earlier ones: many in Francia show a growing carelessness in the opening-up and disposition of new tombs, some in England of greater carelessness in the actual burial sc. the laying-out, of the corpse.[18]

'The graves of kings: an historical note on some archaeological evidence' [1960], in *EMH*, pp. 39–59, pp. 53–56 constituting a 'Postscript' of second thoughts.

[16] Dickinson in Rahtz *et al.*, *Anglo-Saxon Cemeteries*, pp. 21–27; James in *ibid.*, p. 40, citing a 1974 paper of F. Stein which I have not seen.

[17] D. J. Bonney, 'Pagan Saxon burials and boundaries in Wiltshire', *Wilts. Archaeological and Natural History Magazine*, LXI (1966), pp. 25–30; *idem*, 'Early boundaries and estates in southern England', in P. H. Sawyer (ed.), *Medieval Settlement* (London, 1976), pp. 72–82: but location near (which apparently can mean as much as 500 metres away) and on a precisely defined boundary, especially when the latter is on higher ground but on similar soil, are *not* comparable phenomena, and see now C. J. Arnold and P. Wardle, 'Early medieval settlement patterns in England', *Medieval Archaeology*, XXV (1981), pp. 145–9; James, in Sawyer, *Names, Words and Graves*, p. 60. South-facing slopes also seem to be favoured for contemporary cemeteries in Bavaria except along the line of the Danube below Regensburg: see U. Koch, *Die Grabfunde der Merowingerzeit aus dem Donautal um Regensburg* (2 vols, Berlin, 1968). Does this mean anything more, however, than that the settlements which the cemeteries served were established wherever possible on south-facing slopes? The north bank of this part of the Danube was not 'colonized' until the Carolingian period.

[18] B. Young, 'Paganisme, christianisation et rites funéraires mérovingiens', *Archéologie Médiévale*, VII (1977), pp. 5–81, esp. pp. 24–29, 63–5; Meaney in A. L. Meaney and S. C. Hawkes, *Two Anglo-Saxon Cemeteries at Winnall* (Society for Medieval Archaeology, 1970), pp. 29–33. Since in what follows I shall be drawing attention to divergences from Dr Young's interpretations rather than

Only in some areas of the Rhine and in Bavaria does well-furnished burial continue into the eighth century, and in the second-named region it ends quite abruptly in the middle years.[19] By inference, the almost universal abandonment of cemeteries in open country in the (late) seventh and eighth centuries was linked with a widespread adoption of churchyard burials, encouraged if not actually enforced by the clergy.

It has long been recognized that the archaeological evidence for Merovingian and early Anglo-Saxon burial practice fits very ill with the narrative accounts of the conversion of, and organizing a territorial Church among, the invaders of western Romania. *Historiae* and laws are alike indifferent to the phenomenon and, seemingly, to the pressures making for change. Gregory of Tours' writings are, it is true, 'full of tombs', not only in city churches and 'dormitory suburbs of the dead' but also in deserted and living *vici*: in country as well as town, however, they have attracted attention because they provide the setting for some saintly *memoria* which brings healing to the sick and the disturbed. Bede, formed from childhood in a pattern of living and thought far removed from the values of the Gallo-Roman *civitates*, takes us intermittently into the villages of Northumbria but is silent on the places – although not entirely on the manner – of the burial of their dead. The Lindisfarne *Vita Cuthberti*, as well as Bede's revised version, shows the Saint ministering to country distincts both before and after his promotion to the bishopric of Lindisfarne: yet none of his pastoral acts or miracles is linked with any burial place or tomb except, finally, his own.[20] References to graves and burial places in the pre-Carolingian Germanic law-codes are few and predominantly concerned with grave-robbing. They are hardly more frequent, although more

views in common, I should emphasize here that his paper is a major contribution to a better understanding of Merovingian cemetery material which has opened up many new perspectives, not least for myself.

[19] F. Stein, *Adelsgräber des 8. Jahrhunderts in Deutschland* (Berlin, 1967); *idem*, 'Pre-Carolingian graves in south Germany', *Journal of the British Archaeological Association*, ser. 3, XXXI (1968), pp. 1–18.

[20] Brown, 'Relics and social status', the quotations from p. 223; *HE* V.4, V.5, pp. 286–9; the *loculus* in which the thegn's servant was to be buried, in the second of these passages, is clearly a coffin and not merely a grave, which confirms other evidence that coffin burial is not in itself evidence of superior social standing; *corpus defuncti fratris sepeliendum in carro deferrent*: Bede, *Vita Cuthberti* 34, ed. B. Colgrave (1940), p. 264; ministering in country districts: *Vit. Cuth.* II.5, 6, IV *passim, ibid.* pp. 84–7, 112–22; miracles at his tomb: *ibid.* IV.15, 16, 17, pp. 132–8.

varied, in the longer series of Anglo-Saxon laws; and the several
times quoted 'instruction contained in a letter of Boniface to
Ethelbald that the illegitimate children of nuns and other harlots
should be buried in *tumuli*' is a misunderstanding based on a mis-
translation.[21] There is something of the contradiction here,
the seeming lack of any cultural synchrony, implicit in the juxtaposition of the *Beowulf*-poem and Bede's *Historia Ecclesiastica* which
Mr Patrick Wormald has come nearest to resolving in a remarkable
paper.[22]

Just as one school of literary critics and historians has tried to
provide an *interpretatio Christiana* (although by no means always the
same interpretation) of the poem, so current interpretations (usually
referred to as 'models') of 'post-conversion' Merovingian and
Anglo-Saxon cemeteries simultaneously seek evidence of changes in
the disposition of the dead and refer to the continuing force of
'popular religious mentality' or – less commonly now – simply to
'pagan survivals'.[23] Implicit here is that there was a Christian conception of burial, as distinct from a Christian view of the after-life and
the means to its attainment, and definable Christian burial practices
to be set against non-Christian concepts and rites. In fact, the early
Church showed itself surprisingly indifferent to where Christians
were laid to rest, and that in spite of its adoption of the distinctive
new term *coemeterium* – the first to acquire general currency for a
burial *area*. St Peter and other early martyrs were buried and
venerated among the unconverted. Around Rome and some North
African cities land was indeed acquired and set apart as a 'cemetery':
but the primary reasons were practical and charitable, the need to

[21] The laws dealing with grave-robbery are collected and discussed by H. Nehlsen,
'Der Grabfrevel in den germanischen Rechtsaufzeichnungen . . .', in H. Jankuhn *et
al.* (eds), *Zur Grabfrevel in vor- u. frühgeschichtlicher Zeit*, (Göttingen, 1978),
pp. 107–68; for the earliest references to graves in the Anglo-Saxon laws see
below, p. 195. Boniface's letter 73, *MGH,Ep.Sel.* I, ed. M. Tangl, p. 151 is
attacking the infanticide that nearly always follows illegitimate birth – on which he
was almost certainly correct – *with the consequence that* instead of churches being
filled with the adoptive children graves are filled with corpses and hell with
unhappy souls: in eighth-century texts a *tumulus* can be any sort of burial place.
[22] P. Wormald, 'Bede, "Beowulf" and the conversion of the Anglo-Saxon
aristocracy', in R. T. Farrell (ed.), *Bede and Anglo-Saxon England* (BAR XLVI,
1978, pp. 32–95; cf. Wormald above, pp. 102–3.
[23] Young, 'Paganisme, christianisation et rites funéraires', esp. pp. 5–12, 53–66;
P. J. Geary, 'Zur problematik der Interpretation archäologischer Quellen für die
Geistes- u. Religionsgeschichte', *Archaeologia Austriaca*, LXIV (1980), pp. 111–18.

provide for those members of the community who had not the resources to provide for their own or their family's fitting burial. *Saepultura in cymiterio christianorum* in the Marseilles synodal *acta* of 533 is specifically in relation to those who have been lawfully executed, but are not therefore to be excluded from the company of their fellow-Christians in death.[24] A much-discussed letter of Sidonius Apollinaris reveals that his grandfather, 'the first of his line to renounce pagan worship', had none the less been buried on a (rural) site which, when the letter was written, 'had for a long time been so filled up with both ashes from the pyres and with bodies that there was no more room for digging'. His horror at the disturbance of an ancestor's tomb, even unwittingly, was shared by the bishops assembled at Macon more than a century later, when they decreed that corpses forced into the graves of others without the permission of the *domini sepulchrorum* (a traditional Roman legal term but here almost certainly referring to surviving kindred) were to be removed.[25] Indeed, it has been powerfully argued that the severe penalties laid down for the destruction or robbery of graves in many of the Germanic and Romano-Germanic law-codes are not a survival from the supposedly sacral character of pre-Migration burial places but an illustration of the impact of Roman legal thinking, mediated through the Church, on barbarian lawmakers.[26] Burial is a matter of public concern in defence of private or kin-right, not of theological principle.

[24] Pre-Christian Latin prefers to speak of the individual tomb, although Catullus (and no-one else?) uses *sepulchretum* for 'burial area'. *Coemeterium*, from the Greek for 'sleeping-chamber', occurs first in Tertullian: but as a glance at any Medieval Latin dictionary or word-list will show, it is much rarer in early medieval texts than one might suppose – as I believe, because the 'church graveyard' was itself uncommon (and in parts of Celtic Britain, if we believe Charles Thomas, alternative words may have existed: *Early Christian Archaeology*, pp. 85–9, where, however, his account of *cella* in early medieval texts is seriously wrong). For the first specifically Christian cemeteries in the W. Mediterranean region see, most conveniently, R. Krautheimer, *Early Christian and Byzantine Architecture* (London, 1965), pp. 4–14 and notes: and compare Gregory of Tours, *Historiarum Libri* X.31, p. 526, for Gatian of Tours' supposed burial *in ipsius vici cimiterio qui erat christianorum*; at least one third-century bishop created trouble for himself by maintaining family membership of a convivial pagan burial club: see H. Chadwick, *Priscillian of Avila* (Oxford, 1976), p. 1, n. 1. The 533 Marseilles *acta* are ed. C. de Clercq, *Concilia Galliae A.511–A.695*, CCSL CXLVIII A, pp. 84–103, here p. 95.
[25] Sidonius, *Ep.* III.12, ed. F. Luetjohann, *MGH,AA* VIII, pp. 47–8; *Concilia Galliae*, p. 246 (c. 17); see further K. H. Krüger and O. Behrends in Jankuhn, *Zur Grabfrevel* pp. 172–4 (Sidonius' letter), 85–106 (Roman law generally).
[26] Nehlsen, 'Der Grabfrevel', n. 21.

Pagans and Christians did not always draw the line between the sacred and the secular, the permissible and the forbidden, at different points. Sacrifices were unlawful for Christians, ritual meals and recurrent libations at or over the tombs of the dead were not: there is ample archaeological and textual evidence for their continuance in many parts of southern Europe well into the sixth century and perhaps even to the time of Gregory the Great and beyond. An aphorism of St Augustine, pastor as well as theologian, would have been familiar to any reader of the early chapters of the *De Civitate Dei*: a funeral is more a solace to the living than a benefit to the dead.[27] The (rare) depositing of cooked or uncooked food in northern European burials of the sixth or seventh century may be – in the light of a later folkloric evidence – not a part of the provision for the dead man's last and most terrible journey but a symbolic sharing of a final meal with the living who accompany him to his place of burial.[28] The most categoric eighth-century statement of the corporeal, material, needs of the dead is in an unequivocally Christian context. The Lindisfarne *Vita Cuthberti* declares that the deceased bishop 'was robed in his priestly garments, *wearing his shoes in readiness to meet Christ* ("in obviam Christi calciamentis suis praeparatus") and provided with a wax shroud'. I can find no earlier instance of such a statement and Amalarius includes the entire passage in his *Liber Officialis* – with an erroneous attribution to Bede – in the next century but it is unlikely to be original to the anonymous author: in the thirteenth century Durandus records that some say (*quidem dicunt*) that the dead should be laid to rest in hose and slippers *ut per hoc ipsos esse paratos ad iudicium repraesentur.*[29] Sixth/seventh-century conciliar disapproval of the burial of the dead in ecclesiastical vestments or imitations of them – an exaggerated interpretation of being fittingly clad for the tomb, perhaps –

---

[27] Krautheimer, *Early Christian and Byzantine Architecture*, pp. 4–10 and notes; Augustine, *De Civitate Dei*, ed. E. Hoffmann, CSEL, XL (Vienna, 1899), p. 24: but the context in which the statement is made should be read in its entirety.
[28] Young, 'Paganisme, christianisation et rites funéraires', pp. 38–40, has the main references.
[29] *Vita* IV.13, p. 130; for the *oblata super sanctum pectus posita*, ibid., cf. Young, 'Paganisme, christianisme et rites funéraires', pp. 40–43; and note that Bede omits this entire passage; Amalarius, ed. J. M. Hanssens, *Studi e Testi*, CXXXIX (Vatican, 1948), p. 531; G. Durandus, *Rationale Divinorum Officiorum* (ed. pr. 1459), VII, c. 35. For other evidence of shoes (down to the twentieth century!) see N. Kyll, *Tod, Grab, Begräbnisplatz, Totenfeier* (Bonn, 1972), pp. 24–5.

seems to be just that. It was not shared by the monks who prepared the body of Cuthbert, nor by many after them.[30] Not surprisingly we shall look in vain for disapproval or prohibition of burial of laymen and women in their appropriate finery in the Merovingian and early English councils or in those who, from Caesarius of Arles to Boniface, preached and wrote against 'superstitious practices' – fertility rituals, divination, phylacteries and the like.

A clear distinction between 'pagan' and Christian burial grounds has commonly been identified as the consecration of those in the second group, which came increasingly to have a well-defined precinct.[31] Some direct and more indirect evidence suggests, however, that both notion and practice developed only in the Carolingian period. Eighth-century sacramentaries, although providing formulae for *missae in cymeteriis*, and the earliest *ordines* give no hint of the existence of a consecration rite for burial grounds; and there is little or no textual support for the exclusiveness of use which would seem to be its most obvious corollary. Mr Wormald, it is true, has drawn attention to a section of the Penitential attributed to Theodore which he believes 'specifies that when churches are converted, the *cadavera infidelium* interred therein are to be flung out.' This is hardly what the text says. The context is a discussion of the problems that arise when a wooden *ecclesia* where the unbaptized have been buried (in later terminology, a chapel or oratory) must be moved to a new site and/or an altar consecrated so that masses can be celebrated there; where, however, there is already a consecrated altar masses may be said even if religious men are buried there; but if a pagan is there it is better to cleanse it and throw (it? him?) out. Certainly there is no notion here of the redemptive power of prayer for those who had died unbaptized: but Theodore, or the person using his name, apparently envisages a modest equivalent of the old Roman 'cemeterial basilicas', not intended for regular liturgical worship, in cemeteries whose development began in the pagan period and remained unconsecrated.[32] Texts for the ceremony of

[30] *Concilia Galliae*, p. 106 (c. 3) (*s.a.* 535), p. 267 (c. 13) (*s.a.* 561/605).

[31] So, e.g., Thomas, *Early Christian Archaeology*, chapter 3; Hawkes, *Anglo-Saxon Cemeteries at Winnall*, pp. 50–5; R. Bruce-Mitford, *The Sutton Hoo Ship-Burial*, I (London, 1975), pp. 709–13 and esp. p. 713: 'The Christian Church, as we have seen, insisted [?] on the burial of the bodies of Christian royalties in consecrated ground.'

[32] Cf. *The Gelasian Sacramentary*, ed. H. A. Wilson, (Oxford, 1894), III.103, 104, pp. 310–12, with Sicard, *Liturgie de la Mort*, pp. 279–378 *passim*; M. Andrieu, *Les*

benedictio (or *consecratio*) *cymeterii* are not to be found in the earliest
Pontificals; when they first occur, in the early tenth century, form
and language alike point to a Carolingian origin.[33]

Alternative or complementary evidence of the impact of 'conversion' on ordinary community burial has been sought and found in
the orientation of graves, in the strict sense of their alignment along
a west–east axis, specifically with feet to the east. Evidence of the
same practice in various parts of old *Romania* at too early a date for
Christianity to be a convincing explanation, and the evident indifference to alignment that characterizes the major Christian urban
cemeteries of Provence and elsewhere in southern Europe in the
fifth century, are both arguably irrelevant to northern Europe in
the sixth and seventh centuries: at this period the (approximate)
orientation of churches was normal, especially on unencumbered
sites, although by no means universal.[34] But the central argument
latterly deployed in support of a Christian interpretation of
cemetery practice is hardly favourable to it. The alignment of
graves excavated at the early East Anglian mission centre at Burgh
Castle, in a supposedly post-conversion phase at Finglesham

Ordines Romani du Haut Moyen Age, II–IV (Louvain, 1946–51). Accounts of or
references to the consecration of village churches in, e.g., the *Vitae Cuthberti*,
Bede's *HE*, the *Hodoeporicon Willibaldi* by the nun Hugeberc (*MGH, SS* XV/1,
pp. 80–117) and other eighth-century *hagiographica* never allude – so far as I can see
– to the consecration of graveyards, unlike later *Vitae* such as that of Wulfstan of
Worcester, which has a splendid account of why a village cemetery was *not* in fact
consecrated (ed. R. R. Darlington, Camden Series, 1928, pp. 40–1). For the
Theodore text see P. Finsterwalder, *Die Canones Theodori Cantuariensis u. ihre
Überlieferungsformen* (Weimar, 1929), p. 312 and compare Wormald, 'Bede,
"Beowulf" and the conversion of the aristocracy', p. 46.

[33] For the main references, see below, p. 199. At no time, except possibly in the
later Middle Ages and Counter-Reformation period, has the consecration of
cemeteries seemed of any great importance and its title in modern Rituals is
simply 'Benediction'. Anglican Rituals prescribe that a bishop will walk the
bounds saying Psalms or other suitable texts: but the late bishop Barry of South-
well was once heard by his chaplain, who was striving to keep up with him,
muttering 'Half a league, half a league, half a league onward . . .'

[34] See, among other recent contributions, Young, 'Paganisme, christianisation et
rites funéraires', pp. 16–24; P. Rahtz, 'Grave orientation', *Archaeological Journal*,
CXXXV (1978), pp. 1–14 (thoughtful and cautious in its interpretations). For the
urban cemeteries of Provence, where the alignment of tombs was determined – if
at all – by the layout of pre-existing structures, see F. Benoît, 'Cimetières de
Provence', *Cahiers Archéologiques*, II (1947), pp. 7–15. Late Anglo-Saxon burials
on the Minster site at York continued to follow the alignment of Roman buildings
in the area.

(Kent), and in parts of the Cannington cemetery – argued, be it said, without prejudice to alternative explanations – has been explained in terms of the observable azimuth of sunrise which changes daily between the two solstices.

It is implicit here that a wake or watch was maintained at the intending place of burial until the sun rose.[35] Pre-Carolingian evidence for the time of Christian burial and for the venue of any watch (*excubiae funeris*) is not great: but it is incompatible with any such practice as archaeologists are postulating. Narrative sources and *ordines* agree that burial on the day of death was normal, burial on the following day an exceptional alternative – for religious. The relevant section of Theodore's Penitential explicitly follows 'Roman custom': the corpses of monks and clergy are taken into church when they are anointed with chrism and a mass celebrated for them; they are then carried out for burial. There are no corresponding provisions for laity, for whom however commemorative masses may be offered on the third or later days, preferably after a period of fasting by the dead man's kindred. A late eighth-century Frankish adaptation of a Roman *ordo* which does have laity in mind provides that if Sunday burial is unavoidable it must not be before the fourth hour, priest and *parentes* then fasting until the ninth hour. All the evidence for wakes, and the preparation of the corpse which preceded them, is that they took place in the home of the deceased, from which his body was then taken to the place of burial in daylight and in the public gaze.[36] A residual explanation

[35] C. Wells and C. Green, 'Sunrise dating of death and burial', *Norfolk Archaeology*, XXXV (1973), pp. 435–42; S. C. Hawkes, 'Orientation at Finglesham: sunrise dating of death and burial . . .', *Archaeologia Cantiana*, XCII (1976), pp. 33–51; P. Rahtz in Reece, *Burial in the Roman World*, pp. 56–59, and *idem*, 'Grave Orientation', pp. 6–9.

[36] The incomparable Charles Plummer noted the evidence from early England and from contemporary Rome for burial on the day of death: Plummer, II, Index p. 432 *s.vv.*; it is implicit in Ordo XLIX, Andrieu, *Ordines Romani*, IV, pp. 529–30, while a ninth-century East Frankish *agenda mortuorum* says explicitly *in ipso depositionis die vel in altero*: H. Frank, 'Der älteste erhaltene Ordo Defunctorum der römischen Liturgie u. sein Fortleben in den Totenagenden des frühen Mittelalters', *Archiv. f. Liturgiewissenschaft*, VII (1961/2), pp. 360–415, here p. 395; Theodore, ed. Finsterwalder, p. 318 (*secundum Romanam ecclesiam mos*), p. 319; Ordo XV in Andrieu, *Ordines Romani*, III, p. 122 (c. 131): but note also that the third of the *carraria opera* permitted on a Sunday in the *Admonitio generalis* of 789, c. 81 (*MGH, Capit.* I. p. 61) is *si forte necesse erit corpus cuiuslibet ducere ad sepulcrum*; and for the specific documentation of the burial of a layman *in ipso die* in the early ninth century, see below, p. 200. The exceptions seem to be Irish, notably Adomnan's account of the three days and nights' *rite exequiae* which preceded Columba's burial

which would postulate a single gravedigger keeping lonely vigil with his measuring rods until the sun rose may fairly be left to the pseudo-Druids awaiting the summer solstice at Stonehenge.

Ground might be made holy by association, and therefore eagerly sought after by other Christians as a place of burial: but this is something quite different. Seventh-century kings of Kent, like their Merovingian contemporaries and many of their predecessors, were laid to rest in the *porticus* of a suburban church, an option not yet available to kings of the East Angles at the most likely date of Sutton Hoo. The Northumbrian *praefectus* Hildemer, in Bede's account of the Life of Cuthbert (but not in the Lindisfarne *Vita*), sought to have his deranged and dying wife buried with the bishop's permission *in locis sanctis*, presumably at Lindisfarne itself. This privilege would have been even more widely available if it were certain that the lay-burials revealed by excavation at Benedict Biscop's monastic sites belonged to the period when their *vita regularis* flourished.[37]

The early medieval Church, concerned with 'the judgement', Salvation and the means of its attainment – baptism and the prayers of the living supported by the intervention of the very special dead, the *sancti* – was largely indifferent to rites and modes of burial (except as regards cremation), and even confirmed their private or familiar character by Roman-influenced conciliar and secular legislation. They therefore functioned within a framework of values on which theological doctrine and ecclesiastical discipline barely impinged. What, then, were the dynamics of a change that in the eighth and ninth centuries brought the majority of *rustici* into burial grounds around or adjacent to the churches where they had worshipped in their lives?

The evidence must come for the most part from the 'field' cemeteries themselves, whose supposedly 'sacral' character is

---

(although a storm kept away people who would otherwise have crossed to Iona), *Vita Columbae*, ed. A. O. and M. O. Anderson (Edinburgh, 1961), p. 536. Adomnan declares these rites were properly conducted *more ecclesiastico*: was Theodore's *secundum Romanam ecclesiasticam mos* a deliberate counter to Irish practice?

[37] K. H. Krüger, *Königsgrabkirchen der Franken, Angelsachsen u. Langobarden bis zur Mitte des 8 Jh.* (Münster, 1971), esp. pp. 264–89, 40–54, 103–24; Bede, *Vita Cuthberti*, 15, p. 204; R. Cramp, 'Monastic sites', in *The Archaeology of Anglo-Saxon England*, ed. D. M. Wilson (London, 1976), pp. 201–52, here esp. p. 231, and cf. pp. 245–6 for Glastonbury.

unproved and unprovable. Certainly, no argument can be drawn from their spatial separation from the nearest existing village. The English evidence has recently invited the comment that: 'An important factor which has been overlooked . . . is that not only are pagan Anglo-Saxon cemeteries frequently located near parish boundaries, but so also are the excavated contemporary settlements'; and in northern and eastern Francia a sampling of several score cemeteries on elevated sites suggests that distances of 200–400 metres from the communities they may be supposed to have served were the norm.[38] Carefully conducted excavations of burials in western Germany and eastern France in recent decades and the reconsideration of 'rural' cemeteries excavated earlier have shown that in a significant number of instances the larger cemeteries whose use spans the sixth century or extends into the seventh began in the last years of the fifth century or the opening decades of the sixth with a distinctively rich burial or burials; the paradigm is the cemetery of Krefeld-Gellep (Ruhr) and its grave no. 1782. From this point subsequent burials (a few well-furnished, many more with few and modest objects accompanying the skeleton) spread 'like the rings around the heart of a tree': at times this chronological wave-motion may be disturbed by grave-clusters which are commonly interpreted as 'family groups'; and a stricter alignment may be imposed on the later graves. Finglesham, expanding southwards and down-slope from the richly furnished grave of a male who died at about the age of twenty-five within a few years of 525, provides a striking English parallel.[39] These lavishly endowed nuclear burials, whose model among the Franks is probably to be sought in royal

[38] Arnold and Wardle, 'Settlement patterns', p. 145; my own sampling, using such French publications as have been available to me, the excellent site maps in appropriate volumes of the *Führer zu vor- u. frühgeschichtlichen Denkmälern* (Mainz, 1950 et seq.) and volumes of the *Germanische Denkmäle der Völkerwanderungszeit* (Berlin): sites 'as much as a kilometre from the nearest settlement' (James, in Sawyer, *Names, Words and Graves*, p. 69) seem to me very much the exception.
[39] The Frankish evidence is excellently summarized, with reference to the major literature, by James, in Sawyer, *Names, Words and Graves*, pp. 82–4 and by H. Steuer, *Frühgeschichtlicher Sozialstrukturen in Mitteleuropa* (Göttingen, 1982), pp. 342–92: for Krefeld-Gellep no. 1782 see R. Pirling, 'Ein fränkisches Fürstengrab aus Krefeld-Gellep', *Germania*, XLII (1964), pp. 188–216; for the sequence of rich graves in the later-sixth-century phases of the cemetery (notably nos. 2268, 2259) see most conveniently M. Todd's review in *Britannia*, XII (1981), p. 419. Finglesham: S. C. Hawkes, 'The Anglo-Saxon cemetery at Finglesham', *Medieval Archaeology*, II (1958), pp. 1–71; idem, 'Orientation'; idem, in *The Anglo-Saxons*, ed. J. Campbell (Oxford, 1982), pp. 24–5.

burial (e.g. that of Childeric), are best understood as the deliberate removal from circulation of accumulated wealth – 'conspicuous waste' – to demonstrate to the living the superior social standing and, in some cases, authority of the dead man and his kin.

That these early 'rich' burials are almost always intact even in cemeteries where there is ample evidence of grave robbery in the later phases can be explained in several different ways. Either there were no visible indications of the position of the first grave(s), or the kin of the founder (*domini sepulchrorum?*) exercised authority over other users through several generations, or the robbery for which such severe penalties were prescribed in the sixth century ceased to be socially unacceptable subsequently and was normally perpetrated against recent deposits.[40] The first explanation is clearly excluded where, as at Finglesham, the grave was marked by a massive mound – a demonstration of status long outlasting first-hand memory of the 'treasure' and its deposit; the second may not be, even in those cemeteries where (as again at Finglesham) there are implications of social change in the extended imitative use there of smaller barrows over less-well-furnished graves during the seventh century. It is certainly an acceptable interpretation of the similar barrow cemeteries elsewhere in southern England that a numeri-cally larger social group, which had none the less accumulated adequate resources for that purpose, was making the same kind of public demonstration of status that had previously been, or else-where in the country was, the prerogative of a (?narrower and) wealthier group: and that, without regard for or relevance to religi-ous affiliation.[41]

The notion taken over by some archaeologists from anthropologi-cal thought that a burial rite which offered the possibility of con-tinuous reference to ancestors was one way of asserting claims to scarce resources on a basis of heredity has no obvious support in early English (or Frankish) texts; nor has the idea found in other societies that burial on a boundary is itself a safeguard of descendants' rights.[42] Yet the former is certainly compatible with

[40] On the latter, see H. Roth, 'Archäologische Beobachtungen zum Grabfrevel im Merowingerreich', in Jankuhn, *Zur Grabfrevel*, pp. 53–84.
[41] J. Shephard, in Burnham and Kingsbury, *Space, Hierarchy and Society*, esp. pp. 70–7.
[42] See P. Ucko, 'Ethnography and archaeological interpretation of funerary re-mains', *World Archaeology*, I (1969), pp. 262–80; J. Tainter, 'Mortuary practices and the study of prehistoric social systems', in ed. M. Schiffer, *Advances in*

the missionary church's active concern – so illuminated by Mr Eric John more than twenty years ago – to find ways of guaranteeing the perpetual alienation of land and rights from a kindred whose members had prior claims to it. The earliest two references to graves in the Anglo-Saxon law-codes, which even on the most sceptical view of the antiquity of their provisions must be held to go back to the pagan period, do indeed link them with kin-right and property. Aethelbert's code, c.22, declares that the first twenty shillings of the hundred-shilling *wergeld* of a (free) man is to be paid *aet openum graefe*. The reason is entirely practical. The kin who have accompanied the body will still be there: a payment on account before they turn from lamenting the slain will, or should, triumph over vendetta; for those who fail to make this preliminary payment the risks of the latter and the potential threat to the entire community are immeasurably increased. Could grave-goods other than items of personal adornment sometimes have been the form in which such payments were made?[43]

Rather more ambiguous is a provision in the code of Ine of Wessex: a man found in possession of a slave he has bought from a third party may 'vouch the dead man's grave to warranty'. It must be assumed that the grave of a dead man (although not of a long-dead man) has some distinctive feature that allows it to be identified; and it is apparent that in late seventh-century Wessex a cemetery may be the proper setting for a public, legal, transaction. There may be some sacral element here; but essentially it is the truth of the oath that the unwitting purchaser puts to the judgment of a spiritual power; and those who wrote down Ine's laws would certainly have identified that power exclusively with the Christian God.[44]

Their Church in the World – Gregory's Church, Bede's Church –

Archaeological Method and Theory, I (New York, 1978), pp. 105–41; Shephard, in Burnham and Kingsbury, *Space, Hierarchy and Society*, p. 77. Early Irish evidence for boundary-burial as a protection of kin-right is considered by T. Charles-Edwards, 'Boundaries in early Irish law', in Sawyer, *Medieval Settlement*, pp. 83–7, with the striking comment on p. 86 that: 'Relegated to the graveyards of churches the dead lost their power to defend the land which they left to their heirs.'

[43] Abt. 22, *Gesetze,* I, p. 4. Note that Mr P. Grierson has explained the Crondall 'hoard' of gold coins (C. H. V. Sutherland, *Anglo-Saxon Gold Coinage in the Light of the Crondall Hoard*, Oxford, 1948) – found with jewellery now lost and presumably from a grave – as a '100-shilling wergeld', one piece being removed from a necklace to make the sum complete: *Numismatics* (Oxford, 1975), pp. 131–2.

[44] In.53, *Gesetze*, pp. 112–13.

was now offering itself as an alternative destination for accumulated wealth, in forms that even more clearly than the traditional ones perpetuated the reputation of the giver and could make lasting provision for his kinsfolk: Benedict Biscop's concern that hereditary right might be asserted when his communities came to choose a new abbot, and the eighth-century concern with abusive 'family monasteries', are familiar themes. A lead given by monarchs, in the choice of places for ostentatious burial as well as for endowment, could be and was taken up by their *leudes* and *optimates* and in turn by men of lesser although still 'landed' status. There was not necessarily a sharp break between the old ways and the new. Examples of fully-dressed burials with an ample range of precious objects *under* churches are now known from southern Belgium to Alamannian Switzerland: most are seventh-century; and if we accept the most careful and convincing cluster-analysis of grave-finds as evidence of relative wealth and status, they coincide with a decline in the frequency of such clusters in 'field' cemeteries.[45] The relationship between burial and church is not always the same: in some cases they may genuinely be the graves of the founders, although one of the most celebrated examples, Morken (because of its helmet) almost certainly is not.[46]

In England a royal precedent, an example to be imitated, has been found in the supposed early foundation of churches and even churchyards in royal *vici* or *villae*: but there is no certainty how the 'old minsters' of Kent, with their extensive territorial responsibilities in the late Anglo-Saxon period, correspond to the early estate centres and *regiones* of its kings. Eastry, where Mrs Hawkes suggests the successors of the founders of Finglesham were buried, was such a royal centre (later a manor of the church of Canterbury)

---

[45] Stein, *Adelsgräber*, esp. pp. 118–24; R. Christlein, 'Besitzabstufungen zur Merowingerzeit im Spiegel reicher Grabfunde aus West- u. Suddeutschland', *Jahrbuch des Römisch-Germanischen Zentralmuseums, Mainz*, XX (1973), pp. 147–80; idem, 'Merowingerzeitliche Grabfunde unter der Pfarrkirche St. Dionysius zu Dettingen, Kr. Tübingen, u. verwandte Denkmäle in Süddeutschland', *Fundberichte aus Baden-Württemberg*, I (1974), pp. 573–96; a summary with references to further literature in Steuer, *Frühgeschichtlicher Sozialstrukturen*, pp. 393–400: and add the unique example from western France (Touraine), under the parish church of Perrusson (Indre-et-Loire), published by C. Lelong in *Archéologie Mediévale*, VI (1976), pp. 219–32, and discussed there without reference to comparable examples elsewhere in Francia.
[46] H. Hinz, *Die Ausgrabungen auf dem Kirchberg in Morken, Kreis Bergheim (Erft)* (Düsseldorf, 1969), esp. pp. 63–75, 113–20.

but was not one of those minsters; while the identification of one of the structures and associated enclosure from the later phases at Yeavering as a church with churchyard remains a bold and unproven hypothesis. Textual evidence for thegnly foundation of village churches has not, I think, been matched by evidence of 'rich graves': unless we suppose that the Taplow barrow – once, perhaps, second only to Sutton Hoo in lavishness – was deliberately included within a (subsequent) churchyard.[47] The hypothesis that precious metals earlier destined for the tomb were diverted directly into the making of church ornaments and vessels, however plausible in itself, is necessarily undemonstrable.[48] Examples of churches (or oratories) constructed in older cemeteries that were still in use are not numerous and often disputable, but they are clearly demanded by the passage already quoted from Theodore's Penitential. They are apparently not uncommon in parts of Francia, such as the diocese of Trier and further west, although interestingly they only rarely develop later into 'parish' churches.[49]

The pressures and justification for burial in the vicinity of a church in an estate centre, usually with baptismal rights, were considerable. Imitation of urban practice may have played a part in

[47] The substance of the remarks in the text about the Kentish 'minsters' and their relation to royal estates has been kindly provided by my colleague Dr N. P. Brooks: for a detailed examination of the evidence see his *The Early History of the Church of Canterbury* (Leicester, 1983), ch. 9. At Yeavering, Building B – 'a hall-like structure with a western annexe' and 'the focus of burial in the later phases' on pp. 73–4 of Hope-Taylor, *Yeavering*, – is 'certainly a church' on p. 168, although only 'church?' in the index (p. 389); while 'the northern fence of its enclosure [which] observed the curious alignment of the earlier buildings and inhumations, while taking in the site of the wooden post that had long stood at the apparent centre of the barrow. (Paganism, then, can hardly have been dead?)' (p. 279) is elsewhere firmly 'fence of churchyard'. Perhaps.

For the siting and contents of the Taplow barrow see, pending a full publication, Bruce-Mitford, *Sutton Hoo*, I, p. 712 and n., 512 and Index *s.v.*

[48] But see the wills of Erminethrud (*c*.700): J. M. Pardessus, *Diplomata, chartae . . . ad res Gallo-Francicas spectantia*, I (Paris, 1843), no. 413, pp. 211–2; and of the Alamannian Adalhram (806): ed. H. Wartmann, *Urkundenbuch der Abtei St. Gallen*, I (Zurich, 1863), no. 191. Stein, 'Pre-Carolingian graves', pp. 11–13, has drawn attention to some of the known examples of secular and ecclesiastical metalwork apparently produced in the same workshops. There are others.

[49] For England see P. Addyman and R. Morris (eds), *The Archaeological Study of Churches* (London, 1972), with an extensive bibliography. For a part of the Trier diocese, for which both the archaeological and the early written evidence are exceptionally rich, see N. Kyll, 'Siedlung, Christianisierung u. kirchliche Organisation der Westeifel', *Rheinische Vierteljahrsblätter*, XXVI (1961), pp. 159–241, here esp. pp. 181–212.

some areas. The depositing of relics in the altars of lesser churches, reflected in dedications which in Francia and Bavaria – but not in England – are surprisingly often named in early documents, allowed ordinary men and women to be buried *ad sanctos*.[50] The use of the tomb in juridical contexts must have made the inconvenience of cemeteries away from the community increasingly apparent. (Conversely, it has been shown that where in the Westeifel district of the Trier diocese older 'field cemeteries' continued to be used for burials for some considerable time after the last deposits with accompanying grave-goods, the place is distant from and ecclesiastically dependent on an estate centre and parish church, for which the evidence often begins in the ninth century or earlier.[51]) The excavation of 'late' cemeteries in various parts of southern England 'within a stone's throw' of earlier cemeteries may be evidence of a short phase in which families wished to distance themselves from *cadavera infidelium*, although where the not very frequent references to 'heathen burials' in charter-boundaries have been identified topographically they seem to be predominantly barrows.[52] Contemporary continental evidence for a new carelessness in the disposition of bodies and for a disregard of older secular and church law designed to protect the integrity of the tomb (with robbers none the less often leaving untouched objects with Christian connotations) suggests the weakening pull of the attitudes and values the cemeteries corporately express, although whether it also reflects a changing view of the 'personality' of the dead – hitherto regarded as working with the living from beyond the grave – seems to me far less certain.[53] Certainly such developments would have made easier the abandonment of field cemeteries and the crowding (literally) into burial grounds made available beside the village church, henceforth the symbol and setting of the whole span of man's earthly life.

The most immediate and important consequences are quickly apparent in Carolingian texts. The ordinary people whose domestic, familial, funerary rites were still largely outside the

[50] Again, the Trier diocese provides a well-documented exemplar: see *ibid.*, pp. 197–207; and the evidence for dedications assembled in the various volumes by F. Pauly on *Siedlung u. Pfarrorganisation im alten Erzbistum Trier* (Bonn and Trier, c.1950–70). See also the Freising documents quoted below.

[51] Kyll, 'Westeifel', pp. 179, 189–90.

[52] D. Hooke, 'Burial features in West Midland charters', *The English Place-Name Society: Journal*, XIII (1980–81), pp. 1–40.

[53] Roth, '*Archäologische Beobachtungen* . . .' Young, 'Paganisme, christianisation et rites funéraires', pp. 53–7.

Church's purview brought some of their extra-mural ones into the new burial ground: synodal legislation and episcopal inquisition show an understandable concern that funerals are associated with frivolous songs, dancing and other inappropriate behaviour *in atrio ecclesiae*.[54] Yet it was in such acts that the cohesive identity of the bereaved family and of the wider community was most clearly proclaimed. The use of the churchyard as a place of public congress and burial in part of it – very quickly impossibly crowded – without distinction of rank was unlikely to be acceptable for long to those who envisaged the local church as one more expression of their social superiority.[55] Carolingian episcopal synodal decrees and some other texts reveal both the preferred solution in the early years of the ninth century, namely, burial within the church with the maximum of visibility, and the hierarchy's determined opposition to it.[56] Liturgical sources show one part of the response to the worldliness of funerary *solatia* and a possible palliative to those distanced from the saint in the altar: a sacralization of the cemetery itself by a formal ceremony of consecration.[57]

[54] There is an excellent collection of material in Kyll, *Tod, Grab*, pp. 30–7, 95–101. Complaints about women singing in a churchyard are at least as old as Gregory of Tours: see his *Lib. de virt. s. Martini*, II.45, *MGH,SRM* I, p. 625. Note that in Gregory of Tours as in ninth-century texts the *atrium* is nearly always the area round a church, usually but not invariably enclosed, and not part of the structure of the church. At the end of the ninth century Regino of Prüm distinguishes between the *atrium* and the more limited area of the *coemeterium: Libri duo de Synodalibus Causis et Disciplinis ecclesiasticis*, ed. F. G. A. Wasserschleben (Leipzig, 1840), p. 20 (cc. 14, 16), cf. 24.

[55] But for members of a 'noble' family who were still in the wet, outside 'their' church of Wittislingen, in the later tenth century, when their relative bishop Ulrich of Augsburg arranged for them to be moved inside, see Gerhard, *Vita S. Oudalrici, MGH, SS* IV, p. 410.

[56] Characteristic prohibitions are: Theodulf, *Capitulare ad presbyteros suos*, c.9: *PL* CV, c.200; Regino, *De Synodalibus Causis*, ed. Wasserschleben, pp. 80–1.

[57] The Carolingian, even later Carolingian, origin of the *benedictio (al. consecratio) cimeterii* is quite evident in the succinct but carefully-documented account of the early development of pontificals by V. Leroquais, *Les Pontificaux manuscrits des bibliothèques publiques en France* (Paris, 1937), pp. xv–xxiii: it is unknown to the 'primitive' Pontificals of the ninth century (pp. xx–xxi); it is still absent from the Pontifical of Langres, Dijon, Bib. Mus., MS 122 of *s.X²* but is in the later Pontificals which are closely related to it, where it occurs not far from the *Dedicatio ecclesiae*. The earliest text known to me is 'Claudius Pontifical I', ed. D. H. Turner, *The Claudius Pontificals* (London, 1971), pp. 60–1. The first three *orationes* there are also those of the 'Romano–Germanic Pontifical of the tenth century', ed. C. Vogel and R. Elze (Vatican City, 1963), I, pp. 192–3; but here the ceremony begins with the chanting of the Seven Penitential Psalms, which can hardly be earlier than Alcuin.

Two documents from the Freising cartulary give us a rare insight into what the tension between social aspiration and ecclesiastical regulation might mean in practice. The earlier, datable 793/806 and therefore from the early years of Carolingian authority in Bavaria, is a straightforward gift of land to the church of St Lawrence at Maisach: the donors are two brothers from an identifiable well-propertied 'noble' family, the body of whose father 'is buried in that church'. (That he had been its founder is not improbable but unproven.) The deacon writing the document adds, in the name of the giver(s), that they have given the land 'so that each of us shall deserve St Lawrence's compassion [*indulgentia*] and his intercessions with God.'[58] The second, of 821 but recording two separate transactions, is far more elaborate. Isancrim, a relative of Bishop Hitto, had given to the baptismal church of St Martin at Nörting a third part of his *hereditas* whose centre was a *domus* at Hirshbach, two kilometres away, but apparently preserving certain rights to a relative. When he died on 28 April 821, 'many noble kinsfolk gathered on that same day [*in illo die*] to bury the body and carried him to the church'. While his body was laid out there, *orationes et preces legantur*: that is to say, the forms of the *agenda mortuorum* which had once been (and perhaps still properly were) the prerogative of clergy and monks were extended to a prominent layman. But when the earlier transaction or transactions had been formally confirmed at the altar of St Martin 'in the presence of priests and people', Isancrim's body was taken *extra ecclesiam* for burial.[59]

For men like Isancrim, as for abbot Alcuin and bishop Hitto, the revival of the epigraphic tombstone was one possible response to the threat of anonymity, of being forgotten among the graves of *rustici*. But even in cities north of the Alps this was rare in the late eighth and ninth centuries – rarer, probably, than is sometimes realized; and in rural areas it remains rare to the point of invisibility for several centuries more, even in most parts of Mediterranean Europe. Some at least of the familiar 'Anglian' cross fragments must surely have come from the burial places of secular figures,

---

[58] T. Bitterauf (ed.), *Die Traditionen des Hochstifts Freising* I (Munich, 1905), no. 167.

[59] *ibid.*, no. 447. For other references to Isancrim and for some of his relatives, see W. Störmer, *Früher Adel: Studien zur politischen Führungsschicht in fränkish-deutschen Reich*, II (Stuttgart), pp. 369–70. At the date of Isancrim's death, the *agenda mortuorum* used in the diocese of Freising is likely to be that found in one or other of our 'Eighth-century Gelasians': but there can be no certainty.

although the fact that they tend to occur in groups, with a limited chronological span, poses problems of interpretation; and the status of the site in the eighth and ninth centuries is rarely independently documented. Salvation for such men and their families was found in the greater urban churches and above all in monasteries, in their *libri memoriales* and their prayers even more than their burial grounds. All men might be united one day in the great community of the Saved, 'living happily in Eternity': but in the meanwhile the place of rest of their bodies and the intercessions for their souls reflected the social distinctions and the contrasting senses of 'community' which had been their earthly lot.[60]

[60] I am grateful to Professor Malcolm Todd (Exeter) who answered queries relating to cemetery practice in the Roman period and to my colleague Dr N. P. Brooks who discussed aspects of the paper with me on several occasions and read it on completion.

9

Legislation and Consensus in the Reign of Charles the Bald

JANET NELSON

In a recent comment on some Carolingian historical writing, Professor J. M. Wallace-Hadrill spoke of 'a nice mixture of ruthlessness and fantasy'.[1] It is a rare achievement to have coped as he has with this and other early medieval mixtures: he has seemed as much at home at Brebières or Clichy as at St Denis; he has conveyed vividly the excitement of both 'matters of the mind' and 'their startling physical background'; he has explained equally convincingly the bloodfeud's function in Merovingian society, and the interest of Carolingian scholars in *Lex Salica*, and he has discerned in Frankish legal sources 'the public reason of the Franks'.[2] The following notes on the capitularies of Charles the Bald are offered in gratitude for many insights and a generous supply of counsel and aid.

Since F.-L. Ganshof published his fine work on Carolingian capitularies,[3] his views have been developed in two main ways. First, increasing attention has been given to the survival of capitularies in private collections rather than in remnants of an official archive; and while new editions are still urgently needed, much progress has been made in understanding the ways in which

[1] Wallace-Hadrill, *EMH*, p. 17.
[2] Review of W. A. Eckhardt, *Die Kapitulariensammlung Bischof Ghaerbalds von Lüttich* (Göttingen, 1955), in *Tijdschrift voor Rechtsgeschiedenis*, XXIV (1956), pp. 471–2.
[3] F. L. Ganshof, *Recherches sur les Capitulaires* (Paris, 1958), with references to earlier literature.

Charlemagne's capitularies, at least, were produced and preserved.[4] Second, Ganshof's contrast between Charlemagne's capitularies, given binding force 'by the ruler's ban alone', and those of Charles the Bald, where the consent of the aristocracy has become a condition of validity, has been refined by the argument that the written text in the case of Charles the Bald's capitularies, unlike his predecessors', had come to possess a 'dispositive character' and was no longer merely an *aide-mémoire* to orally-promulgated legislation.[5] On the whole, however, recent research has tended to focus, as Ganshof did, on Charlemagne's reign at the expense of his successors, and to reaffirm Ganshof's belief that the references to 'consent' in Charles the Bald's capitularies signify the progressive weakening of the Carolingian monarchy from *c*.830 onwards.[6] But these later capitularies, though quarried for historical data, have never been systematically explored; nor have they been looked at in the context of political practice, as collective 'public reason'. Even a brief and preliminary survey seems timely.

Over fifty capitularies have survived from the reign of Charles the Bald, including fourteen which are records of meetings between

[4] A start was made by S. Stein, '*Lex* und *Capitula*: eine kritische Studie', *MIÖG*, XLI (1926), pp. 289–301, and 'Étude critique des capitulaires francs', *Le Moyen Age*, LI (1941), pp. 1–75. Although he reached the wrong conclusions, he directed attention to the MSS. See also W. A. Eckhardt, 'Die *Capitularia Missorum Specialia* von 802,' *DA*, XII (1956), pp. 498–516; R. Schneider, 'Zur rechtlichen Bedeutung der Kapitularientexte', *DA*, XXIII (1967), pp. 273–94; D. Hägermann, 'Zur Entstehung der Kapitularien', in *Festschrift P. Acht* (Kallmütz, 1976), pp. 12–27; G. Schmitz, 'Wucher in Laon. Eine neue Quelle zu Karl der Kahlen und Hinkmar von Reims', *DA*, XXXVII (1981), pp. 520–58; the best discussion in English is R. McKitterick, *The Frankish Church and the Carolingian Reforms* (London, 1977), pp. 18 ff.; also W. Ullmann, *Law and Politics in the Middle Ages* (London, 1961), pp. 203 ff. and *The Carolingian Renaissance and the Idea of Kingship* (London, 1969), pp. 30–5; for capitularies in the broad context of early medieval legislation and kingship, P. Wormald, '*Lex Scripta* and *Verbum Regis*', in P. H. Sawyer and I. N. Wood (eds), *Early Medieval Kingship* (Leeds, 1977), pp. 105–38.
[5] Schneider, 'Rechtliche Bedeutung'.
[6] Hägermann, 'Entstehung', makes important qualifications to this argument, but concludes (p. 27) that instead of 'a fundamental constitutional change', there was 'a significant shift of accent'. E. Magnou-Nortier, *Foi et fidelité* (Toulouse, 1976), pp. 98 ff., offers a more radical reassessment with a remarkable analysis of the ideological content of four of Charles the Bald's capitularies. But I am not convinced by her interpretation of the term *convenientia* (which does not recur in Charles' later capitularies and seems unlikely to be an import from Roman law via the Midi), or by her general account of a 'restructuring of the French monarchy' in this reign.

Charles and (one or more) other Carolingian rulers.[7] Though a
number of these texts have not been transmitted in the form of
capitula, i.e. are not divided into numbered sections or 'chapters',
nearly all of them fall within Ganshof's broad substantial definition
of capitularies as 'prescribing rules of law and ordering their
implementation, and/or prescribing measures in particular cases'.[8]
What proportion has survived of the total number that may have
been produced? We can only begin to answer that question by
looking at how our texts have been preserved. Early in Charles'
reign, at the Council of Ver in 844, it looks as if no agreed 'official'
text was produced there and then.[9] Some months later, Lupus of
Ferrières in a letter to Hincmar of Rheims regretted that the king
'had not agreed in the first place to the recommendations which he
sought and got at Ver', and recalled: 'I sent you [Hincmar] these
same canons, or, as you call them, *capitula*, which I then marshalled
with my pen. Posterity will, I think, judge them fair, and God will
not be unmindful of my devotion.'[10] Hincmar, present at Ver, had
evidently had to wait for Lupus to produce the capitulary text.
From the early 850s, efforts were made to have a given capitulary
text available at the palace from the time of issue, for copying by
'the archbishops and their counts'(!)[11] This rule does not suggest
that many copies were envisaged, and the copying itself was evidently left to scribes attached to the archbishops and counts – hardly
a surprising arrangement, given the very small number of chancery

---

[7] See R. Schneider, *Brüdergemeine und Schwurfreundschaft* (Lübeck–Hamburg,
1964).

[8] Ganshof, *Recherches*, p. 12. Appendix 1 lists these texts. All were edited by
A. Boretius and V. Krause, *MGH, Capit.* II, except for no. 58, which falls within
Ganshof's classification of 'capitulary-like texts' (*Recherches*, pp. 11–12), and has
been edited by Schmitz, 'Wucher in Laon', pp. 556–8. That *ordines* of royal
consecration should also be thus classified has been well argued by Ullmann, *Law
and Politics*, pp. 207–8.

[9] No doubt the council had worked from a written agenda and some record of
proceedings was kept. cf. McKitterick, *Frankish Church*, pp. 23–5, on ecclesiastical
councils.

[10] Lupus, *Ep.* 43, in *Correspondance*, ed. L. Levillain (2 vols. Paris, 1927–35), I,
p. 182.

[11] As originally prescribed by Louis the Pious in 825, *MGH, Capit.* I, no. 150,
c.26, which reappears in the collection of Ansegis, ed. A. Boretius in *MGH, Capit.*
I, Bk II, c.24, p. 419, and was cited from there in the capitularies of Servais (853)
and Pîtres (864), *MGH, Capit.* II, no. 260, c.11 and no. 273, c.36 (appendix 1,
nos. 17, 39).

notaries operating at any one time.[12] We have no way of knowing how regularly the repeated directives about the keeping of a palace text were carried out. No example of such a text survives.[13] An episode in 862 where 'counsellors' tried to suppress a capitulary text suggests that, at this date anyway, the drawing-up of capitularies was in the hands of a very small group of close royal advisers who, especially if a capitulary was not promulgated, could have taken texts away with them to 'private' archives.[14]

I would like to pursue further the question of capitularies' survival by considering three manuscripts:

1. Hague 10 D 2, written at Rheims in the third quarter of the ninth century, contains a series of West Frankish capitularies dating from between 843 and 856, and including virtually every capitulary known from these years.[15] The last piece in the collection contains references to ten of the earlier items. I have suggested elsewhere that Hincmar may have been responsible both for this last capitulary, and for the collection of which Hague 10 D 2 is an early copy.[16] If so, ought we to ask whether he was acting in a 'public capacity', 'entrusted' with the construction of a state archive, or in a private capacity as one interested in collecting, preserving and even composing capitularies (among other legal texts)? The question is, I think, *mal posé*: it presupposes a hard and fast dividing line which was constantly transgressed in ninth-century practice. I shall return to this point.

2. Most of Yale Beinecke 413[17] is in the hand of a scribe,

---

[12] cf. Ganshof, *Recherches*, p. 64. On the chancery of Charles the Bald, see G. Tessier, *Receuil des Actes de Charles le Chauve* (3 vols, Paris, 1944–55), III, pp. 46 ff.

[13] And see below, p. 206, for reservations about the alleged link between a copy of Ansegis and Charles the Bald. If there was a copy of Ansegis in Charles' palace archive late in the reign, was anyone there to use it as a legislative data-bank? The mandate tentatively dated by Schmitz to 868 (1, no. 58) tells Hincmar to prepare a dossier of Ansegis-citations on a particular issue (usury).

[14] *Annales de Saint-Bertin*, ed. F. Grat, J. Vielliard and S. Clemencet (Paris, 1964), (hereafter cited as *Annales*), pp. 94–5.

[15] See appendix 1. This MS was cited by the *MGH* editors as Haagensis 1. For details (and dating by B. Bischoff) see P. Classen, 'Die Verträge von Verdun und Coulaines, 843, als politische Grundlagen des west-fränkischen Reiches', *HZ* CXCVI (1963), pp. 28 *et seq.*

[16] 'Kingship, law and liturgy in the political thought of Hincmar of Rheims', *EHR*, XCII (1977), pp. 256–7.

[17] See appendix 1. This MS, formerly Chester Beatty 11, and before that Phillipps 10190, was listed by the *MGH* editors as Cheltenhamensis 10190 and cited as

Ingobert, who also copied out a bible apparently presented to
Charles the Bald by Hincmar c.870.[18] The manuscript consists of a
fine copy of the capitulary collection of Ansegis, followed by six
capitularies of Charles the Bald. Ingobert wrote in the last of the
additional capitularies at a later date than the rest, which probably
means that the manuscript remained in its original Rheims
scriptorium from c.864 to c.873. The rationale behind this particular
series of six seems to be that all these capitularies cite from Ansegis'
collection, the first of them being the earliest of Charles the Bald's
capitularies to do so.[19] This Ansegis connection is important, for
no fewer than four Ansegis-manuscripts can be attributed to
Hincmar's Rheims scriptorium.[20]

3. A manuscript still extant at Beauvais in the early seventeenth
century, and used by Sirmond in his remarkable edition of Charles
the Bald's capitularies,[21] has since been lost, but two copies of it
survive in the Vatican library, both made in the early modern

---

Middlehill. It has been very thoroughly described by E. G. Miller, *The Library of
A. Chester Beatty* (2 vols, Oxford, 1927), I, pp. 50–2, II, plates xxviii–xxx; and in
less detail in Sotheby's catalogue, 24 June 1969, pp. 20–3. I am grateful to Yale
University Library for lending me a microfilm of the MS.

[18] See Sotheby's catalogue, 24 June 1969, p. 21, for the identification by Bischoff
of Ingobert's hand. On the San Paolo Bible, see R. McKitterick, 'Charles the Bald
and his library', *EHR*, XCV (1980), pp. 41–2. As against the strong paleographical
links with Rheims, the arguments that have been adduced for a Soissons origin for
this manuscript seem to me weak. There may be another pointer towards Rheims
in the list of addressees of the Quiersy capitulary in 857 (appendix 1, no. 26) in this
manuscript: Bishop Hunfrid (of Thérouanne), and Counts Ingiscalc and Berengar.
Clearly the original of this text was destined for the Ternois *missaticum* (cf. the list
of *missi* here in the Servais capitulary of 853, appendix 1, no. 17: Bishop Folcoin
(succeeded by Hunfrid in 856), Ingiscalc and Berengar): a likely explanation is that
Hincmar's *scriptorium* was responsible for multiplying and distributing capitulary
texts throughout the Rheims province, and an exemplar that happened to contain
the Ternois names had remained in the Rheims archive to be copied by Ingobert in
the 860s.

[19] See appendix, no. 14, *MGH, Capit.* II, no. 259, c.4. On the proceedings at this
assembly, see J. Devisse, *Hincmar, archevêque de Reims, 845–882* (3 vols, Geneva,
1975–6), I, p. 91.

[20] See Devisse, *Hincmar.* III, p. 1078, and *idem, Hincmar et la Loi* (Dakar, 1962),
pp. 64–9; and Schmitz, 'Wucher in Laon', pp. 540–1. Interestingly, Hincmar cites
from Ansegis quite often in *De Ecclesiis et Capellis*, written in 857 or 858 (ed. W.
Gundlach, 'Zwei Schriften des Erzbischofs Hinkmars von Reims', *Zeitschrift für
Kirchengeschichte*, X (1889), pp. 92–145.

[21] J. Sirmond, *Capitula Caroli Calvi et successorum* (Paris, 1623); Ganshof,
Recherches, pp. 7 ff., thinks this work unworthy of mention.

period: Vaticanus reginae Christinae 291 and Vaticanus 4982.[22] The coverage of capitularies in the lost manuscript overlaps to a small extent with, but largely continues, that of Hague 10 D 2: taken together, these manuscripts could suggest an attempt at the systematic preservation of Charles the Bald's capitularies. I am tempted to make this juxtaposition, first because the lost manuscript contained a number of capitularies in whose composition Hincmar seems to have been involved;[23] second because none of the capitularies preserved in the lost manuscript is of later date than 876,[24] in other words, all fall within the period when Hincmar can plausibly be assigned a major role in the composition of capitulary texts; and third because several other manuscripts containing capitularies of Charles the Bald have been traced to a Rheims origin or exemplar.[25]

In appendix 1, I list Charles the Bald's capitularies chronologically, as do the manuscripts, rather than using the categories of the *Monumenta* editors (though for convenience I also give *Monumenta* numbers).[26] The appendix shows in which of the four manuscripts

[22] See Boretius' conspectus in *MGH, Capit.* II, p. xxviii (where, however, the Servais capitulary of 853 (appendix 1, no. 17) has been accidentally omitted from the contents of Vat. 4982). The contents of these two MSS are very similar indeed, but Vat. 4982 is probably closer to the exemplar as it includes the capitularies of Epernay (appendix 1, no. 10) and Meersen 847 and 851 (appendix 1, nos. 11 and 12) where Vat. Reg. 291 omits these. Further, Vat. Reg. 291 contains two additional capitularies which suggest the use of other sources in an attempt at more complete coverage: the *Decretio Childeberti* (596) and the *Conventio* of Furon (878). These other sources could well be of Rheims origin: the *Decretio* occurs (twice) in the Rheims MS Paris BN Lat. 10758, while the Furon text is given by Hincmar in the *Annales*, pp. 230–4.
[23] Especially the Quiersy oaths and the Quiersy letter of 858 (appendix 1, nos. 29, 30) and the Pact of Tusey (appendix 1, no. 40). Hincmar's hand in no. 29 is likely: see J. Devisse, 'Essai sur l'histoire d'une expression qui a fait fortune: *consilium et auxilium* au IXe siècle', *Le Moyen Age*, LXXIV (1968), pp. 187–8; and in no. 30, is certain: Hincmar *Ep*. 126, *MGH, Ep*. VIII, p. 64. For no. 40, cf. *Annales, s.a.* 865, p. 116, and see Devisse, *Hincmar*, I, pp. 449 ff., (where, however, as elsewhere in Devisse's work, Tusey near Toul is confused with Douzy, near Sedan.)
[24] This is true on the assumption that Vat. 4982 is nearer the original collection: see above, n. 22.
[25] Paris BN Lat. 4638; 4761; 9654; and cf. 10758 (with capitularies of Charlemagne and Louis the Pious, and Ansegis' collection). The Rheims connection was already noted by E. Bourgeois, *Le Capitulaire de Quierzy-sur-Oise (877)* (Paris, 1885), pp. 23, 25: still a valuable study; and by Stein, 'Étude critique', pp. 51–2. (Stein's implied inference that Hincmar forged the capitularies of Charles the Bald's predecessors is absurd, yet Stein had a feel for the grain of the evidence).
[26] Like the *MGH* editors, I have taken 'capitulary' in a broad sense, to include 'capitulary-like texts': see above, n. 8. Such a classification clearly corresponds to the view of ninth-century compilers.

just discussed each capitulary was preserved. Out of 58 capitularies, only 12 are not found in one (or more) of these four manuscripts, and of those 12 texts, 6 can be associated with Hincmar as author or preserver.[27] Of the 46 capitularies in one or more of our four manuscripts, Hincmar's authorship has been suggested, in whole or in part, for 19,[28] and I would think it likely for at least a further 5.[29] In other words, Hincmar's hand can perhaps be seen in the writing-up of 30 out of the 58 surviving capitularies, and, if a Hincmar-connection for the four manuscripts is accepted, in the preservation of a further 23. Now it is clear that Hincmar was not the only author or preserver of capitularies in Charles the Bald's reign. But what seems beyond doubt is the major role of Hincmar in the maintenance and indeed the climaxing (whether judged on formal or substantial criteria) of the Carolingian capitulary tradition. Other Carolingian contemporaries of Charles the Bald 'prescribed and ordered the application of rules of law' and took 'measures for particular cases':[30] it was no difference in political practice but a highly differential degree of interest in written law on the part of the clerical elite, and specifically of Hincmar, as compared with prelates in other kingdoms, which accounted for the distinctiveness of the West Frankish capitularies between c.840 and c.880.

[27] The twelve texts not in any of the four manuscripts (numbers refer to appendix 1): 4, 27, 33, 43, 51, 55–7, 58, 22, 42 and 46. The six that can be linked with Hincmar: 22, 42 and 46 (on these royal consecration *ordines*, see C. A. Bouman, *Sacring and Crowning* (Groningen, 1957), pp. 8–9, 112 ff.); 33 (on the *Libellus contra Wenilonem*, see Nelson, 'Kingship, law and liturgy', p. 250 and n. 3); 43 (on the Pacts made at Metz either in 867 or 868, see Devisse, *Hincmar*, I, p. 453, and P. McKeon, *Hincmar of Laon and Carolingian Politics*, Urbana, 1978, pp. 210–1); and 58 (on the preservation of this text, see Schmitz, 'Wucher in Laon', esp. p. 552).

[28] See Devisse, '*Consilium et auxilium*', for appendix 1, nos. 2, 12, 18, 20, 28, 29, 31, 32, 33, 34, 38, 40, 43; and the *MGH* editors for nos. 22, 26, 30, 42, 45, and 46.

[29] Appendix 1, nos. 36, 37, 39, 44 and 50; also possibly 13, 14, 15, 16 and 17. Detailed discussion of Hincmar's role awaits further study.

[30] See n. 8; on capitularies in the Italian kingdom, see C. Wickham, *Early Medieval Italy* (London, 1981), pp. 60–2. The possibility that capitularies were issued by Louis the German, but have been lost, was suggested by H. Conrad, *Deutsche Rechtsgeschichte* (Karlsruhe, 1954), I, p. 187. The kind of occasion on which capitularies might well have been promulgated is noted frequently by Hincmar in the *Annales*: e.g., *s.a.* 872, p. 186; 873, pp. 190, 193; 875, p. 197 (East Francia); and *s.a.* 864, p. 105, 866, pp. 132–3 (Middle Kingdom). As Ganshof stressed (*Recherches*, p. 102), the positive evidence for the persistence of the capitulary tradition after 840 really comes only from the reign of Charles the Bald; but that fact has of course specific significance for the way in which the relevant texts were preserved.

This is not the place for anything more than a brief indication of the scope and formal sophistication of these texts. The Capitulary of Servais (November 853: see appendix 1, no. 17) has been held to signify 'a remarkable restoring to order of the kingdom'.[31] Here was affirmed the principle of the collective liability of free Franks to denounce and pursue criminals in their locality; practical means to enforce this were the oaths required of free men and the hundredman's role in linking local and central measures to suppress disorder.[32] A total of forty-three *missi* were named in a dozen *missatica* in Francia and Burgundy.[33] The Edict of Pîtres (June 864: see appendix 1, no. 39) was conceived on a grand scale in thirty-seven *capitula* (which run to seventeen pages of *Monumenta* text).[34] The single largest topic was coinage reform (cc.8–24):[35] the siting of mints, the duties of moneyers, penalties for rejecting new coin (including careful specification of type of flogging to avoid permanent health damage), were all spelled out in detail. As for the formal characteristics of this capitulary, the frequent reference to Ansegis is very striking, and allowed the author(s) to place the measures taken at Pîtres solidly within the framework of recent Frankish legislation.[36] Yet there is no sense here of merely formulaic repetition: the older provisions were often modified or supplemented, and as in the capitularies of Charlemagne and Louis the Pious we find a wealth of data about quite specific governmental problems: for instance the need to secure the supply of horses both for military and communications purposes; the difficulties posed for royal estate-managers by the growth of a peasant land-market and the consequent dismemberment of tenurial units that were also fiscal

[31] Devisse, *Hincmar*, I, p. 290 with n. 26.
[32] *MGH, Capit*, II, p. 274. cf. *Capit. de missis instruendis* (829), *ibid.*, p. 8.
[33] *ibid.*, pp. 275–6. The first *missaticum* here covers the Rheims area, and Hincmar is the first *missus* named.
[34] *ibid.*, pp. 310–28. cf. *Annales* p. 113: 'Generale placitum habet in quo annua dona . . . recipit . . . Capitula etiam ad triginta et septem consilio fidelium more praedecessorum ac progenitorum suorum regum constituit et ut legalia per omnem regnum suum observari praecepit'.
[35] See P. Grierson, 'The *Gratia Dei Rex* coinage of Charles the Bald', in M. Gibson and J. Nelson (eds), *Charles the Bald: Court and Kingdom*, (BAR International Series, CI, 1981), pp. 41–2; D. M. Metcalf, 'A sketch of the currency in the time of Charles the Bald', *ibid.*, pp. 73–4.
[36] There are 24 references to, or citations from, Ansegis, plus 1 reference to the collection of Benedict the Levite, and 5 to Roman law, as well as several others to previous capitularies of Charles the Bald (notably appendix 1, nos. 17 and 26).

units; conflicts of interest between lords and peasants over labour
services and the earnings of migrant workers.[37]

As always with medieval legal sources, we are left with the
question of how far rules reflect social reality: how widespread or
long-term were the problems dealt with at Pîtres in June 864? In this
and other capitularies, we can sometimes suspect that remedies are
being prescribed for quite local and/or short-term problems. For
instance, peasant migration, here said to be 'recent' and the result of
'the persecution of the Northmen', may have been affecting only
the lower Seine valley, and perhaps even there only certain estates,
and we have no way of telling whether it was more widespread than
that here referred to (via Ansegis) as having occurred in the time of
Charlemagne and Louis the Pious[38] (when, presumably, it was due
to factors other than the Vikings). Again, peasant resistance to
lords' new demands for the cartage of marl may have been quite
widespread, or may have been merely a local phenomenon. We
have two near-contemporary cases where charters show that
groups of peasants have appealed to the king and lost, and in the
earlier of these it is polyptych evidence that clinches the lord's
case.[39] Could it be that the 864 capitulary is another kind of reflection of the outcome of a single similar case, an apparent generalizing
of the particular?[40] It looks very much as if such an interpretation
might work for the famous denunciation of lay abbots by the
Council of Ver:[41] in this case, we know the author, Lupus, and his
particular grievance against the lay-abbot Odulf at the time of this
council – and indeed, he himself makes the connection explicit in his
letter to Hincmar, cited above.[42] It is obvious, too, that a specific
factional conflict, centring on the court, lies behind the references
in the Capitulary of Coulaines (843) to persons pursuing private
interests and influencing the king improperly.[43] Again, external,

---

[37] cc.26, 30; 29 and 31: *MGH, Capit.* II, pp. 321, 323–4.
[38] c.31, with reference to Ansegis III, 18.
[39] Pippin I of Aquitaine, charter no. XII, in L. Levillain (ed.), *Receuil des Actes de
Pépin I et de Pépin II* (Paris, 1926), pp. 44–7 (original dated 828); Charles the Bald,
charter no. 228, in Tessier, *Receuil*, ed. Tessier, II, pp. 7–9 (original dated 861).
[40] P. Wormald, '*Lex Scripta*', pp. 112–13; cf. some early modern Scottish
parliamentary legislation and the illuminating comments of J. Wormald, *Court,
Kirk and Community* (London, 1981), p. 27.
[41] Appendix 1, no. 6, c.12, *MGH, Capit.* II, pp. 385–6.
[42] Lupus, *Ep.* 43, in *Correspondance*, ed. Levillain.
[43] Appendix 1, no. 2, and cf. also no. 1: *MGH, Capit.* II, pp. 254–5, 402.

this time charter, evidence points fairly clearly to at least one of the individuals concerned: the chamberlain Vivian.[44]

To see why any particular topic was the subject of a capitulary, we have to understand the text as the residue – all that survives – of the proceedings of an assembly. The agenda would be the product of initiatives not only from the king and his close advisers but also from individuals and groups among the aristocracy. Collective deliberations and decision-making could translate private concerns and grievances into public law: thus, in the Edict of Pîtres, statements on peasant labour services and migrants' earnings appear alongside the decrees on coinage reform and the defence of the realm. Politics is the common denominator, in as much as dealings involving king and aristocracy lie behind all these affairs, and the assembly is the forum in which power is negotiated. A lively impression of the assembly's central role in the earlier part of the reign is conveyed in some of Lupus' letters: the operation of networks of patronage and the activity of favoured magnates as brokers between the king and other nobles supplement but are no substitute for personal participation at assemblies. Lupus regards these occasions with a keen anticipation that sometimes carries more than a hint of anxiety. Attendance is at once a burden and an opportunity: a summons is a demand for service, specifically military service, and for gifts, but also a personalized signal of the king's attention. Refusal of such a summons, on whatever excuse, is dangerous.[45]

How large was the attendance at the summer assembly which still in Charles the Bald's reign was a gathering of the Frankish host for campaign? Enough information even to hazard a guess is very rare. In late summer 843, most of the bishops and abbots of Francia proper, Neustria, northern Aquitaine and Burgundy seem to have been present, and we can name five lay magnates probably with the king through the autumn and present at Coulaines in November. In this case, we can piece together evidence from the list of subscribers to a monastic privilege plus several charters.[46] Occasionally,

---

[44] Tessier, *Receuil*, I, nos. 24, 28, 30, 31. See also F. Lot and L. Halphen, *Le Règne de Charles le Chauve* (Paris, 1909), pp. 86, 88, 153 n. 2.

[45] Lupus, *Epp.* 15, 16, 17, 28, 36, 41, 45, 47, 58, 60, 67, Levillain, *Correspondance*, I, 72, 74, 111, 112, 123, Levillain, *Correspondance*, II.

[46] Synodal privilege for St Lomer: Mansi XIV, cc.795–6: see Lot and Halphen, *Règne*, p. 85, n. 4, 86, n. 1. For the charters see n. 44 above: evidence for Harduin, Vivian and (in conjunction with Lupus *Ep.* 32) Adalard (who also appears in the St

charters can be linked with assemblies;[47] but even in the early years
of the reign when charters are relatively plentiful, the absence of lists
of subscriptions severely limits the usefulness of charters as indi-
cators of attendance at assemblies.[48] Royal judgements, though
very rare, do carry lists of subscribers and this makes the three such
texts we have from Charles the Bald's reign particularly significant.
Two dated within a week of each other can be read as showing 18
counts as well as 25 archbishops and bishops and 6 abbots with the
king at the palace of Verberie in late October/early November
863.[49] The third shows the king attended by nine counts at Rouy
(near Laon) in April 868.[50] Unfortunately neither occasion can be
linked with a capitulary nor indeed identified with an assembly; but
both hint at the numbers of magnates that could be present when
important business was being discussed. In two cases, the scale of an
assembly is indicated in the capitulary emanating from it: it is clear
that most of the forty-three *missi* named in the capitulary of Servais
were present there.[51] They represent a majority of the bishops and
perhaps also of the counts in the Frankish and Burgundian parts of
the kingdom. In the capitulary of Quiersy (June 877; see appendix 1,
no. 56), 10 bishops, 4 abbots[52] and 16 counts are named, all but
three of whom were at the assembly,[53] and the list certainly includes
only a proportion of those present.[54]

Lomer text). The Capitulary of Coulaines, *MGH, Capit.* II, pp. 253–4: evidence
for Warin and Richwin.

[47] The one striking case relates to attendance at St Sernin's, Toulouse, in May/June
844: cf. Tessier, *Receuil*, nos. 36–56. But one or two charters can be linked with a
number of other assemblies: e.g. Tessier, no. 157 with the Synod of Verberie
(appendix 1, no. 15); Tessier, nos. 191–193bis with the Assembly of Quiersy in
857 (appendix 1, no. 26); see also appendix 2.

[48] Contrast the Anglo-Saxon charter evidence discussed by S. Keynes, *The
Diplomas of King Aethelred 'the Unready' 978–1016* (Cambridge, 1980).

[49] Tessier, *Receuil*, II, nos. 258, 259.

[50] *ibid.*, no. 314.

[51] Appendix 1, no. 17, *MGH, Capit.* II, p. 271: the prologue addressed to the *missi*
specifies that if anyone has had to be absent from the assemblies of Valenciennes
(appendix 1, no. 16) or Servais where this capitulary was agreed, still he is to carry
out its instructions.

[52] For their importance, see K.-F. Werner, 'Gauzlin von Saint-Denis', *DA*,
XXXV (1979), pp. 395–462.

[53] *MGH, Capit.* II, cc.12, 15, p. 359. Hincmar's letter to Louis the Stammerer, *PL*
CXXV, c.987.

[54] Only those magnates staying in Francia with Louis the Stammerer are
mentioned; but some, at least, of those present at Quiersy would be going with
Charles to Italy.

Nearly all Charles the Bald's assemblies, especially in the latter half of the reign, were held in Francia proper, usually at one of the palaces on the Oise or the Seine.[55] Enemies of the king might be captured in the provinces but were brought back to Francia to be sentenced at an assembly by the judgement of the Franks.[56] Disputes between magnates might be settled in the assembly-forum, as at Pîtres in 862 when Charles 'at the request of his faithful men' forestalled an outbreak of violence by reconciling two such opponents.[57] Similar rivalries and reconciliations are attested at another great summer assembly at Pîtres in 864.[58] Here too, the royal changes in, or confirmations of, comital personnel that were the outcomes of such manoeuvring, were publicly announced.[59] While aristocratic politics remained centripetal with the court still the natural forum for competition between nobles and for peaceful resolution of conflicts by king and faithful men acting in concert, equally, the king could use the assembly as a convenient locale for orchestrating support. It is clear that political arrangements of this kind continued in practice throughout the reign of Charles the Bald.

The fragmentary evidence makes it hard to draw up a full list of the assemblies during the reign. We no longer, as in the reigns of Charlemagne and Louis the Pious, have the Royal Frankish Annals with their consistent interest in the where and when of assemblies. The Annals of St Bertin, which cover Charles's reign and are in some sense a continuation of the Royal Frankish Annals, are essen-

---

[55] See appendices 1 and 2. See also C.-R. Brühl, *Fodrum, Gistum, Servitium Regis* (Cologne, 1968), p. 40 with nn. 145–7, and cf. the evidence for Anglo-Saxon assemblies discussed by Sawyer, below pp. 277, 286–99.

[56] This was prescribed at Quiersy, 857 (appendix 1, no. 26), *MGH, Capit.* II, cc.4, 6, p. 287. For actual cases, see *Annales, s.a.* 849, p. 58. (Charles of Aquitaine); 852, p. 64 (Pippin II of Aquitaine); 866, p. 130 (William, son of Odo); 870, p. 171, and 871, p. 184 (Carloman). Probably another case is Gauzbert in 853 (Regino of Prüm, *Chronica, s.a.* 860, *MGH, SRG*, p. 78). Bernard of Septimania was condemned by judgement of the Franks, but Prudentius thinks it worth noting that he was executed in Aquitaine, not Francia: *Annales, s.a.* 844, p. 45.

[57] *ibid.*, pp. 92–3.

[58] *ibid.*, pp. 113–14. In one case, conciliation was unsuccessful: hostility between Bernard, son of Bernard, and Robert flared immediately afterwards. Perhaps there is an allusion to this episode in Hincmar's *De Ordine Palatii*, c.31, ed. V. Krause, *MGH, Capit.* II, p. 528. But the reconciliation of Egfrid proved more lasting.

[59] *Annales, s.a.* 864, p. 114; 865, p. 124; 867, p. 137; 868, p. 151; 872, pp. 185–6; 877, pp. 212–13. Cf. the role of the Merovingian court noted by Wood, above, pp. 42–6.

tially a private work.[60] Under Prudentius' authorship, up to 861, they contain only a few random mentions of assemblies: for instance, neither Coulaines, 843, nor Servais, 853, appears. Several summer assemblies are known only from a chance reference in a letter of Lupus', or from the Chronicle of St Wandrille with its curious attempt at 'official' coverage from 847–51.[61] But from 861 until the end of Charles' reign, a fairly complete list (see appendix 2) of twice-yearly assemblies can be constructed from the Annals of St Bertin – for we are now back with Hincmar (when can we ever be far from him in Charles the Bald's reign?), this time as contemporary historian, consciously reverting to the pattern of the Royal Frankish Annals.[62] Information on assemblies becomes more detailed and systematic than ever in the annals from 868–77. In 868, for instance, the king is said to have received the annual gifts at Pîtres in mid-August, and to have 'summoned certain leading men of his kingdom, both some of the bishops, and others' to meet him at Quiersy at the beginning of December. The term 'counsellors' is used increasingly frequently for the clearly small group of leading men who advises on major decisions. Under 874, Hincmar records: 'Charles held a meeting with his counsellors on the feast of the Purification of Holy Mary [2 February] at the monastery of St. Quentin . . . He held the general assembly at the manor of Douzy on 13 June and received the annual gifts.'[63]

Another piece of evidence can now be brought into the picture: Hincmar's description in the last few chapters of the *De Ordine Palatii* of how 'the healthy condition of the whole realm was

---

[60] See J. L. Nelson, 'The Annals of St Bertin', in Gibson and Nelson, *Charles the Bald*, pp. 15–36. By 'private work', I mean that the annals were not written at court, had no 'official' status, and were never intended for circulation.

[61] Lupus, *Epp.* 28, 67; *Chronicle of St. Wandrille*, ed. J. Laporte, (Rouen-Paris, 1951), pp. 78–85.

[62] Nelson, 'Annals', in Gibson and Nelson, *Charles the Bald*, p. 24. The work and the author have recently been reconsidered with characteristic insight by J. M. Wallace-Hadrill, 'History in the mind of Archbishop Hincmar', in R. H. C. Davis and J. M. Wallace-Hadrill (eds), *The Writing of History in the Middle Ages. Essays presented to R. W. Southern* (Oxford, 1981), pp. 43–70.

[63] See appendix 2 for these and other references to the *Annales*. The role of the counsellors was stressed particularly by Hincmar in his later years: see H. Löwe, 'Hinkmar von Reims und der Apocrisiar. Beiträge zur Interpretation von *De Ordine palatii*', in *Festschrift für H. Heimpel* (Göttingen, 1972), pp. 197–225, esp. 221 ff., and cf. the comments on the term *primores regni* in the *Annales*, idem, 'Geschichtsschreibung der ausgehenden Karolingerzeit', *DA*, XXIII (1967), p. 10 with n. 39.

maintained' by the holding of twice-yearly assemblies whose business was dealt with by means of 'lists of separately-headed chapters' (*denominata et ordinata capitula*).[64] At the general assembly, 'the whole aristocracy' (*universitas maiorum*), lay and clerical, attended, 'the more influential to frame counsel, the less important men to hear that counsel and sometimes similarly to deliberate on it, and to confirm it, not because they were forced to do so, but from their own understanding and freely-expressed opinion.'[65] Such assemblies were also the occasions for the aristocracy to hand over their gifts to the king. The other assembly was attended only by the more influential men, the leading counsellors. It was held in winter, to take stock of what would have to be done in the coming year. Its transactions were confidential: the same matters would be brought up again at the general summer assembly, where, 'as if nothing had been previously worked out concerning them, they were now subject to the new counsel and consent of the people, policies were found, and, under God's leadership, arrangements made along with the magnates, for putting good order into effect.'[66] The next chapter (c.31) details the qualities required in counsellors: loyalty, wisdom, the ability to withstand pressures of political friends and relatives, and a commitment to confidentiality. Recruitment should be by merit, from among the pool of the king's palace servants (*ministeriales palatini*). After explaining how the palace officers should conduct less important affairs, Hincmar describes in detail (c.34) how the counsellors dealt with assembly business:

[64] The edition by Krause in *MGH, Capit.* II, pp. 517–30, has been superseded by that of T. Gross and R. Schieffer, *MGH, Fontes Iuris Germanici Antiqui* (Hanover, 1980), with a German translation and notes by Schieffer. The passages I refer to are in cc.29–36, pp. 82–93. See H. Anton, *Fürstenspiegel und Herrscherethos in der Karolingerzeit* (Bonn, 1968), pp. 288 ff.; Löwe, 'Apocrisiar'. The text is translated in D. Herlihy, *History of Feudalism* (New York, 1970), pp. 208–27. But I use my own translation to bring out the ambiguities of the original.

[65] *De Ordine*, c.29, pp. 84–5. 'Counsel' translates Hincmar's *consilium*, which Herlihy renders misleadingly as 'decisions', and Schieffer as 'Beschlüsse' (conclusions, decrees), though further down the same page he translates as 'Rat' (counsel, advice). (Schieffer complains, p. 83, n. 195 of Hincmar's 'schwankende Terminologie'!)

[66] *ibid.*, c.30, pp. 86–7. The implication here that legislation was promulgated only at summer assemblies, though obviously an oversimplification, holds true in general: see appendix 1.

So that it should not look as if [the counsellors] had been summoned without good reason, at the outset, both those matters which
the king (through God's inspiration) had found to be in need of
attention, and those which, since the counsellors' departure from the
last assembly, had been brought to the king's notice from far and
wide as especially important, were laid before them by the king's
authority to be discussed and carefully pondered. The documents
consisted of lists of chapters each with a separate heading. When the
counsellors had received these chapters, they considered each sometimes for a day, sometimes for two days, or even three or more, as
the gravity of the matter required. Messengers chosen from the
palace servants went back and forth between them and the king
supplying them with answers on whatever queries they thought had
to be asked. All this time, no outsider came near them. Finally each
matter on which a conclusion was reached was explained orally to
the glorious prince in his presence, and whatever his divinely-
bestowed wisdom might choose, all would follow. The same process was gone through once, twice or as many times as the number of
chapters demanded, until, by God's mercy, all the problems that had
had to be dealt with on that occasion were smoothed out.[67]

The difficulty of translating certain words and phrases in this and
other passages reflects what may appear to us as the ambiguous,
even contradictory, nature of Carolingian political action: who is
making the decisions here, and who is taking initiatives? The king
'finds' the agenda, the counsellors 'find counsel', the people 'find
what is required, by their counsel and consent'. The counsellors
'reach conclusions'; the king 'chooses'; all 'follow'. It seems to me
artificial to claim that there is a special insistence here on the king's
authority, to contrast this with Hincmar's 'accent on the collaboration of the counsellors' in another near-contemporary work, and to
infer that c.34 of the De Ordine Palatii reflects conditions in the reign
of Charlemagne rather than that of Charles the Bald.[68] I am not
convinced, either, by the argument that c.29 describes the assem-

[67] ibid., pp. 90–3.
[68] So Schieffer, p. 93, n. 219, following Löwe, 'Apocrisiar', p. 223, where the De
Ordine is compared with the Acta of the Synod of St Macra-de-Fismes, PL CXXV,
cc, 1069–86, esp. 1085. On these Acta as 'the end-product of the development of
Hincmar's thought', see Anton, Fürstenspiegel, pp. 236 ff. cf. Nelson, 'Kingship,
law and liturgy', pp. 247–8, n. 5. But for the political context of Fismes, see now
Schmitz, 'Hinkmar von Reims, die Synode von Fismes 881 und der Streit um das
Bistum Beauvais', DA, XXXV (1979) pp. 463–86. For a perceptive comment on
De Ordine, c.34, see F. Kern, Gottesgnadentum und Widerstandsrecht (rev. edn Darm-
stadt, 1954), pp. 266–7.

blies of Louis the Pious, rather than those of Charles the Bald.[69] Such claims have, of course. been lent colour by the well-known fact that some, at least, of the De Ordine Palatii was, as Hincmar asserted, not his own work but that of Adalard of Corbie (d.826). But it is equally clear that much of it was Hincmar's own composition.[70] I believe the chapters on assemblies and capitularies are more likely to fall into that latter category, and that Hincmar had in mind the practice of the 860s and 870s.

As far as assemblies are concerned, the twice-yearly pattern and the specific forms of attendance and deliberation, at winter and summer meetings respectively, can be seen from appendix 2 to correspond rather well with what the Annals of St Bertin record, especially for the last decade of Charles the Bald's reign. And since Hincmar, as author of these Annals, was concerned that this information should be recorded, it seems reasonable to expect a similar interest to be reflected in his reworking of, or additions to, the De Ordine Palatii. Equally noteworthy is the correspondence between c.34's very detailed interest in the nature and function of capitula in assembly business, the references to capitula in the Annals of St Bertin, and Hincmar's role in the composing and keeping of capitulary texts (we recall Lupus' 'canons, or as you, [Hincmar], call them, capitula').[71] But most significant of all is the complex way in which the action, and interaction, of assembly participants is described. I do not hear in c.34 just one 'accent' on the king's role: on the contrary, the counsellors' 'collaboration' sounds an equally strong note, while the 'understanding' of the people provides a ground-bass with which king and counsellors harmonize. Lines of communication, and of influence, run between all these participants. Initiatives might come from one or several different points. There is no doubting the king's central role: the assemblies physically centred, after all, on the king's palace. But the king operated through a generalized 'authority' and a series of informal pressures

[69] Löwe, 'Apocrisiar', pp. 221–2. J. T. Rosenthal, 'The public assembly in the time of Louis the Pious', Traditio XX (1964), pp. 25–40, is a useful discussion, but his distinction between military and other assemblies seems to me artificial.
[70] Admirably demonstrated by Löwe, 'Apocrisiar', with reference to recent literature.
[71] Above, p. 204. cf. also Charles the Bald's order to Hincmar (appendix 1, no. 58) to prepare his dossier of canonical and Carolingian legislation on usury capitulatim. Was the king teasing Hincmar for this penchant? I think Schmitz, 'Wucher in Laon', p. 543, is right to detect 'a malicious undertone' in Charles' telling Hincmar that where canons and capitularies are concerned, 'you know better'.

on individuals. 'Counsel' engaged a select group of magnates, then a wider range of greater and lesser nobles, in collective deliberation:[72] hence, whatever the origin of a given item on the agenda, each participant could feel himself involved in decision-making. This is not to suggest that the system was 'democratic': rather, that assemblies were natural forums for the exertion of magnate influence and of the demands of the 'less important' for protection and support;[73] for the interplay of interest between patrons and clients, and of competition between patrons and between clients; and, last but not least, for royal contact with and influence on individuals and groups among both greater and lesser aristocracy. The formation of 'opinion' was the product of these complex and multiplex interactions of people in a locale where the king's peace prevailed: in a society where so many transactions directly involved coercion, meetings of the assembly seem to have stood out in Hincmar's mind as occasions when men, even *minores*, did not act 'because they were forced to do so'. The picture may have been idealized, but it did, I think, accurately represent a contemporary reality: assembly politics were consensus politics, and that consensus – achieved through political processes of persuasion and brokerage, of authority as well as power, of what Balandier has called, in another context, 'the dialectic of contestation and conformity'[74] – is what is represented , quite literally, in the

---

[72] Clearly evidenced in the surviving form of the Capitulary of Quiersy (877) (appendix 1, no. 56): 'Haec capitula constituta sunt a domno Karolo . . . cum consensu fidelium . . . de quibus ipse definivit et de quibusdam a suis fidelibus responderi iussit.' These responses have been preserved along with the *capitula*: as the *MGH* editors observe, p. 355, the capitulary can hardly have been promulgated in this form. The exchange recorded in c.4, pp. 356–7, seems especially revealing of the direct style of assembly proceedings: *Charles* 'How can we be sure that when we get back (from Italy) our kingdom will not have been disturbed by anyone?' *Fideles* 'As far as that is concerned . . . our answer is that there are the oaths we made to you, and the profession that all of us, clerics and laymen, gave to you at Quiersy . . . we have kept these up till now, and we intend to go on keeping them. So you certainly can believe us [Unde pro certo nos veraciter credere potestis].' In this same c.4, when Charles asks how he can feel confident about his son (Louis the Stammerer), he is told: 'None of us can or should do more than you can to keep him safe . . . so it is up to you to make the right arrangements.' There seems no reason to see anything new in these frank and familiar dealings. On assembly proceedings and the formulation of capitularies through discussion, see Ganshof, *Recherches*, pp. 22–9, and for the political background to Quiersy, Werner, 'Gauzlin', pp. 410 ff.

[73] A nice example: Tessier, *Receuil*, no. 228, cf. n. 39 above.

[74] G. Ballandier, *Political Anthropology* (London, 1972), p. 66.

terminology of 'consent', 'consultation', 'counsel and aid' in the capitularies of Charles the Bald. It was not just that changes in the procedures and penalties of Frankish law required the formal expression of the people's consent as well as royal promulgation.[75] An apparently classic statement of this principle does indeed occur in the 864 capitulary: 'law comes into being by the consent of the people and by the establishment of the king.'[76] (Less often remarked is the context – a change in the procedures for delivering summonses – and the mention of consensus in five other procedural contexts elsewhere in the same capitulary.)[77] But more significant, and to the capitulary's redactor(s) evidently quite compatible with this technical application of consent to legal change, is the invocation of the 'consent of the faithful men' in the prologue of the 864 text, and in several other capitularies of this period, with reference to political decision-making in general. It is important to stress that there was nothing new in such usage: a number of examples can be found in the capitularies of Charlemagne and Louis the Pious.[78] Therefore if it appears – and no more frequently – in Charles the Bald's capitularies, it need not, surely, be understood in terms of a 'shift of legislative initiative from the kingship to the aristocracy':[79] rather, in the context I have described, it at once expresses and appeals to a sense of 'common utility'[80] on the part of all, or most,

[75] For important qualifications to previous hypotheses about the distinction between *Volksrecht* and *Königsrecht*, see E. Kaufman, *Aequitatis Iudicium. Konigsrecht und Billigkeit in der Rechtsordnung des frühen Mittelalters* (Frankfurt, 1959), pp. 60–92; also Ganshof, *Recherches*, pp. 30 ff.; Wormald, 'Lex Scripta', pp. 109–10.
[76] c.6, *MGH, Capit.* II, p. 313.
[77] cc.15, p. 316 (differentials in punishments for refusing coin), 25, p. 321 (capital penalty for those selling to Vikings), 33, p. 325 (standardizing calculation of lifting of bann for returning warriors), 34, p. 326 (rules about redemption or release of slaves), 34, p. 327 (penalty for selling Christians into slavery).
[78] The texts are assembled and ably discussed by Hägermann, 'Entstehung', pp. 19–22.
[79] So Hägermann, 'Enstehung', p. 27. There are certainly more references to *consensus*, in this general sense, in Louis the Pious's capitularies than in Charles the Bald's. Kern. *Gottesgnadentum*, pp. 142–3 with n. 305, rightly stresses that the meaning of 'consensus' varies with political circumstances.
[80] This phrase, which occurs in *De Ordine*, c.31, has appeared in Charlemagne's capitularies: *MGH, Capit.* I, pp. 162, 208. In such contexts, 'usefulness' assumed a genuinely political, and not only moral, content in the later eighth and ninth centuries: see E. Peters, *The Shadow King* (Yale, 1970), pp. 47–72. cf. such terms as *utilitas populi, utilitas publica*. Of course these expressions, like the concept of the state (*res publica*), derive from Roman law and political theory, but they were resurrected in the ninth century, I think, less because of their potential for hierocratic theorists, than precisely because they reflected contemporary political realities as perceived by lay as well as ecclesiastical participants. This point scarcely

members of a political community which really did remain a going concern throughout Charles the Bald's reign.

In c.35 of the *De Ordine Palatii*, Hincmar gives a vignette of the king's role during the general assembly. Interestingly, it is at this point that we are told that 'if the weather was set fair, the assembly would be held outdoors . . .' If requested, the king would join the counsellors in their closed session, and in an atmosphere of good-fellowship (*familiaritas*) would listen to their debates. Otherwise,

> he would be occupied with the rest of the assembled people, receiving gifts, greeting important men, swapping stories with people he didn't see often, expressing sympathy with the old, sharing their pleasures with the young, and so forth, involving himself in spiritual as well as secular affairs.[81]

This could, of course, be any Carolingian king about his business: perhaps it is an idealized Charlemagne, or even a composite royal image. But Hincmar could also be drawing on his memories of Charles the Bald's assemblies, and of Charles' speeches on those occasions. For instance, in his *adnuntiatio* at Pîtres in 864, Charles thanked his faithful men for their attendance 'fully and in peace', adding wryly: 'even if not all of you, as we wanted, have been keeping the peace since our last assembly, still most of you have'.[82]

---

emerges from the otherwise admirable discussion of L. Wehlen, *Geschichts-schreibung und Staatsauffassung im Zeitalter Ludwigs des Frommen* (Lübeck-Hamburg, 1970), pp. 8–11; 91–104.

[81] Hincmar, *De Ordine*, c.35, pp. 92–3. The meaning of *familiaritas* has to be inferred not only from this passage but from its two other appearances in the *De Ordine*, cc.27 and 32, pp. 80, 88. (cf. also *familiarius* in c.18, p. 66, and *familiariter* in c.31, p. 86.) In the *De Ordine*, Hincmar consistently uses 'familiarity' in something like its colloquial sense in modern English, i.e. 'intimate acquaintanceship'. This sense of the word is not taken account of in J.-F. Niermeyer, *Mediae Latinitatis Lexicon Minus* (Leiden, 1976), *s.v.* 'familiaris', 'familiaritas'.

[82] *MGH, Capit.* II, p. 311. For another possible instance of Charles' irony, see above, n. 71. cf. Hincmar's letter to Charles, *PL* CCXXVI, c.97, where Devisse, *Hincmar*, II, p. 727, n. 6, sees a veiled allusion to a royal taunt: 'some people', says Hincmar, 'accuse us bishops of wanting to spend all day parabling through written communications' (*per scripturas parabolare* – the pun is lost in translation). The best example of Charles' black humour is his treatment of Archbishop George of Ravenna after the battle of Fontenoy, recorded, I think from eye-witness sources (perhaps George himself), by Agnellus, *Liber Pontificalis Ecclesiae Ravennatis*, c.174, *MGH, SRL*, p. 390. For the young Charles' close and informal relationship with his faithful men, see Nithard, *Histoire des fils de Louis le Pieux* II.4, ed. P. Lauer (Paris, 1926), p. 46. There is no real evidence that Charles' political style changed in later life, despite the hostile remarks about his 'Greek' imperial costume in the Annals of Fulda, *s.a.* 876, *MGH, SRG*, p. 86.

In context, Charles, repeated assurances that he will 'preserve to each man his law and justice'[83] should be interpreted not as symptoms of weakness (of monarchy 'descended from its throne' in Halphen's sense),[84] nor as statements of new constitutional principle (of 'the birth of contractual monarchy' in Magnou-Nortier's sense),[85] but as affirmations of a thoroughly traditional ideal relationship of mutual trust and collaboration between king and aristocracy: the 'familiar face' (in both senses) of Frankish politics. This image, this ideology, has been preserved for us – thanks, not least, to Hincmar's efforts – in the capitularies of Charles the Bald. It was in his reign, and probably at Rheims, that a scribe headed Ansegis' collection: 'capitula episcoporum, regum et maxime omnium nobilium francorum'.[86] For each of the noble Franks, his 'law' in the subjective sense[87] was his status, his social standing, his fair treatment according to 'the law(s)' in the objective sense of customary norms and procedures including the judgement of his peers. Hence Charles the Bald's care in having political enemies condemned 'by the judgement of the Franks'. Hence the evident requirement that any change in those customary procedures as practised in public courts should be made, should 'come into being', 'with the consent of the Franks', as well as 'by the establishment of the king'. Capitularies, duly consented to and established, themselves became laws, part of that law (in the general sense), composed of both statute and codified 'gentile' custom, which was the collective possession of the king's faithful men.[88] The law of all constituted the framework that guaranteed and preserved the law of each. Bishops, and still more kings with authority, had a crucial function in law-making that maintained 'the stability of the king-

---

[83] For such promises at Coulaines (843), Quiersy (858) and several other occasions through the reign, see Nelson, 'Kingship, law and liturgy', pp. 255 ff.

[84] In Lot and Halphen, *Règne*, p. 96.

[85] *Foi et fidelité*, pp. 98 ff.

[86] Beinecke 413, fol. 2b. For other MSS with this *incipit*, see *MGH, Capit.* I, p. 394, n.(a).

[87] For the sense of 'lex unicuique competens', see above, n. 83. cf. the closely related meaning of 'iustitia' in, for instance, the capitularies of Servais, c.2, *MGH, Capit*, II, p. 271, and Quiersy (858), *ibid.*, p. 296.

[88] For examples of these various meanings of law (*lex, leges*), see the Edict of Pîtres, c.2, *MGH, Capit.* II, p. 312 (divine and human law in general); c.3, p. 312 (the due law of each); c.6, p. 313 (customary procedures of Frankish law); c.33, p. 325 (law-makers: *conditores legum*).

dom';[89] but it was not surprising if for one well-informed contemporary – perhaps Hincmar himself? – the capitularies belonged
in a special way – *maxime* – to 'all the noble Franks'.

---

[89] *Stabilitas regni*, a traditional phrase in Merovingian and Carolingian charters,
gained a new lease of life in ninth-century capitularies.

APPENDIX 1
Capitularies of Charles the Bald

No.	Date	MGH no.	MGH title	Hague 10 D 2	MS transmission Vat. reg 291/ Vat. 4982	Beinecke 413
1	Oct 843	[293]	Capitula in synodo acta quae habita est apud Lauriacum			
2	Nov 843	254	Conventus in villa Colonia	x		
3	Jun 844	255	Capitulare Septimanicum apud Tolosam datum	x		
4	Jun 844	256	Praeceptum pro Hispanis			
5	Oct 844	227 [293]	Synodus ad Theodonis villam habita	x		
6	Dec 844	291	Concilium Vernense	x		
7	Apr 845	292	Synodus Bellovacensis	x		
8	Jun 845 }	293	Concilium Meldense–Parisiense	x (in part)		
9	Feb 846					
10	Jun 846	257	Notitia de conciliarum canonibus in villa Sparnaco a Karolo rege confirmatis	x		
11	Feb 847	204	Conventus apud Marsnam primus	x	x	
12	summer 851	205	Conventus apud Marsnam secundus	x	x	
13	Apr 853	258	Conventus Suessionensis	x		
14	Apr 853	259	Capitulare missorum Suessionense	x	x	x
15	Aug 853	294	Synodus Vermeriensis	x		

No.	Date	MGH no.	MGH title	Hague 10 D 2	MS transmission Vat. reg 291/ Vat. 4982	Beinecke 413
16	Nov 853	206	Conventus apud Valentianas	x	x	
17	Nov 853	260	Capitulare missorum Silvacense	x	x	x
18	Feb 854	207	Conventus apud Leodii habitus	x (in part)	x	
19	Jun 854	261	Capitulare missorum Attiniacense	x	x	
20	Jul 856	262	Capitula ad Francos et Aquitanos missa de Carisiaco	x		
21	Aug 856	295	Concilium optimatum Karolo II datum	x	x	
22	Oct 856	296	Coronatio Iudithae Karoli II filiae	x	x	
23	Jul/Sept 856	263	Primum missaticum ad Francos et Aquitanos directum		x	
24	Sept 856	264	Secundum missaticum ad Francos et Aquitanos		x	
25	Sept/Oct 856	265	Tertium missaticum ad Francos et Aquitanos		x	
26	Feb 857	266	Capitulare Carisiacense		x	x
27	post-Feb 857	267	Allocutio missi cuiusdam Divionensis			
28	Mar 857	268	Conventus apud Sanctum Quintinum		x	
29	Mar 858	269	Sacramenta Carisiaci praestita		x	
30	Nov 858	297	Epistola synodi Carisiacensis ad Hludowicum regem Germaniae directa		x	
31	May/June 859	298	Synodus Mettensis		x	
32	Jun 859	299	Synodus apud Saponarias habita		x	
33	Jun 859	300	Libellus proclamationis adversus Wenilonem		x	
34	Jun 860	242	Conventus apud Confluentes			

#	Date	No.	Title		
		270	Capitula post conventum		
36	Jun 861	271	Confluentinum missis tradita	x	
37	Jun 862	272	Constitutio Carisiacensis de moneta	x	
38	Nov 862	243	Capitula Pistensia	x (in part)	x
39	Jun 864	273	Conventus apud Saponarias	x	
40	Feb 865	244	Edictum Pistense	x	x
41	Feb 865	274	Pactum Tusiacense	x	x
			Capitulare Tusiacense in Burgundiam directum		
42	Aug 866	301	Coronatio Hermintrudis reginae	x	
43	867 or 868	245	Pactiones Mettenses		
44	Jul 869	275	Capitula Pistensia		
45	Sept 869	276	Electionis Karoli capitula in regno Hlotharii factae	x	
46	Sept 869	302	Ordo coronationis Karoli	x	
47	Mar 870	250	Pactiones Aquenses	x	
48	Aug 870	251	Divisio regni Hlotharii II	x	
49	Sep 872	277	Sacramenta apud Gundulfi-villam facta	x	
50	Jan 873	278	Capitulare Carisiacense	x	
51	Jun/Jul 874	303	Synodus Attiniacensis		x
52	Feb 876	220	Karoli II imperatoris electio		
53	Feb 876	221	Karoli II capitulare Papiense	x	
54	Jun/Jul 876	279	Synodus Pontigonensis	x	
55	May 877	280	Edictum Compendiense de tributo Nordmannico	x	
56	Jun 877	281	Capitulare Carisiacense		
57	Jun 877	282	Capitula excerpta in conventu Carisiacensi coram populo lecta		
58	853–75 (?868)		Mandate to Archbishop Hincmar		

APPENDIX 2

Assemblies of Charles the Bald, 860–77

	Date and place	Capitulary(ies) issued (see appendix 1)	Annals of St Bertin ref. (see n. 14 for Grat edn)	Charters issued (see n. 12 for Tessier edn)
860	Jun: Coblenz	34, 35	83	221, 222
	?Nov: Ponthion			229, 230
861	Jul: Quiersy	36		237
862	?Jan: Senlis		88: regni primores consulens.	
862	Jun: Pîtres	37	91: omnes primores . . . convenire fecit.	
	Nov: Savonnières	38	94	
			98	
863	? : Soissons		104: consilio fidelium suorum.	261
	?Nov: Auxerre			
864	Jun: Pîtres	39	113–4: generale placitum habet in quo annua dona . . . recipit.	269
865	Feb: Douzy	40, 41	116: cum fidelibus consideratis . . .	
865	?Jul: Attigny		118	
	?Dec: Rouy		124	
866	?Jun: Pîtres		127: hostiliter ad locum . . . pergit.	
867	(Aug: Chartres)		136: placitum suum . . . condixit.	
	Aug: Compiègne		137: populus . . . hostiliter veniat.	
868	Aug: Pîtres		150–1: anna dona . . . accepit . . . placitum.	
	Dec: Quiersy		151: quosdam primores . . . sibi accersivit.	

Year	Location	Entry		
869	Jul: Pîtres		44	
	Nov: Gondreville	153: placitum.		326
		167: denuntians se . . . venturum . . . ut . . . ad se venturos suscipiat.		
870	Jul: Meersen		48	
	Nov: Rheims	171–5: colloquium.		330
871	Aug: Douzy	177: plurimos fidelium . . . convenire faciens.		
	Dec: Senlis	181–2: synodum.		349
872	?Jun: Senlis	184: placitum cum suis consiliariis habuit.		
		185		
873	Sept: Gondreville	188: placitum.	49	
	Jan:Quiersy	189: cum consilio fidelium suorum . . . leges . . . promulgavit.	50	365
874	? ? (Neustria)	192: hostem denuntiat versus Brittaniam.		
	Feb: St Quentin	195–6: cum suis consiliariis placitum . . . tenuit.		
	Jun: Douzy	196: generale . . . placitum . . . tenuit, ubi et annua dona sua accepit.		369, 370, 371, 372
875	?Dec: Herstal	197: placitum . . . conlocutio.		
	Aug: Ponthion	198: quoscumque potuit de vicinis suis consiliariis obviam sibi venire praecepit . . . et suppetias in itinere suo accepit.		
876	Jan: Pavia	200: placitum suum.	52, 53	402, 403
	Jun: Ponthion	201–16: synodum . . . indixit.	54	
	Nov: Samoussy	210: placitum suum . . . condixit.		409, 410, 411
877	Jun: Quiersy	212–14: placitum suum generale habuit, ubi per capitula . . . ordinavit . . .	55, 56, 57	428

10

The Carolingian Kings and the See of Rheims, 882–987

ROSAMOND McKITTERICK

Hincmar, archbishop of Rheims (845–82), had made Rheims great.[1] From the troubles of the time of Charles Martel, several times bitterly referred to by Hincmar,[2] and the unhappy muddle resulting from the deposition of Ebbo,[3] Hincmar had made the pre-eminence of the see of the great Remigius a reality, had successfully exercised its metropolitical prerogatives, and had linked his authority with that of the west Frankish kings, particularly in the sphere of law and legislation,[4] as well as providing crucial guidance to Charles the Bald, Louis the Stammerer, Carloman and his brother Louis III.[5] Rheims' position under Hincmar, however, cannot be assumed to have endured under his successors. The pre-eminence he had achieved for Rheims became the ideal for the archbishops of the tenth century; the reality was quite different. Yet in Dumas' classic article, ideal has been confused with reality. His interpreta-

[1] J. Devisse, *Hincmar, archevêque de Reims, 845–882* (3 vols, Geneva, 1975–6) is the seminal study, but see also J. Nelson, 'Kingship, law and liturgy in the political thought of Hincmar of Rheims', *EHR*, XCII (1977), pp. 241–79, and her references. Professor Wallace-Hadrill has himself made many contributions to our understanding of Hincmar's achievement, the most recent being 'History in the mind of Archbishop Hincmar', in R. H. C. Davis and J. M. Wallace-Hadrill (eds), *The Writing of History in the Middle Ages. Essays presented to R. W. Southern* (Oxford, 1981), pp. 43–70.

[2] See for example, *MGH, SRM* III, p. 250, and *MGH, Capit.* II.2, p. 468.

[3] See Devisse, *Hincmar*, pp. 71–96.

[4] See Nelson, above, pp. 202–22.

[5] Wallace-Hadrill discusses this briefly in his 'History in the mind of Archbishop Hincmar', pp. 58–61. Rheims' importance for educating the ruler in the ninth century can be compared with that of Trier for the Merovingian kings in the sixth: see Collins, above, pp. 16–18, 23–24.

tion of the history of Rheims as a central factor in the 'struggle between Robertian and Carolingian' is thus overly simplistic and in need of revision (see appendices 2 and 4).[6]

Our understanding of the relations between Rheims and the Carolingian kings is limited by the nature of the sources. Just as Clermont's uniquely rich Merovingian sources enable us to understand something of the realities of episcopal power in Merovingian Gaul,[7] so the richness of the historiographical tradition in tenth-century Rheims means that we are particularly well informed about Rheims. Yet we know very little about anywhere else, not even Rheims' supposed chief ecclesiastical rival, Sens. Moreover, apart from the surviving royal charters issued between 882 and 987, very few of which relate to Rheims,[8] we have barely any information written from the Carolingian point of view. Most of the principal sources – Flodoard's *Annales* and his *Historia ecclesiae Remensis*, Richer's History and the letters of Gerbert – are written from a Rheims perspective and are, in the cases of the last two named, distinctly anti-Carolingian. The relations existing between the archbishops and their rulers in the tenth century, therefore, are rarely clear, and in the absence of alternative sources it is often difficult to determine precisely how important each was to the other. Nevertheless, as I shall suggest below, the main themes can be made out.

As far as can be determined from the surviving sources, Rheims, with its city, cathedral church and monasteries, was unique in the west Frankish kingdom, not only because of the prestige of the see of the great Remigius, but also for its immense wealth. Quite apart from its lands north of the Seine, many of the monastic and diocesan estates of Rheims extended into Lotharingia, Aquitaine, Provence, Limoges and Lyons. The close association between the archbishops and the principal monasteries of Rheims, moreover, added significantly to the wealth the former could command. Until 945, for

---

[6] A. Dumas, 'L'église de Reims au temps des luttes entre Carolingiens et Robertiens', *Revue d'Histoire de l'Église de France*, XXX (1944), pp. 5–38.
[7] See I. Wood, above, pp. 34–57.
[8] R. H. Bautier (ed.), *Recueil des actes d'Eudes, roi de France 888–898* (Paris, 1967), nos. 31 and 47; P. Lauer (ed.), *Recueil des actes de Charles III le Simple, roi de France 893–923* (Paris, 1940–9), nos. 1, 18 and 54; *idem* (ed.), *Recueil des actes de Louis IV, roi de France 936–954* (Paris, 1914), nos. 13, 47 and 53; L. Halphen and F. Lot (eds), *Recueil des actes de Lothaire et de Louis V, rois de France 954–987* (Paris, 1908), nos. 6, 17 and 63.

example, when the community of the suburban monastery of St
Remigius finally gained its independence of archiepiscopal control
and a regular abbot was installed, the monastery seems to have been
part of the archbishop's patrimony.[9] Thereafter, the lands of St
Remigius, concentrated between the Aisne and Marne rivers and
after 968 including estates round Kusel and Meersen in Lotharingia,
belonged to the monks. St Remigius was also important to the
Carolingians. Frederuna, Charles the Simple's first wife, Louis IV
and his wife Gerberga, and Lothar were all buried there. The
country monasteries of Rheims were also under the archbishop's
authority. St Peter's, Avenay, for example, probably a royal convent, had been dominated by archbishop Hincmar and his successor Fulk. Odo conceded it to the church of Rheims at Fulk's
request.[10] Later interventions on the part of the archbishops
to institute reform at the abbeys of St Theuderic (Thierry), St
Remigius, St Basle and Notre Dame of Mouzon are further evidence of their influence.

The landed wealth of Rheims also meant that it had considerable
military resources at its disposal. Prinz has stressed how important a
military role Rheims played within the kingdom under both Fulk
(882–900) and Heriveus (900–22).[11] Fulk renewed the ramparts of
Rheims and fought against both King Odo and count Baldwin of
Flanders. Heriveus renewed the walls of the *castrum* of Mouzon on
the Meuse and built fortifications near Coucy le Chateau and
Epernay. When the Magyars invaded Champagne in 919, Heriveus
led a force of 1500 warriors to assist the king. Subsequent
archbishops continued to fortify strongholds in Rheims and its
environs, such as the wall Seulf (922–25) built round St Remigius,
and were clearly capable of mustering an army when necessary.

Of the seven archbishops of Rheims (see appendix 1) who held
office in succession to Hincmar, none appears to have held as
dominating a position within the kingdom or in relation to the
Frankish kings as their illustrious predecessor had done. This was
not only due to the changes in the structure of the kingdom and in
the exercise of royal authority;[12] the position of the see of Rheims

---

[9] F. Poirier-Coutansais, *Gallia Monastica* I: *Les abbayes bénédictins du diocèse de Reims* (Paris, 1974).

[10] Bautier, *Eudes, Recueil*, no. 31.

[11] F. Prinz, *Klerus and Krieg im früheren Mittelalter* (Stuttgart, 1971), pp. 147–73.

[12] See R. McKitterick, *The Frankish Kingdoms under the Carolingians, 751–987* (London, 1983), pp. 305–9.

itself during the tenth century was complicated by its subservience to the house of Vermandois between 922 and 946, by the see's landed and ecclesiastical interests in Lotharingia and elsewhere, and by the personal jealousies, aristocratic connections and private ambitions of the archbishops themselves (see appendix 3).

Fulk's incumbency is the best documented.[13] Although he lacked both Hincmar's political acumen and his breadth of vision, he appears to have had every intention of continuing Hincmar's policies with regard both to Rheims and the king. Yet his initial support of his kinsman Guy of Spoleto's candidacy for the west Frankish throne and his subsequent intrigues on behalf of Charles the Simple indicate that his political manoeuvres were not entirely motivated by either loyalty to the Carolingians or the wish to maintain peace within the kingdom. Fulk was obliged in 888 to acknowledge the Robertian Odo as ruler, and recrowned him at Rheims on 13 November 888. This may have been an attempt to assert Rheims' claim to constitute kings, a claim as yet imperfectly founded, though there was no suggestion that the earlier consecration of Odo by Archbishop Walter of Sens in June 888, had been in any way invalid. For the next few years Fulk remained a reluctant supporter of Odo, while successfully resisting the latter's efforts to interfere in episcopal elections. In January 893, however, taking advantage of Odo's absence in Aquitaine, Fulk led the revolt against Odo and was joined by Odo's chancellor, bishop Askericus of Paris, Herbert, a direct descendant in the male line of Bernard, king of Italy (d.817) and later count of Vermandois, and some minor northern counts. The rebels raised their own king, the eleven-year-old Carolingian, Charles the Simple, and by promising Arnulf, king of the east Franks, 'superiority' over the west Frankish kingdom (a superiority but ill defined) Fulk induced Arnulf to recognize Charles as king. He also gained the approval of pope Formosus.[14] It is significant that the justification for the revolt was not that Odo was an usurper – he was never formally deposed – but that he had abused his power. This either referred to Odo's attempts to trespass on episcopal prerogative, or, as some commentators have suggested, it represented a protest at Odo's gift of royal and ecclesiastical land and offices to his brother Robert.[15] Once Odo had returned

[13] G. Schneider, *Erzbischof Fulco von Reims 883–900 u. das Frankenreich* (Munich, 1973).

[14] Schneider's comments on Fulk's difficult relations with pope Formosus, *ibid.*, pp. 121–3.

[15] See E. Favre, *Eudes, comte de Paris et roi de France (882–898)* (Paris, 1893), p. 96.

to Francia and besieged Rheims, the rebels soon dispersed, though Fulk and his closest allies did not capitulate until 896. Odo remained in control until his death in 898, but designated Charles the Simple as his heir. Fulk's rebellion had proved to be a false move. Rather than enhancing the power and prestige of Rheims and its archbishop, it diminished them. Even the post of archchancellor was out of Fulk's grasp for the whole of Odo's reign; it was held in turn by the abbot of St Germain-des-Prés and the bishops of Paris, Autun and Sens.[16] Fulk himself was murdered in 900 by Winemar, a retainer of Baldwin II of Flanders. The assassination itself is a comment on the extent to which Fulk had become embroiled in local ecclesiastical politics and family rivalries. As I have commented elsewhere, Baldwin II had had Fulk eliminated because of the latter's initial success in acquiring the rich abbacies of St Bertin and St Vaast after the death of their abbot Ralph, both of which Baldwin had wanted for himself as part of the extension of his control over Flanders.[17] Despite his being the undoubted instigator of the murder of the archbishop of Rheims, Baldwin II was subsequently rewarded with the abbacy of St Bertin by Charles the Simple. Thereafter, St Bertin remained in the control of the counts of Flanders, and was lost to Rheims.

Although Heriveus (900–22) was possibly appointed to succeed Fulk as archbishop of Rheims by the king,[18] had a clear wish to emulate Archbishop Hincmar,[19] and remained a staunch supporter of Charles the Simple, Rheims ceased after 900 to play as central a role in the west Frankish kingdom. Instead, local interests were predominant. Flodoard recorded Heriveus' effectiveness as archbishop, not only as a religious leader in his diocese and province but also in restoring Rheims' property to the see. Heriveus recovered land that Fulk had granted out in precaria but promptly gave it to members of his own family, his brother Odo and nephew Heriveus.[20] Schmitz argues that this was not just a blatant boosting

[16] Bautier, *Eudes, Recueil*, pp. XVIII–XLI.

[17] McKitterick, *Frankish Kingdoms*, pp. 250–1.

[18] Richer, ed. and trans. R. Latouche, *Histoire de France 888–995* (2 vols, Paris, 1967; hereafter Richer, *Historia*), I.19, pp. I.46–9, says this, but Flodoard does not mention it in either the *Annales* or the *Historia ecclesiae Remensis*.

[19] See R. H. Bautier, 'Un recueil de textes pour servir à l'histoire de l'archevêque de Reims Hervé (xe siècle)', *Mélanges Halphen* (Paris, 1951), pp. 1–6 and G. Schmitz, 'Heriveus von Reims (900–922). Zur Geschichte des Erzbistums Reims am Beginn des 10 Jahrhunderts', *Francia*, VI (1978), pp. 59–106.

[20] Flodoard, *Historia ecclesiae Remensis*, IV.11, *MGH, SS* XIII, pp. 575–6.

of the archbishop's family fortunes but a means of securing church property so that he would be able to exert some influence over it during his lifetime.[21] This may be so, but it was a shortsighted policy; neither Odo nor Heriveus was willing to relinquish newly acquired estates on his benefactor's death. A long struggle ensued between them and Heriveus' successors which, as we shall see, enabled the counts of Vermandois to gain control of the archbishopric. Heriveus, moreover, was not always successful in recovering Rheims' property; he failed, for example, to get back lands in the Lyons area. Where necessary he was ready to use force to prevent lay usurpation of ecclesiastical property. He succeeded in retrieving Mezières from Count Erlebald of the *pagus Castricensis*,[22] and fortified a number of Rheims churches and monasteries. How large the problem of retaining a hold on church property was, is clear from the proceedings of the Council of Trosly, summoned by Heriveus in June 909. The prologue is packed with the standard complaints about a world full of impurity, adultery, sacrilege, theft from churches, murder and violence against the poor, and refers feelingly to the plight of the kingdom, riven with dissension and invasion, with the cities depopulated, monasteries destroyed, the countryside laid waste and virtue gone. Yet the decree forsakes generalities in its attack on laymen who had taken church land, and the encroachment on ecclesiastical property, offices and privileges by the king and lay magnates.[23] Heriveus was contending against such encroachment throughout his term of office. In the religious sphere he was no less active. In marked contrast to Fulk's attitude towards the Vikings,[24] Heriveus supported Wido, archbishop of Rouen, in the attempt to convert the Vikings in the lower Seine basin to Christianity.[25] This enterprise, probably to be dated 900–11, is important evidence of the Viking presence in the region and the Franks' relations with them.

Nothing much of political importance is recorded for the first decade of Heriveus' archbishopric, and it was probably in these years, the most peaceful and fruitful of Charles the Simple's reign,

[21] Schmitz, 'Heriveus von Reims', p. 65.
[22] Flodoard, *Historia*, IV.16 p. 577; and see A. Longnon, *Études sur les pagi de la Gaule* (Paris, 1872), pp. 34–46.
[23] Mansi, *Concilia* XVIII, cc. 263–308; and see G. Schmitz, 'Das Konzil von Trosly', *DA*, XXXIII (1977), pp. 341–434.
[24] Flodoard, *Historia* IV.5, pp. 563–7.
[25] See *PL* CXXXVI, cc. 661–74.

that Heriveus was able to concentrate on his property, church building and promotion of the religious life. Thereafter, as well as acting as chancellor (910–19), Heriveus twice came to Charles' aid, sending troops to assist the king against the Magyars in 919 and, when the Frankish counts deserted the king in 920, it was Heriveus who remained loyal and who provided Charles with a refuge at Rheims for seven months. When Charles' authority was next challenged, Heriveus lay on his deathbed and was in no position to help. Charles and his favourite, the Lotharingian Hagano, fled to Lotharingia in June 922. In their absence, Robert, Odo's brother, was elected king and crowned by Walter, archbishop of Sens, in the monastery of St Remigius and under the very nose of the dying Heriveus. The use of St Remigius, whose status as a place for the consecration of kings was no greater than that of any other, has often been taken as proof that even the loyalty of Heriveus foundered and that he acquiesced in the coronation of Robert. This does not necessarily follow, though Charles the Simple's devotion to Hagano may have tried Heriveus' patience too far. Although an archiepiscopal monastery, St Remigius was without the Rheims city walls and a favoured royal residence. There was little Heriveus could do, ill as he was, to prevent the monastery being used by the rebels, and there is no reason to suppose either that Heriveus' support was essential (Odo, after all, had succeeded in gaining his throne without support from the archbishop of Rheims) or that Heriveus was anything but loyal to Charles the Simple to the end. In contrast, his successor Seulf (922–25), although a nominee of King Robert, had little contact with him or with King Ralph.

Seulf spent much of his short incumbency endeavouring to recover Rheims land from the brother and nephew of Heriveus. In this he was aided and abetted by Count Herbert of Vermandois who hoped thereby to gain control of Rheims. Seulf was weak enough to promise Herbert that the next archbishop would not be elected without the count's sanction and he died suspiciously soon afterwards. Flodoard indeed states quite baldly that Herbert had Seulf poisoned.[26] Immediately after Seulf's death, Herbert convoked an assembly and persuaded the clergy and people of Rheims and the bishops of Soissons and Châlons, both his creatures, to elect Herbert's five-year-old son Hugh archbishop. As Herbert had had the foresight to take the deposed Charles the Simple prisoner in 923,

[26] Flodoard, *Historia* IV.19, p. 578.

the acquiescence of the then king, Ralph, was secured. Pope John X even went so far as to endorse Herbert's position as 'lay administrator' of the temporal of Rheims.[27] Abbo, bishop of Soissons, was appointed to conduct the services in Rheims and regulate spiritual affairs as proxy for the infant archbishop. Odalric, bishop of Aix-en-Provence, who had been driven from his own see by the Saracens, later took over the spiritual direction of Rheims.

For the next twenty years the count of Vermandois retained his hold on Rheims; he conferred Rheims land on his supporters and ruthlessly quelled any opposition from the diocesan clergy. Flodoard, for example, was deprived of his benefices and ecclesiastical offices. During this period, Herbert attempted further to extend his position by proclaiming the unfortunate Charles the Simple king, but failed to win sufficient support. Only after the death of Charles did Ralph feel able to challenge Herbert's supremacy north of the Seine, and in 931 Ralph, with the help of Hugh the Great and his army, besieged Rheims and forced a new archbishop, a monk of St Remigius called Artald, on the people. In the presence of eighteen bishops the child Hugh was declared deposed and Artald consecrated. A compliant pope John XI in 933 sent the *pallium* to Artald, who remained undisturbed in his see until 940.[28]

Information about communication between Rheims and the Frankish kings Ralph (923–36) and the Carolingian Louis IV (936–54) is sparse, but on a formal level relations were close. Between 936 and 940, and again from 949 to 961, Artald acted as archchancellor. Before that, the caretaker bishop of Rheims, Abbo of Soissons, had acted as chancellor until 24 March 931; he was replaced by Ansegis of Troyes who stayed until 936. Generally however, the relationship between Rheims and the royal chancery was much disturbed in the course of the tenth century, not only on account of the Vermandois seizure of Rheims but also because neither of the Robertian rulers seemed anxious to rely on the Rheims archbishop to act as head of the chancery. It was precisely during this period that the chief notary emerged as the real head of the writing office and the office of archchancellor became a sinecure.[29]

[27] ibid., IV.20, pp. 578–9.   [28] ibid., IV.24, p. 580.
[29] This development had begun by the last few years of Charles the Bald's reign. Compare G. Tessier, *Diplomatique royale française* (Paris, 1962).

Louis IV's relations with the archbishop of Rheims were some-what warmer than had existed under Robert and Ralph. The king took the monastery of St Remigius under his protection in 940 and granted immunity to the monks. Artald had consecrated Louis king on the latter's return to his kingdom from his exile in England in 936, and in 940 Louis ceded the *comitatus* of Rheims and the right to mint coins to the archbishop. Louis probably hoped thereby to strengthen the ties between Rheims and the crown on his own terms as well as reinforcing the archbishop's ability to resist the house of Vermandois, but the precise extent of the secular authority thus conferred, in the absence of secure knowledge concerning the counts or county of Rheims, remains obscure.[30] Nor is it clear how Artald maintained secular authority over the city and its environs. There may have been a viscount and certainly in 987 there was a *vicedominus*.[31]

Whatever the case, Herbert of Vermandois was able to capture Rheims once more; with the assistance of Hugh the Great, now *dux francorum*, he attacked Rheims, drove out Artald and convoked a synod of the bishops and clergy of Rheims. Artald was deposed and Hugh was reinstated. It is significant that Flodoard gave a careful and exact account of the clerical orders Hugh had received; Abbo of Soissons had initiated him into the minor orders, after which he had been educated at Auxerre and ordained deacon by the bishop.[32] Again the pope co-operated and sent the *pallium* to Hugh in 942. On Artald was bestowed the consolation prize of the country monasteries of St Basle and St Peter's Avenay to the south of Rheims.

According to Flodoard, Hugh by no means disgraced himself as archbishop.[33] Apart from a single appearance as archchancellor in a charter dated 1 August 943, there is no evidence of a close associa-tion with Louis IV.[34] It was Hugh in 945 who made the monks of St Remigius independent of the archbishop, gave them the right to

[30] Lauer, *Louis IV, Recueil*, no. 13; and see P. Desportes, 'Les Archevêques de Reims et les droits comtaux du xᵉ et xiᵉ siècles', in *Économies et Sociétés au moyen age. Mélanges offerts à Edouard Perroy* (Paris, 1973), pp. 79–89. Corpus Christi College, Cambridge, MS 272, may contain evidence of a count of Rheims at the end of the ninth century, or of a count of a *pagus* in the Rheims area, for it was written at Rheims during Fulk's term of office and belonged to a Count Achadeus.
[31] See below, p. 243.
[32] Flodoard, *Historia* IV.28, pp. 581–2.
[33] *ibid.*, IV.32, pp. 583–4.
[34] Lauer, *Louis IV, Recueil*, no. 21.

elect a regular abbot, and, with the help of Archambald, the Cluniac abbot of Fleury, restored Benedictine observance to the monastery. (Whether this affected the monks' relationship with the king, established in 940, is not clear.) Hincmar, a monk of St Remigius, became abbot and led the Benedictine revival among the monasteries of Rheims.[35] Even on Count Herbert's death Hugh maintained his position and Louis IV was persuaded to acknowledge Hugh's election and receive his homage.[36] Louis apparently thought of providing Artald with another bishopric. Emulating his predecessors and following the injunctions of Trosly, Hugh endeavoured to regain Rheims estates from a number of the minor nobles who had installed themselves thereon. These included Artald's brother Dodo.[37] The injured nobles called on the king for assistance and, rather than protecting Rheims, Louis chose to take the nobles' part. In 944 he, and in 945 an army led by northern nobles including Bernard of Senlis and ex-Archbishop Artald, attacked Rheims. In the latter year Louis, however, was a prisoner of Hugh the Great. The army sent by his brother-in-law Otto and led by Conrad of Burgundy secured both his release and the see of Rheims. At the Council of Ingelheim in June 948, presided over by Otto, Louis IV and the papal legate Marinus, and attended by the bishops of Lotharingia and the east Frankish kingdom (with the bishops of Laon and Rheims as the sole representatives of the western kingdom), Hugh was declared an usurper, deposed and excommunicated. The council's decision was ratified by pope Agapetus II.[38] The stronghold at Mouzon where Hugh had taken refuge was destroyed by a Lotharingian army in 948. Louis IV's motives for deciding against Hugh even after he had acknowledged him are obscure, especially as by that time Hugh's brothers, the heirs to Herbert of Vermandois, had made their submission to the king. It may be that Louis thought it would be easier if a more compliant and weaker man, such as Artald clearly was, were the incumbent of Rheims, and thus that he was resistant to the strong-willed Hugh, a man capable of resisting even his own brothers' encroachments on ecclesiastical property.[39] Artald's subsequent activities, however, would suggest that this was not the case. He not only resumed his office of archchancellor and promoted, with the help of Rotmar of

[35] Flodoard, *Historia* IV.32, pp. 583–4.
[36] *ibid.*, IV.30, pp. 582–3.
[37] *ibid.*, IV.30, pp. 582–3.
[38] *ibid.*, IV.35, pp. 585–9.
[39] *ibid.*, IV.30, pp. 582–3.

Hautvillers, the monastic reform begun under Hugh by restoring the Benedictine Rule to St Basle; he also continued the archiepiscopal attack on lay encroachment on Rheims' territory and excommunicated Count Herbert III of Vermandois for taking *oppida* and *villae* belonging to Rheims.[40]

On Artald's death in 961, Count Herbert III made it clear that he wished his brother Hugh to be restored to the archbishopric. At a synod summoned by King Lothar (956–86), Gibuin of Châlons and Rorico of Laon opposed Hugh's re-election, even though the influential Bruno of Cologne was willing. The synod eventually resolved to be bound by the pope's ruling and pope John XII, no doubt recognizing that to elect the same man to the same see for the third time would be stretching the canons too far, and in this case actually being in a position to prevent this happening rather than being presented with a *fait accompli*, pronounced that Hugh could not be reinstated. Instead Odalric, a canon of Metz, was consecrated as Artald's successor.

There is no evidence that Odalric's Lotharingian origin made the slightest difference to the exercise of his archiepiscopal functions, despite Dumas' assertion that his election marked the beginning of the 'Lotharingian captivity' of the church of Rheims.[41] Apart from his position as archchancellor, Odalric was not involved in political affairs and proved a good ecclesiastical choice, continuing his predecessors' policies both with regard to the retrieval of sequestered estates and in promoting the religious life of Rheims. He succeeded, for example, in gaining Epernay from the house of Vermandois, and excommunicated Ragnold of Roucy for the depredation of Rheims' property and Theobald the Trickster, count of Blois, in 964 for taking Coucy and other estates in the Remois, despite the fact that both were vassals and supporters of Lothar. Lothar indeed assisted Odalric in his effort to protect Rheims' territory rather than letting himself be bullied by disgruntled nobles: when Hadouin, a vassal of Count Theobald, entrenched himself in the Rheims fortress of Coucy, it was Lothar who drove him out and obliged Hadouin to submit to him.

Odalric was succeeded by another canon of Metz, Adalbero, brother of Count Godfrey of Verdun, and for the first time, Lotharingia became a major preoccupation of the archbishop of

---

[40] Richer, *Historia* II.82, and cf. III.20, pp. I, 264–9, II, 26–9.
[41] Dumas, 'L'église de Reims', but the phrase is my own.

Rheims. Until then, Lotharingia's contiguity with the province of Rheims, the possession by both the cathedral church and the monasteries of Rheims of land in Lotharingia and the fact that its suffragan see Cambrai, apart from a brief period between 870 and 880, had been within the Lotharingian kingdom since 843, had simply enhanced both Rheims' interests in Lotharingia and east Frankish interest in Rheims. Only rarely, however, is there any indication that this 'interest' became more specific. There is some evidence, for example, that Rheims had contact with and could even act in the ecclesiastical affairs of the Lotharingian dioceses of the provinces of Cologne, Trier and Mainz. An agreement was reached between Heriveus of Rheims and Hatto of Mainz that Rheims lands in the diocese of Mainz should be placed under Mainz protection.[42] Following Louis IV's capture of Verdun, the archbishop of Rheims also formed a connection with the see of Verdun, for in 940, Berengar, bishop of Verdun, was consecrated by Artald,[43] and among the bishops present at Odalric's consecration was Wicfred, bishop of Verdun.[44] The bishops of Cambrai after 972 on the other hand were Ottonian nominees.[45] Adalbero of Rheims, moreover, was apparently in close sympathy with the archbishops of Mainz and Trier. To Egbert of Trier Adalbero offered Rheims as a refuge should he need it, and Willigis of Mainz was requested to assist in the protection of the property of St Remigius near Mainz (a renewal of the earlier agreement between Heriveus and Hatto).[46] This sympathy, however, was exceeded by Adalbero's involvement with the fortunes of his family; Adalbero seems to have put family loyalties above all else. Because of Lothar's attack on Lotharingia and capture of Verdun and members of Adalbero's family (including his brother Count Godfrey), Adalbero's family interests brought him into conflict with the Carolingian king. Indeed, the support Adalbero rendered Hugh Capet after the death of the last Carolingian king, Louis V, in May 987 is usually regarded as the vital factor which determined the fate

---

[42] Schmitz, 'Heriveus von Reims', p. 68.
[43] P. Lauer (ed.), *Les Annales de Flodoard* (Paris, 1905), *s.a.* 940. See also E. Hlawitschka, *Lotharingien und das Reich an der Schwelle der deutschen Geschichte* (Stuttgart, 1968).
[44] Richer, *Historia* III.19, pp. II, 26–7.
[45] L. Trenard (ed.), *Histoire des Pays-Bas français* (Toulouse, 1972), pp. 83–4.
[46] F. Weigle (ed.), *Die Briefsammlung Gerberts von Reims. MGH, Die Briefe der deutschen Kaiserzeit* II, *Epp.* 26 and 27.

of the Carolingians and ensured Hugh's elevation to the throne. Dumas went so far as to label Adalbero the 'master of the hour'. It is necessary therefore to ask how essential Rheims' backing was to Hugh.

Adalbero had been educated at Gorze, and for the first few years of his incumbency proved an exemplary archbishop. He installed Gerbert as a master of the school of Rheims, re-established a Benedictine community at Mouzon and gave the monks Lotharingian land and vineyards in the Meuse and Metz regions; a canon's rule was reintroduced for the cathedral canons and regular monks were restored to the monastery of St Theuderic. The richness of Rheims' library under archbishop Hincmar and the productiveness of its *scriptorium* at that time are well attested,[47] and there is ample evidence that in these respects at least, Rheims retained its importance in the tenth century, and that the fame of its school attracted students from far and wide. Although I have yet to document the manuscript production of Rheims in the tenth century fully, it is clear that the *scriptoria* of the monasteries of St Remigius and St Theuderic were particularly active, producing a wide range of books of high quality.[48] From the inscription on ff. 2v–3r of Rheims, Bibliothèque Municipale MS 133 – a glossed text of the Psalms, moreover, which records that the book was a gift from archbishop Adalbero to the church of St Mary, Rheims – it seems that Adalbero at least continued Hincmar's patronage of the cathedral library. Adalbero also devoted his resources to embellishing existing churches and building a new one in Rheims itself.[49]

Relations between the see of Rheims and the king were closer than they had been for many decades. Lothar's natural sons Otto (later a canon of Rheims), Richard and Arnulf (later archbishop of Rheims) were educated in the school at Rheims, as was his nephew Bruno, later bishop of Langres. Lothar's mother Gerberga be-

[47] F. L. Carey, 'The Scriptorium of Reims during the archbishopric of Hincmar', in L. W. Jones (ed.), *Classical and Mediaeval Studies in Honor of Edward Kenneth Rand* (New York, 1938), pp. 41–60.

[48] The library and *scriptorium* of Rheims in the tenth century will form part of a larger study of the tenth-century church that I am preparing. A few examples of manuscripts produced at Rheims during this period are described in *Les Plus Beaux Manuscrits de la Bibliothèque Municipale de Reims* (Rheims, 1967); while some indications of the resources of St Theuderic are to be found in Rheims, Bibliothèque Municipale MS 427, ff. 12v–13; see the *Catalogue Générale des Manuscrits* XXXVIII (Paris, 1904), p. 540.

[49] Richer, *Historia* III.22–3, pp. II, 28–31.

queathed all her property, including Meersen, to the monastery of St Remigius. Adalbero acted as archchancellor to Lothar from 949. At Adalbero's invitation in December 976, Lothar performed the solemn elevation of the relics of St Theuderic.[50] Coolidge has suggested that Adalbero may have had an ulterior motive in inviting Lothar to call off his campaign in Lotharingia.[51] This would make better sense if we accept the justness of Louis V's accusation against Adalbero, recorded by Richer in an ambiguously worded phrase, that Adalbero provided guides to lead Otto's army safely from the west Frankish kingdom after the east Frankish ruler's invasion in 978.[52] When Lotharingia became once again central to west Frankish interests in 984, after the death of Otto II, Adalbero, egged on by the wily Gerbert, then became embroiled in political intrigue.

Gerbert, a master of the school at Rheims from 974 to 980 had then been appointed abbot of Bobbio by Otto II. His installation there was so unpopular that in 984, despite his zeal for the Ottonians, he was obliged to leave Italy and return to Rheims. At first his and Adalbero's efforts were devoted to preventing Henry of Bavaria securing the east Frankish throne and to promoting Lothar as guardian to the young Otto III.[53] Gerbert's letters (many of which, it must be remembered, he wrote on his own behalf) reveal his patron Adalbero preoccupied with the Lotharingian question and in particular with the fate of his own family before and after the capture of Verdun. At Rheims in June 984, Adalbero received Lotharingian hostages who were to act as surety for the Lotharingian nobles' fidelity to Lothar as guardian of Otto III; the hostages included his nephew Adalbero.[54] Gerbert reiterated Adalbero's loyalty to Otto III and Theophanu,[55] manifest in Adalbero's involvement in the attempt to get his own nephew Adalbero, a nominee of Otto III, elected bishop of Verdun. Archbishop Adalbero permitted his nephew to leave his custody at Rheims, and Egbert, archbishop of Trier was eventually induced to consecrate Adalbero bishop of Verdun in December 985 or January 986. By

[50] F. Lot, *Les Derniers Carolingiens* (Paris, 1891), p. 86.
[51] R. T. Coolidge, 'Adalbero of Laon', *Studies in Medieval and Renaissance History*, II (1965), pp. 1–114 at p. 17, n. 69.
[52] Richer, *Historia* IV.2, pp. II, 146–7.
[53] See, for example, Gerbert, *Epp.* 22, 26, 27, 30, 37, 38, 39.
[54] *ibid., Ep.* 49.
[55] *ibid., Ep.* 37 and cf. *Epp.* 41 and 43.

that time Lothar had been in possession of the city of Verdun for
six months, while Count Godfrey had been taken prisoner and
entrusted to the counts of Chartres and Vermandois. Adalbero's
consequent dilemma, between his loyalty to his kindred and to his
king, seems to have been exploited fully by Gerbert for his own
ends. Many letters ensued on behalf of the captives.[56] Lothar
suspected Adalbero and Gerbert of treason and called on the former
to answer for his conduct at Compiègne on 11 May 985. Although
Lothar, apparently unable to gather sufficient evidence to support
his case, let the matter drop, Adalbero's aggrieved defence survives.
In it he protested constant fidelity to the king.[57]

Yet despite their activities on behalf of east Frankish interests,
neither Adalbero nor Gerbert directed their energies to the under-
mining of Lothar's position in the west Frankish kingdom. The
overtures to Hugh Capet, usually regarded as highly significant
evidence of Rheims' new alignment to the Robertian house, are, on
careful reading, simply efforts to gain the esteem of a powerful
noble, with no clear objectives in view, and with apparently no
response from Hugh Capet himself.[58] Gerbert's famous references
to Hugh as the king of the west Frankish kingdom in fact though
not in name are sheer bombast.[59] The initiative for the approach to
Hugh Capet, moreover, came primarily from Gerbert. In other
words, the evidence is insufficient to support the supposition that
either Adalbero or Gerbert was actively intriguing for Hugh Capet
and against the Carolingians. This did not become a possibility until
after Louis V's death in May 987.

During Louis V's short reign (March 986–May 987) the chronology of the shifting alliances is extremely difficult to unravel, owing
to the latitude given the dates of the most crucial of Gerbert's letters.
Gerbert evidently decided to leave the west Frankish kingdom[60] but
Hugh Capet supported Louis. Louis' mother Queen Emma, on the
other hand, sought an alliance with the east Frankish ruler through
her mother Adelaide, widow of Otto I,[61] as well as with archbishop
Adalbero, himself anxious about the fate of Verdun and of his
family.[62] Louis, however, cast his mother off and turned against

---

[56] ibid., for example, Epp. 47, 48, 50, 51, 52, 53, 54, 55.
[57] ibid., Ep. 57.   [58] ibid., for example Epp. 60 and 61.
[59] ibid., Epp. 41 and 48: Lotharius rex franciae praelatus est solo nomine, Hugo vero non
nomine sed actu et opere.
[60] ibid., Ep. 91.   [61] ibid., Ep. 74.   [62] ibid., Ep. 85 and cf. Ep. 99.

Adalbero.[63] With the support of Hugh Capet's army Louis attacked Rheims in February 987 and delivered his ultimatum to the archbishop.[64] If Adalbero would deliver up hostages, swear fidelity, destroy his castles of Mouzon and Mezières (both were in east Frankish territory) and come to answer the charges against him (these included the treasonable assistance supposedly rendered Otto II in 978) he would be pardoned. Otherwise he would forfeit his see and be exiled. Adalbero gave his *vicedominus* Ragnald as hostage and promised to come to trial at Compiègne on 18 March 987.[65] The assembly was postponed to 11 May, but before Adalbero's case could be heard, Louis V was killed in a hunting accident. As *dux francorum* and leading magnate in the kingdom, Hugh Capet assumed the presidency of the assembly and Adalbero was acquitted. At some stage before this, Hugh Capet seems either to have 'changed sides' or to have been hedging his bets, for he appears to have accorded asylum to Queen Emma. It is only at Compiègne that Adalbero came out in unequivocal support of Hugh, so recently his enemy. Whatever Adalbero's motives – acknowledgement of Hugh's power within the kingdom, his anxiety for the release of his brother and the relinquishment of Verdun – his advocacy of Hugh's candidacy was decisive. The problem of the succession was raised, and to avoid the accusation of unseemly haste the assembly was reconvened at Senlis a fortnight later. There Adalbero made a rousing speech – or at least, Richer provides him with one – in favour of the elective principle of kingship and against that of legitimacy.[66] A number of transparently spurious reasons were adduced for setting aside the claims to the throne of Charles of Lotharingia, Lothar's younger brother. Hugh Capet was thereupon elected king and crowned by Adalbero at Noyon on 3 July 987. By September 987 Count Godfrey had been released and Verdun had been returned to the east Frankish kingdom. It is tempting to think that this was the price Hugh Capet paid for Adalbero's support and east Frankish restraint from backing the claim of Charles of Lotharingia. On the other hand, Hugh could not have foreseen the early demise of Louis, and the events after the latter's death hardly left time to negotiate with the east Franks.

[63] *ibid.*, *Ep.* 97. The letter is dated by Weigle to October 986–February 987; it is thus not clear whether Louis had repulsed his mother before or after his attack on Rheims. It is more likely that it was before.
[64] Richer, *Historia* IV.3–5, pp. II, 148–53.
[65] Gerbert, *Ep.* 89.   [66] Richer, *Historia* III.11, pp. II, 18–21.

Adalbero's backing for Hugh was important, but there is little doubt that Hugh could probably have succeeded without it. Yet he lacked the approval of the archbishop of Sens as well, the archbishop of Rheims' peer,[67] and we need to consider how significant this was.

In assessing Sens' position in relation to the Robertians, the Carolingians, and to Rheims during the tenth century we are bedevilled by the sources; apart from the ninth-century annals of St Columba of Sens, the narrative sources for Sens are eleventh-century or later and both derivative and partisan. Neither Odorannus[68] nor Clarius[69] reveal much concerning the archbishops of Sens before 1015, so that in matters such as Sens' 'primacy of Gaul',[70] its 'rivalry' with Rheims over the consecration of kings, and whether and when Sens supported the Carolingians or Robertians, the evidence is depressingly sparse. That Sens was at least sympathetic towards the Robertian family in the late ninth and early tenth centuries may be concluded from the fact that Walter, archbishop of Sens, consecrated Odo, Robert and Ralph in 888, 922 and 923 respectively and acted as archchancellor in Odo's chancery. But political circumstances rather than overt rivalry between the two sees determined which bishop consecrated each new king between 882 and 987. William of Sens fetched Louis IV from England but Artald of Rheims crowned him. Lack of political involvement on Sens' part thereafter may simply be due to its ill fortune in its archbishop. Archembald (958–67), for example, a relative of the count of Sens, was, according to Odorannus and Clarius, bishop only in name. He sold the churches of Sens as well as their lands and treasure, and used what remained for his private enjoyment; he turned the refectory of St Peter's monastery into a brothel for his pleasure and kept his dogs in the monastic precincts. Only under Anastasius (968–76) was there the beginning of recovery, while the real work of restoration and renewal was organized by Seguin (977–99).

Despite the anti-Capetian tone of the *Historia francorum*

---

[67] See A. Fliche, 'La Primatie des Gaules depuis l'époque carolingienne jusqu'à la fin de la querelle des investitures (876–1121)', *RH*, CLXXIII (1934), pp. 329–42.

[68] Odorannus, *Opera Omnia*, ed. and trans. R. H. Bautier and M. Gilles (Paris, 1972).

[69] Clarius, *Chronicon sancti Petri Vivi Senonensis*, ed. and trans. R. H. Bautier and M. Gilles (Paris, 1979).

[70] Fliche, 'Primatie des Gaules'.

Senonensis,[71] there is no evidence that the archbishop of Sens was particularly pro-Carolingian at the end of the tenth century. From a letter written by Gerbert on behalf of Hugh Capet, it seems that Seguin of Sens was tardy in acknowledging Hugh Capet as king.[72] On the other hand, Seguin does not feature among the supporters of Charles of Lotharingia in his bid for the west Frankish throne in 988; and his sympathy towards Charles' ally and nephew Arnulf, archbishop of Rheims (989–91) at the council of St Basle in 991 was more a product of the maintenance of ecclesiastical dignity and prerogative against Hugh Capet and possibly an aversion to the bullying Gerbert who wanted Rheims for himself.[73] Seguin, moreover, had undoubtedly made his submission to Hugh by 991. All our information about Sens in the tenth century, meagre as it is, indeed indicates that local and ecclesiastical interests were predominant, just as they were for Rheims.

These local preoccupations on Rheims' part were also, in a sense, part of Hincmar's legacy to the see. As Professor Wallace-Hadrill has stressed, Hincmar provided the faithful of Rheims, in his *Life of St Remigius*, with 'a local saint strengthened in his dealings with local problems by his exceptional connection with national affairs'.[74] Throughout the last century of Carolingian rule, Rheims strove to preserve its lands from lay encroachment, to promote the religious life, to defend its wealth and its interests. National interests were subordinate; the archbishops' first loyalty was to Rheims. Their aristocratic connections and ecclesiastical priorities dominated their policies. From the examples of Clermont, discussed by Ian Wood above, Auxerre and Le Mans in the eighth century,[75] and Rheims and Sens in the tenth century, it is evident that a common theme, that of the interdependence of royal political power and local ecclesiastical and aristocratic interests, runs through the history of the Frankish kingdoms. But the precise

[71] See J. Ehlers, 'Die *Historia francorum Senonensis* und der Aufstieg des Hauses Capet', *Journal of Medieval History*, IV (1978), pp. 1–26.
[72] Gerbert, *Ep.* 107.
[73] Richer, *Historia* IV.51–7. pp. II, 230–43; see too A. Fliche, 'Seguin, archevêque de Sens, primat des Gaules et de Germanie (977–999)', *Bulletin de la Société archéologique de Sens*, XXIV (1909), pp. 149–206.
[74] Wallace-Hadrill, 'History in the mind of Archbishop Hincmar', p. 68.
[75] On Auxerre and Le Mans, see briefly J. Semmler, 'Pippin III. und die fränkischen Klöster', *Francia*, III (1975), pp. 88–146 at 95–7 and 123–7 respectively. Wormald's comments on the importance of Canterbury in relation to the English kings, above, pp. 125–9, should also be borne in mind.

relationships between the different groups or individuals within this interdependence differed, as we have seen in the case of tenth-century Rheims, according to particular circumstances. If the success of the Carolingian kings had offered a useful political context for the spiritual authority of the bishop of Rheims in the ninth century, one Hincmar at least was quick to exploit, so the problems which beset the Carolingian kings in the tenth century had their complement in those which confronted the see of Rheims; each had their effect upon the other.

APPENDIX 1

Archbishops of Rheims and Sens

Archbishops of Rheims, 882–1021

Fulk   (882–900)
Heriveus   (900–22)
Seulf   (922–25)
Hugh   (925–32, 940–48)
Artald   (932–40, 948–61)
Odalric   (962–69)
Adalbero   (969–88)
Arnulf   (988–91, 996–1021)

Archbishops of Sens, 871–999

Ansegis   (871–83)
Evrard   (883–87)
Walter I   (887–923)
Walter II   (924–27)
Audald   (927–32)
William   (932–38)
Gerland   (938–54)
Hildeman   (954–59)
Archembald   (959–68)
Anastasius   (968–77)
Seguin   (977–99)

APPENDIX 2 *The Robertians*

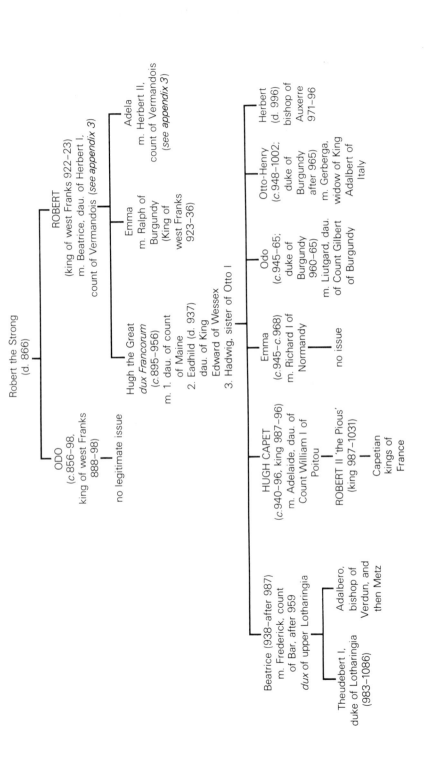

Robert the Strong
(d. 866)

ODO
(c.856–98,
king of west Franks
888–98)

no legitimate issue

ROBERT
(king of west Franks 922–23)
m. Beatrice, dau. of Herbert I,
count of Vermandois *(see appendix 3)*

Hugh the Great
dux Francorum
(c.895–956)
m. 1. dau. of count
of Maine
2. Eadhild (d. 937)
dau. of King
Edward of Wessex
3. Hadwig, sister of Otto I

Emma
m. Ralph of
Burgundy
(King of
west Franks
923–36)

Adela
m. Herbert II,
count of Vermandois
(see appendix 3)

HUGH CAPET
(c.940–96, king 987–96)
m. Adelaide, dau. of
Count William I of
Poitou

ROBERT II 'the Pious'
(king 987–1031)

Capetian
kings of
France

Emma
(c.945–c.968)
m. Richard I of
Normandy

no issue

Odo
(c.945–65;
duke of
Burgundy
960–65)
m. Liutgard, dau.
of Count Gilbert
of Burgundy

Otto-Henry
(c.948–1002;
duke of
Burgundy
after 965)
m. Gerberga,
widow of King
Adalbert of
Italy

Herbert
(d. 996)
bishop of
Auxerre
971–96

Beatrice (938–after 987)
m. Frederick, count
of Bar, after 959
dux of upper Lotharingia

Theudebert I,
duke of Lotharingia
(983–1086)

Adalbero,
bishop of
Verdun, and
then Metz

APPENDIX 3 The house of Vermandois

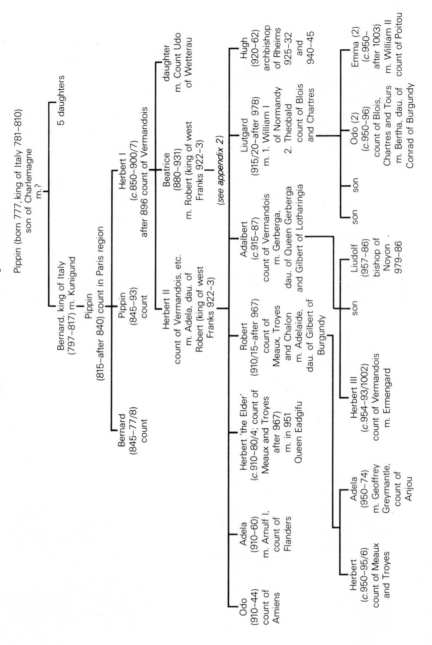

APPENDIX 4 The Carolingians in the tenth century: descendants of Charles the Simple

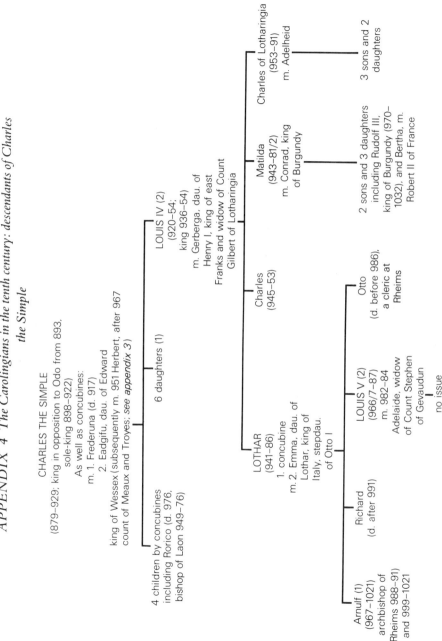

CHARLES THE SIMPLE
(879–929: king in opposition to Odo from 893, sole-king 898–922)
As well as concubines:
m. 1. Frederuna (d. 917)
2. Eadgifu, dau. of Edward king of Wessex (subsequently m. 951 Herbert, after 967 count of Meaux and Troyes; *see appendix 3*)

4 children by concubines including Rorico (d. 976, bishop of Laon 949–76)

6 daughters (1)

LOUIS IV (2)
(920–54; king 936–54)
m. Gerberga, dau. of Henry I, king of east Franks and widow of Count Gilbert of Lotharingia

LOTHAR
(941–86)
1. concubine
m. 2. Emma, dau. of Lothar, king of Italy, stepdau. of Otto I

Charles
(945–53)

Matilda
(943–81/2)
m. Conrad, king of Burgundy

Charles of Lotharingia
(953–91)
m. Adelheid

Arnulf (1)
(967–1021)
archbishop of Rheims 988–91)
and 999–1021

Richard
(d. after 991)

LOUIS V (2)
(966/7–87)
m. 982–84
Adelaide, widow of Count Stephen of Gevaudun

no issue

Otto
(d. before 986),
a cleric at Rheims

2 sons and 3 daughters including Rudolf III, king of Burgundy (970–1032), and Bertha, m. Robert II of France

3 sons and 2 daughters

11

The Making of
King Aethelstan's Empire:
an English Charlemagne?

MICHAEL WOOD

No other Anglo-Saxon reign poses so acutely as Aethelstan's the early English historian's familiar problem of the discrepancy between what he knows and what he is tempted, if not entitled, to guess. Compared to his grandfather, Aethelstan is poorly documented, and his achievement, the spectacular military and diplomatic successes apart, remains obscure. Yet on almost any reading of the evidence available, he was the most powerful ruler that Britain had seen since the Romans.[1] Exactly fifty years after Alfred built his stockade at Aethelney, his grandson was proclaimed 'rex Anglorum' in the royal hall at Exeter, in the presence of Welsh 'subreguli': perhaps the first unchallengeable instance of the title (above, pp. 110–11). Within a short time, his charters and coins reflect a new imperial style: 'florentis Brytaniae monarchia praeditus rex', as an 'original' of 931 puts it.[2] In the 980s, his relative, Aethelweard, in a work designed for a kinswoman in Germany, provides a brief but coherent background to the *pax* of Edgar in the same way that Adalbert of St Maximin or Widukind of Korvey do for the *imperium* of Otto I: following the 'immense battle against the barbarians' at Brunanburh (which, he adds, the man in the street still calls the 'great war'), 'the barbarian forces . . . held the

---

[1] Wormald, above, p. 119, as against J. Campbell, *The Anglo-Saxons* (Oxford, 1982), p. 54. I wish to thank Dr J. J. G. Alexander for reading this paper and for advice on the 'Aethelstan' manuscripts.

[2] S 400; S 416; cf. C. Blunt, 'The coinage of Aethelstan, 924–39: a survey', *British Numismatic Journal*, XLII (1974).

superiority no more . . . The king drove them off the shores of the ocean . . . The fields of Britain were consolidated into one, (*uno solidantur Brittanidis arva*) there was peace everywhere.'[3] Aethelstan impressed foreigners too. In a poem modelled on one once addressed to Charlemagne, a Frankish cleric at his court spoke of 'ista perfecta Saxonia'.[4] For a Frankish correspondent, he 'excelled in fame and praise all earthly kings of modern times'.[5] A contemporary annalist at Clonard or Armagh called him 'roof-tree of the dignity of the western world' (a *topos* perhaps, and the 'western world' had shrunk since Charlemagne's day, but nevertheless a *topos* evoking Charlemagne and the Roman emperors before him).[6] While the Carolingian and Breton royal families sheltered in Aethelstan's court, the rising stars, Capetians and Ottonians, engaged in diplomacy and extravagant gift-giving in a bid to mingle their blood with that of the West Saxon dynasty, who now ruled a '*regalis imperium*', to which '*omnes gentes* were subject' (in the words of Aethelstan's chaplain, the future archbishop Oda).[7]

Something dramatic had happened in Aethelstan's England, and contemporaries knew it. Historians have often been less sure, and the extravagant language of the king's diplomas and correspondence has generally been viewed with caution. Yet, as is observed elsewhere in this book, the imperial style inaugurated by Aethelstan is at least consistent (above, p. 111). It invites speculation on its ideological basis. Charlemagne and Alfred had seen that the realities of early medieval power demanded their ideal dimension. To maintain an *imperium* a king needed not only military force, but also councillors in kingship and ritual, technicians of the sacred, craftsmen, illuminators, poets and scribes, a 'think tank' of *gesceadwise men* in constant attendance on him. Professor Wallace-Hadrill has written of how 'Alfred turned for help to the experts on kingship – Charlemagne's descendants, whose would-be supplanters, twenty-

[3] The *Chronicle of Aethelweard*, ed. and trans. A. Campbell (London, 1962), p. 54; cf. K. Leyser, 'Henry I and the beginnings of the Saxon Empire', *EHR*, LXXXIII (1968), p. 1 ff.

[4] M. Lapidge, 'Some Latin poems as evidence for the reign of Aethelstan', *ASE*, IX (1981), p. 89. W. H. Stevenson was the first to see that this poem was closely modelled on a Carolingian work addressed to Charlemagne: 'A Latin poem addressed to King Aethelstan', *EHR*, XXVI (1911), pp. 482–7; Dr Lapidge's discussion shows that it was written in northern England in 927, not in Francia as Stevenson thought.

[5] William of Malmesbury, *Gesta Pontificum*, ed. N. Hamilton (RS, 1870), p. 399.

[6] *AU*, I, p. 459.   [7] *Gesta Pontificum*, p. 23.

seven years after Alfred's death, could think of no gift more fitting
for his grandson than Charlemagne's own lance.' This essay will
argue, building on foundations laid sixty years ago by Armitage
Robinson, that Aethelstan continued, even intensified, Alfred's
Kulturpolitik, and that Charlemagne's lance was a not unfitting
reflection of his efforts. Although the paucity of our sources suggests
that his success was limited, these efforts form an essential bridge
between the work of Alfred on the one hand and that of the
tenth-century reformers on the other.[8]

Throughout the heyday of the Anglo-Saxon 'empire' the actual
number of the relevant experts was tiny. Even at the peak of Edgar's
patronage of the monastic reform, we can only point to around a
dozen *scriptoria* trained in the Caroline minuscule that was by then
the 'official' tool of government.[9] In Aethelstan's day we must
suspect that there was a mere handful of such houses, and a very
small pool of scribes capable of writing a trained square minuscule,
Aethelstan's 'official' script and the first reformed script of the
tenth-century revival. Of this small group, it seems that some spent
at least part of their time in the king's company as he crossed his
kingdom from one royal *tūn* to the next (below, pp. 286–7).

The key manuscripts of the second quarter of the tenth century
have such clear similarities of script that they very likely all emanate
from a small and related circle of writers.[10] The most important is
Corpus Christi College, Cambridge, MS 173, the Parker Chronicle.
This consisted originally of a *res gestae* of the house of Cerdic down
to 891, continued early in Aethelstan's reign to 920. The main hand
of this later section also wrote BL Add. MS 47967, the OE Orosius.
The Orosius shows that impetus behind the copying of 'Alfredian'
translations persisted under Aethelstan, as we can also see from the

[8] Wallace-Hadrill, *EMH*, p. 214; J. Armitage Robinson, *The Times of St Dunstan*
(Oxford, 1923), pp. 51–80.
[9] T. A. M. Bishop, *English Caroline Minuscule* (Oxford, 1971), p. xv.
[10] In what follows, I have relied on N. R. Ker, *A Catalogue of Manuscripts
containing Anglo-Saxon* (Oxford, 1957), nos 39, 42, 133, 259, 335, 351; on the
articles of P. Chaplais, *Journal of the Society of Archivists*, III (1965–9), pp. 59–60,
163; on T. A. M. Bishop, 'An early example of the square minuscule', *Transactions
of the Cambridge Bibliographical Society*, IV (1968), pp. 246–52; and on M. Parkes,
'The palaeography of the Parker Manuscript of the *Chronicle*, laws and Sedulius',
ASE, V (1976), p. 146 ff.; many of the manuscripts are illustrated in E. Temple,
Anglo-Saxon Manuscripts, 900–1066 (London, 1976). An important forthcoming
article by D. Dumville may necessitate some modification for the 'Winchester'
thesis.

now lost leaf of Bodleian Junius MS 86, a Boethius in a hand apparently similar to the Orosius, and from Bodleian Tanner MS 10, an OE Bede with script and ornament closely resembling the Orosius and a contemporary Psalter, Bodleian Junius MS 27. The origin of Junius 27 is uncertain, but it is linked to the Orosius, for the same artist did the initials of both.[11] Moreover, the Psalter incorporates part of a metrical calendar adapted from the Irish *feliri* in early tenth-century Wessex, probably by itinerant *Scotti* whom we know to have resided with Alfred and his successors;[12] its royal connection is suggested by the entry of the obits of Alfred and his wife in the calendar. Now this *martyrologium poeticum* is found in full, with the royal *obits*, in BL Cotton MS Galba A xviii, added to a Frankish Psalter which belonged to Aethelstan , and to which were also added at this time an important cycle of pictures, and liturgical material in a hand very like one in a contemporary Aldhelm (BL Reg. MS 7 D xxiv).

It is likely that this whole group of manuscripts is directly or indirectly linked with Winchester. The first hand of Corpus 173 also wrote the bounds of a housing-plot in Winchester into BL Harleian MS 2965 (f. 40v), which belonged to Nunnaminster, the convent in the city founded by Alfred's widow.[13] There is evidence of its subsequent association with bishop Frithestan of Winchester (909–31); it may have become 'the bishop's book'. But the next two bishops of Winchester, Beornstan and Aelfeah, were very close to Aethelstan, and the next addition to Corpus 173 is perhaps evidence of a connection with the court. This was a copy of the laws of Alfred and Ine; together with the preceding *Chronicle*, the MS now reflected the peaceful as well as the warlike activity of the West Saxon dynasty, perhaps 'a conscious attempt . . . to present the tradition of the West Saxon royal house in its purest form.'[14] The script of the first page of the laws resembles that of a late Aethelstan charter; the remainder is in a hand like that of 'Chaplais, scribe (3)', who wrote Aethelstan's personal inscription into a manuscript which he gave to Canterbury.[15]

[11] F. Wormald, 'Decorated initials in English MSS', *Archaeologia*, XCI (1945), p. 118.   [12] E. Bishop, *Liturgica Historica* (Oxford, 1918), p. 140 ff., 254 ff.
[13] Ker, *Catalogue*, 237.
[14] Parkes, 'Parker MS', pp. 164–7; cf. P. Wormald, '*Lex Scripta* and *Verbum Regis*', in P. H. Sawyer and I. N. Wood (eds), *Early Medieval Kingship* (Leeds, 1977), pp. 121, 130, 132, 134.
[15] S 447(939); Chaplais, *Journ. Soc. Arch.*, p. 163.

Two other important books can be added to this group. One is the manuscript of Bede's two *Lives of Cuthbert* which Aethelstan gave to Chester-le-Street between 934 and 937 (Corpus 183). The main hand reappears in ff. 82–127 and 136–62 of the above-mentioned Aldhelm, which, like the language of the king's charters, testifies to the reviving interest in an author whose abbey of Malmesbury was especially favoured by Aethelstan.[16] Some of the initials in both manuscripts were probably by the same artist. There are thus significant links between seven important manuscripts. Corpus 173, with its royal *gesta*, genealogies and laws, shares a scribe with the Orosius (containing geographical information given to Alfred), which shares an illuminator with Junius 27, a de luxe Psalter with royal *obits*. In its turn, Junius 27 shares an Irish calendar with a Psalter which is intimately connected with Aethelstan; the handwriting of these manuscripts bears an unmistakable resemblance to that of scribes in the Tanner Bede, the Royal Aldhelm and the royal charter series; the Aldhelm shares a scribe (and probably an artist) with Corpus 183, which with its king-lists and genealogies was presented by Aethelstan to St Cuthbert's. The implication of this admittedly circumstantial evidence is that we may as well call these books 'royal' as anything else. Corpus 183 was commissioned by the king and bears his picture on its frontispiece (Plate VI), and we shall see that the new pictures in Galba A xviii reflect his interest.

We cannot show that such scribes worked in a royal workshop rather than an episcopal *scriptorium*: most likely, they worked in both, borrowed by the king when he needed them. This is also suggested by the other important group of the royal scribes, the charter writers. Dr Chaplais has argued that the 'chancery' scribes of Aethelstan and his immediate successors were, for the most part, members of the Winchester *scriptorium*; one ('scribe (4)') almost certainly was, and five others are so similar in style 'that one cannot even be sure that some of the works [ascribed to] different hands were not in fact written by the same scribe.'[17] Clearly, however, as Dr Keynes stresses, these scribes moved about with the king: the charters of 'scribe (1)' were *perscripta* at places as far apart as Lifton

---

[16] For reservations about the Winchester connection of these manuscripts, see D. Dumville, 'The Anglian collection of royal genealogies', *ASE*, V. (1976), pp. 25–6. For the identity of hands in Corpus 183 and Royal 7 D xxiv, Bishop, 'Early example', p. 247.

[17] Chaplais, *Journ. Soc. Arch.*, pp. 59–60.

(Devon) and Winchester.[18] Travel with the king is also indicated by book inscriptions. At the top of f. 15r of the Durham *Liber Vitae* (BL Cotton MS Domitian vii), what may be a tenth-century West Saxon hand wrote Aethelstan's name above a list of Northumbrian kings, probably when the king visited the shrine in 934. The scribe used a horned 'a', resembling 'ac', a feature otherwise confined to Corpus 183 among 'Aethelstan' manuscripts, though, because the script is imitative, we cannot be sure that the same man was involved. The charred square minuscule inscription in BL Cotton MS Otho B ix, also given to St Cuthbert's by Aethelstan, reads 'Kl. iul. bdictus evernensicus pingere feci in honore sci cudbrechti'.[19] Aethelstan may indeed have been at Chester-le-Street on 1 July 934, and it is thus likely that the inscription was penned in the royal tent; it is again not impossible that the scribe of Corpus 183 was responsible, because both use the near-uncial 'r', but the fragment is too blackened and shrunk for a firm conclusion. At any rate, there is nothing implausible about itinerant scribes: a note on f. 167r of Durham MS A iv 19 says that four collects in the MS were written 'at Oakley near Woodyates in Wessex on Wednesday, St Lawrence's day, by Aldred the provost in Bishop Aelfsige's tent' (probably 970).[20]

It has recently been suggested that one solution to the controversy over the later Anglo-Saxon chancery may lie in an analogy with what Professor Fleckenstein has demonstrated for the chapel of Ottonian kings.[21] Ottonian *capellani* accompanied their royal masters whilst retaining a close relationship with the cathedrals where they had been educated or served, and where they often still held benefices. Such men were not only the court's clerical staff; they also went on diplomatic or relic-collecting missions and even presided over *placita*. Asser, who elsewhere writes of Alfred's 'priests and *capellani*', describes an organized rotation of court personnel in Alfred's day, which applied not only to secular officials but also to

[18] S 416; S 425; S. D. Keynes, *The Diplomas of King Aethelred 'the Unready'*, 978–1016 (Cambridge, 1980), p. 39 ff.
[19] Wanley in Hickes, *Thesaurus*, II (1705), p. 238, gives 'Euernenficus', but this is very likely an error by his compositor at the Sheldonian; the MS clearly has '-sicus', giving a formulation on 'Evernia', the older form of 'Hibernia'.
[20] Ker, *Catalogue*, 106.
[21] P. Wormald, review in *History*, LXVII (1982), p. 310; J. Fleckenstein, *Die Hofkapelle der deutschen Könige*, II (Stuttgart, 1966), p. 119 ff.

the king's craftsmen.[22] It is at least possible that the scribes who 'published' Alfred's translations were sometimes at court and sometimes in their home churches. Although the only definite statement that royal scribes were organized in this way comes from a late and notoriously unreliable passage in the *Liber Eliensis*, it makes sense of the palaeographical evidence to suppose that Aethelstan had a chapel which was integrally linked with his chief churches.[23]

In a charter of 4 September 925, and a manumission of the same day entered into BL Reg. MS 1 B vii (f. 15v), we find that the king's clerical entourage on his coronation day included Aelfeah 'mass priest', Beornstan 'mass priest' and Aelfeah 'priest and monk'.[24] The list of Aethelstan's court circle in the Durham *Liber Vitae* includes 'Odo presbyter' and Cenwald 'monachus'. There can be little doubt that we have here the men respectively appointed to the key bishoprics of Wells (926), Winchester (931), Winchester again (934), Ramsbury (927, ultimately Canterbury, 942) and Worcester (928). All these prelates remained in frequent attendance on the king after their promotion. Oda and Cenwald were sent on important diplomatic missions. Bishop Theodred of London was also close to the king throughout his reign; he is said to have accompanied Aethelstan to Brunanburh, apparently bought relics in Pavia and took messages from the king to law-making councillors.[25] The gifted young men in Aethelstan's tightly knit circle were to dominate the intellectual and ecclesiastical life of the English kingdom for the next three decades.

From the point of view of the charters themselves, a perhaps Winchester phase may be detected from 931, when royal diplomas acquire distinctively elaborate styles and remarkable uniformity; examples of both main proems ('Flebilia fortiter . . .' of 931–3, and 'Fortuna fallentis . . .' of 934–5) survive as originals by 'Chaplais scribe (1)'.[26] The phase coincides with the episcopate of Beornstan

---

[22] Asser, *Life of Alfred*, ed. W. H. Stevenson (Oxford, repr. 1959), pp. 62, 86–7; cf. the unduly neglected discussion in L. M. Larson, *The King's Household in England before the Norman Conquest* (Wisconsin, 1904), pp. 138–9.

[23] *Liber Eliensis*, ed. E. O. Blake (London, Camden 3rd ser., XCII, 1962), p. 146. The rotation in *Liber Eliensis* is apparently in blocks of four months, that in Asser is every third month, but each involves a tripartite division of responsibilities.

[24] *S* 394.

[25] D. Whitelock, *Some Anglo-Saxon Bishops of London* (London, 1971), pp. 17–21; *Gesetze*, I, pp. 182–3; cf. Nelson, above, p. 216.

[26] Above, n. 18.

'mass priest'. A new phase begins in 935, in which the bishop of Winchester is ranked second only to Canterbury, and its one surviving original is by 'Chaplais scribe (2)'.[27] It is again tempting to associate this phase with bishop Aelfeah, another ex-'mass priest', who was 'previsor in electione sua' at the end of 934 and consecrated in 935, and who played the crucial role in the education of Dunstan and Aethelwold.[28] Before this, there are traces of a Worcester phase. It would have made sense for Aethelstan. He had been brought up in Mercia, and elected by the Mercians in opposition to the West Saxon establishment. Worcester had supplied his grandfather with scholars, it could produce good manuscripts like BL Reg. MS 5 F iii, and its scribes were still producing private charters during the West Saxon diplomatic 'hiatus' from 909 to 924.[29] Bishop Cenwald is now thought to have inspired an important series of alliterative charters, many from the archives of Burton Abbey, extending from 939 to 957 (when Cenwald died).[30] But two of Aethelstan's book inscriptions and at least one of his early charters have several affinities with this series. For example, S 404 (930) is alliterative, it varies the titles of its witnesses, pairing them and sometimes using English words like 'biscup' and its royal title is unusually specific about the peoples ruled by Aethelstan.[31] This last feature also recalls the title 'rex angulsaxonum et mercianorum' in MS Veste Coburg 1 (f. 168r), which Cenwald probably took with him to Germany (below, p. 260). The 'rex et rector Angulsaexna' title in several alliterative charters should be compared with 'Anglosaexana rex et rector' in the alliterative inscription of Lambeth MS 1370 (f. 3v), another Aethelstan gift-book; Robinson noted long ago that this poetic inscription with its Aldhelmian *topos* ('per triquadrum' – S 404 has 'triquadri orbis') is too close to the charters for this to be coincidence. We may suppose that Cenwald *monachus* wrote the Lambeth inscription when in the king's chapel;[32] that, as

[27] Above, n. 15.
[28] S 427.
[29] e.g. S 1289.
[30] *Charters of Burton Abbey*, ed. P. H. Sawyer (Oxford, Anglo-Saxon Charters, II, 1979), pp. xlvii–xlix.
[31] Note also that the bishop's name is here spelt 'koenwald', as in some others of the series, and compare the inscription 'koenwald monachus' in the Worcester MS, Bodleian Hatton MS 20, f. 98v. On all this, Robinson, *Dunstan*, pp. 57–8.
[32] Maelbrighde, coarb of Armagh, who gave the MS to Aethelstan, and who was seemingly alive when the inscription was written, died on 22 February 927, before Cenwald became a bishop.

head of the Worcester *scriptorium*, he was behind some royal documents from 928–30; and that, when the king's itinerary took him to the Worcester diocese in the last month of his reign, he inaugurated the alliterative series proper with a royal grant to a Mercian thegn.[33]

Aethelstan's small but very significant group of *clerici* can thus be seen as a kind of intellectual *comitatus*, whose members were 'farmed out', like veterans, to positions of local responsibility, whilst retaining a close connection with the king.[34] Cenwald, Aelfeah and Oda were all monks; and like Ottonian royal clergy they were all learned.[35] Aethelstan surrounded himself with other such men: the continental cleric Petrus, from the New Minster, who composed *Carta Dirige*, the 'Charlemagne' poem, when in the North with the king in 927;[36] Benedict, the (Irish ?) painter of Cotton Otho B ix, perhaps identical with the man who witnesses among Aethelstan's bishops at King's Worthy;[37] the deacon Edward, who repaired an Irish gospel-book (BL Add. MS 40618) in fine square minuscule (Winchester style paintings were also added), who may have been with the king at Colchester in March 931 and at Lifton the following November;[38] even the Norse skald, Egil Skallagrimson, fragments of whose *drapa* in praise of the king survive.[39] Elsewhere at court we meet an Irish scribe and bishop, a Breton anchorite and Frankish and Italian scholars.[40] It was in this atmosphere that the young *palatinus* Aethelwold 'learned from the king's councillors many things useful to him . . . and at length was tonsured by the king's orders and consecrated by Aelfeah, bishop of Winchester, whom he zealously served for some time'.[41] In all this, the king's aim seems

[33] S 392.

[34] D. Whitelock, *The Audience of Beowulf* (Oxford, 1951), pp. 89–92.

[35] The post-Conquest *Vita Odonis* describes Oda as one of the king's *secretores*, H. Wharton, *Anglia Sacra* (1690), II, p. 78; for his learning, cf. his Pastoral Epistle (above, n. 7), his canons (ed. G. Schoebe, *Bulletin of the Institute of Historical Research*, XXXV, 1962, p. 75 ff.), and above all his preface to Frithegoda's *Life of Wilfred*, on which see M. Lapidge, 'The hermeneutic style in tenth-century Anglo-Latin literature', *ASE*, IV (1975), p. 78.

[36] n. 4 above.   [37] n. 19 above, S 413.

[38] F. Wormald, 'The "Winchester School" before St Aethelwold', in P. Clemoes and K. Hughes (eds), *England before the Conquest: Studies presented to Dorothy Whitelock* (Cambridge, 1971), pp. 309–10; S 412; S 416.

[39] *Egils Saga*, ed. S. Nordal, *Islenzk Fornrit*, IIb (1933), p. 146; cf. A. Campbell, *Skaldic Verse and Anglo-Saxon History* (London, 1971), pp. 5–7.

[40] For the Breton, *Memorials of St Dunstan*, ed. W. Stubbs (RS, 1874), p. 381; for the others, below, p. 263.

[41] Aelfric, *Life of St Aethelwold*, ed. M. Winterbottom, *Three Lives of English Saints* (Toronto, 1972), pp. 18–19; trans. *EHD*, pp. 904–5.

clear. According to Asser, Alfred proposed to allocate a fourth part of his revenue to a *schola* of young men under his watchful eye; Alfred himself stipulated that, after learning to read English well, 'let those be instructed in the Latin language whom one wants to teach further and bring *to hierran hade*' (which may mean not only 'holy office' but high office of any kind).[42] Aethelstan, who must have seen, and possibly attended, his grandfather's school, carried on in that vein.

It is already evident that the staffing and library of Aethelstan's court school depended in considerable measure on foreign contacts, and it is to this chapter in the as yet unwritten history of 'England and the Continent in the Tenth Century' that we should now turn.[43] In 929 an English embassy visited 'all the churches of Germany', bringing rich donations of silver and presents from Aethelstan himself; it seems plausible to connect this event with the wedding of Otto to the West Saxon Edith, which took place that year at Quedlingburg, and lists of English names preserved at St Gall and Reichenau show that Aethelstan entered into confraternity with these houses, along with many of his bishops, chiefs and kinsfolk.[44] German sources also describe an embassy to Canterbury by a Cologne nobleman who brought back stories of the British saints, Ursula and her Virgins, which took root in Cologne and helped to inspire the greatest cult of the later medieval city.[45] The embassy of 929 is also described by Hrotsvit of Gandersheim, who implies that it brought a story of the Northumbrian St Oswald's connection with Edith's maternal line.[46] According to Hrotsvit, precious gifts were exchanged to seal the alliance, and scholars generally accept that two books still surviving in London and Coburg were among the gifts given then or at Otto's coronation in 936. One, BL Cotton

---

[42] H. Sweet, *King Alfred's West Saxon version of Gregory's Pastoral Care* (Oxford, 1871–2), p. 7; trans. *EHD*, p. 889; cf. the important remarks of D. A. Bullough, 'The educational tradition in England from Alfred to Aelfric', *Settimane*, XIX (1972), pp. 455–6.

[43] D. A. Bullough, 'The continental background', in D. Parsons (ed.), *Tenth Century Studies* (London, 1975), p. 20.

[44] *MGH,LC* I (ed. P. Piper (1884), pp. 100, 136, 238, 363: the last from Pfäfers, written after the king's death.

[45] *Analecta Bollandiana*, III (1884), pp. 8–9.

[46] Hrotsvit, *Opera*, ed. H. Homeyer (Munich, 1970), pp. 408–10; the teenage Aethelstan had very likely witnessed his aunt's translation of Oswald's relics to Gloucester: William of Malmesbury, *Gesta Regum*, ed. W. Stubbs (RS, 1887), p. 136.

MS Tiberius A ii, a gospel-book from Lobbes in Lotharingia, was a present from Otto, whose name, with that of his mother Mihthild, it bears in OE letters.[47] A Latin inscription and a poem written in England show that Aethelstan had the book ornamented with jewelled covers and given to Christ Church, Canterbury.[48] The other book, MS Veste Coburg 1, was in Gandersheim abbey at the turn of the tenth century, perhaps given by Otto. Its last folio carries an inscription in untidy English square minuscule, naming Aethelstan 'king of the Anglo-Saxons and Mercians' with a queen, Eadgifu, who is more probably the king's redoubtable step-mother than his half-sister.[49]

The Coburg MS was executed at Metz in the 860s, and is adorned with lavishly illustrated canon tables and a beautiful ivory cover depicting the Ascension. That Metz ivories formed one of the inspirations of tenth-century English art has long been recognized, and it is therefore interesting to note that the other cover of the MS is preserved in the Victoria and Albert Museum: a crucifixion originally set with gold studs and precious stones, it was detached before the sixteenth century.[50] It is possible that this Carolingian masterpiece remained in tenth-century England to provide a model for English artists. If so, it may not have been alone. The Brunswick Casket, which, like Coburg 1, was at Gandersheim by the end of the century, was perhaps in England before the 970s, for, in the opinion of some scholars, its famous scene of the Baptism in the Jordan was the direct model for the same scene in the Benedictional of St Aethelwold.[51] Though it is only a conjecture that the casket was given to Aethelstan by Otto, it suggests the kind of artistic

[47] Lapidge, 'Some Latin poems', p. 93.

[48] See ibid., pp. 93–7.

[49] I. Hubay, Die Handschriften der Landesbibliothek Coburg (Coburg, 1962), pp. 9–16, and plates I–II (the inscription is on f. 168r); for Eadgifu, see Hubay, p. 11: she appears in the Pfäfers list as 'Odgiva' (MGH, LC I, p. 363). But S 1211 suggests that she was out of public life for much of her stepson's reign. For the canon tables and ivory cover of the MS, see excellent illustrations in P. Schramm and F. Mütherich, Denkmäle der deutschen Könige (Munich, 1962), pp. 273–4.

[50] The opinion of A. Goldschmidt, Elfenbeinskulpturen I (Berlin, 1914), I, 88; recently illustrated in colour by P. Williamson, An Introduction to Medieval Ivory Carving (London, 1982), p. 25. The plaque shows Longinus with the lance and Stephaton with the sponge: see below, pp. 267–8.

[51] H. Swarzenski, Monuments of Romanesque Art (London, 2nd edn, 1974), fig. 121, and cf. fig. 124; the casket is from Metz or Saxony. In spite of the 'extremely close similarity', Dr Alexander has reservations about a direct debt: Parsons, Tenth Century Studies, p. 177; but he tells me that he would not dismiss it.

borrowings which certainly grew out of the diplomacy of the period. We might imagine that the Metz crucifixion, the Brunswick casket and the Galba Psalter (also closely studied by the Benedictional artists) were preserved after the king's death in a treasury similar to 'the chest with all the *halidom* that was with King Aethelstan's gems'.[52]

The obvious upshot of such transactions was exchanges of personnel between English and German houses. There is evidence of Englishmen in Germany;[53] but Germans are much more evident in Aethelstan's England. Within two years of Cenwald's embassy, Aethelstan had put a German *sacerdos* called Godescalc in charge of a newly restored church at Abingdon.[54] Before 933, three Germans, Gundlaf, Waltere and Hildewine, appear in the New Minster *familia*, and a fourth may be concealed in the Latin name Petrus.[55] It was a German at Christ Church who entered the poem in praise of Aethelstan into Tiberius A ii.[56] But it is in London and its associated diocese of East Anglia that we find the clearest signs of a German presence. Bishop Theodred's name was German, and he was surrounded by clerics with German names: Gundwine, Odgar, Theodred and Gosebriht.[57] It is possible that Theodred was German or of German descent, and that he reinforced his clergy from Germany in order to restore the sadly dilapidated East Anglian Church. If Aethelstan was as short of literate clergy as would appear, he may well have wished to recruit from abroad, and perhaps Cenwald's 929 mission was also given that very task.

We should expect to find evidence of such men's activities, and it is a remarkable fact that copies of the two major works of Aldhelm had apparently to be imported from Germany: the English transmission of the verse *De Virginitate* is entirely dependent on East Frankish manuscripts, including one which passed through Dunstan's

---

[52] cf. *Liber Vitae*, ed. W. de Gray Birch (Hants. Record Society, 1892), p. lxv.

[53] e.g. Gregory, the English abbot of Einsiedeln in the 960s: *Vita Wolfgangi*, ed. G. Waitz, *MGH,SS* IV, p. 530, and for his insular Boethius commentary, M. Parkes, 'A note on Vatican MS. Bibl. Apost. Lat. 3363', in M. Gibson (ed.), *Boethius: Studies in his Life, Thought and Influence* (Oxford, 1981), pp. 425–7.

[54] F. M. Stenton, *The Early History of the Abbey of Abingdon* (Reading, 1913), p. 38; *S* 409.

[55] Lapidge, 'Some Latin poems', p. 93, n. 143; *S* 1417.

[56] Chaplais, *Journ. Soc. Arch.*, p. 163; Lapidge, 'Some Latin poems', pp. 93–7; the Conrad who appears among Aethelstan's court in the St Gall lists (*MGH,LC* I, pp. 100, 136) was perhaps another German.

[57] Above, n. 25; cf. *EHD*, pp. 552–4, and Stenton, *ASE*, p. 438.

hands and which contains an acrostic addressed to Aethelstan by John the Old Saxon; its prose counterpart likewise descended from German manuscripts, especially from Würzburg, whither English missionaries had taken them in the eighth century.[58] But most intriguing in its implications is the Anglo-Saxon translation from Old Saxon of part of a poem on Genesis, which was incorporated in the early eleventh-century poetic codex, Bodleian Junius MS 11. The last editor of *Genesis* B thought that the translation dated from the early tenth-century and was known to the author of *Judith*, a poem roughly contemporary with *Brunanburh*.[59] There is no known OE translation of the Old Saxon *Heliand*, but an Anglo-Saxon manuscript *is* known, the late tenth-century BL Cotton Caligula A vii. The manuscript was written by a German scribe who had been long enough in England to use common Anglo-Saxon words, and, according to Professor Priebsch, these characteristics were shared by its exemplar, a square minuscule copy perhaps dateable to the early tenth century.[60] As it happens, the *Heliand* and Saxon *Genesis* were once united in a single MS, now the fragmentary Vatican Pal. Lat. MS 1447, which was written at Metz in the early ninth century; and, on the basis of a late but probably genuine preface, scholars have speculated that a similar manuscript was once sent abroad as a presentation volume, perhaps to England, as is suggested by the preface's use of OE *vitteas* for *lectiones*.[61] Such a manuscript would have been an artistic treasure on a par with the great Bibles of Charles the Bald; and Barbara Raw has recently shown that an illustrated Genesis cycle did indeed reach England by the late tenth century, for the illustrations in the Junius MS were designed for the Old Saxon text, and were therefore, in all probability, present in the continental exemplar.[62]

Further clues as to the date when the German cycle was 'Anglicized' depend on hypotheses about the style of the miniatures in the

[58] *Aldhelmi Opera*, ed. R. Ehwald, *MGH,AA* XV, pp. 211–25, 327–48; M. Lapidge, in A. C. de la Mare and B. C. Barker-Benfield (eds), *Manuscripts at Oxford: an exhibition in memory of Richard William Hunt* (Oxford, 1980), pp. 19–20.

[59] B. J. Timmer, *The Later Genesis* (Oxford, 1948), p. 43; *idem, Judith* (London, 2nd edn, 1961), pp. 6–8, 10.

[60] R. Priebsch, *The Heliand Manuscript* (Oxford, 1925), p. 28 ff.

[61] O. Behagel, *Heliand und Genesis* (Halle, 1948), pp. 1–3; cf. Priebsch, *Heliand MS*, p. 37; Bischoff, *Mittelalterliche Studien*, III (1982), pp. 104–5.

[62] B. Raw, 'The probable derivation of most of the illustrations in Junius 11 . . .', *ASE*, V (1976), pp. 133–48.

Junius MS. Francis Wormald considered that they were copied from an Aethelstan period manuscript, and Dr Alexander points out to me that the manuscript's initials are very old-fashioned, as if the artist set out to copy a treasured older text faithfully.[63] The idea that this treasured text dated from Aethelstan's time may gain slight support from Dr Lucas's recent attribution of the Junius MS to Aethelstan's favoured Malmesbury.[64] In the end, we can only say that such hypotheses square with other evidence for a strong German presence in Aethelstan's England, and at least we can see that the impetus of John the Old Saxon did not fade with his death.

There are two interesting footnotes to this question. First, Tyndale claimed, in his *Obedience of a Christian Man*, that Aethelstan ordered a translation of the Gospels; his authority was 'the Old English Chronicle'. Tanner's *Bibliotheca* supplies the date 930, and says that the translation was 'from the purest founts of the Hebrews, by certain Hebrews converted to Christianity in his kingdom'.[65] It is hard to see in what sense such a work might literally have been done from Hebrew, and the tale seems to verge on the kind of bibliophile fiction beloved of M. R. James; but, by a remarkable coincidence, a note in an eleventh-century Irish gospel-book, Corpus Christi College, Oxford, MS 122, describes how an Irish bishop of Bangor met in Aethelstan's *domus* a Frankish scholar and an Italian Jew who was 'remarkably skilled in the Gospels'.[66] Such were the conversational possibilities of early medieval courts. Further evidence of such interests is the fact that, in the early tenth century, a manuscript of Philo Judaeus, *On the Interpretation of Hebrew Names*, came from St Médard Soissons to Malmesbury.[67]

The other footnote also has a Malmesbury connection. It is William of Malmesbury who claims that Alfred translated the first

---

[63] F. Wormald, *English Drawings of the tenth and eleventh centuries* (London, 1952), p. 76.

[64] P. Lucas, 'MS. Junius 11 and Malmesbury', *Scriptorium*, XXXIV (1980), pp. 197–200.

[65] J. F. Mozley, *William Tyndale* (London, 1937), p. 8; Tanner's *Bibliotheca Britannico-Hibernica* (1748), p. 267: Tanner cites William of Malmesbury as his authority, I do not know on what basis.

[66] f. 5v; cf. Robinson, *Dunstan*, pp. 173–4.

[67] R. Thomson, 'Identifiable books from the pre-Conquest library of Malmesbury Abbey', *ASE*, X (1981), p. 16. Though Aethelstan and two of his cousins were buried at Malmesbury, and William, *Gesta Pontificum*, p. 397 ff., shows that he was very generous to the abbey, there is as yet no sign of the books he must have given it, as he did to other foundations.

fifty Psalms, but died before the rest were finished.[68] Scholars have long assumed that William's authority for this assertion was a manuscript that he had seen, and Janet Bately has now shown that the prose version of the first fifty Psalms in a Paris MS was indeed Alfred's work.[69] Some time later, all the Psalms were translated into rather pretentious OE verse, in a centre, it has been suggested, that cultivated hermeneutic Latin, replete with overblown word-play and neologisms.[70] The verse translation was done in time to be quoted in the *Menologium*, and, in the Paris MS, the Alfredian fifty are combined with the last hundred of this collection. Our only clue to the provenance of the verse Psalms – or at least of the Paris MS – lies in the litany, where the presence of Aldhelm and Paternus points to Malmesbury.

Such speculation at least serve to remind us that there are still many unanswered questions about royal patronage of learning between Alfred and Edgar, not only Latin but also vernacular;[71] they remind us too that foreign scholars, especially Old Saxons, could be useful to the English king in both languages. Biblical translation was an important intellectual current in ninth-century Francia, especially in the East, where major works like *Genesis*, *Heliand* and Otfrid of Weissenberg's *Evangelienbuch* were produced under royal patronage.[72] It would not then be surprising if kings like Alfred and Aethelstan, as they recruited German scholars, were ambitious to initiate biblical translations into OE. Alfred was

---

[68] *Gesta Regum*, p. 132.
[69] BN Lat. 8824 (s. XI med.): *The Paris Psalter*, ed. B. Colgrave *et al.* (Early English Manuscripts in Facsimile, VIII, Copenhagen, 1958); J. Bately, 'Lexical evidence for the authorship of the prose psalms in the Paris Psalter', *ASE*, X (1981), pp. 69–95.
[70] J. Tinkler, *The Vocabulary and Syntax of the OE Version of the Paris Psalter* (The Hague, 1971): over 200 words appear here and nowhere else. cf. also G. Krapp, *The Paris Psalter* (New York, 1932), p. xvii.
[71] cf. K. Sisam, *Studies in the History of Old English Literature* (Oxford, 1953), pp. 61–108, 137–8, for very suggestive remarks about the dates and motivation of the original compilation of the major OE poetical codices. Was Aethelstan collecting 'age-old poems', like Charlemagne? – Einhard, *Vita Caroli*, ed. O. Holder-Egger, *MGH,SRG*, p. 33.
[72] Behagel, *Heliand and Genesis*, pp. 1–3 for Louis the Pious and the *Heliand; Otfrids Evangelienbuch*, ed. O. Erdmann (Halle, 1882), pp. 1–2, for the dedication of this work to Louis the German. The *Gospel Harmony* of Tatian was translated into OHG at Fulda between 832–42 after a visit by Louis the Pious; cf. F. Pickering, *Literature and Art in the Middle Ages* (London, 1970), pp. 329–30.

clearly thinking this way at the end of his life.[73] It is not impossible that one of his successors, perhaps Aethelstan, as late tradition asserts, sponsored a vernacular translation of the Gospels. If so, he may have been consciously emulating Louis the Pious.

We might have a more coherent impression of the Carolingian strand in Aethelstan's kingship if we still had the *Gesta* of the king which William of Malmesbury discovered in the twelfth century, perhaps at Glastonbury, where a thirteenth-century library catalogue records a 'bella ethel[s]tani regis' in a volume prefaced by the correspondence of Alcuin and Charlemagne.[74] The work, of which William gives a précis, was, he implies, written in the hermeneutic Latin which is now seen as characteristic of the 'Aethelstan phase' of English learning; and, to judge from the content as recorded by William, it was also thoroughly influenced by *Lives* of ninth-century continental kings, as Asser was.[75] It is thus important to determine the nature of William's 'very old book'. Dr Lapidge has recently suggested that the two verse extracts which William gives are twelfth-century concoctions, which have no connection with the ancient work from which he excerpted his prose text.[76] But William clearly says that the verses were 'the account of that poet from whom we have excerpted *all* these particulars';[77] in other words, there was one source both for William's prose and his verse. But if the old book was in hermeneutic Latin, how is it that William's verse is in twelfth-century language, as Dr Lapidge proves? The simplest solution is that William's verses are twelfth-century *translations* of the hermeneutic poem.[78] Some of their contents also support this view. In the account of Brunanburh, Aethelstan is actually criticized for sloth, which is incredible for a twelfth-century

[73] cf. *Liber Eliensis*, ed. Blake, p. 54, for a passage to the effect that Alfred learned so well from Grimbald and John that he was able to translate the Old and New Testaments into English: a garbled memory of his translation of the Psalms? Further linguistic examination of the West Saxon Gospels would be welcome.

[74] *Gesta Regum*, pp. 144–52; trans. *EHD*, pp. 303–10. The catalogue entry, noticed by Lapidge, 'Some Latin poems', p. 61, n. 6, is Trinity College, Cambridge, MS R S 33 (f. 103v); I am grateful to Dr Keynes for a photostat of this folio.

[75] See Bullough, 'Educational tradition', pp. 454–9.

[76] Lapidge, 'Some Latin poems', pp. 62–71. Dr Lapidge kindly allowed me access to his important article before its publication.

[77] *Gesta Regum*, p. 151: 'tempus est ut illius versifici, de quo omnia haec excerpsimus, sententiam ponamus'.

[78] A practice followed by William elsewhere, as also by his literary hero Cicero; cf., to cite a work that William knew, *Tusculani Disputationes*, II.8 and 10.

poet at Malmesbury of all places, but quite conceivable in a work seeking to persuade Aethelstan's immediate successors that kings should be 'provident and militant . . . seated on a high watchtower', in readiness for war.[79] Such details as Olaf Guthfrithson's brief heyday in 940 (a fact not recorded in the southern manuscripts of the *Anglo-Saxon Chronicle*) are likewise implausible as twelfth-century inventions. William's verse, like his prose, is based on a contemporary account.

What, then, does the *Gesta* seem to have said? Beginning with the king's illustrious descent, election and consecration, it went on to tell of his military conquests, his restoration of cities and his generosity to his military following; it listed the foreign races who submitted to him and the tribute in precious metals, cattle, hawks and hounds paid by the Welsh kings: just as Frankish kings were 'imperatores plurimarum nationum', so the West Saxon *basileus* could name nine or ten kings who acknowledged him as a 'king who ruled other kings'. After a brief sketch of the king's character and looks, it then, in an obvious echo, direct or indirect, of Einhard, described how Aethelstan's victories and 'greatness of soul' attracted the attention of foreign kings, who 'rightly considered themselves fortunate if they could buy his friendship either by marriage alliance or gifts . . . all Europe proclaimed his praises'. A lengthy and lavish account of Aethelstan's diplomacy and gift-exchanges follows, and here we reach an incident which has attracted much attention from students of kingly regalia and cult objects in the early Middle Ages.[80] In 926 at Abingdon, the king's kinsman, Adelolf of Flanders, pressed the suit of Hugh, duke of the Franks, for Aethelstan's sister. His gifts included 'perfumes hitherto unknown in England', a classical or Byzantine onyx vase carved with pastoral scenes, the

[79] See my 'Brunanburh revisited', *Saga Book of the Viking Society*, XX iii (1980), pp. 203–4, which unfortunately could not take Dr Lapidge's article into account. That William thought the poem written while 'the king was still alive' (Lapidge 'Some Latin poems', p. 63) is not a serious objection: though its last line mentions the king's death, it was plainly based on detailed contemporary panegyrical material.
[80] L. Loomis. 'The holy relics of Charlemagne and King Aethelstan', *Speculum*, XXV (1950), pp. 447 ff.; P. Schramm, *Herrschaftszeichen und Staatssymbolik* (3 vols, Stuttgart, 1954–6), II, pp. 392, 522–3, 534, 562. The Holy Lance was brought from St Riquier to Sens in around 888, and William of Sens is found negotiating with Aethelstan in 936; P. Lauer, *Le Règne de Louis IV d'Outremer* (Paris, 1900), p. 12. See McKitterick, above, pp. 244–5, for the relations of the Robertians with Sens.

alleged sword of Constantine with a Holy Nail in its hilt, and portions of the True Cross and Crown of Thorns set in crystal. But three items stand out even in this catalogue: the standard of Maurice, the warrior saint, which Charlemagne was said to have carried to victory against pagans; 'the lance of Charles the Great, which, whenever that *invictissimus imperator*, leading an army against the Saracens, hurled it against the enemy, never let him depart without the victory; it was said to be the same which, driven by the centurion's hand into Our Lord's side, opened by the gash of that precious wound paradise for wretched mortals'; and finally a gold and bejewelled diadem 'so splendid that it threw out flashes of light and dazzled onlookers': it was possibly a Carolingian royal crown from the cathedral treasury of Sens.

Karl Leyser has unravelled some of the implications of this extraordinary account. He suggests that Hugh was imitating Byzantine diplomatic usage; onyx chalices were the currency of Byzantine embassies to the West, and similar vases and rare perfumes feature in Widukind's descriptions of embassies in Otto's time. But another aspect of the transaction was evidently important to the unknown panegyricist, the connection of some artefacts with Charlemagne himself. Hugh may have thought it politic to deliver some of the hereditary treasure of the Carolingians to the host of the exiled Carolingian heir. In English eyes, however, such gifts may have implied a *translatio imperii*, such as Widukind later ascribed to the Ottonians: some of Charlemagne's own divine favour and *virtus* now passed to Aethelstan, who was certainly entitled to think that there was no continental king to rival him. A late tradition portrays the king fighting the pagans at Brunanburh with what was perhaps one of Hugh's relics around his neck.[81]

We can in fact trace the intellectual impact of the exchange right to the king himself, and show that he embraced their Carolingian associations. Cotton MS Galba A xviii has good claims to have been the king's own Psalter; it was written in ninth-century Francia, and contains Carolingian *obits*, including Charles himself, 'piissimus imperator' (f. 28r). The English material added in the tenth century

---

[81] K. Leyser, 'The tenth century in Byzantine-Western relationships', in D. Baker (ed.), *Relations between East and West in the Middle Ages* (Edinburgh, 1973), pp. 42–3, nn. 78–9; *idem, Rule and Conflict in an Early Medieval Society* (London, 1979), p. 88. For the king's wearing the relic, *Eulogium Historiarum III* ed. F. S. Haydon (RS, 1863), pp. 10–11.

included not only the calendar with obits of Alfred and his wife, but also a prayer to the Holy Cross, a Greek Litany transliterated into Latin, and a cycle of paintings done in a court atelier (or at Winchester).[82] The cycle now comprises a Last Judgement showing Christ with the relics of his Passion, the spear, cross and sponge (f. 2v) (Plate IV); a Christ in Majesty by a different artist with the spear wound exposed (f. 21r) (Plate V); and an Ascension (f. 120v). A Nativity cut out opposite Psalm 1 at f. 35v is now Bodleian MS Rawlinson B 484 (f. 85r).[83] Paint rubbing on f. 80r shows that another miniature has been lost opposite Psalm 51, probably the Crucifixion of which BL Cotton MS Titus D xxvii (f. 65v) is an eleventh-century copy.[84] The cycle's obvious allusions to the relics acquired by Aethelstan in 926 add to the Psalter's 'royalist' tone, and they suggest that the implications of *Carta Dirige Gressus* (above, p. 251) are unlikely to have been lost on him.

The impression is confirmed by the two manuscripts bearing pictures of the king. The frontispiece of Corpus 183, showing Aethelstan presenting the book to St Cuthbert, is thoroughly Carolingian in style (Plate VI); Peter Bloch has shown that its inspiration lies in ninth-century Frankish depictions of Hrabanus Maurus and Charles the Bald.[85] Although completely destroyed in the Cottonian fire, the presentation picture in Cotton Otho B ix can be reconstructed from the detailed descriptions in the catalogues of Smith and Wanley.[86] The king was shown crowned with a *diadema* and carrying a *sceptrum* as he genuflected *flexo poplite* before the enthroned saint, and an inscription recorded the gift of Aethelstan 'Anglorum piissimus rex'. This kind of presentation picture has no known OE parallels, but ample Frankish prototypes, both for the

[82]   F. Wormald, 'The Winchester School', pp. 305, 308–9.

[83]   J. Alexander, *Anglo-Saxon Illumination in Oxford Libraries* (Oxford, 1971), p. 6, plate Ic.

[84]   Dr Alexander tells me that this was also the opinion of the late Francis Wormald. The extraordinary 'Quinity' on f. 75v of the Titus MS may also be from a lost miniature in the Aethelstan Psalter, either at Psalm 109 or after Psalm 150; but cf. E. Kantorowicz, 'The Quinity of Winchester', in his *Selected Studies* (New York, 1965), p. 105. For the Psalter's influence on the artists of St Aethelwold, cf. Alexander in Parsons, *Tenth Century Studies*, pp. 172, 176, 178. And for the later significance of the association of kings with Christ's Passion see John, below, pp. 312–3.

[85]   P. Bloch, 'Zum Dedikationsbild in Lob des Kreuzes des Hrabanus Maurus', *Das erste Jahrtausend* (Dusseldorf, 1961), I, pp. 471–94.

[86]   Above, n. 19; and T. Smith, *Catalogus Librorum Manuscriptorum Bibliothecae Cottonianae* (1696), p. 70.

architectural setting and for the king's posture.[87] A picture of Charles the Bald in the Munich Schatzkammer (Plate VII) is very close in style to that of Corpus 183: both kings wear not dissimilar three-pronged crowns, and their calf-length cloaks clasped at the shoulder, leggings and shoes are also similar. The frame of the Corpus miniature is an entirely Carolingian styled inhabited vinescroll.[88] Whether or not painted in a royal atelier, these pictures are conspicuous English essays in the Frankish fashion of Aethelstan's court, and the function of such *imagines regum* was probably the same in England as in Francia. In a Tours gospel-book, Paris BN Lat. 266, the emperor Lothar 'is duly depicted on that page, so that whoever at any time looks on the face of the Emperor shall say in supplication: "Praise be to Almighty God, may Lothar earn eternal rest through our Lord Jesus Christ".'[89] Similar prayers appear in Aethelstan manuscripts, notably the first person inscription in Tiberius A ii, and shorter notes in BL Cotton MS Claudius B v (f. 5r) and BL Reg. MS 1 A xviii (f. 3v): 'quisquis hoc legerit omnipotenti pro eo proque suis fundat preces.'

A detailed and more closely dated catalogue of the large number of Frankish manuscripts which were in England by the later tenth century may yet prove that more foreign material was available in English houses under Aethelstan than appears at present, and that they were a rich source of the tenth-century intellectual revival.[90] Even now, however, Aethelstan's court seems to stand at the centre of the web of learning. And if the king dealt mostly in Frankish, Irish and Breton manuscripts (illuminated Frankish gospel-books were perhaps the appropriate currency for a would-be *imperator*), English scribes, especially those in or near the royal circle, were developing the expertise to make worthy repairs or insertions in

[87] cf. the Martyrology of Wandelbert of Prüm, in Schramm and Mütherich, *Denkmäle*, 36, and Charles the Bald's giftbook in the Munich Schatzkammer, *ibid.*, 43.

[88] F. Wormald, 'Decorated initials', p. 117.

[89] The translation is that of D. A. Bullough, '*Imagines Regum*, and their significance in the early medieval West', in G. Robertson and G. Henderson (eds), *Studies in Memory of David Talbot Rice* (Edinburgh, 1975), p. 223 ff.

[90] Given Aethelstan's important Breton connections, his reign supplies an appropriate context for the import of the many Breton MSS in tenth-century England: see, e.g., F. Wormald, *An Early Breton Gospel Book*, ed. J. Alexander (London, Roxburghe Club, 1977), p. 12, p. 13 n.1. Another serious candidate is Bodleian Hatton MS 42, which Professor Whitelock and Patrick Wormald have both suggested to me was a source of Oda's canons, and, in Wormald's view, of Aethelstan's quotation in his 'Tithe Ordinance' also: *Gesetze*, I, pp. 146–7.

such books, and to produce something of their own like Corpus
183. Manuscripts from this period which would repay further study
include Boulogne MS 10, a fine gospel-book whose main hand
resembles one of those in the Tanner Bede;[91] Brussels MS 8558–63, a
square minuscule MS of that Carolingian classic, the short rule of
Chrodegang;[92] and Leningrad PL Lat. O v xvi 1, a grammatical
tract likewise in square minuscule.[93] Trinity College Cambridge B
16 3, a massive and handsome Hrabanus, *De Laudibus Sanctae Crucis*,
whose illustrations are copied from a Fulda archetype, cannot date
to Aethelstan's time, as its scripts are Anglo-Caroline of s. x. med.[94]
But it may have an indirect connection with Aethelstan's intense
devotion to the Cross and with Dunstan's picture of himself
prostrated before Christ in his Glastonbury class-book.[95] The
general impression made by the manuscripts of standard Carolingian
authors like Hrabanus, Chrodegang and Smaragdus is that, while
the reproduction of the 'Alfredian' translations continued, the
scribes of Aethelstan's period were also assimilating some of the
intellectual legacy of the Carolingian Renaissance, and in at least
some cases with royal encouragement.

If the results seem small beer by comparison with the *Hofbiblio-
theken* of Charlemagne, Louis the Pious and Charles the Bald, that is
partly because, by such standards, they were.[96] But it is also
because, in the nature of the evidence, Aethelstan is eclipsed by the
glaring light of his grandfather and nephew. It is easy to ascribe
manifestations of German culture in tenth-century England to John

[91] Alexander, in Parsons, *Tenth Century Studies*, pp. 169–70, plate III; the initials
are of the same type as those in the Helmingham Orosius and the Junius Psalter; the
hand is second quarter of the tenth century.

[92] Ker, *Catalogue*, 10.

[93] N. R. Ker, 'A supplement to "Catalogue of Manuscripts containing Anglo-
Saxon"', *ASE*, V (1976), p. 127.

[94] Temple, *Anglo-Saxon Manuscripts*, 14; Alexander, in Parsons, *Tenth Century
Studies*, pp. 172–3.

[95] J. Higgitt, 'Glastonbury, Dunstan, monasticism and manuscripts', *Art History*,
II. 3 (1979), pp. 275–90, esp. pp. 278–80. Alexander, in Parsons, *Tenth Century
Studies*, pp. 174–5 suggests the Utrecht Psalter as a possible model for the Dunstan
drawing (it is not known when the Psalter arrived in England). H. Gneuss inde-
pendently arrived at the same conclusion as Higgitt: 'Dunstan und Hrabanus
Maurus', *Anglia*, XCVI (1978), pp. 136–48. Note also that the Smaragdus which is
Cambridge UL MS Ee 2.4 was done at Glastonbury in the mid-tenth century from
a continental exemplar: Bishop, *English Caroline Minuscule*, p. 2.

[96] R. McKitterick, 'Charles the Bald and his library', *EHR*, XCV (1980),
pp. 28–47, and references.

the Old Saxon rather than Theodred, and to deny intellectual and artistic attainment to the 'evil-living clerics' expelled by Aethelwold from Winchester. It is a sobering thought that, but for German sources and the *Gesta* discovered and used by William of Malmesbury, we should not know enough of Aethelstan's foreign contacts to make sense of the largely diplomatic and artistic evidence that we otherwise have. But the evidence as it stands surely suffices to rebut the recent assertion that, before Aethelwold, 'intellectual and spiritual life seems to have been in a state of stagnation; there was nobody to take over where Alfred left off.'[97] There is a good case, as Robinson thought, for continuity through Aethelstan between Alfred and the makers of monastic reform. The royal chapel where the learned and monastically inclined churchmen of Aethelstan's reign began their careers, and the court school where Dunstan and Aethelwold were educated, both perpetuated Alfredian traditions. There are now new reasons to believe William of Malmesbury that Aethelstan himself was learned;[98] it is at least tempting to see a connection between the spectacularly Aldhelmian elements in the king's diplomas and his burial at Malmesbury.[99] From the scribes of the Hatton MS of Alfred's *Pastoral Rule*, learning their trade as they went along, through the square minuscule of Aethelstan's books and charters to the onset of Caroline minuscule in the context of tenth-century reform, the story of development is writ plain: it took Alfred's dynasty over half a century not only to secure their *imperium* but also to train the scholars who could provide its theological, liturgical and ideological foundations; and until royal patronage established reformed houses at Glastonbury and Abingdon, only the king could supply the requisite drive.

It can also be argued that there was more to Aethelstan's *imperium* than sonorous diplomatic formulae, more even than the 'warfare and deeds' which Aethelweard, like Widukind, made central. Aethelstan was remembered at Exeter (Bodleian MS Auct. D 2 16, f. 8r) as the king 'who by the Grace of God ruled all of England singly, which prior to him many kings had shared between them'.

[97] H. Gneuss, 'The origin of standard Old English', *ASE*, I (1972), p. 69; according to *Liber Eliensis*, ed. Blake, p. 415, Aethelwold regarded Aethelstan as 'his lord'; and cf. n. 41 above.

[98] *Gesta Regum*, p. 144: 'Nemo literatius rempublicam administravit'; see now the acrostic addressed to him by John (the Old Saxon ?): Lapidge, 'Some Latin poems', pp. 72–83.

[99] But cf. Bullough, 'Educational tradition', pp. 466–78.

Like the Carolingians, his dynasty were hard-headed and practical men, with a gift for far-sighted improvisation, and they mastered their 'empire' by ruthlessly effective use of their landed wealth (below, pp. 279–81). But, as with the Carolingians, their patronage of art and learning was equally important, and they addressed themselves to it just as seriously, drawing on the widest range of sources not only to enhance their prestige and wealth but also to establish true Christianity and just kingship. Aethelstan and his advisers knew that Carolingian power meant Carolingian responsibilities. It may not be fortuitous that in the 920s a Frankish poet and a Frankish potentate both implicitly compared Aethelstan with Charlemagne; or that William's lost *Gesta* called him *Magnus Adelstanus*.[100]

[100] *Gesta Regum*, p. 145.

12

The Royal *Tun* in Pre-Conquest England

PETER SAWYER

It is perhaps in the study of royal residences and what happened in them that we come closest to the realities of early medieval kingship.[1] Much was written at the time about what kings ought to do and the judgement of God was sometimes manifested on battlefields but it was in royal palaces and *villae* that contemporaries witnessed the routines of royal power, routines that included the noble pursuit of hunting as well as the celebration of solemn festivals, and discussions, both private, even in the king's chamber as he washed his hands,[2] and public, in great assemblies.

Eugen Ewig and Carl-Richard Brühl, among others, have shown how the study of royal residences and the use made of them can illuminate early medieval politics and improve our understanding of 'the material basis of medieval kingship'.[3] The topic is no less interesting or significant in England than in Francia but students of early English history have not found it easy to develop their own *Pfalzenforschung*.[4] The most notable advances in recent years have

[1] I should like to thank Simon Keynes for advice in writing this paper. The key to the abbreviations used in these notes and the appendix, other than those standard to the volume as a whole, is on pp. 289–90.

[2] S 1445.

[3] E. Ewig, 'Résidence et capitale pendant le Haut Moyen Age', *RH*, CCXXX (1963), pp. 25–72; C.-R. Brühl, *Fodrum, Gistum, Servitium Regis* (3 vols, Köln-Graz, 1968); J. M. Wallace-Hadrill, review of Brühl, *EHR*, LXXXV (1970), pp. 601–3.

[4] D. A. Bullough's paper on the English evidence, contributed to the Compiègne-Paris conference of 1973 on 'Royal residences in Western Europe in the early and high Middle Ages', unfortunately remains unpublished; see P. Rahtz and D. A. Bullough, 'The parts of an Anglo-Saxon mill', *ASE*, VI (1977), p. 27, n. 2.

been made by archaeologists, at Yeavering and Cheddar,[5] and there is a somewhat over-optimistic tendency to interpret every large and elaborate structure of the period as a royal palace.[6] The relative neglect of the subject in England is understandable for, although the importance of royal vills has long been recognized, the systematic study of them is hampered by the inadequacy of the available evidence.[7] *Gerefa* hardly fills the place of the *Capitulare de Villis* and no English text rivals the *Brevium exempla* in either detail or date.[8] Domesday Book, it is true, provides a comprehensive account of royal resources at the Norman Conquest but very few royal vills are named in earlier sources and it is therefore difficult to trace their previous development. There are, fortunately, some indirect indications which, taken together with explicit references, have made it possible to compile the list of pre-conquest royal vills that is appended to this paper. This list provokes thought about various matters, such as the alienability of royal estates and the consequences of conquest, in particular the West Saxon expansion of the ninth and tenth centuries. It is, however, first necessary to explain the criteria adopted in making the list, the reasons for identifying these places as royal vills.

Bede names only five,[9] although he mentions several others, and the *Anglo-Saxon Chronicle* describes only one place, which it does not name, as *cyninges tūn*. Aethelweard implies that it was Dorchester in Dorset and further amplifies the *Chronicle* by describing the four *tūnas* captured by Cuthwulf in 571 – Aylesbury,

[5] B. Hope-Taylor, *Yeavering. An Anglo-British Centre of Early Northumbria* (London, 1977); P. Rahtz, *The Saxon and Medieval Palaces at Cheddar* (BAR. LXV, 1975).
[6] P. Rahtz, 'A possible Saxon palace near Stratford-on-Avon', *Antiquity*, XLIV (1970), pp. 137–43; J. K. St Joseph, 'Air reconnaissance: recent results, 39', *Antiquity*, XLIX (1975), pp. 293–5: buildings at Atcham, Shropshire; M. J. Swanton, 'A "lost" crop-mark site at Westenhanger', *Archaeologia Cantiana*, LXXXVIII (1973), pp. 203–7; D. Benson and D. Miles, 'Crop-marks near the Sutton Courtenay Saxon site', *Antiquity*, XLVIII (1974), pp. 223–6. This paper went to press before the remarkable recent discoveries at Northampton were publicized.
[7] H. M. Chadwick, *Studies on Anglo-Saxon Institutions* (Cambridge, 1905), pp. 228–62; H. M. Cam, '*Manerium cum Hundredo*: the hundred and the hundredal manor', and 'Early groups of hundreds', in her *Liberties and Communities in Medieval England* (Cambridge, 1944), pp. 64–106.
[8] *Gesetze*, I, pp. 453–5.
[9] Bamburgh, *Campodunum*, Millfield (*Maelmin*), Rendlesham and Yeavering (*Adgefrin*); references for these and the following royal vills are *s.v.* in the appendix to this chapter.

Benson, Eynsham and Limbury – as *regiae villae*. He uses the same term for Somerton when reporting its occupation by Aethelbald in 733. Asser similarly amplified the *Chronicle* by calling Chippenham, Reading and Wedmore royal vills and additionally mentions others at Dean where he first met Alfred, at Wantage, where the king was born, and at *Leonaford*. Less weight can be put on post-Conquest identifications of royal vills for later writers may simply have assumed that the events in question are likely to have happened in such a place. That could well explain both Florence of Worcester's description of Pucklechurch, where Edmund was murdered, as a *villa regia* and the use of the same term by the Annals of St Neots when describing the burial of Guthrum at Hadleigh.

Charters are a little more helpful. Authentic texts specifically describe at least nineteen places as royal vills, five of which are unidentified,[10] and one grant was made in an un-named *villa puplica*.[11] Offa's charter describing the tribute owed from Westbury says that it was to be delivered *ad regalem vicum* but does not specify which, and a charter of Cenwulf which apparently named a royal *vicus* to which criminals should be delivered has unfortunately been damaged and the name is lost.[12] Charters make it possible to identify some other royal property. Best known, perhaps, are the exchange whereby Aethelbert acquired land at Mersham in Kent and turned it into folkland, and that booking twenty hides in south Devon to King Aethelwulf.[13] Others provide information about the former ownership of land held by kings, such as Offa's claim that Bath, Stratford and other places rightly belonged to the inheritance of King Aethelbald while another shows that he inherited land from his grandfather Eanwulf.[14] A charter of Aethelred shows that Edgar gave some land that should have been reserved for king's sons to Abingdon Abbey and that it was recovered after his death on behalf of Aethelred.[15] Wills, several of which record bequests to kings, are also instructive and, most valuable of all, there are the

[10] *Bearuwe, Bydictun, Escant*, *Freoricburna* and *Werburgwic*.
[11] *S* 268.
[12] *S* 146; *S* 1861; doubts about the former charter, voiced by Whitelock, *EHD*, p. 512, and Wormald, above, ch. 5, n. 49, need not affect its value for present purposes.
[13] *S* 328; *S* 298.
[14] *S* 1257; *S* 146.
[15] *S* 937; some references in spurious texts to royal vills may well derive from authentic models, but only *S* 133, *S* 245 and *S* 173, concerning Tamworth, Everley and Southampton, are included in the appendix.

wills of two kings, Alfred and Eadred, although neither is a complete statement of the land they held.[16]

It is also possible to identify some royal residences. Several of Edward the Confessor's are known, including Britford, Westminster and Windsor, and he also had a hunting lodge built at Brill. The Fonthill letter implies that Wardour was one of Alfred's residences and that Edward the Elder had one at Chippenham, although Alfred had bequeathed it to Aelfthryth, who certainly retained land in England after her marriage to Count Baldwin.[17] Most places in which kings died were probably royal residences, for those who survived battle are likely to have died at home. Edward the Confessor certainly did. The fate of Oswine, murdered while staying *in domum comitis Hunualdi* shows that there were exceptions, but the attempt on Edwin's life was certainly made in a *villa regalis*,[18] and Tamworth, where Aethelflaed died in 918, was a favourite residence of Mercian rulers. It is likely that Farndon, where her brother died six years later, was also a royal vill; it was shared between the bishop and the earl in 1065. Driffield, where King Aldfrith died in 705, had a similar 'official' character in 1065 for it was then held by Earl Morcar and it was, moreover, the centre of both a soke and a hundred. Many of the places in which kings were killed are also likely to have been royal residences, but none appears to have been royal property in Domesday Book. Edward the Martyr was killed at Corfe Gap, apparently very near the place in which Aethelred and his mother were staying, possibly the Kingston which included the site of Corfe Castle and was held by Shaftesbury Abbey in 1065.[19] At that date Pucklechurch, where Edmund was murdered, was held by Glastonbury Abbey who claimed that it had been given to them by Edmund.[20] Seckington, where Aethelbald was killed in 757, was held by two men, Godric and Ernui, in 1065. None of the sites of royal killings reported in the eighth-century Northumbrian annals can be identified with any confidence, nor can *Merantun*, where Cynewulf was killed in 786. Possibly such unlucky places were not retained by the victim's successors.

[16] S 1484–6, S 1503; S 1526; royal wills: S 1507, S 1515.
[17] Stenton, *ASE*, p. 344.
[18] *HE* III. 14, II.9, pp. 155, 99.
[19] *ASC* (DE), *s.a.* 978; *Vita Oswaldi*, ed. J. Raine, *The Historians of the Church of York and its Archbishops* (3 vols, RS. 1879), I, p. 448; R. B. Pugh (ed.), *The Victoria History of the County of Dorset, III* (London, 1968), p. 83, n. 26.
[20] S 553.

There were also royal residences in towns but the evidence for them is slight. A king's hall is mentioned in seventh-century London but there is no other pre-Conquest reference to it and the first mention of a royal 'palace' in Winchester is in the late tenth century.[21] Kings visited both places but they did not necessarily stay in them; there were royal residences near both. Domesday Book's description of the arrangements to protect and serve the king when he stayed in Canterbury, Sandwich or Shrewsbury suggest that such visits did occur, but most pre-Conquest kings seem to have preferred their country estates.[22]

Royal assemblies were occasionally held in towns but most of the meetings of the *witan*, like many Carolingian councils (above, p. 220), seem to have been in royal residences in the countryside. Some charters explicitly state that the assembly at which a grant was made was held in a royal vill, and many other places in which royal councils met can be shown to have been royal property at some time. Thus Amesbury, where councils were held in 858, 932 and 995, was owned by Alfred, Eadred and by Edward the Confessor. Domesday Book names the pre-Conquest owners of 51 of the 63 identifiable places of assembly and 39 of these were held, completely or partly, by the king or queen in 1065. There is, additionally, pre-Conquest evidence that seven others had been royal vills at some time.

Another clue to the location of some early royal vills is provided by the churches that were later known as old minsters. These appear to have been the original parish churches that were established on, or near, royal vills. Some, perhaps many, were founded in the course of the conversion. Bede relates how Aidan used royal vills as bases for his missionary work and a church had been built on at least one of these before Aidan's death. In time some of these churches were served by members of the bishop's *familia* and many appear in Domesday Book as communities of secular canons. They were supported not only by such spiritual dues as tithes and church-scot but also had a landed endowment.[23] Some were richer than others and achieved a degree of independence but many are listed in

[21] *Gesetze*, I, p. 11; M. Biddle (ed.), *Winchester in the early Middle Ages* (Oxford, 1976), p. 289.
[22] DB I.1, 252.
[23] *HE* III.17, pp. 159–60; F. Barlow, *The English Church, 1000–1066: a Constitutional History* (London, 1963), pp. 190–6.

Domesday Book among the possessions of bishops. Others had become, or been granted to, monastic communities, and both processes continued after the Norman Conquest.[24] Others remained closely linked with royal families, a connection that was clearly shown by the choice of royal burial places. A few, later known as royal free chapels, resisted episcopal jurisdiction.[25] Domesday Book also described a number of churches with property that was separately assessed for the geld, often a hide or more, frequently on royal, comital or episcopal estates, and, as Frank Barlow remarked, 'it is easy to believe that most of them once belonged to the king.'[26] In many areas there tended to be one such church in each hundred, sometimes associated with the hundredal manor, and in some counties these were the only churches mentioned in Domesday Book.[27] At least three churches that are listed under the royal demesne in Wiltshire, Highworth, Heytesbury and Avebury, all with substantial endowments, appear to be independent of any secular estate although two were clearly hundredal churches.[28]

Royal ownership is also implied by such place-names as Kingston, Kingsclere and Conisbrough, as well as by similar names given to landscape features in charters indicating, for example, a quarry or a wood that marked the boundary with a neighbouring royal estate.[29] Some of the places whose royal ownership is indicated in this way were held by King Edward in 1065, but others were not.[30]

[24] R. Lennard, *Rural England, 1086–1135* (Oxford, 1959), pp. 396–404.
[25] J. H. Denton, *English Royal Free Chapels, 1100–1300. A Constitutional Study* (Manchester, 1970).
[26] Barlow, *English Church*, p. 188.
[27] W. Page, 'Some remarks on the churches of the Domesday Survey', *Archaeologia*, 2nd ser., XVI (1915), pp. 61–102.
[28] DB I.65b; cf. R. B. Pugh and E. Crittall (eds), *The Victoria History of the County of Wiltshire, II* (London, 1955), pp. 33–4.
[29] M. Gelling, *The Place-Names of Berkshire, III* (Cambridge, English Place-Name Society, 1976), p. 828.
[30] The pre-Conquest ownership of places in DB with settlement-names implying ownership by a king is as follows (numbers refer to DB I):
 (a) Wholly or partly owned by king or queen: Coningsby, Li 339; Kineton, Wa 238; Kingscote, Gl 163; Kingston, Ca 189b; Kingston-on-Thames, Sr 30b; Kingstone nr Hereford, He 179b; Kingstone nr Ross, He 163, 182b; Kingsthorpe, YN 299; Kington, He 181.
 (b) Comital or ecclesiastical owners: Conesby, Li 349; Coney Weston, Sf II 365; Conington, Hu 206b; Consibrough, YW 321; Coniston, YE 323b; Coniston Cold,

It is clear that kings acquired land in various ways and also disposed of it; the royal demesne was constantly changing. It does, however, appear that some land remained in royal hands for centuries. Three of the four *tūnas* won by Cuthwulf in 571, for example, were held by King Edward in 1065, as were 20 of the places bequeathed by Alfred. Whether Aylesbury, Benson and Limbury remained in royal hands all the time cannot, of course, be determined. Benson, which was captured by Offa in 777, was described as a *villa regia* in a charter about a century later but land at Aylesbury was bequeathed to King Edgar by Ealdorman Aelfheah along with land in several other places that were royal demesne in 1065. Aelfheah was, however, a member of the royal family and, like most bequests, the extent of the land is not stated and need not necessarily have been the whole estate. It is, therefore, possible, even probable, that some places were continuously held by kings, their kinsmen or their agents. One possible explanation, that all land originally belonged to the king but that most had been given away by the eleventh century, has little to commend it. It requires the assumption that most royal charters were grants of the king's own land. Some certainly were, but others were grants of land that had been forfeited and many were grants of royal rights over land or, more simply, of freedom to dispose of it. There were certainly other landowners than the king in the seventh century and the description of some places as royal vills implies that others were not.

A more satisfactory explanation is that some land was thought to belong to the crown in contrast to the king's personal property, whether inherited or acquired in other ways, which could be disposed of more easily. Such a distinction is implied by Asser when describing the arrangements made by Aethelwulf for the disposal of his property. He provided that the kingdom (*regnum*) should be divided between his two eldest sons, that his own inheritance

---

YW 301b; Kingsbury, Mx 128b; Kingsbury Episcopi, So 89; Kingston in Corfe, Do 78b; Kingston, Sf II 386.

(c) Others: Conington, Ca 197ab, 199; Conistone in Burnsall, YW 331b; Keinton Mandeville, So 92b, 94; Kineton Green, Wa 243; Kingthorpe, Li 351ab, 362, 364; Kingsthorpe, Np 221b; Kingston, Sx 26b, 28b (of Harold); Kingston, Wt 52b; Kingston Bagpuize, Brk 60b, 61; Kington St Michael, W 72b; Kingston Seymour, So 89; Kington, Do 80b, 82, 84; Kington, Wa 240; Kington, Wo 176b.

(d) No 1065 owner named: Congerstone, Le 233, 234b; Kingsland, Sf II 425; Kingston Blount, O 159ab.

(*propria hereditas*) should be divided among his sons, daughter and other relatives, and that his money (*pecunia*) should be devoted to the needs of his soul, his sons and his nobles.[31] Alfred, in his will, distinguished between the land that Aethelwulf left jointly to his sons and that was apparently kept undivided, and other lands and treasures that Alfred and his brother agreed should be granted to their children by the one who lived longest. Lands acquired by kings in the tenth century certainly seem to have been disposed of with relative ease and very few of the bequests made to tenth-century kings were in royal hands in 1065. There are also several charters granting confiscated estates.

By the eleventh century some former royal vills, or parts of them, had been acquired by churches or by laymen. Kings did not, however, have complete freedom to alienate their lands. Some-times a king recovered land that had been given away by a predeces-sor and even Alfred, who claimed to have been allowed the right to give or bequeath land to kinsmen or strangers as he wished, gave only two estates to a church, Winchester Cathedral, and the rest to members of his family. Eadred tried to be more generous but with little success; none of his bequests to New Minster or Nunnaminster were held by those churches at the Norman Conquest and the one bequest to Old Minster that that church did hold in 1065, Downton, had been the subject of charters of both Edgar and Aethelred.

A king could, perhaps, more easily give away part of an estate. Some charters appear to do that, and in 1065 the king shared many estates with a church or with laymen, sometimes called king's thegns. It was obviously in the king's interest to retain centres at which food-rents were delivered as long as they were paid by most land. This obligation could be remitted but it appears that the burden was still common in eighth-century Mercia. The land at Westbury that Aethelbald granted to Offa's grandfather was still expected to pay a heavy food-rent, called both *vectigal* and *gafol*, to the royal vill even after Offa had given that estate to the church of Worcester.[32] By the eleventh century this ancient obligation had almost entirely disappeared. Most land then owed the *trinoda necessitas* and geld. Traces of the old obligation apparently survived in the form of hundred pennies and varied renders of honey, iron,

[31] Asser, 16, pp. 14–15.
[32] *S* 146; see n. 12 above.

animals and other produce that are occasionally recorded in Domesday Book and later as owing to certain manors.[33]

When food-rents were no longer a general burden there was no need to retain royal vills as collecting centres, but the same places also served as centres of government, controlled by reeves whose importance as agents of kings increased greatly in the tenth century.[34] The alienation of such places was likely to weaken royal authority to some extent even when the recipient was a church that could be expected to act in the royal interest. Another cause of change was the incorporation of Mercia and the Danelaw in the West Saxon kingdom. This made control more difficult – even William I suffered from the depredations of his agents – but the enlarged resources also made it easier for kings to be generous. At the same time some places, former Roman towns as well as royal vills, were developed as especially important centres of royal authority and either became, or were closely associated with *burhs*. On the eve of the Norman Conquest an impressive network of estates remained in the hands of the king, the queen or the earls, and many of these royal vills were administrative centres for the hundreds or wapentakes in which royal reeves supervised the collection of dues and penalties owing to the king from the people who lived on land that the king did not own.

This network of royal estates, with various modifications, extended throughout England and the system can perhaps be seen in its simplest form in the Domesday account of the lands between the Ribble and the Mersey.[35] Most of the landowners, called thegns or radmen, were obliged to pay a cash farm (*firma*) to the king and also to provide customary services which included making the king's houses (*domos regis*) and other duties apparently connected with hunting, and they were also expected to send men to help harvest the king's crops. Some had been excused these *consuetudines* but all paid geld. The area was divided into six hundreds, each with a royal vill, consisting of a manor with berewicks, controlled by a reeve who had responsibility for maintaining the peace and imposing penalties. Four are explicitly said to have a church and they probably all did. The thegns commonly held a hide or carucate, some had more. They clearly had their own tenants, some of whom

[33] E. B. Demarest, 'The hundred-pennies', *EHR*, XXXIII (1918), pp. 62–72.
[34] Chadwick, *Studies*, pp. 228–39.
[35] DB I.269b–70.

were freemen. There were no great ecclesiastical foundations or major landowners to confuse this simple, and probably archaic, pattern.

Further south, in Shropshire, the situation described in Domesday Book was more complicated but a similar pattern can easily be recognized. There were twelve hundreds and for nine of them Domesday specifically indicates the manor at which the king's share of hundredal revenues was due; all these manors were held by King Edward.[36] They also all had churches, mostly with substantial endowments. Two of the hundreds, *Culvestan* and *Patintune*, were grouped together under one manor, Corfham. Similar groups of hundreds are found elsewhere, most clearly in Oxfordshire where, for example, four and half hundreds rendered church-scot at the royal manor of Benson.[37] Church-scot payments are particularly revealing and point to other groups, such as the two hundreds attached to Fawsley in Northamptonshire or the eight hundreds associated with Aylesbury,[38] both royal manors in 1065.

These indications of early groups of hundreds are one of the reasons for believing that many of the hundreds and wapentakes described by Domesday Book were rearrangements, by subdivision or otherwise, of earlier territories. Some of these, like their hundredal successors, were named after a prominent natural feature, commonly a hill, river or wood, and the same name was sometimes used for the vill that functioned as its centre. Alfred's will offers several good examples, such as Meon and Yeovil, both named from rivers, or Wedmore which probably means 'moor for hunting'.[39] Other centres were simply called the *tūn* of their district. This Alfred bequeathed land at *Heortigtūn*, referring to the *tūn* of Hartland, originally *Heorot īeg* 'stag island'. Similarly Carhampton (*Carumtun*) appears first, in the *Chronicle*, as simply *aet Carrum* 'at the rocks'. A similar explanation underlies many other names, including Chewton, from the river Chew, Cannington, from the Quantocks, and the *Aeweltun* named in Alfred's will next after Leatherhead is likely to be the *tūn* of Ewell, which was in Domesday Book a royal manor to which the church of Leatherhead belonged.

[36] DB I.253ab.
[37] DB I.154b; Cam, *Liberties*, pp. 91–106.
[38] DB I.143b; Stenton, *ASE*, p. 154.
[39] O. S. Anderson, *The English Hundred-Names: the South-Western Counties* (Lund, 1939), 49, 58, 183.

This supports the suggestion made by James Campbell that the word *tūn* had a special sense referring to the functions of a royal vill as a local centre.[40]

Some districts were, on the other hand, named after places within them, presumably their centres. An early example of this occurs in the anonymous *Life* of St Cuthbert which describes the saint stopping *in regione qui dicitur Ahse*, between Hexham and Carlisle, a name that has most plausibly been interpreted as referring to *Aesica*, now Great Chesters.[41] Many Domesday hundreds appear to be named in this way after their hunded vills. Others were named after the places in which the freemen of the hundred assembled, commonly at a named tree, a burial mound, a cross or at a ford.[42] These two types of hundred or wapentake name do not reflect a fundamental difference but are rather two ways of referring to the same thing. Domesday Book, as a record of royal rights, naturally tended to use the name of the royal vill, but the alternative name was often used elsewhere and in many hundreds that were named, or renamed, after a royal vill, the freemen continued to meet in their traditional places of assembly long after the Norman Conquest.

The fact that many battles were fought at, or close to, royal vills underlines their importance as local centres. Some may have been little more than skirmishes as at Pinhoe in 1001 and possibly at Dean in the same year.[43] Others must have been much like the fighting described at *Merantun* in 786. There were also sieges, some of which seem to have ended in burnings; had Aethelwold not escaped there could well have been a battle at Wimborne after Alfred's death. Some battles associated with royal vills, such as Offa's victory at Benson or Alfred's at Edington, had far-reaching consequences. It is particularly interesting that in 871 at least three battles were fought at royal vills, Reading, Basing and Wilton, and a fourth, at *Meretun*, was perhaps the place Cynewulf was killed a century earlier. A royal *tūn* was the obvious place in which forces could be assembled, or an enemy trapped. What is more, the seizure of such a

[40] J. Campbell, 'Bede's words for places', in P. H. Sawyer (ed.), *Names, Words and Graves: Early Medieval Settlement* (Leeds, 1979), pp. 48–50.
[41] *Two Lives of Saint Cuthbert* IV.5, ed. and trans. B. Colgrave (Cambridge, 1940), p. 116; cf. p. 332.
[42] O. S. Anderson, *English Hundred Names* (Lund, 1939), pp. 156–208.
[43] Teignton and Clyst (?Broad), D, and (Bishop's) Waltham, Ha, were attacked in the same year (*ASC A, s.a.* 1001), and may have been royal vills, but there is no supporting evidence. At Pinhoe two royal reeves gathered an army.

centre could also mean the conquest of the region that was tributary to it. A new ruler was naturally eager to gather the tribute and services that his defeated rival had enjoyed and in this way the old structure tended to survive despite conquests.

The Scandinavian conquests of the ninth century were certainly disruptive but even in the Danelaw there are signs of continuity. Driffield and Aldborough were still local centres in the eleventh century as they had been long before, and Conisbrough was held by Wulfric whose close interest in Tamworth suggests that he inherited some Mercian royal rights.[44] In Lincolnshire the sokes described in Domesday Book seem often to preserve ancient arrangements. So, for example, Waltham whose name may well indicate that it was used at an early date as a centre for hunting,[45] or Kirton in Lindsey both appear to have been important before the Scandinavian invasions. Grantham and Horncastle are perhaps even more revealing. Both were held by the queen in 1065 and were the centres of very large parishes. In the twelfth century both these churches had rights over many dependant chapels in surrounding settlements, rights that can hardly have been newly created after the Scandinavian conquests.[46]

A similar continuity may span the English conquest of British areas. That is clearly implied by Alfred's bequest to Edward of *Straetneat on Triconscire*. Triggshire was later divided into the three hundreds of Trigg, Lesnewth and Stratton but the original British name suggests that it was a grouping of three units in the first place.[47] It appears in the geld accounts included in the *Liber Exoniensis* as the hundred of Stratton, apparently an English misunderstanding or adaptation of the Cornish name in which the first element refers not to a *straet* in the sense of a paved road but to a *strat*, or broad valley. This is both a good example of the use of alternative names and also of the antiquity of these arrangements. Whether *Straetneat* was a centre of *Triconscir*, as Stratton was later, cannot be proved, but Alfred's specific mention of it suggests that it

[44] P. H. Sawyer, *Charters of Burton Abbey* (Oxford, Anglo-Saxon Charters, II, 1979), pp. xxi, xxv.
[45] R. Huggins, 'The significance of the place-name wealdhām', *Medieval Archaeology*, XIX (1975), pp. 198–201.
[46] D. Owen, *Church and Society in medieval Lincolnshire* (Lincoln, 1971), pp. 1–2.
[47] Anderson, *Hundred Names (SW)*, pp. 151–2; K. Jackson, *Language and History in early Britain* (Edinburgh, 1953), p. 587. I am grateful to Simon Keynes for advice on this point, and for passing on comments by Oliver Padel.

was. There is, however, no doubt that the district was an ancient territory that survived the English conquest.

The area appurtenant to a vill could be changed. Domesday Book has many examples of land being transferred from one hundred to another, and similar adjustments are likely to have been made earlier. The grouping of royal estates could also be changed. It has been suggested recently that the arrangements described in Domesday Book for the collection of farm from the royal estates was the result of a relatively recent reorganization, and that the groupings of Dorset in particular are artificial and probably recent.[48] That may be so, but they could alternatively be the remnants of territories that were once much larger. The existence of such extensive rights is indicated by, for example, Amesbury's rights in the Isle of Wight.[49] The compact estates of the Wiltshire Domesday may have once been component parts of much larger units that had been broken up. That seems to have happened with the estate of Bedwyn. In the late tenth century Lambourn church was a daughter church of Bedwyn's but in Domesday Book these estates had the same status.[50]

The royal estates of the eleventh century do therefore seem to reflect arrangements of great antiquity that survived centuries of alienation and illegal seizures, as well as other changes such as the ending of the universal obligation to render a heavy food-rent to the king. There was a continued need for local centres in which royal power could be asserted or displayed. That was best done by the king himself. When he was accompanied by his household spacious accommodation must have been needed for a variety of functions, both public and private, ranging from the provision of a prison to a hall for feasts and assemblies. The *Chronicle* account of the fight at *Merantun* shows that the buildings were surrounded by a fence with a gate that could be closed against attack and the fact that the king's companions were woken by the screams of his mistress and not by the fight may mean that they were sleeping some distance away from the *bur*, but they could, of course, simply have been sound asleep after a feast.

[48] P. A. Stafford, 'The "Farm of one night" and the organization of King Edward's estates in Domesday', *Economic History Review*, 2nd ser., XXXIII (1980), pp. 491–502.
[49] DB I.64b.
[50] H. Merritt, 'Old English entries in a manuscript at Bern', *Journal of English and Germanic Philology*, XXXIII (1934), p. 344.

We can hardly suppose that kings had residences on all their estates. They certainly had no need to visit them all to collect food-rents. Churches were able to gather food from distant estates[51] and royal agents could do likewise, collecting what was needed at the residences favoured by the king. The accommodation needed for the king's normal retinue was large but assemblies attended by bishops, abbots and lay lords, many with their own retinues, required even more. The two royal residences that have been excavated and published give some idea of the size of royal halls and of some of the subsidiary buildings, but neither site was completely excavated and there may well have been many other structures, permanent or temporary.[52] In good weather discussion probably took place out of doors, as in ninth-century Francia, (above, p. 220) but the halls presumably had room for all those entitled to attend assemblies. Additional accommodation must also have been required, either in tents or in temporary structures that were perhaps erected by the men who owed the king building services. Later evidence shows that very large structures could be put up to meet temporary needs, as at Leicester where in 1414 Henry V had a hall measuring 120 by 40 feet built in 24 days for a meeting of Parliament.[53]

Royal residences were not permanent. *Campodonum* and Yeavering were abandoned after destruction and Asser explicitly stated that Alfred moved royal residences built of stone from their old sites to more suitable locations.[54] Some places were clearly favourite residences. Many Mercian assemblies, including some at Christmas and at Easter, were held at Tamworth and it was there that Aethelflaed died. The West Saxons, however, seem to have been less consistent. They are known to have celebrated Christmas at Amesbury, Chippenham and Dorchester and Easter at Amesbury, Calne, Sherborne and Somerton.

It is rarely possible to trace the movement of pre-Conquest kings in any detail and we have no means of telling how long they stayed in any one place. One charter describes assemblies in quick succession at Calne and Wantage.[55] Others suggest that Aethelstan

---

[51] Lennard, *Rural England*, pp. 131–41.
[52] Hope Taylor, *Yeavering*; Rahtz, *Cheddar*; above, p. 274.
[53] H. M. Colvin (ed.), *The History of the King's Works*, II (London, 1963), p. 703; and, for a similar temporary structure at Westminster in 1397, *ibid*., pp. 532, 1004. I owe these references to Maurice Barley.
[54] Asser, 91, p. 77.   [55] *S* 891.

progressed with a very large company from Winchester to Nottingham between 28 May and 7 June 934, that is at a rate of about 20 miles a day, much the same as when the Exchequer was moved from London to York in 1322.[56] There is no information about the stages of Aethelstan's journey to Nottingham. He continued north to reach Chester-le-Street by about 1 July and after reaching Scotland returned to an assembly at Buckingham on 12 September.[57] This journey, like all movements of the royal court, must have required some system of messengers giving advance notice of the king's plans so that appropriate arrangements could be made. Aethelstan's journey north in 934 was a military expedition against the Scots, but kings also travelled for political or religious purposes and the main objective of many journeys appears to have been hunting. Alfred, like Edward the Confessor, seems to have greatly enjoyed hunting and, as in Merovingian Francia, Carolingian Aquitaine and Angevin England, royal assemblies were sometimes held in hunting lodges. In 904 an assembly was held in the *villa venatoria* called *Bicanleag*, possibly one of the Devon Bickleighs, and Edmund's decision not to exile Dunstan was made during a hunt while the royal party was staying at Cheddar, which in Domesday Book was associated with the royal vill of Wedmore.[58] In the century before the Norman Conquest several important assemblies were held in what appear to have been hunting lodges. Woodstock, where two of Aethelred's legal codes were produced, is described in Domesday Book as royal forest, while Whittlebury and Woolmer, neither of which is named in Domesday Book, were both later parts of royal forests. This may explain why it has not been possible to identify some places of assembly.

Large estates had many components, not all of which are named in Domesday Book. Chalton in Hampshire, for example, according to the will of the atheling Aethelstan, included eight hides at Catherington, but the latter does not appear in Domesday Book.[59] A king might sometimes choose to hold an assembly elsewhere on a

[56] *S* 407; *S* 425; D. Broome, 'Exchequer migrations to York', in A. G. Little and F. M. Powicke (eds), *Essays in Medieval History presented to T. F. Tout* (Manchester, 1925), pp. 291–300.

[57] For the date and inscription on the now almost wholly destroyed manuscript of the Gospel-book presented to St Cuthbert by Aethelstan, see above, p. 255. I owe advice on this point to Simon Keynes.

[58] *Vita Dunstani*, ed. W. Stubbs, *Memorials of St Dunstan* (RS, 1874), p. 36.

[59] *S* 1503.

royal estate than in the royal vill itself. That is apparently what
Aethelred did when he met his *witan* at Enham rather than
Andover, of which it formed a part and where both he and his father
held several assemblies. A few royal vills, including Snaith,
Tamworth and Yeovil, were not described in Domesday Book,
possibly by mistake for the inquiry does seem to have been an
attempt to record all royal rights. Alfred's will was certainly not a
complete list of his property. One omission, *Leonaford*, where Asser
visited Alfred, may have been part of another estate but that can
hardly be the explanation for the omission of Reading and
Wardour, or of Wimborne and *Twinham* which Aethelwold seized
on the king's death. It is also significant that few of the *burhs*
listed in the Burghal Hidage are mentioned in the will, while in Kent
Alfred specifically bequeathed his booklands but did not refer to
folklands. It is therefore possible that some vills, together with the
burhs and the royal folkland, formed part of the royal demesne that
his successors could expect to inherit with the kingdom. It may
even be that the places named in the will were all acquired in
other ways. Some were later absorbed into the crown property;
Chippenham, which he left to a daughter, and Wantage, which he
left to his wife, were both held by King Edward in 1065. It is,
however, possible that Alfred was simply allocating crown property, possibly for what was understood to be a limited period,
perhaps a life.

The great extension of royal lands in the tenth century made it
possible for the restraints on alienation to be loosened and by the
eleventh century the process of granting even *burhs* had begun. The
Norman Conquest enlarged the royal demesne still more and the
rulers of Anglo-Norman England could therefore afford to relinquish rights that their predecessors had jealously guarded. The
rubric in the Exon Domesday *Dominicatus Regis ad regnum pertinens*
may have had little significance in 1086[60] but it did preserve an echo
from a past in which lands that pertained to the kingdom were
distinguished from other lands that a king might have. The land so
described in the Exon Domesday were the king's hundredal manors
in Devonshire, the royal vills, that were very much like those
described in Shropshire, Lancashire and, indeed, in most parts of

[60] R. S. Hoyt, *The Royal Demesne in English Constitutional History, 1066–1272*
(Ithaca, N.Y., 1950), pp. 10–24, 50–1.

England. The network of royal vills and regalian rights revealed by Domesday Book was not a recent creation, it had deep roots that extended even beyond the English conquests.

APPENDIX
Royal Vills in pre-Conquest England

This list includes places in which royal assemblies were held, excluding such major religious centres as Glastonbury or *Medeshamstede* and the towns of Canterbury, Lincoln, London, Rochester and Winchester. Unidentified places are listed separately at the end. Normally only one charter is listed for each assembly. For further details of those held after 900, see S. D. Keynes, *The Diplomas of King Aethelred 'the Unready', 978–1016* (Cambridge, 1980), pp. 269–73. The identifiable places in which Alfred and Eadred bequeathed land in their wills (S 1507, S 1515) are listed with the appropriate abbreviation at the beginning of an entry. Other indications of royal ownership, discussed above, are also noted, and explicit references to royal vills in pre-Conquest sources are indicated by an *. Place-name evidence is considered above, n. 30. The main DB references are given, together with the name of the principal landowners of 1065. The abbreviations used for counties (pre-1974) are those adopted by the English Place-Name Society, and used by E. Ekwall, *Concise Oxford Dictionary of English Place-Names* (Oxford, 4th edn, 1960). Chronicle sources are cited *s.a.*, and laws by the abbreviations standardized in Liebermann's *Gesetze*. Abbreviations other than those in use for the whole book are:

A	King Alfred's Will (S 1507)
Aethelweard	*The Chronicle of Aethelweard*, ed. and trans. A. Campbell (London, 1962)
Arbp	Archbishop
ASN	*Annals of St Neots*, ed. W. H. Stevenson in his Asser (*q.v.*), pp. 117–45
ass.	assembly
Asser	Asser, *Life of Alfred*, ed. W. H. Stevenson (Oxford, repr. 1959)
Bp	Bishop
DB	Domesday Book, referred to by folio, b indicating verso
E	King Eadred's will (S 1515)

FW   *Florentii Wigorniensis Monachi Chronicon ex*
                  Chronicis, ed. B. Thorpe (2 vols, London,
                  1848–9)
K.   King
NM   New Minster, Winchester
OM   Old Minster, Winchester
Q.   Queen
VAE   *Vita Aedwardi Regis*, ed. and trans. F. Barlow
                  (London, 1962)

Abingdon, Brk   ass. *c.*930 (*S* 1208); royal building at (*S* 876);
                  not in DB,? under Barton, DB I.58b – K.
Aldingbourne, Sx A,E; DB I.16b – Bp of Chichester.
Amesbury, W   A,E; ass. 858 (*S* 1274), 24 Dec.932 (*S* 418),
                  977 (*FW*), Easter 995 (*ASC* F); DB I.39,
                  64b – K.
Andover, Ha   E; ass. 959x963 (IV Edg.1.4, pp. 208–9,
                  referring to II and III Edg.), 980★ (Wulfstan
                  Cantor, *Narratio de Sancto Swithuno*, ll.
                  75–80, ed. A. Campbell, *Frithegodi Monachi*
                  Breuiloquium Vitae Beati Wilfredi et Wulfstani
                  Cantoris Narratio Metrica de Sancto Swithuno,
                  Zürich, 1950, p. 67), 994 (*ASC* F); DB
                  I.39 – K.
Angmering, Sx   A; DB I.24b – Earl Godwine.
Arreton, Wt   A; DB I.39b – K.
Axminster, D   ass. 901 (*S* 364); atheling Cyneheard buried at
                  (*ASC* 757); DB I.100 – K.
Axmouth, D   A; DB I.100b – K.
Aylesbury, Bk   captured (*ASC* 571, Aethelweard★);
                  bequeathed to Edg. (*S* 1485); DB I.143 – K.
Aylesford, K   Eadric met K. Edmund at (*ASC* C 1016);
                  DB I.2b – K.
Bamburgh, Nb   *regia civitas* (*HE* III.12), *urbs regia* (*HE* III.6,
                  16); Bp Cynewulf imprisoned at (*HR* 750);
                  K. Alhred flees to (*HR* 774).
Bapchild, K   ass. 696x716 (*S* 22), 803 (*S* 290); not in DB
                  but *Domesday Monachorum of Christ Church*
                  Canterbury, ed. D. C. Douglas (London,
                  1944), p. 78 records a church there, *Bacelde*,
                  pertaining to Milton, a royal estate in
                  DB I.2b.
Basing, Ha   E; K. Edmund granted land at B. to

	Aethelnoth 945 (*S* 505), cf. grant by Aethelnoth to NM (*S* 1418); DB I.43 – NM, 45 – *Altei*? for Aelfheah.
Bath, So	captured (*ASC* 577); ass. 796 (*S* 148), 864 (*S* 210), Whitsun 973 (*ASC*), 1009 (VII Atr.); DB I.87 – borough.
Beaduricesworth, later Bury St Edmunds, Sf	St Edmund buried in B.★ Abbo of Fleury, *Passio Sancti Eadmundi, Three Lives of English Saints*, ed. M. Winterbottom (Toronto, 1972); p. 82, DB II.372 – St Edmund's Abbey.
Beckley, Sr	A; not in DB.
Beddingham, Sx	A; DB I.20b – K. For a *monasterium* at B. in Offa's reign, see *S* 158, 1435.
Bedwyn, W	A; granted by Edg. to Abingdon Abbey 968 (*S* 756); granted to Atr. as atheling (*S* 937); DB I.64b – K. In 778 K. Cynewulf granted land at B. to Bica, *comes* (*S* 264), but the bounds show that this was Little Bedwyn, which was not included in *S* 756, O. G. S. Crawford, 'The Anglo-Saxon bounds of Bedwyn and Burbage', *Wiltshire Archaeological Magazine*, XLI (1921), pp. 281–301.
Beeding, Sx	A; DB I.28 – K.
Benson (formerly Bensington), O	captured (*ASC* 571, Aethelweard★); captured by Offa (*ASC* 779); *Dux* Aethelred granted six men, formerly belonging *ad villam regiam in* B.887 (*S* 217); DB I.154b – K.
Bradford, W	E; Atr. granted *cenobium* and land to Shaftesbury Abbey 1001 (*S* 899); DB I.67b – Shaftesbury Abbey.
Branscombe, D	A; DB I.102 – Exeter Cathedral.
Brentford, Mx	ass. 780 (*S* 116), 718 (*S* 1257); not in DB.
Brill, Bk	royal palace built for K. Edward (*VAE* p. 64); DB I.143b – K.
Britford, W	ass. 1065★ (*VAE* p. 52); DB I.65 – K.
Buckingham, Bk	ass. 934 (*S* 426); DB I.143 – borough.
Bures, Sf	K. Edmund crowned at 856 (*ASN*★); DB II.392 – Wihtgar, 421b – Earl Aelfgar, 435b – Wulfric, son of Brihtric.
Burnham, So	A; DB I.95 – *Brixi* for Brihtsige.
Calne, W	E; ass. 977 (*ASC*), Easter 997 (*S* 891); DB I.64b – K.

Candover, Ha	A; DB I.40b – Bp of Winchester, 42 – NM, 44b – *Aluric* from Earl Harold, 45b – Godwin from K., 49b – Sberne from Q. etc.
Cannington, So	A; DB I.86b – K.
Carhampton, So	A; battle 836 (*ASC*): Edward the Elder recovered land at C. from community at Cheddar (*S* 806); DB I.86b – K.
Catterick, YN	*vicus* (*HE* II.14, 20, III.14); K. Aethelwold married at (*HR* 762); burnt by Beornred (*HR* 769); DB I.310b – Earl Edwin.
Cheddar, So	ass. 956 *in palatio regis* (*S* 611); DB I.86 – K.
Chelsea, Mx	ass. from 785 (*S* 123) to 816 (*BCS* 358); DB I.130b – *Wluuene* (for Wulfwine) *homo regis*.
Chewton Mendip, So	A; DB I.87 – Q.
Chippenham, W	A; ass. 930 (*S* 405), 933 (*S* 422), 940 (*S* 473); K. Burgred married at 853 (Asser c.9,★ p. 8); Asser c.52,★ p. 40; *S* 1445; DB I.64b – K.
Chiseldon, W	A; DB I.67b – NM.
Cholsey, Brk	Aethelflaed bequeathed land at C. to K. 962x991 (*S* 1494); Atr. given land at C. by his mother (*S* 877); DB I.56b – K.
Cirencester, Gl	captured (*ASC* 577); battle at (*ASC* 628); ass. 935 (*S* 1792), 956 (*S* 633), 985 (*S* 896, 937), 1020 (*ASC* CDE); DB I.162b – K.
Colchester, Ess	ass. 931 (*S* 412), 940 (*S* 472); DB II.104–7b – borough.
Colyton, D	ass. 939x946 (III Em., p. 190); DB I.100b – K.
Cookham, Brk	given by K. Aethelbald to Canterbury, taken by K. Cynewulf, recovered and retained by Offa and in 798 confirmed to abbess Cynethryth, ?Offa's widow (*S* 1258); ass. 997 (*S* 939); blinding of Wulfheah and Ufegeat at C, where Atr. was staying (*FW* 1006); Aelfheah bequeathed land at C. to Edg. (*S* 1485); DB I.56b – K.
Cosham, Ha	Atr. ill at 1015 (*ASC* CDE); DB I.38 – K.
Crewkerne, So	A; DB I.86b – *Eddeua*, probably for Q. Edith (cf. O. von Feilitzen, *Pre-Conquest Personal Names of Domesday Book*, Uppsala, 1937, p. 231). The estate was unhidated and in 1065 was royal, DB I.87b under *Seveberge* for Seaborough, Do and 92 under *Estham*.

Croft, Le	ass. 836 (*S* 190); DB I.231b, 232b – no 1065 owner named.
Crondall, Ha	A; Aelfheah and Bp Aelfsige bequeathed land at C. to OM (*S* 1485, 1491); DB I.41 – OM.
Cropthorne, Wo	? ass. 841 (*S* 196, *scripta est in loco* . . . C); DB I.174 – Bp of Worcester.
Cullompton, D	A; DB I.104 – *Turbert*.
Damerham, W (later Ha)	K. Alfred desired that the community of D. be given their charters and freedom to choose their lord (*S* 1507), E; K. Edmund and Aethelflaed granted D. to Glastonbury Abbey (*S* 513, 1494); DB I.66b – Glastonbury Abbey.
Dean, Sx	A; Asser c.79★, p. 64; battle at *Aethelingadene* 1001 (*ASC* A); land at D., formerly Q. Aelfthryth's, granted to Wherwell Abbey 1002 (*S* 904); not in DB.
Ditchling, Sx	A; DB I.26 – K.
Dorchester, Do	ass. 26 Dec. 833★ (*S* 277), 26 Dec. 864★ (*S* 333); attempt to force Northmen *to thaes cyninges tun* (*ASC* 789) identified as D. (Aethelweard, p. 27); DB I.75 – borough.
Downton, W	E; Atr. restored land at D. to OM 997 (*S* 891); DB I.65b – Bp of Winchester.
Driffield, YE	K. Aldfrith died at (*ASC* DE 705); DB I.299b – Earl Morcar.
Droitwich, Wo	ass. 888 (*S* 220), c.903 (*S* 1446); DB I.172ab – K., Earl Edwin.
Eashing, Sr	A; borough in Burghal Hidage (A. J. Robertson, *Anglo-Saxon Charters*, Cambridge, 1939, p. 247); not in DB, apparently part of Godalming, *q.v.*
Edington, W	A; battle at 878 (*ASC*); ass. 957 (*S* 646); granted by Edg. to Romsey Abbey 968 (*S* 765); DB I.68 – Romsey Abbey.
Enham, Ha	ass. Whitsun 1006x1011 (VI Atr. Latin, cf. X Atr., pp. 247, 269); King's Enham not in DB, royal thegns in Knight's Enham, DB I.50.
Everley, W	ass. ? 704 (*S* 245, spurious but genuine witness list 705x709); not in DB.
Ewell, Sr	A (*aet Aeweltune*); DB I.30b – K.
Exminster, D	A; DB I.100 – K.
Eynsham, O	captured (*ASC* 571, Aethelweard★);

foundation of E. Abbey confirmed 1005
(*S* 911); DB I.155 – Bp (of Dorchester).

Farndon, Chs   K. Edward died at 924 (*ASC* BCD); DB I.263
                    – Bp of Chester, 266b – Earl Edwin.

Faversham, K   grants of lands *in regione* . . . F. 812, 815
                    (*S* 170, 178); ass. 924x939 (III As., p. 170);
                    DB I.2b – K.

Felpham, Sx   A; K. Eadred granted land at F. to his mother
                    953 (*S* 562); DB I.17b – Shaftesbury Abbey.

Gillingham, ? Do   battle at Penselwood, near G. 1016 (*FW*); ass.
                    993 (*S* 876), ? 1042 (William of Malmesbury,
                    Gesta Regum I, ed. W. Stubbs, London, 1887,
                    p. 238); DB I.75 – K.

Glenn, Le   ass. 848 (*S* 1272); DB I.232b – 1065 owner not
                    named.

Gloucester, Gl   captured (*ASC* 577); ass. 896 (*S* 1441), 1051
                    (*ASC* DEF); Aethelflaed buried at 918 (*ASC*
                    BCD); DB I.162 – borough.

Godalming, Sr   A; DB I.30b – K.
Grately, Ha   ass. 924x939 (II As. p. 166); not in DB.
Guildford, Sr   A; DB I.30 – borough.
Gumley, Le   ass. 749 (*S* 92), 772 (*S* 109), ? 779 (*S* 114); DB
                    I.234, 236 – 1065 owner not named.

Hadleigh, Sf   K. Guthrum buried at 890 (*ASN**); DB
                    II.372b – Christ Church Canterbury.

Hamsey, Sx   ass. 924x939 (*S* 1211); DB I.22b, 27b – *Vlueua*
                    for Wulfgifu.

Hartland, D   A; DB I.100b – Gytha, Harold's mother.
Headington, O   ass. 1004 (*S* 909); DB I.154b – K.
Hellesdon, Nf   K. Edmund stayed at 869 (Abbo of Fleury,
                    Passio S. Eadmundi, p. 73).

Hurstbourne   A; DB I.41 – Bp of Winchester.
Priors, Ha

Hurstbourne   A; granted by Edg. to Abingdon Abbey 961
Tarrant, Ha   (*S* 689); granted to Atr. as atheling (*S* 937);
                    DB I.39 – K.

Irthlingborough, Np ass. 787x796 (*S* 1184); DB I.221b, 222 –
                    Peterborough Abbey.

Kilton, So   A; DB I.96 – *Aluuard, Leuric*.
Kingsclere, Ha   A, E; DB I.39 – K.
Kingston, Do   see p. 276 and n. 19.
Kingston-on-Thames, Sr   ass. 838 (*S*1438), 972 (*S*1451), 1016x1020
                    (*S* 1461); for coronations of As. Eadred, Atr.

	and possibly others see Keynes, *Diplomas of King Aethelred*, pp. 270–1; DB I.30b – K.
Kirtlington, O	ass. 943x946 (*S* 1497), 977 (*ASC* BC); DB I.154b – K.
Lambeth, Sr	K. Harthacnut died at 1042 (*ASC* E); DB I.34 – *Goda*, K. Edward's sister and Waltham Abbey, from Harold.
Lambourn, Brk	A; Aethelflaed bequeathed land at L. to K. 962x991 (*S* 1494); DB I.57b – K., 61b – *Bristec*, 62 – *Esgar*.
Leatherhead, Sr	A; estate not in DB but church of *Leret* (DB I.30b) pertains to Ewell, *q.v.*
Lifton, D	A; ass. 931 (*S* 416); DB I.100b – Q.
Limbury, Bd	captured (*ASC* 571, Aethelweard★); not in DB, ?part of Luton, a royal estate, DB I.209.
Lyminster, Sx	A; ass. 930 (*S* 403); DB I.24b – K, 24b – *Esmund presbiter* held *Nonneminstre*=L. from K., 28 – *Aluuin* held *Clopeham* from K., *jacuit in* L.
Meon, Ha	A; *Meanuarorum prouinciam (HE* IV.13); grants of land in E. and W. Meon, 932–67 (*S* 417, 619, 754), replacement charter by Edg. for Eadgifu, his grandmother, for 65 hides at E. Meon, 959x963 (*S* 811); DB I.38 – Arbp Stigand *ad opus monachorum* (E. Meon), 40b – Bp of Winchester (W. Meon).
Mereworth, K	ass. 843 (*S* 293); DB I.14 – Norman.
Micheldever, Ha	ass. 862 (*S* 335★); DB I.42b – NM.
Millfield, Nb	*villa* at *Maelmin* built in seventh cent. in place of Yeavering (*HE* II.14).
Milton, ?K	ass. 903 (*S* 368), 932 (*S* 417); DB I.2b – K.
Passenham, Np	K. Edward stayed at P. 917 (*ASC* A); DB I.220 – K.
Penkridge, St	ass. 958 (*S* 667); DB I.246 – K., 247b – royal clerks.
Petherton, So	ass. *aet Peddredan* 1061x1066 (*S* 1116); DB I.86 (*Nort* and *Sud Peret*) – K. The alternative identification of P. in *S* 1116, N. Perrott, So (DB I.92b – *Algar*), seems less likely.
Pewsey, W	A; grant by K. Edmund of 30 hides to NM 940 (*S* 470); DB I.65b – K. (church), 67b – NM (30 hides).

Pinhoe, D	battle at 1001 (*ASC* A); DB I.101 – Earl Leofwine.
Pucklechurch, Gl	K. Edmund killed at 946 (*ASC, FW★*); DB I.165 – Glastonbury Abbey.
Puddletown, Do	ass. 976 (*S* 830); DB I.75 – K.
Reading, Brk	Asser, c.35★ p. 27; Aethelflaed bequeathed R. to K. 962x991 (*S*1494); DB I.58 – K.
Rendlesham, Sf	*HE* III.22★; DB II. many references but no royal associations.
Risborough, Princes, Bk	ass. 884 (*S* 219); DB I.143b – *Asgar Stalre* from Christ Church Canterbury, Earl Harold.
Rotherfield, Sx	A; DB I.16 – Earl Godwine.
Seckington, Wa	K. Aethelbald killed at, 757 (*ASC* 757); DB I.240, 243 – 1065 owners not named.
Shaftesbury, Do	K. Cnut died at 1035 (*ASC*); DB I.75 – borough.
Shalbourne, Brk (later W)	E; DB. I.57b – K.
Shrewsbury, Sa	ass. 901 (*S*221); DB I.252 – borough.
Slaughter, Gl	ass. 975x983 (*Liber Eliensis*, ed. E. O. Blake, London, 1962, p. 80); DB I.162b – K.
Somerton, So	taken by K. Aethelbald 733 (*ASC*, Aethelweard★); ass. 860 (*S* 329), Easter 949 (*S* 549); DB I.86 – K.
Southampton, Ha	ass. 26 Dec. 825 *in Omtune* (*S* 273, some authentic basis), 840 (*S* 288★), 903 (*S* 369), 1016 (*FW*); DB I.52 – borough.
Steyning, Sx	A; K. Aethelwulf buried at (*ASN* 857); DB I.17 – Harold.
Stratton, Co	A; DB.I 121b – Bp Osbern, Alfred *marescal*.
Sturminster, Do	A; DB I.80 – Arbp Stigand.
Sutton Courtenay, Brk	? ass. 1042 (*S* 993★); DB I.57b – K.
Sutton, Sx	A; DB I.23b – five thegns.
Tamworth, St	ass. 675x692 (*S* 1804 *Tomtun*), 26 Dec. 781 (*S* 120★), Easter 790 (*S* 133, authentic basis), 799 (*S* 155★), Easter 808 (*S* 163), Christmas 814 (*S* 172), Easter 840 (*S* 192), Christmas 841 (*S* 193–6), Christmas 845 (*S* 198★), 849 (*S* 199), 855 (*S* 207), Easter 857 (*S* 208); Aethelflaed died at 918 (*ASC* BCD); As and Sihtric met at, Sihtric married sister of As,

	926 (*ASC* D); DB I.238, 246ab – incidental references in *Terra Regis*, no description.
Taunton, So	Q. Aethelburh demolished T., which K. Ine had built (*ASC* 722); Bp of Winchester granted land to K. Edward in exchange for privileges for T. monastery 904 (*S* 1286), bequest by Bp Aelfsige (Winchester) of land at T. to K., who had let it to him (*S* 1491); DB I.87b – Arpb Stigand as Bp of Winchester.
Thame, O	ass. 672x674 (*S* 1165); DB I.155 – Bp (of Dorchester).
Thatcham, Brk	E; Aelfheah bequeathed land at T. to Edg. (*S* 1485); DB I.50b – K.
Thunderfield, Sr	A; ass. 924x939 (IV As, p. 171, cf. VI As. 10, p. 182); not in DB.
Tiverton, D	A; DB I.100b – Gytha, Harold's mother.
Twinham, now Christchurch, Ha	seized by Aethelwold (*ASC* 900); DB I.38b – K.
Walbottle, Nb	*HE* III.21★, 22★, pp. 170, 172.
Wantage, Brk	A,E; Alfred born at (Asser. c.1, p. 1★); ass. 997, soon after Easter (*S* 891), 978x1008 (III Atr., p. 228); DB I.57 – K.
Wardour, W	K. Alfred at (*S* 1445); DB I.68 – Wilton Abbey.
Wareham, Do	K. Brihtric and K. Edward buried at (*ASC* 786, 978D); DB I.75 – borough.
Warminster, W	Edward at 899x924 (*S* 1445); DB I.64b – K.
Wedmore, So	A; K. Alfred and Guthrum at 878 (*ASC*, Asser c.56★, p. 47); K. Edward granted W. to Bp Giso for canons of Wells, 1061x1066 (*S* 1115); DB I.86, 89b – Bp of Wells as part of royal estate of Cheddar.
Wellesbourne, Wa	ass. 840 (*S* 192), 862 (*S* 209★); DB I.238 – K.
Wellow, Ha	A; ass. 934 (*S* 1604★); DB I.50 – Agemund from K.
Wellow, Wt	A; DB I.52 – *Coolf* from K.
Wherwell, Ha	E; grant by Atr. to Wherwell Abbey 1002 (*S* 904); DB I.44 Wherwell Abbey.
Whitchurch Canonicorum, Do	A; grant by K. Edward of land in W. 1044 (*S* 1004); DB I.78b – St Wandrille holds church, estate not described.
Willenhall, St	ass. ? 733 (*S* 86); DB I.246 – K, 247b – canons of Wolverhampton.

Wilton, W

ass. 838 (*S* 1438★); DB I.64b – borough.

Wimborne, Do

minster founded by Cuthburh, K. Ine's sister (*ASC* 718); K. Aethelred buried at, 871 (*ASC*); seized by Aethelwold (*ASC* 900); K. Sigeferth buried in (*ASC* A 962); DB I.75 – K.

Winchcombe, Gl

ass. 942 (*S* 479); DB I.162b – borough.

Windsor, Brk

K. Edward at 1065 (*S* 1042, *VAE*, p. 50n.); DB I.56b – K.

Woodstock, O

ass. 978x1008, and ?1008x1016 (I and IX Atr., pp. 216–17, 269); DB I.154b – royal forest.

Woodyates, Do

ass. ? 869 *in publico loco* (*S* 334), for possible assembly 970 or 981 see *Rituale Ecclesiae Dunelmensis*, ed. A. H. Thompson and U. Lindelöff (Surtees Society CXL, 1927), p. 185; DB I.77b – Glastonbury Abbey.

Woolmer, Ha

ass. 898 (*S* 350), Easter 970 (*S* 776★, 779★), *c*.990 (*S* 1454); not in DB.

Worthy, King's, Ha

ass. 931 (*S* 413); DB I.38b – berwick of royal estate of Barton Stacey.

Wychbold, Wo

ass. 815 (*S* 178★), 831 (*S* 188★); DB I.176b – Earl Godwine.

Wye, K

762 (*S* 25★); ass. 839 (*S* 287★), 845 (*S* 296), cf. *S* 1473; DB I.11b – 1065 owner not named, but it was royal, cf. f. 1.

Yeavering, No

HE II.14★.

Yeovil, So

A; DB I.93 – four thegns, 96b – 1065 owner not named, ?borough.

Unidentified places

Unless otherwise indicated, the following were places of assembly. No attempt has been made to give all variant forms of names.

Acleah 787 (*S* 127) to 810 (*S* 1439) and ?824 (*S* 283); *Andredeseme* 842 (*S* 292); *Arcencale* 709x716 (*S* 65); *aet Astran* 839 (*S* 1438); *Bearuwe* 743 (*S* 99★), 814 (*S* 177★): Barrow, Li (DB I.360 – Earl Morcar) and Barrow, Le (DB I.237 – Earl Harold) are both possible, but neither Barrow, Gl nor Sa is in DB; *Beorchore* 1007 (*S* 915); *Berghamstyde* 695 (Wi), 696 (*S* 17): Bearstead, K. is possible but not in DB; *Besingahearh* 685x687 (*S* 235); *Bicanleag* 904 *in villa venatoria* (*S* 373, 1286): Bickleigh, D near Silverton (DB I.105b – *Aluuard*) and Bickleigh, D near Plymouth (DB I.111b – *Brismar*) are both possible; *in monte Biohthandoune* ?791 (*S* 1178); *Birenefeld* 863 (*S* 332); *Bradford* 957 (*Vita Dunstani*, ed. W. Stubbs, *Memorials of St Dunstan*, London, 1874, p. 36); *Bregford* 683 (*S* 1169); *Bromdun* 987x?997, cf. I Atr. 1.2., III Atr. 4, pp. 216–7, 228–9; *in Broninis*, Wilfrid imprisoned in *urbe regis* (*The Life of Bishop Wilfred by Eddius Stephanus*, ed. B. Colgrave, Cambridge, 1927, pp. 72–3★); *Bydictun* 822 (*S* 186★); *Campodonum* church in *uilla regia* burnt 633 (*HE* II.14★); *Clofeshoh* 716 (*S* 22) to 825 (*S* 1435); *Colleshyl* ?802 (*S* 154); *Escant* 852 (*S* 202★); *Freoricburna* 757x796 *in regione Suthregeona* (*S* 144★), 838 (*S* 280★); *villam Fritheuuoldi juxta* . . . *fossatum Fullingadich* 672x674 (*S* 1165); *Godgeocesham* 761x764 (*S* 33); *Hursteshevet* ?1041 (*Quadripartitus Argumentum* 9, ed. Liebermann, *Gesetze*, I.533); *Iortlaford* 779 (*S* 114); *Iudanbyrig* Arbp Wulfstan imprisoned at, 952 (*ASC* D); *Langanden* early in Alfred's reign (*S* 1507); *Leonaford* (Asser c.81★); *Medilwong* Cuthbert preached *in quodam uico* . . . *M* (*Vita Sancti Cuthberti auctore anonymo* IV.6, ed. B. Colgrave, *Two Lives of St Cuthbert*, Cambridge, 1940, p. 118), K. Oswulf killed *a sua familia juxta Mechil Wongtune* (*HR* 758); *Merantun* K. Cynewulf killed at 786 (*ASC* 757), battle at *Meretun* (*ASC* 871); *Mirafeld atque Stapulford* 691 (*S* 10); *Oswaldesdun* 855 (*S* 206); *Pencrik* 729 (*S* 253); *Pincanheale* Aethelwold deposed at (*HR* 765), cf. synods at (*HR* 787, 798); *Scythlescester* K. Aelfwold killed at (*HR* 788) possibly Chesters, Nb; *Seletun* Ealdorman Beorn burnt in, at Christmas (*ASC* DE 779, *HR* 780); *Swinbeorg* 866x871 (*S* 1507); *Weardburg* 878 (*S* 225), *burh* built at (*ASC* BCD 915); *Werburgewic c.*845 (*S* 88★), 823 (*S* 187★); *Wihtbordestan* 962x963 (IV Edg., pp. 208–9); *Willherestrio* 862 (*S* 331).

13

The World of Abbot Aelfric

ERIC JOHN

Aelfric has been much studied but no overview of his work and importance as a whole has been attempted, nor is one likely to be attempted for some years to come. It is one of my tasks in this paper to explain why. Some of the reasons are obvious. It will be necessary first to edit all the Old English homilies as yet unpublished, and then to make detailed comparisons between the various strands of Aelfric's thought and the rest. Some progress has been made. Professor Clemoes and Professor Pope have established the canon and chronology of Aelfric's writings, and no serious revision is likely to be necesary.[1] Professor Pope has edited the homilies that do not form part of the linked series of *Catholic Homilies* and *Saints' Lives*.[2] A series of studies of the utmost value by Professor Ó'Carragáin of Cork deal with what, from the Aelfrician point of view, is the pre-history of some of his themes.[3] So far, however, the main thrust of Aelfrician studies has been philological – in the broad rather than the narrow sense. The main debate has been that initiated by R. W. Chambers in his classic study, 'On the continuity of

[1] *The Anglo-Saxons: Studies . . . presented to Bruce Dickens*, ed. P. Clemoes (London, 1956), pp. 212–47, and J. C. Pope, *Homilies of Aelfric, A Supplementary Collection* (Early English Text Society, 1967/8), I, pp. 136–45.

[2] *Catholic Homilies*, ed. B. Thorpe (London, 1843); *Aelfric's Lives of the Saints*, ed. W. W. Skeat (Early English Text Society, 1881–5). I have generally followed Thorpe and Skeat's translations, with small variations.

[3] See *Studies in English Language and Early Literature in honour of Paul Christopherson* (Coleraine, 1981), pp. 63–104. Professor Ó'Carragáin kindly allowed me to read portions of his new book on the Vercelli Book in manuscript. The drift of his work suggests that representations of the Crucifixion were not common in the pre-Aelfrician period, but see M. Wood above, p. 270.

English prose'.[4] But there are now some signs that interest is being shown in Aelfric's thought and his theology.

A recent important study is that of Dr Gatch, on *Preaching and Theology in Anglo-Saxon England*.[5] He quotes the late C. L. Wrenn: 'It is generally rightly assumed that Anglo-Saxon theology was mainly derivative in doctrine, pastoral in approach, and practical in the application of inherited teaching and the devising of effective ecclesiastical administrations, especially in the mission field.'[6] With important reservations, Dr Gatch is in broad agreement with this judgement when it is applied to Aelfric, though in his summing up he does allow him some originality. Dr Gatch has, however, weighted the scales heavily on the side of the conservative Aelfric by restricting his book to the eschatological homilies, and studying them in a context provided by the writings of other authors on the same themes. But eschatology was not – if the *double entendre* may be excused – a burning topic for Aelfric, and its function in his work is only revealed by a study of his other themes. There is another side to Aelfric's theology that, though derivative all right and dependent on other, more original, thinkers, exhibits radical discontinuity with the kind of text Dr Gatch uses, and in which Aelfric treated themes unfamiliar and very unwelcome to many of his contemporaries.[7] It is this radicalism I wish to discuss here, though it will not be possible to place the tension between the radical and the conservative in Aelfric in its correct perspective until late Old English theological writing has been reviewed as a whole.

It is worth beginning by looking at Aelfric's intentions in composing his *Catholic Homilies* and *Saints' Lives*.[8] Aelfric tells us that the *Catholic Homilies* represent 'the Passions and Lives of those Saints whom that illustrious nation celebrates by honouring their festival'. The *Lives* celebrate 'those Saints whom, not the vulgar, but the monks, honour by special services'.[9] Both collections were associated with Ealdormen Aethelweard and Aethelmaer;[10] but the

---

[4] Early English Text Society, 1932; M. McC. Gatch, *Preaching and Theology in Anglo-Saxon England* (Toronto, 1977), p. 176, gives a useful bibliography of work on this topic published since Chambers' essay.

[5] *ibid.*   [6] *ibid.*, p. 6.

[7] Aelfric was himself aware of this to some extent. In the preface to *Saints' Lives* II.43–8, he disclaims the intention of saying anything new, but admits that laymen will find some of it unfamiliar.

[8] A new edition of the *Homilies* is being produced by M. Godden, of which only vol. I has so far appeared.

[9] *Saints' Lives*, preface   [10] *loc. cit.*, and *Homilies* I, p. 8.

Catholic Homilies were for a general audience, as Aelfric makes clear
in his letter to Sigeric: they were written deliberately in simple
English, 'ob aedificationem simplicium, qui hanc norunt tantum-
modo locutionem, sive legenda, sive audienda'.[11] The *Lives* were
for a more select audience because it was not fitting that many
should be translated into English, 'lest the pearls of Christ be held in
disrespect'.[12] This does not mean that Aelfric had a purely monastic
audience in mind. He was writing for an elite that would not include
all monks, and would include Aethelweard and Aethelmaer.[13] It is
obvious that the reforming monks did preach publicly on occasion,
because Wulfstan's famous *Sermo Lupi*, whether or not it was a
reworking of a homily by Abbo of St-Germain-des-Prés, only
makes sense if we suppose that it was aimed at a mainly lay
audience. Dr Gatch has convincingly argued that Aelfric's purposes
were manifold: exegesis of the Gospel pericopes on fairly frequent
occasions; devotional study; monastic liturgical use in fulfilment of
c. ix of the *Rule of St Benedict*.[14] We must remember that the circles
Aelfric was brought up in were highly politicized and polemical;[15]
the charters demonstrate this very well.[16]

The motives behind this polemic are by now fairly well known:
the aggressive and thrusting policy of extending the lands and rights
of the reformed monks; the depression in status of the lay-tenants of
these same churches, especially marked in Aethelwold's sphere of
influence; the expulsion or monachization of the married clerks,
most of whom must have been of good family.[17] The opposition
was a miscellaneous assortment of major and minor landholders,
especially in western Mercia, where, from the ealdorman down-
wards, they were harshly discriminated against. Even in East Anglia,

---

[11] Published by Thorpe in *Homilies* I, pp. 1–2.
[12] *Saints' Lives*, p. 3.   [13] *ibid.*, p. 5.
[14] I suspect that Aelfric also had in mind a collection in the spirit of the *Rule*,
c. lxxiii, that would be more relevant to his own day.
[15] E. S. Duckett, *St Dunstan of Canterbury* (London, 1955), pp. 160 ff., for the
weight placed on prayers for the royal family in the liturgy of the new monks, and
E. John, *Orbis Britanniae* (Leicester, 1966), pp. 154–80.
[16] S 731, which must have attained its present doctored form before the compilation of the *Liber Wigorniensis*, E. John, 'War and society in the 10th century: the
Maldon campaign', *TRHS*, 5th ser., XXVII (1977), pp. 192–5: '. . . eliminatis
clericorum neniis et spurcis lasciviis . . .'; and the unquestionably authentic New
Minster codex, S 745: 'clericos lascivientes repuli', and the lengthy diatribes in cc. iv
and ix. S 745 is particularly important as it comes from the circles in which Aelfric
was brought up.   [17] John, *Orbis Britanniae*, pp. 176 ff.

where the ealdorman was pro-monastic, it is evident from the records of lawsuits collected in the *Liber Eliensis* that lesser land-holders were very disgruntled.[18] Thus Aelfric was writing in a world deeply divided about the wealth and role of the churches. He was himself very much of the high church party, which in turn depended on the exaltation of the status of the king: royal support was the trump card of 'reform'. It is becoming increasingly clear that they had solid reasons for their regard for royal power, that King Edgar, in whose reign the reform movement really took off, was one of the most powerful English kings of the Middle Ages, and that this very great power rested on foundations laid earlier in the century. In other words, royal power in Edgar's day looked as though it was built to last, as in a sense it did.[19] In this situation a writer as celebrated as Aelfric was, with the kind of connections he had, could not help but be polemical. Nor could he avoid being an innovator.

The reformers frequently pretended that they were restoring a lost age of innocence, and some of them may even have believed this; but when it came to defending their claims with canonical texts they were in some difficulty because the canon law, as it then stood, did not give them much justification for their policies. Some, like Burchard, bishop of Worms, simply altered the texts to make them read as they thought they should.[20] Others, more honestly, though they had authorities all right, simply failed to cite them at all, like the English archbishop Wulfstan.[21] The best solution was that of Abbo of Fleury, who anticipated some of what were to become accepted practices in making collections of canons in the twelfth century.[22] The principle he used was that the *utilitas* of the Church

---

[18] ed. E. O. Blake (Camden Series XCII, 1962). See especially the late Professor Whitelock's comments in the foreword.

[19] J. Campbell, 'Observations on English government from the tenth to the twelfth centuries', *TRHS*, 5th ser. XXV (1975), pp. 39–54, and J. Campbell, *The Anglo-Saxons* (Oxford, 1982), chapters 6, 7, and 10.

[20] P. Fournier and G. Le Bras, *Histoire des collections canoniques en Occident* (Paris, 1931), I, p. 373. The most notorious forger of texts was of course Cardinal Humbert, Leo IX's chief adviser.

[21] See the introduction to D. Bethurum, *Homilies of Wulfstan* (Oxford, 1952).

[22] Fournier and Le Bras, *Collections Canoniques*, pp. 320–30. We are fortunate in having the opinions of a conservative – and intelligent – contemporary of Abbo in the satirical poems of Adalbero of Laon, ed. G. A. Hückel, *Les Poèmes satiriques d'Adalberon* (Paris, 1901), with the corrections of C. Erdmann, *Die Entstehung des Kreuzzugsgedankens* (Stuttgart, 1935), pp. 345–7. Adalbero points out the weak-nesses of the reforming party in the matter of canon law (vv. 30 ff.), where he

ought to have priority over what was customary. This is well illustrated by the opening remarks in his *Collectio Canonum*.[23] Defending his use of imperial – and fairly recent – *decreta* as authoritative, he writes:

> Sed de externis quid loquor, et loquendo immoror, cum ad dispensationem reipublicae et utilitarum ecclesiarum tanta fuerat pietas ac prudentia Caroli, et filii eius Ludovici. Certi utrique pro tempore ac ratione noverant parcere subiectis et debellare superbos.[24]

What Abbo, Burchard and Wulfstan had in common – and they were certainly the three most important canonists of the early reform movement – was a radical attitude towards tradition. What mattered to them was the well-being of the Church as they saw it, and, if only Abbo made this explicit, the other two, by their actions, showed that it was the utility of the Church, not the traditions of the Churches, that mattered to them.

This was the essential feature of the education Aelfric received in the first generation of reformed English monasticism, and not only he. We need to recall that from the time of Edgar a remarkable number of English bishops were monks, and that even secular bishops had been educated in the same reforming principles, whether in England or on the continent. We know that this had some important consequences for the way they conceived their offices.[25]

Aelfric was, as he was proud to admit, a pupil of Aethelwold. Abbo of Fleury was a close associate of Oswald. Through the influence of the late Dean Armitage Robinson, it has been customary to contrast the fierce Aethelwold with the gentle Oswald; but the gentle Oswald will not survive half an hour's study of the charters. I have written at length about this elsewhere; here I shall merely cite the numerous loan charters of lands of the church of Worcester, drawn up for the benefit of his relatives or connections. Oswald's family was East Anglian, and he had no links with the West Country before he became bishop of Worcester. He must have imported his tenants, and there must have been some dis-

---

makes sarcastic remarks on the *Lex Antiquissimus* of the reformers. Hückel is surely right in supposing that Abbo was the target aimed at, here and elsewhere.
[23] *PL* CXXXIX, c. 477.
[24] Abbo evidently liked this Vergilian *topos*, since he used it again with powerful ironic effect of the Viking leader who killed Edmund of East Anglia: *Three Lives of English Saints*, ed. M. Winterbottom (Toronto, 1972), p. 74.
[25] F. Barlow, *The English Church 1000–1066* (London, 1963), pp. 62–73.

placement of the original tenants. I cannot see that Oswald's policies as bishop of Worcester differed very much from Aethelwold's at Winchester, except in degree.[26] There seems no real reason to doubt that Aethelwold and Oswald were collaborators and allies, as Byrhtferth's *Vita Oswaldi* shows.[27] There is nothing, then, to be surprised at when we find how strong Abbo of Fleury's influence on Aelfric was, especially in the *Catholic Homilies* and *Saints Lives*, which are particularly important because it was in these books that Aelfric laid out his ideological programme.

In his *Life* of Saint Edmund, King and Martyr, Aelfric tells us that 'a certain very learned monk came from the South, over the sea, from St Benedict's place . . . to Archbishop Dunstan, three years before he died; and the monk was called Abbo.'[28] Abbo was told the story of St Edmund by Dunstan personally.[29] His own rendering is a major text in the formation of the ideology of the Crusade,[30] and is in turn the source of Aelfric's *Life* of Edmund. Faced with a very sophisticated text,[31] Aelfric greatly simplified it for his far from sophisticated audience; but there is little of Abbo's ideological concern in his *Passio* that does not occur somewhere in Aelfric. When Aelfric speaks of Abbo coming from 'St Benedict's place', he is not referring to the dedication of Fleury, but to the tradition, unquestioned in reforming circles north of the Alps, that St Benedict's bones had at some point been translated to Fleury.[32] The relationship between Abbo and Aelfric, as represented by their accounts of

[26] Athelwold occasionally conceded a loan for one life to a sitting tenant, Oswald conceded quite a number for three lives, though it is clear that not all of these went to sitting tenants or their families. I do not think this was because Oswald was gentler than Aethelwold but because, in an area that had comparatively recently recognized the authority of the West Saxon royal house and where there was a bitterly hostile ealdorman, Oswald had to go rather more carefully than Aethelwold needed to in the heartland of Wessex.

[27] e.g. *Vita Oswaldi*, ed. J. Raine, *Historians of the Church of York* (RS, 1879–94), I, p. 434.

[28] *Saints' Lives* II, p. 314. There is a better text in Aelfric, *Lives of Three English Saints*, ed. G. I. Needham (London, 1966), p. 43.

[29] Winterbottom, *Three Lives*, p. 67.

[30] Erdmann, *Entstehung des Kreuzugsgedankens*.

[31] For Abbo's very effective use of irony, G. A. Bezzola, *Das Ottonische Kaisertum in der französischen Geschichtsschreibung* (Cologne-Graz, 1956), pp. 148–9. Bezzola has a more favourable view of Gerbert than McKitterick, above.

[32] cf. Byhrtferth, *Vita Oswaldi*, p. 422. Earlier, p. 413, he speaks of archbishop Oda sending Oswald to Fleury: 'Praecepit pater venerandus ut ad beatissimi et luculentissimi [this curious locution has a certain currency in these circles, occuring in the epilogue to the *Concordia* as well] confessoris atque abbatis Benedicti properaret arcisterium.'

the career of King Edmund, neatly illustrates the family feeling of the reform movement. This feeling, based on common experience of exile shared by many of the early monks – Dunstan and Abbo had both experienced banishment from their monasteries and native lands, and many others, such as Oswald and some of his pupils, had gone into voluntary exile – created a common sense of *Heimatlösigkeit*.[33]

Abbo's influence is again shown by Aelfric's choice of subjects. There are very few English saints celebrated in his pages: two of these, Aethelthryth and Swithun, are obviously both included because of Aethelwold's appropriation of their cults for Ely and Winchester respectively. On the other hand, the foundation of Fleury, in the shape of a *Life* of St Maur, gets more than three times as much space as Aethelthryth.[34] Further evidence of a Frankish dimension in the ideology of the English monks will appear in the course of the discussion.

Even a first reading of Aelfric will reveal his very strong sense of the Church, the universal Church. 'All churches in the world are reckoned one Church, and it is called the congregation of God because we are all called together to God's kingdom. Now this congregation is God's bride, and continues a maiden like the holy Mary.' On the same page: 'Also the whole Church of God, that is all Christian people, is consecrated to one maiden.'[35] Sir Richard Southern has devoted some classic pages to the rise of a sense of the Church, and its connection with the extension of the cult of Mary, in his *Making of the Middle Ages*.[36] Abbo lays an emphasis on the relationship of Peter and the Church which, though found in Aelfric too, is by him more muted. This is not, I think, a sign of Aelfric's insularity or proof of his indifference to papal authority. Abbo is naturally more strident about Peter because Fleury depended on a papal privilege of exemption for its freedom from wreck by the bishop of Orleans.[37] The English monks captured the

---

[33] The important theme of homelessness is well treated by Bezzola, *Ottonische Kaisertum*.

[34] *Saints' Lives* I, pp. 148–69. It is worth noting here that the contemporary drawing of Jesus dead upon the Cross illustrated from the Harley Psalter (Plate VIII) is by the same artist who drew the constellation Aquarius in BL Harley 2506, f. 38v, made at Fleury.

[35] *Homilies*, II, p. 10.   [36] (London, 1953), pp. 246 ff.

[37] See the opening of Abbo's *Apologeticus* and c. 1 of his *Collectio Canonum*, *PL* CXXXIX, cc. 462 and 46. If the emphasis on the Petrine claims is more muted in

episcopate very early in the history of the reform movement, and no stress was placed on papal privileges of this kind, though genuine ones did exist.[38] Nonetheless, Petrine authority did matter for Aelfric: 'Then said Peter, thou art the Christ, son of the living God. One answered for the many because unity was in the many'; Aelfric goes on to point out that Peter signifies the Church, 'in which, under Christ, he is the head.'[39] The special authority of Peter in connection with his possession of the keys of the Kingdom is also treated.[40]

Aelfric is clear that there is an important division between the roles of clerks and lay people; although he does not elaborate a fully-fledged theology of the laity and the clergy in the corporate sense, as was usual in the writers of a century later, he does have the concept of Christendom, the English equivalent of *Christianitas*, which goes with this theology.[41] He was especially against what was later to be called the heresy of simony, and what Aethelwold had already, in the *Concordia*, called *secularium prioratus*. 'Let every Christian know that no man shall take money for God's Church; but if anyone do so, he that gives God's Bride for money shall be like to Judas . . . let no layman presume to hold direction or authority over God's servants. How can, or how dares, any layman draw to him by violence Christ's monasteries? Not even an ordained man shall represent Christ over his holy community unless the office be committed to him by God's teachers.'[42] And again: 'Very many shun the treachery of Judas, and yet fear not to betray the truth for money. Jesus himself is all truth, and he who sells truth for money will be the companion of Judas in fiery torments.'[43] Aelfric and Gregory VII would have understood one another very well.

Aelfric, his Mariolatry is not. In addition to incidental references, there are homilies for the Purification and the Assumption.

[38] C. P. Wormald, *Famulus Christi*, ed. G. Bonner (London, 1976), pp. 146 ff. I would now accept Wormald's argument n. 45, as substantially correct.

[39] *Homilies*, II, p. 388.   [40] *ibid.*, p. 370.

[41] J. Rupp, *L'Idée de Chrétienté dans la pensée pontificale des origines à Innocent III* (Paris, 1939), pp. 2 ff.; *Lives*, I, p. 422 and 488. Rupp has taught us that *christianitas* was coming to mean the community of Christians here and now, and I think there is a flavour of this in Aelfric's use of the term. It is noticeable in view of Abbo's importance as a proto-ideologist of crusade, that Aelfric in these passages opposes christendom to the heathens, as does the *Code of Edward and Guthrum* 2, *Gesetze*, I, pp. 130–1.

[42] *Homilies*, II, p. 593.   [43] *ibid.*, p. 245.

If Aelfric is not as hostile to bishops as Abbo of Fleury was, he is not as uncritical of them as was Wulfstan of York.[44] Wulfstan, being a bishop himself, was a member of a much more distinguished group of bishops than Abbo usually had to do with, and wanted no truck with the anti-episcopal sentiments some of the reforming monks entertained.[45]

Aelfric has decided and not very flattering views on the laity. He shared the traditional but not hitherto dominant strand in sexual morality that was being given new emphasis by the reformers. Laymen might marry, but sexual intercourse was permitted only for the procreation of children. 'The chastity of a layman is that he hold to his marriage, and lawfully for the increase of people beget children'; laymen must, however, cease from cohabiting with their wives, 'when they can no longer procreate'.[46] A generation or so earlier, a prominent reformer, bishop Rather of Verona, taught the same sort of thing in his widely distributed *Praeloquia*, a copy of which certainly reached France and was probably known to Abbo.[47] Though this moral teaching goes back very much earlier, to conservative-minded men it appeared as an unwelcome novelty and a ridiculous one, as the satires of Adalbero of Laon show.[48] It seems to me to have unfortunate consequences, which the reformers did not intend. If a layman, especially a prince, had a barren marriage, it was not easy to find grounds on which the refusal of a divorce or an annulment could be based. It is difficult to estimate just what effect this sexual morality had on the rather cavalier attitude to divorce and annulment that is noticeable amongst the contemporary establishment, but it must have had some.

[44] In his *Life* of Edmund it is the bishop who urges the coward's course. Abbo's hostility to the episcopate of his day is conveyed best by what he does not say in his *Collectio Canonum*, but is explicitly stated in the letter XIV, *PL* CXXXIX, cc. 440 ff. Adalbero of Laon was aware of this, and attacks what he called Robert the Pious's lowborn, uncouth bishops for lack of learning, vv. 44–50.

[45] That Wulfstan's attitude to bishops was entirely traditional is obvious from the *Canons*, 5, 7, 22, and from the *Institutes of Polity*, ed. K. Jost (Berne, 1959), pp. 59–77. Aelfric's view may be inferred from his *Sermo de Die Judicii*. cf. Gatch, *Preaching and Theology* p. 91.

[46] *Homilies*, II, p. 95; 'The lowest degree is of believing laymen, who live in lawful marriage more for the sake of a family of children than of lust.'

[47] *PL* CXXXVI, cc. 191 ff. for Rather's teaching, and for its dissemination, see F. Weigle (ed.), *Die Briefe des Bischofs Rather von Verona*, in *MGH*, *Briefe der deutschen Kaiserzeit*, e.g. epp. 2 and 8. Few bishops have ever courted publicity for their wrongs or their books as much as Rather.

[48] Hückel, *Adalberon*, v. 24, seems to refer to this teaching.

In Aelfric's circle, the king was not exactly a layman. Aelfric does not say much about this directly. He himself and the most important part of his audience were living in an environment saturated with royalist sentiment. Aelfric had of course been the pupil of Aethelwold, whose comparison of King Edgar with the Good Shepherd was one of the high points of this royalism.[49] In the *Concordia*, Aethelwold also contrasts the *dominium* of the king with the mere *saecularium prioratus* of the lay magnates, suggesting that the royal power was in some sense sacramental.[50] Aelfric's contemporary, Archbishop Wulfstan, takes comparisons between lawful kings and Christ for granted in his legal writings.[51] The account of Edgar's coronation at Bath in 973 given by Byrhtferth of Ramsey is significant here.[52] Edgar's consecration was delayed until Edgar was in his twenty-ninth year, like Christ's entry into his public ministry, and this also suggests a quasi-priestly, even a quasi-episcopal, role for the king. Aelfric clearly accepted this teaching, in particular Abbo of Fleury's version of it. 'We will give an illustration: no man can make himself king, but the people has the power to chose as king whom they please, but after he is consecrated as king, he has dominion over the people, and they cannot shake his yoke from their necks.'[53] In his *Life* of Swithun, Aelfric calls the reign of Edgar a golden age, and recalls, quite inappositely in the context, Edgar's 'imperial durbar', when eight kings submitted to him shortly after his coronation proper.[54] It is altogether likely that Aelfric shared the christocentric view of kingship current in the political theology of the reformers. It is important, then, to ask what view of Christ did Aelfric hold; in particular, what was his Christology, and his view of the atonement?

He of course inherited a theology of the atonement created originally by the Cappadocian fathers. The thesis is succinctly summed up by Sir Richard Southern in his *Making of the Middle Ages*: 'Man was a

[49] *Regularis Concordia*, ed. T. Symons (London, 1953), p. 2.
[50] cf. Abbo, *Passio Eadmundi*, ed. Winterbottom, pp. 75–6, on Edmund's triple consecration: baptism, confirmation and royal consecration. Abbo used the verb *consecrare*.   [51] VIII Aethelred 2.i, *Gesetze*, I, p. 263.
[52] *Vita Oswaldi*, pp. 436–8.
[53] *Homilies*, I, p. 212, and cf. Abbo, *PL* CXXXIX, cc. 477–8, part of his *Collectio Canonum* that deals with royal authority in a virtually identical way.
[54] *Lives*, I, p. 468; cf. Florence of Worcester, *Chronicon* ed. B. Thorpe (London, 1848), I, p. 142 – if Florence can be believed, by rowing him upon the Dee at Chester. My former pupil, Mrs Mary Syner, in an unpublished thesis, examined the topography of medieval Chester, and concluded he was probably right.

helpless spectator in a cosmic struggle which determined his chance
of salvation. The war was one between God and the Devil, and God
won because he proved himself the master-strategist. That God
should become man was a great mystery, a majestic awe-inspiring
act, justly acclaimed in such a triumphant expression of victory as
the *Te Deum*. But there was little or no place for tender compassion
for the sufferings of Jesus.'[55] As is well known, Sir Richard made an
important connection between the feeling that the traditional view
of the atonement was inadequate and the cult of devotion to the
crucifix: a type of crucifix, moreover, in which Jesus is shown as
nearly naked and clearly dead after much suffering (though not until
the middle of the thirteenth century with a crown of thorns[56]).
There are clear signs that Aelfric, at least, and he is unlikely to have
been alone in his views for long given the distribution of his
sermons, felt the current Christology wanting, and that the cult of
the suffering and crucified Christ was very much a part of his
ideological world. The crucifixion scene in the Harley Psalter (plate
VIII) is a fine example.[57]

On the atonement Aelfric is at first sight traditional enough, but
with important qualifications.[58] 'Now some men say that it must
happen to them even as it was determined for them and ordained in
the beginning, and that they cannot avoid acting amiss. Now we
say truly that if this be so it is a useless command that God com-
manded through David: "Turn away from evil and do good."'[59]
Aelfric hardly felt free to offer a fundamental recasting of the
doctrine of the atonement he had inherited. He was not a theologian
of the originality of an Anselm or a Bernard, but he saw, I think, as
they did, some of the limitations of the traditional theory. He is
especially concerned to highlight the part the individual has to play
in his own salvation. 'He hath given us our own choice. He gave a
most steadfast gift, and a most steadfast law together with the gift,
to every man until his end, both to poor and rich. This is the gift,

---

[55] *The Making of the Middle Ages* (1955) p. 235.
[56] G. Thoby, *Le Crucifix* (Nantes, 1959), p. 156, thinks the earliest example is
French, and dates it between 1230 and 1250.
[57] Thoby thought this was the first representation of Christ dead upon the Cross. I
think some earlier Ottonian representations were also meant to portray Christ as
dead, e.g. the Gero crucifix in Cologne Cathedral.
[58] *Homilies*, I, p. 216. He insists redemption has been earned for us by the traditional method of God fishing for the Devil, and baiting the hook with Jesus.
[59] *Saints' Lives* I, p. 378.

that a man may do what he will, and this is the law, that God recompenses every man according to his works, both in this world and in that which is to come, whether good or evil, whichsoever he practises . . .'[60] Aelfric is clear that if God has achieved the atonement by becoming man, men have still to earn their salvation; and here he is nearer to Anselm than to tradition.

He is also clear about the kind of thoughts Christians ought to have about Christ and the place the Crucifixion ought to take in the pattern of Christian devotion. He has no time for representations of the triumphant Christ on the cross. 'Verily to his beloved disciple Jesus entrusted his mother, when, suspended on the cross, he redeemed mankind';[61] 'he fled from worldly honour when he was chosen king; but he fled not from reproach and scorn when the Jews would hang him on a cross. He would not encircle his head with a golden crown, but with one of thorns . . .'[62] He states baldly, drawing the moral specifically from Christ's sufferings: 'He who will suffer nothing in this life shall suffer against his will in the life to come.' His eucharistic teaching has a similar emphasis. 'Now if you believe that Christ the son of God who was hanged on a cross is true God, then I will show you how the Lamb continued undefiled in his kingdom, after it is offered and its flesh eaten and its blood drunken'.[63] In other places we are bidden to recall Jesus' wounds, his blood, his crown of thorns. It soon becomes apparent that Aelfric has a special, and, for England, a very new, role for the Cross to play in Christian devotion.

For the feast of the exaltation of the Holy Cross, which as a late seventh-century papal innovation had as yet little place in the Latin homily tradition, he says: 'When that heavenly king, Christ, himself entered in through this same gate to his own passion, he was not clothed in purple, nor adorned with a royal crown, nor rode he through this stone gate upon a horse but upon the back of an ass'.[64] In this same homily, we are told of an emperor whose piety took this point, so that he 'took off his purple . . . then went he with naked feet and took the Cross, praising God with the shedding of tears.' When he came to write a *Life* of St Martin, Aelfric predictably could not resist the story of the Devil appearing to St Martin in the guise of Christ. He found the story in Sulpicius Severus, and

[60] *ibid.*, p. 383.   [61] *Homilies*, I, p. 58.
[62] *ibid.*, p. 162.   [63] *ibid.*, p. 590.
[64] *Saints' Lives*, II, p. 150.

follows him pretty closely, but in the context of Aelfric's general teaching the story has a Christological significance not found in the original *Vita*. 'Then perceived the saintly man by the Holy Ghost that it was the same Devil, and not his Lord, and said: "Our Lord said not that he would come with a crown or clothed in purple, and I believe he will not come to us except in the same form wherein he suffered." '[65] In another place, Aelfric specifically recommends devotion to the Crucifix: 'My brothers, let us behold the crucified Christ, that we may be healed of venomous sins. Truly, as the people of Israel looked on the brazen serpent and were healed of the serpent's bite, so will now be healed of their sins who look with belief on the death of Christ and his resurrection.'[66] It is not surprising that a feature of Aelfric's world should be important representations of the crucifixion, often of a surprisingly intimate character.[67]

This kind of spirituality was meant for very general consumption, but it had particular and important implications for the reformers' political theology, radiating as it did around the idea of kingship. It seems to me implicit in Aelfric that it was with the suffering Christ that kings were expected to identify themselves, and not only in Aelfric. Byrhtferth, in his account of Edgar's coronation, pointed out that the king was decorated with roses and lilies.[68] Roses and lilies are ancient Christian symbols, but Aelfric shows that they have acquired a new significance for his circle, the roses representing martyrdom and the lilies chastity. The two lives of royal saints that provide subjects for Aelfric, Oswald and Edmund, were both martyrs. Abbo's *Passio* of Edmund lays much more stress on the religious than the political context of his death. If Dr Smyth is correct in his view of the circumstances of Edmund's death, this

---

[65] *ibid.*, p. 266. For the original story see Sulpicius Severus, *Vita Martini*, ed. J. Fontaine, *SC* CXXXIII, pp. 1, 306–8.   [66] *Homilies*, II, p. 240.
[67] F. Wormald, *English Drawings of the Tenth and Eleventh Centuries* (London, 1952), is still the classic work; cf. K. Hallinger in *Revue Mabillon* XLVI (1965), pp. 128–30. Hallinger pointed out that the fashion of drawing attention to Christ's human rather than his divine attributes commences with the Carolingians. He also gave Cluny an important role in the transmission of this tradition. St Odo anticipated Aelfric in much of this, and may, through Abbo, have had a direct influence on him.
[68] Byhrtferth must be referring to parts of the regalia that had undergone drastic changes as part of Dunstan's recasting of the *ordo*. What the roses were I do not know, but the lilies are surely the new – to England – lily crown, and the change connected with the reformers' view on chastity.

would underlie still further the appropriateness of presenting Edmund as a Christian martyr.[69]

It is sometimes argued that the replacement of Old Testament models for kingship by christocentric ones is a move towards caesaropapism'. For some kings and some polemicists, this new model was an invitation to take just such a line, an invitation that they were tempted to accept. But something very different from flattery was built into the new model. If kings compared to David should persecute the Church, the model offered no grounds for resistance. But an unsatisfactory Christ-modelled king could be labelled as a monster, a tyrant, whom it would be blasphemy *not* to resist. There is no doubt that there was such a radical streak in the reforming theology, though it only came into the open as reforming monasteries provided see after see with bishops of a very different calibre and outlook from those Abbo had known. The 'critical' theories can be found developing from the anonymous treatise that stands first in the *MGH Libelli de Lite*, through Cardinal Humbert – who, as the late Dr Michel pointed out, was much influenced by Abbo of Fleury – to the ideologues who surrounded Gregory VII. Neither Abbo nor Aelfric ever envisaged resistance to a legitimately elected king, though, when they affirm that such a king must be obeyed, what they have in mind is the obedience of a king's lay subjects to unpopular measures of 'reform'. What they would have said of a king who persecuted monks is not known or knowable, but both, of course, lived under reasonably pious monarchs and had no occasion to develop their thoughts in this dangerous direction.

Apparent by now will be the particular importance of the traditional eschatological themes deployed by Aelfric, to which Dr Gatch has drawn attention. Hellfire, damnation and the Last Judgement were, for Aelfric, sanctions to persuade his hearers or readers to live their lives in the way he thought proper. Dr Gatch notes a passage that illustrates this well, even if it can hardly be called felicitous:

> Rather different . . . is a very short passage probably translated by Aelfric from the *Liber de Visione et Obitu Wetini Monachi*, which survives only as introduction to a short piece on ordination by Wulfstan. It describes the fate of priests and deacons who have not

---

[69] A. P. Smyth, *Scandinavian Kings in the British Isles, 850–880* (Oxford, 1977), pp. 201 ff.

fulfilled the requirements of celibacy. They stand bound to stakes in hellfire up to their waists; facing them their partners in sin are also bound to stakes in fire up to their navel. Their genitalia are regularly flogged by the Devil.[70]

Aelfric has anticipated Gilbert's Mikado in making the punishment fit the crime. It is impossible for a historian to estimate how effective such sanctions were, but they should not be too lightly written off; this was a world in which people believed in Hell as those of us today, who have never been there, believe in Australia.

This is as much as I want to say here of the radical strand in Aelfric's thought. Professor Wrenn was evidently right in saying that Aelfric's writings were derivative, but wrong in thinking that this made them conservative and traditional. His thought has a context that was radical as well as traditional; and even a final unsystematic glance at the strands that made up that context throws a fascinating light on the location of the republic of letters in the world of the monastic reformers.

Byrhtferth of Ramsey was, of course, as Dr Hart has pointed out, deeply influenced by Abbo of Fleury, whom he must have known, and by whom he was probably taught. His account of Edgar's coronation contains the *topos* of the marriage of a king to his kingdom, and he likens the whole coronation service to a marriage feast.[71] Common in the high Middle Ages, this *topos* is rare at so early a date, and yet it crops up in some interesting places. Flodoard of Rheims called the emperor *consors imperii Romani*.[72] This theme persisted in the Rheims tradition. When in 1025 King Hugh died, his epitaph says that France was widowed.[73] Hugh, like Edgar, was crowned on Whitsunday. Some scraps of annals from Fleury say, *s.a.* 1017: 'rotbertus rex filium suum hugonem consortem regni factit apud conpendium.'[74] The key to the transmission of this *topos* was surely Abbo. He was at least partly educated at Rheims and must have known Flodoard's work, which seems to have been seminal. Written in the early tenth century, Flodoard's *History of the Church of Rheims* is a pioneer in the composition of the history of a particular church as a microcosm of the universal Church, a theme

[70] Gatch, *Preaching and Theology*, p. 73.
[71] *Vita Oswaldi*, p. 427.   [72] *PL* CXXXV, c. 810.
[73] *Recueil des historiens de France*, X, p. 326.
[74] A Vidier, *L'Historiographie à St Benoît-sur-Loire et les miracles de St Benoît* (Paris, 1965), p. 220, printing the fragmentary *Annales Floriacenses*.

dear to both Abbo and Aelfric as we have seen.[75] His *History* seems to have been the model for histories of some lower Lotharingian churches. One of the features of the genre is the quoting of relevant documents verbatim. It seems to me that a case can be made out for thinking that Byrhtferth's *Vita Oswaldi* is influenced by this genre, especially in the sections relating to Ramsey. Byrhtferth certainly quoted the Dunstan *Ordo*, probably also a line from what lay behind the Oswaldslow charter, and certain other passages read very like quotations from diplomas.[76]

Aelfric belonged, then, as much to a minority of thinkers, mostly from west Francia and perhaps east Francia too, as he did to a local English context. The newness of monastic reform, and the speed with which Edgar pushed it through, gave Aelfric a unique importance. His writings are a primer of the new theology that, if properly used, can throw light on the more sophisticated continental authors, who could take more for granted than Aelfric could. Aelfric looked to Abbo, and this took him back directly or indirectly to Rather of Verona and Flodoard. I do not think we should have to probe very far before we found ourselves in the presence of Hincmar of Rheims.[77] To unravel all this, to move from informed guesswork to secure ground, we need to recognize that the world of abbot Aelfric is a development from what, on this occasion at least, we may call the world of Michael Wallace-Hadrill. What is needed to make a more

[75] W. Wattenbach and R. Holtzmann, in F. J. Schmale (ed.), *Geschichtsquellen deutscher Kaiserzeit* (Cologne-Graz, 1967), pp. 290–4. C. R. Hart, 'The *B* text of the Anglo-Saxon Chronicle', *Journal of Medieval History*, VIII (1982), p. 291, points out that 'amongst the works of Abbo was an *Epitome de xci Romanorum pontificum vitis* (*PL* CXXXIX cc 535–70), an abridgement of an earlier *Liber Pontificalis* begun by Anastasius, librarian of the papal library, and added to by Flodoardus, the chronicler of Rheims (who died in 966) and by Liutprand, bishop of Cremona . . . it is quite possible that the text edited by Migne represents a late revision of the *Epitome*, which has been worked over and extended by Abbo.' Dr Hart thinks Abbo had a limited but very important influence on the compilation and dissemination of the Anglo-Saxon Chronicle. cf. also *Die Briefsammlung Gerberts von Rheims*, ed. F. Weigle, *MGH*, *Briefe*, II, *ep*, 86, which is a friendly letter written to the schoolmaster of Fleury during Abbo's exile at Ramsey, asking for works of Cicero, thus bringing another famous tenth-century scholar into the picture.

[76] cf. passage on p. 425 beginning *Rex 'armipotens' Eadgar*, which sounds like an excerpt from a diploma to me. There is an explicit quotation on p. 426. One of Aelfric's important sources was the homiliary of Haymo of Auxerre, see Pope, *Homilies*, I, p. 157.

[77] Hallinger, see n. 67 above, must give us a hint to look in this direction. See also J. Nelson, 'Kingship, law and liturgy in the political thought of Hincmar of Rheims', *EHR* XCII (1977), pp. 241–79, in the light of the discussion.

precise intellectual map is an enterprise modelled on the work that he and his pupils have done over the last generation, in which the understanding of English history has been greatly advanced by looking at that history in a continental and Carolingian context.[78]

---

[78] Especially Professor Wallace-Hadrill's Ford Lectures (Wallace-Hadrill, *EGK*), and the collection of papers, most of whose authors by a happy 'chance' also appear in this volume, in P. H. Sawyer and I. N. Wood (eds), *Early Medieval Kingship* (Leeds, 1977).

A Bibliography of the Historical Writings of J. M. Wallace-Hadrill

IAN WOOD

In addition to the abbreviations used elsewhere in this book, the following are used here:

ABHL   *Annual Bulletin of Historical Literature*
BJRL   *Bulletin of the John Rylands Library*
JEcH   *Journal of Ecclesiastical History*
JTS, ns   *Journal of Theological Studies* new series
Med.Aev. *Medium Aevum*
TLS   *Times Literary Supplement*

1947

Review of J. Calmette, *Charlemagne – sa vie et son oeuvre*, in *French Studies Review*, I, pp. 258–61.

1948

Review of R. N. Walpole, *Philip Mouskés and the Pseudo-Turpin Chronicle*, in *Med. Aev.*, XVII, pp. 37–45.
Review of *Opus Epistolarum Des. Erasmi Roterodami* XI, ed. H. M. Allen and H. W. Garrod, in *The Pelican Record*, XXVIII, pp. 40–2.
Review of C. Delisle Burns, *The First Europe*, in *Time and Tide*, 26 June, p. 668.

1949

'Alfred the Great, 849–899, his European setting', in *The Manchester Guardian*, 15 October, p. 6.
Review of L. Dupraz, *Le Royaume des Francs et l'ascension politique des maires du palais (656–680)*, in *Bulletin of the Institute of Historical Research*, XXII, pp. 162–4.
'Earlier medieval history, 500–1200', *ABHL*, XXXV, pp. 12–18.

1950

'The Franks and the English in the ninth century: some common historical interests', *History*, XXXV, pp. 202–18, repr. in Wallace-Hadrill, *EMH*, pp. 201–16.

Review of H. Fichtenau, *Das karolingische Imperium: soziale und geistige Problematik eines Grossreiches*, in *EHR*, LXV, pp. 390–1.

Short notice of H. Wiedemann, *Karl der Grosse, Widukind und die Sachsenbekehrung*, in *EHR*, LXV, pp. 273–4.

Short notice of Y. Bongert, *Recherches sur les cours laïques du Xe au XIIIe siècle, in EHR*, LXV, p. 401.

Short notice of E. Zöllner, *Die politische Stellung der Völker im Frankenreich*, in *EHR*, LXV, pp. 537–8.

'Earlier medieval history, 500–1200', *ABHL*, XXXVI, pp. 17–22.

1951

'The work of Gregory of Tours in the light of modern research', *TRHS* 5th ser., I, pp. 25–45, repr. in Wallace-Hadrill, *LHK*, pp. 49–70.

Review of E. A. Thompson, *A History of Attila and the Huns*, in *History*, XXXVI, pp. 112–13.

Review of *Martini Episcopi Bracarensis Opera Omnia*, ed. C. W. Barlow, in *JTS*, ns II, pp. 208–11.

Review of A. L. Poole, *From Domesday Book to Magna Carta*, in *The Pelican Record*, XXX (1), pp. 13–15.

Short notice of L. Halphen, *A travers l'histoire du Moyen Age*, in *EHR*, LXVI, pp. 430–1.

Short notice of H. L. Mikoletzky, *Die Regesten des Kaiserreiches unter Otto II 955 (973)–983*, in *EHR*, LXVI, pp. 431–2.

Short notice of J. de Pange, *Le Roi Très Chrétien*, in *EHR*, LXVI, p. 440.

Short notice of H. Beumann, *Widukind von Korvei*, in *EHR*, LXVI, p. 610.

'Earlier medieval history, 550–1200', *ABHL*, XXXVII, pp. 11–15.

1952

The Barbarian West, 400–1000 (London).

Review of R. Folz, *Le Souvenir et la légende de Charlemagne dans l'Empire germanique mediéval*, and *idem, Études sur le culte liturgique de Charlemagne dans les églises de l'Empire*, in *EHR*, LXVII, pp. 83–6.

Review of *Gregorii Episcopi Turonensis Libri Historiarum X*, fasc. iii, ed. B. Krusch and W. Levison, in *EHR*, LXVII, pp. 402–4.

Review of C. W. Previté-Orton, *The Shorter Cambridge Medieval History*, in *The Journal of Education*, LXXXIV, pp. 590–1.

Review of D. Knowles, *The Episcopal Colleagues of Thomas Becket*, in *Med. Aev*, XXI, pp. 43–5.
Short notice of *The Burgundian Code*, trans. K. Fischer, in *History* XXXVII, p. 69.
'Earlier medieval history, 500–1200', *ABHL*, XXXVIII, pp. 10–15.

1953

'Archbishop Hincmar and the authorship of *Lex Salica*', *Tijdschrift voor Rechtsgeschiedenis*, XXI, pp. 1–29, repr. in Wallace-Hadrill, *LHK*, pp. 95–120.
Review of R. W. Southern, *The Making of the Middle Ages*, in *The Journal of Education*, LXXXV, pp. 445–6.
Review of H. Homeyer, *Attila, der Hunnenkönig von seinen Zeitgenossen dargestellt*, in *Journal of Roman Studies*, XLIII, p. 170.
Short notice of W. Wattenbach and W. Levison, *Deutschlands Geschichtsquellen im Mittelalter, Vorzeit und Karolinger*, I, in *EHR*, LXVIII, pp. 301–2.
Short notice of F. Oppenheimer, *Frankish Themes and Problems*, in *EHR*, LXVIII, pp. 454–5.
Short notice of F. Oppenheimer, *The Legend of the Sainte Ampoule*, in *EHR*, LXVIII, p. 631.
'Earlier medieval history, 500–1200', *ABHL*, XXXIX, pp. 11–15.

1954

'Manuscripts of Frankish Gaul', review of E. A. Lowe, *Codices Latini Antiquiores* VI, in *TLS*, 19 February, p. 120.
Review of R. Folz, *L'Idée d'Empire en Occident du Ve au XIVe siècle*, in *EHR*, LXIX, pp. 426–8.
Review of T. Schieffer, *Winfrid-Bonifatius und die christliche Grundlegung Europas*, in *EHR*, LXIX, pp. 619–22.
Review of W. H. C. Frend, *The Donatist Church: A Movement of Protest in Roman North Africa*, in *History*, XXXIX, pp. 102–3.
Review of E. S. Duckett, *Alcuin, Friend of Charlemagne*, in *History*, XXXIX, p. 268.
Review of D. Talbot Rice, *English Art, 871–1100*, in *History*, XXXIX, pp. 268–9.
Review of C. A. Macartney, *The Medieval Hungarian Historians*, in *Med. Aev.*, XXIII, pp. 61–3.
Short notice of W. Wattenbach and W. Levison, *Deutschlands Geschichtsquellen im Mittelalter, Die Karolinger vom Anfang des 8 Jahrhunderts bis zum Tode Karls des Grossen*, and R. Buchner, *Die Rechtsquellen*, in *EHR*, LXIX, pp. 138–9.

Short notice of *Études Mérovingiennes*, in *EHR*, LXIX, pp. 646–7.

Short notice of P. Riché, *Les Invasions Barbares*, in *History*, XXXIX, pp. 294–5.

1955

Articles in *Encyclopedia Britannica*.

Review of *Lex Ribvaria*, ed. F. Beyerle and R. Buchner, in *EHR*, LXX, pp. 440–3.

Short notice of H. Helbling, *Goten und Wandalen: Wandlung und der historischen Realität*, in *EHR*, LXX, pp. 472–3.

Short notice of G. W. Greenaway, *Saint Boniface*, in *EHR*, LXX, pp. 657–8.

1956

Review of *Sankt Bonifatius. Gedenkgabe zum zwölfhundertsten Todestag*, in *EHR*, LXXI, pp. 630–4.

Review of P. Hunter Blair, *An Introduction to Anglo-Saxon England*, in *JEcH*, VII, p. 246–7.

Review of W. A. Eckhardt, *Die Kapitulariensammlung Bischof Ghaerbalds von Lüttich*, in *Tijdschrift voor Rechtsgeschiedenis*, XXIV, pp. 470–3.

'Ancient Latin Manuscripts', review of E. A. Lowe, *Codices Latini Antiquiores* VII, in *TLS*, 23 November, p. 699.

Short notice of J. Herrick, *The Historical Thought of Fustel de Coulanges*, in *History*, XLI, p. 295.

Short notice of A. Cabaniss, *Amalarius of Metz*, in *JEcH*, VII, p. 270.

1957

The Barbarian West, 2nd edn (London); Spanish trans. (1962); Italian trans. (1963).

'Frankish Gaul', in J. M. Wallace-Hadrill and J. McManners (eds), *France: Government and Society* (London), pp. 36–57. repr. in Wallace-Hadrill, *LHK*, pp. 1–24.

Review of C. Verlinden, *L'Esclavage dans l'Europe médiévale*, I *Peninsule Ibérique-France*, in *The Economic History Review*, 2nd ser., IX. pp. 517–18.

Review of P. Goubert, *Byzance avant l'Islam, II; Byzance et l'Occident sous les successeurs de Justinien*: I, *Byzance et les Francs*, in *JEcH*, VIII, pp. 221–2.

Review of M. L. W. Laistner, *Thought and Letters in Western Europe, AD 500–900*, in *JEcH*, VIII, pp. 226–7.

Short notice of M. Deanesly, *A History of Early Medieval Europe, 476–911*, in *EHR*, LXXII, pp. 352–3.

Short notice of P. Vaccari, *Studi sull' Europa Precarolingia e Carolingia*, in *EHR*, LXII, p. 521.
Short notice of G. A. Bezzola, *Das ottonische Kaisertum in der französischen Geschichtsschreibung des 10 und beginnenden 11 Jahrhunderts*, in *EHR*, LXII, pp. 727–8.

1958

'Fredegar and the history of France', *BJRL*, XL, pp. 527–50, repr. in Wallace-Hadrill, *LHK*, pp. 71–94.
Review of M. L. W. Laistner, *The Intellectual History of the Early Middle Ages*, in *History*, XLIII, pp. 220–1.
Review of *Sancti Columbani Opera,* ed. and trans. G. S. M. Walker, in *JEcH*, IX, pp. 90–1.
Short notice of G. Schnürer, *Church and Culture in the Middle Ages*, trans. G. Undreiner, in *EHR*, LXXIII, p. 129.
Short notice of I. Zibermagr, *Noricum, Baiern und Oesterreich*, in *EHR*, LXXIII, pp. 131–2.
Short notice of H. Fichtenau, *The Carolingian Empire*, trans. P. Munz, in *EHR*, LXXIII, p. 342.
Short notice of B. Branston, *The Lost Gods of England*, in *JEcH*, IX, p. 268.

1959

'The bloodfeud of the Franks', *BJRL*, XLI, pp. 459–87, repr. in Wallace-Hadrill *LHK*, pp. 121–47.
Review of *Defensoris Logociacensis Monachi Liber Scintillarum*, ed. D. H. M. Rochais, in *JEcH*, X, pp. 99–101.
Review of N. K. Chadwick (ed.), *Studies in the Early British Church*, in *JEcH*, X, pp. 101–3.
Short notice of J.-P. Bodmer, *Der Krieger der Merowingerzeit und seine Welt*, in *EHR*, LXXIV, p. 336.
Short notice of *Ekkehard IV: Die Geschichten des Klosters St. Gallen*, trans. H. Helbling, in *EHR*, LXXIV, pp. 716–17.

1960

The Fourth Book of the Chronicle of Fredegar, ed. and trans. J. M. Wallace-Hadrill (London; repr. Westport, Conn., 1981).
'Rome and the Early English Church: some questions of transmission', *Settimane*, VII, pp. 519–48, repr. in Wallace-Hadrill, *EMH*, pp. 115–37.
'The graves of Kings: an historical note on some archaeological evidence', *Studi Medievali*, 3rd ser., I, pp. 177–94, repr. in Wallace-Hadrill, *EMH*, pp. 39–59.

Review of A. Bergengruen, *Adel und Grundherrschaft im Merowingerreich*, in *EHR*, LXXV, pp. 483–5.
Review of *Adomnan's De Locis Sanctis*, ed. and trans. D. Meehan, in *JEcH*, XI, pp. 112–13.
Short notice of H. Hartmann, *Untersuchungen zur karolingischen Annalistik*, in *EHR*, LXXV, pp. 325–6.
Short notice of P. W. A. Immink and H. J. Scheltema, *At the Roots of Medieval Society*, in *EHR*, LXXV, pp. 509–10.

1961

'Gothia and Romania', *BJRL*, XLIV, pp. 213–37, repr. in Wallace-Hadrill, *LHK*, pp. 25–48.
Review of L. Wallach, *Alcuin and Charlemagne*, in *EHR*, LXXVI, pp. 87–9.
Review of *Notkeri Balbuli Gesta Karoli Magni Imperatoris*, ed. H. F. Haefele, in *EHR*, LXXVI, pp. 490–2.
Short notice of J. Fleckenstein, *Die Hofkapelle der deutschen Könige*, I, in *EHR*, LXXVI, pp. 117–18.
Short notice of R. Boutruche, *Seigneurie et féodalité*, in *EHR*, LXXVI, p. 120.
Short notice of B. Blumenkranz, *Juifs et Chrétiens dans le monde occidental, 430–1096*, in *EHR*, LXXVI, pp. 510–11.

1962

The Long-haired Kings (London; repr. Toronto, 1982).
Bede's Europe (Jarrow Lecture), repr. in Wallace-Hadrill, *EMH*, pp. 60–75.
'France: the Gallo-Roman period', *Encyclopedia Americana*, II, pp. 718–20.
Review of R. Latouche, *The Birth of the Western Economy*, in *History*, XLVII, pp. 52–3.
Review of R. H. M. Dolley (ed.), *Anglo-Saxon Coins*, in *History*, XLVII, p. 54.
Review of G. Holzherr, *Regula Ferioli: ein Beitrag zur Enstehungsgeschichte und zur Sinndeutung der Benediktinerregel*, in *JTS*, ns XIII, pp. 440–1.
Review of W. Ullmann, *Principles of Government and Politics in the Middle Ages*, in *JTS*, ns XIII, pp. 441–2.
Review of *Son of Charlemagne: a contemporary life of Louis the Pious*, trans. A. Cabaniss, in *Med. Aev.*, XXXI, pp. 52–4.
Short notice of P. Lehmann, *Erforschung des Mittelalters*, I–III, in *EHR*, LXXVII, pp. 130–1.
Short notice of W. Metz, *Das karolingische Reichsgut*, in *EHR*, LXXVII, pp. 341–2.
Short notice of F. Merzbacher, *Die Bischofsstadt*, in *JEcH*, XIII, p. 120.

1963

'St Aidan in England', in J. Ryan (ed.), *Irish Monks in the Golden Age* (Dublin), pp. 31–43.

Review of M. Bloch, *Feudal Society*, trans. L. A. Manyon, in *EHR*, LXXVIII, pp. 116–21.

Review of W. Lange, *Texte zur germanischen Bekehrungsgeschichte*, in *Med. Aev.*, XXXII, pp. 91–2.

Short notice of P. Lehmann, *Erforschung des Mittelalters*, IV–V, in *EHR*, LXXVIII, pp. 756–7.

1964

Short notice of R. Wenskus, *Stammesbildung und Verfassung: das Werden der frühmittelalterlichen Gentes*, in *EHR*, LXXIX, pp. 137–9.

Short notice of H. Dannenbauer, *Die Entstehung Europas von der Spätantike zum Mittelalter*, II, *Die Anfänge der abendländischen Welt*, in *EHR*, LXXIX, pp. 392–3.

Short notice of P. H. Sawyer, *The Age of the Vikings*, in *EHR*, LXXIX, pp. 818–19.

1965

'The *Via Regia* of the Carolingian Age', in B. Smalley (ed.), *Trends in Medieval Political Thought* (Oxford), pp. 22–41, repr. in Wallace-Hadrill, *EMH*, pp. 181–200.

'Charlemagne and England', in H. Beumann (ed.), *Karl der Grosse*, I (Düsseldorf), pp. 683–98, repr. in Wallace-Hadrill, *EMH*, pp. 155–80.

Review of A. H. M. Jones, *The Later Roman Empire*, in *EHR*, LXXX, pp. 785–90.

Review of G. Faider-Feytmans, *La Belgique à l'Époque mérovingienne*, in *History*, L, p. 68.

Short notice of L. Weinrich, *Wala, Graf, Mönch und Rebell* in *EHR*, LXXX, pp. 813–14.

Short notice of *Renovatio Imperii*, in *EHR*, LXXX, pp. 814–15.

1966

Short notice of K. F. Morrison, *The Two Kingdoms*, in *EHR*, LXXXI, pp. 577–8.

Short notice of D. Talbot Rice, *The Dark Ages*, in *EHR*, LXXXI, pp. 805–6.

Short notice of *Annales de Saint-Bertin*, ed. F. Grat *et al.*, in *EHR*, LXXXI, p. 806.

1967

The Barbarian West, 3rd edn (London).

Review of *I Collectanea di Eirico di Auxerre*, ed. R. Quadri, in *JTS*, ns XVIII, pp. 246–8.

Review of F. Kempf, H.-G. Beck, E. Ewig and J. A. Jungmann, *Die mittelalterliche Kirche*, in *JTS*, ns XVIII, pp. 507–8.

Short notice of R. Latouche, *Gaulois et Francs de Vercingétorix à Charlemagne*, in *EHR*, LXXXII, p. 143.

Short notice of F. S. Lear, *Treason in Roman and Germanic Law*, in *EHR* LXXXII, pp. 143–4.

Short notice of J. Vansina, *Oral Tradition*, in *EHR*, LXXXII, p. 211.

Short notice of E. Kantorowicz, *Selected Studies*, in *EHR*, LXXXII, pp. 590–1.

Short notice of S. Mazzarino, *The End of the Ancient World*, trans. G. Holmes, and A. Momigliano, *Studies in Historiography*, in *EHR*, LXXXII, pp. 816–17.

1968

'Gregory of Tours and Bede: their views of the personal qualities of kings', *Frühmittelalterliche Studien*, II, pp. 31–44, repr. in Wallace-Hadrill, *EMH*, pp. 96–114.

Review of *Dicuili Liber de Mensura Orbis*, ed. and trans. J. J. Tierney with L. Bieler, in *JTS*, ns. XIX, pp. 348–9.

Review of W. Goffart, *The Le Mans Forgeries*, in *Speculum*, XLIII, pp. 719–22.

Short notice of E. A. Thompson, *The Visigoths in the Time of Ulfila*, in *EHR*, LXXXIII, pp. 146–7.

Short notice of R. W. Hanning, *The Vision of History in Early Britain*, in *EHR*, LXXXIII, pp. 147–8.

Short notice of B. Bischoff, *Mittelalterliche Studien* I, in *EHR*, LXXXIII, pp. 368–9.

Short notice of F. Prinz, *Frühes Mönchtum im Frankenreich*, in *EHR*, LXXXIII, pp. 370–1.

Short notice of L. Falkenstein, *Der 'Lateran' der karolingischen Pfalz zu Aachen*, in *EHR*, LXXXIII, pp. 815–16.

Short notice of H. Wolfram, *Intitulatio: Lateinische Königs- und Fürstentitel bis zum Ende des 8. Jahrhunderts*, in *EHR*, LXXXIII, p. 816.

1969

Review of *Recueil des travaux historiques de Ferdinand Lot*, I, in *EHR*, LXXXIV, pp. 786–8.

Short notice of P. E. Schramm, *Kaiser, Könige und Päpste*, I, in *EHR*, LXXXIV, p. 143.
Short notice of B. de Gaiffier, *Études critiques d'hagiographie et d'iconographie*, in *EHR*, LXXXIV, pp. 147–8.
Short notice of B. Bischoff, *Mittelalterliche Studien*, II, in *EHR*, LXXXIV, pp. 143–4.
Short notice of *The Earliest Life of Gregory the Great*, ed. B. Colgrave, in *EHR*, LXXXIV, pp. 376–7.
Short notice of J. Svennung, *Jordanes und Scandia*, in *EHR*, LXXXIV, pp. 819–20.
Short notice of P. E. Schramm, *Kaiser, Könige und Päpste*, II, in *EHR*, LXXXIV, p. 820.

1970

J. M. Wallace-Hadrill and J. McManners (eds), *France: Government and Society*, 2nd edn (London).
Short notice of W. Kienast, *Studien über die französischen Volkstämme des Frühmittelalters*, in *EHR*, LXXXV, pp. 599–600.
Short notice of D. Lohrmann, *Das Register Papst Johannes' VIII*, in *EHR*, LXXXV, pp. 600–1.
Short notice of C. Brühl, *Fodrum, Gistum, Servitium Regis*, in *EHR*, LXXXV, pp. 601–3.
Short notice of E. Boshof, *Erzbischof Agobard von Lyon*, in *EHR*, LXXXV, pp. 828–9.

1971

Early Germanic Kingship in England and on the Continent (Oxford).
'A background to St. Boniface's mission', in P. Clemoes and K. Hughes (eds), *England before the Conquest: Studies in primary sources presented to Dorothy Whitelock* (Cambridge), pp. 35–48, repr. in Wallace-Hadrill, *EMH*, pp. 138–54.
'Sir Frank Stenton', review article, *History*, LVI, pp. 55–9.
Review of K. Hauck, *Goldbrakteaten aus Sievern*, in *EHR*, LXXXVI, pp. 559–61.
Short notice of I. Haselbach, *Aufstieg und Herrschaft der Karlinger in der Darstellung der sogenannten Annales Mettenses priores*, in *EHR*, LXXXVI, pp. 154–6.
Short notice of *Recueil des travaux historiques de Ferdinand Lot*, II, in *EHR*, LXXXVI, pp. 600–1.
Short notice of E. Zöllner, *Geschichte der Franken bis zur Mitte des 6. Jahrhunderts*, in *EHR*, LXXXVI, p. 601.

Short notice of W. Wehlen, *Geschichtsschreibung und Staatsauffassung im Zeitalter Ludwigs des Frommen*, in *EHR*, LXXXVI, p. 601.

1972

Review of F. L. Ganshof, *The Carolingians and the Frankish Monarchy*, in *EHR*, LXXXVII, pp. 106–7.
Review of *Césaire d'Arles: Sermons au Peuple*, ed. and trans. M.-J. Delage, in *JTS*, ns XXIII, pp. 508–10.
Short notice of P. Llewellyn, *Rome in the Dark Ages*, in *EHR*, LXXXVII, pp. 154–5.
Short notice of *Liber Memorialis Romaricensis*, ed. E. Hlawitschka, K. Schmid and G. Tellenbach, in *EHR*, LXXXVII, pp. 160–1.

1973

'Early Medieval', *Civilisation* (Del Mar, Cal.), II.
Review of A. de Vogüé, *La Règle de Saint Benoît: Commentaire historique et critique*, (3 vols), in *JTS*, ns XXIV, pp. 267–71.
Review of *La Règle de Saint Benoît*, ed. and trans. A. de Vogüé and J. Neufville (3 vols), in *JTS*, ns XXIV, pp. 599–600.
Review of A. J. Zuckerman, *A Jewish Princedom in Feudal France, 768–900*, in *Med. Aev.*, XLII, pp. 189–92.
Short notice of H. V. Livermore, *The Origins of Spain and Portugal*, in *EHR*, LXXXVIII, pp. 159–60.
Short notice of *Viator*, I, in *EHR*, LXXXVIII, p. 160.
Short notice of P. Demolon, *Le Village mérovingien de Brebières*, in *EHR*, LXXXVIII, p. 161.
Short notice of R. Folz, A. Guillou, L. Musset and D. Sourdel, *De l'Antiquité au monde médiéval*, in *EHR*, LXXXVIII, p. 410.
Short notice of K. H. Krüger, *Königsgrabkirchen*, in *EHR*, LXXXVIII, p. 410.
Short notice of P. D. King, *Law and Society in the Visigothic Kingdom*, in *EHR*, LXXXVIII, pp. 873–4.
Short notice of *Anglo-Saxon England*, I, in *EHR*, LXXXVIII, p. 874.
Short notice of B. de Gaiffier, *Recherches d'hagiographie latine*, in *EHR*, LXXXVIII, pp. 874–5.

1974

Articles in *Encyclopedia Britannica*.
Short notice of R. Weiss, *Chlodwigs Taufe: Reims 508*, in *EHR*, LXXXIX, p. 144–5.
Short notice of J. Autenrieth and F. Brunhölzl (eds), *Festschrift Bernhard Bischoff*, in *EHR*, LXXXIX, pp. 145–6.

Short notice of *Recueil des travaux historiques de Ferdinand Lot* III, in *EHR*, LXXXIX, p. 413.
Short notice of W. H. Fritze, *Papst und Frankenkönig*, in *EHR*, LXXXIX, p. 414.
Short notice of B. S. Bachrach, *A History of the Alans*, in *EHR*, LXXXIX, pp. 649–50.

1975

Early Medieval History (Oxford).
The Vikings in Francia (Stenton Lecture, 1974), (Reading), repr. in Wallace-Hadrill, *EMH*, pp. 217–36.
'War and peace in the earlier Middle Ages' (Prothero Lecture), *TRHS*, 5th ser., XXV, pp. 157–74, repr. in Wallace-Hadrill, *EMH*, pp. 19–38.
Review of G. Duby, *Guerriers et paysans, VII–XIIe siècle*, in *Archives internationales d'histoire des sciences*, XXV, pp. 141–3.
Review of H. Fuhrmann, *Einfluss und Verbreitung der pseudoisidorischen Fälschungen* I–II, in *EHR*, XC, pp. 116–18.
Short notice of V. Mudroch and G. S. Couse (eds), *Essays on the Reconstruction of Medieval History*, in *EHR*, XC, p. 156.
Short notice of H. Jankuhn, W. Schlesinger and H. Steuer (eds), *Vor- und Frühformen der europäischen Stadt im Mittelalter*, I, in *EHR*, XC, pp. 158–9.
Short notice of H. Ebling, *Prosopographie der Amtsträger des Merowingerreiches von Chlothar II (613) bis Karl Martell (714)*, in *EHR*, XC, pp. 419–20.

1976

'Bede and Plummer', in G. Bonner (ed.), *Famulus Christi* (London), pp. 366–85, previously published in Wallace-Hadrill, *EMH*,. pp. 76–95.
Review of *The Hisperica Famina: I, The A-Text*, ed. and trans. M. Herren, in *JTS*, ns XXVII, pp. 235–6.
Short notice of H. Jankuhn, W. Schlesinger and H. Steuer (eds), *Vor- und Frühformen der europäischen Stadt im Mittelalter*, II, in *EHR*, XCI, pp. 405–6.
Short notice of H. Fuhrmann, *Einfluss and Verbreitung der pseudoisidorischen Fälschungen*, III, in *EHR*, XCI, pp. 406–7.
Short notice of *Le Polyptique de l'Abbaye de Saint-Bertin (844–859)*, ed. F. L. Ganshof, in *EHR*, XCI, pp. 884–5.

1977

Review of H. Mordek, *Kirchenrecht und Reform im Frankenreich*, in *JTS*, ns XXVIII, pp. 200–3.

Short notice of W. Ullmann, *The Church and the Law in the Earlier Middle Ages*, in *EHR*, XCII, p. 410.

Short notice of *Dhuoda: Manuel pour mon Fils*, ed. and trans. P. Riché, in *EHR*, XCII, pp. 640–1.

Short notice of M. Rissel, *Rezeption antiker und patristischer Wissenschaft bei Hrabanus Maurus*, in *EHR*, XCII, p. 882.

1978

'A Carolingian Renaissance Prince: The Emperor Charles the Bald', (Raleigh Lecture), *Proceedings of the British Academy*, LXIV, pp. 155–84.

Review of J. Devisse, *Hincmar, Archevêque de Reims, 845–92*, in EHR, XCIII, pp. 100–5.

Review of O. Eberhardt, *Via Regia: der Fürstenspiegel Smaragds von St Mihiel und seine literarische Gattung*, in *EHR*, XCIII, pp. 845–6.

Review of A. de Vogüé, *La Règle de Saint Benoît, VII: commentaire doctrinal et spirituel*, in *JTS*, ns XXIX, pp. 239–41.

Short notice of *Documents comptables de Saint-Martin de Tours à l'époque mérovingienne*, ed. P. Gasnault, in *EHR*, XCIII, pp. 427–8.

Short notice of U. Penndorf, *Das Problem der 'Reichseinheitsidee' nach der Teilung von Verdun (843)*, in *EHR*, XCIII, pp. 898–9.

1979

Review of M. Heinzelmann, *Bischofsherrschaft in Gallien*, in *JTS*, ns XXX, pp. 573–4.

Review of *Césaire d'Arles: Sermons au Peuple*, II, ed. and trans. M.-J. Delage, in *JTS*, ns XXX, pp. 574–5.

Short notice of B. de Gaiffier, *Recueil d'Hagiographie*, in *EHR*, XCIV, p. 622.

Short notice of E. Ewig, *Spätantikes und fränkisches Gallien*, I, in *EHR*, XCIV, pp. 622–3.

1980

'The Ghost goes West', review of W. Horn and E. Born, *The Plan of St Gall*, in *New York Review of Books*, XXVII, 6 November, pp. 46–9.

Review of *Rabani Mauri, Martyrologium*, ed. J. McCulloh, and *De Computo*, ed. W. M. Stevens, in *JEcH*, XXXI, pp. 212–13.

Review of *Grégoire le Grand, Dialogues*, I, ed. A. de Vogüé, in *JTS*, ns XXXI, pp. 224–6.

Short notice of O. G. Oexle, *Forschungen zu monastischen und geistigen Gemeinschaften im westfränkischen Bereich*, in *EHR*, XCV, p. 195.

Short notice of P. Riché, *Les Écoles et l'enseignement dans l'occident chrétien de la fin du Ve siècle au milieu du XIe siècle*, in *EHR*, XCV, pp. 400–1.

Short notice of K. F. Werner, *Structures politiques du monde franc (VIe–XIIe siècles)*, in *EHR*, XCV, p. 401.

1981

'History in the mind of Archbishop Hincmar', in R. H. C. Davis and J. M. Wallace-Hadrill (eds), *The Writing of History in the Middle Ages: Essays presented to Richard William Southern* (Oxford), pp. 43–70.

Review of M. Rouche, *L'Aquitaine des Wisigoths aux Arabes 418–781*, in *EHR*, XCVI, pp. 131–3.

Review of R. Kottje, *Die Bussbücher Halitgars von Cambrai und des Hrabanus Maurus*, in *EHR*, XCVI, pp. 846–8.

Review of J. Autenrieth, D. Geuenich and K. Schmid (eds), *Das Verbrüderungsbuch der Abtei Reichenau, Einleitung, Register, Faksimilae*, in *JEcH*, XXXII, pp. 519–21.

Review of *Grégoire le Grand, Dialogues*, II, ed. and trans. A. de Vogüé, in *JTS*, ns XXXII, pp. 275–7.

Review of *Grégoire le Grand, Dialogues*, III, ed. A. de Vogüé, in *JTS*, ns XXXII, pp. 531–2.

Short notice of E. Ewig, *Spätantikes und fränkisches Gallien*, II, in *EHR*, XCVI, pp. 428–9.

1982

Review of F. J. Felten, *Äbte und Laienäbte*, in *JEcH*, XXXIII, pp. 114–17.

Forthcoming

The Frankish Church (Oxford History of the Christian Church) (Oxford).

List of Contributors

DONALD BULLOUGH is Professor of Medieval History, University of St Andrews and a Corresponding Fellow of *MGH*. He was Ford's lecturer in English history at Oxford, 1979–80, and is author of *The Age of Charlemagne* (Elek, 1965).

ROGER COLLINS is author of several articles, mostly on Visigothic history, and of *Early Medieval Spain: Unity in Diversity, 400–1000* (Macmillan, 1983).

DAVID GANZ is Assistant Professor of Latin at the University of North Carolina, Chapel Hill. He was co-editor of *Charles the Bald, Court and Kingdom* (BAR, Int. CI, 1981), and is working on the Abbey of Corbie in the ninth century.

ERIC JOHN was formerly Reader in History, University of Manchester. He is author of *Land Tenure in Early England* (Leicester UP, 1960), and *Orbis Britanniae and Other Studies* (Leicester UP, 1966), and a co-author of J. Campbell (ed.), *The Anglo-Saxons* (Phaidon, 1982).

JUDITH McCLURE is head of history, St Helen's School, Abingdon. She is author of various articles on the Latin Bible and early medieval exegesis, and of *The Bible in the Middle Ages* (Macmillan, forthcoming).

ROSAMOND McKITTERICK is a fellow of Newnham College Cambridge and University Assistant Lecturer in History. She is author of *The Frankish Church and the Carolingian Reforms, 789–895* (Royal Historical Society, 1977) and *The Frankish Kingdoms under the Carolingians* (Longmans, 1983).

JANET NELSON is Lecturer in History at King's College, London. She is author of a series of articles on early medieval kingship, and was co-editor of *Charles the Bald, Court and Kingdom* (BAR, Int. CI, 1981).

PETER SAWYER was formerly Professor of Medieval History, University of Leeds and is still a Senior Fellow of the University. He is the author of various Domesday studies, and of *The Age of the Vikings* (Arnold, 2nd edn, 1971), *Anglo-Saxon Charters: an annotated list and bibliography* (Royal Historical Society, 1968), *From Roman Britain to Norman England* (Methuen, 1978), *The Charters of Burton Abbey* (British Academy, 1979) and *Kings and Vikings* (Methuen, 1982); he was co-editor of *Early Medieval Kingship* (Leeds UP, 1977).

CLARE STANCLIFFE is a freelance early medieval historian and Honorary Lecturer in the Department of Theology, Durham University. She is author of 'Kings and Conversion', *Frühmittelalterliche Studien*, XIV (1980), and of *St Martin and his Hagiographer* (Oxford Historical Monographs, 1983).

ALAN THACKER is Assistant Editor, *Victoria County History (Cheshire)*. He is author of *Saints and Cults in Early England* (Batsford, forthcoming).

IAN WOOD is Lecturer in History, University of Leeds. He is the author of articles on the late Roman and Merovingian periods in Britain and Gaul, and was co-editor of *Early Medieval Kingship* (Leeds UP, 1977).

MICHAEL WOOD makes documentary films for the BBC, and wrote and presented *In Search of the Dark Ages*, now published by the BBC (1981). He is author of *King Aethelstan and the Anglo-Saxon Empire* (British Museum, forthcoming).

PATRICK WORMALD is Lecturer in Medieval History, University of Glasgow, and a Fellow of All Souls College, Oxford. He was a co-author of J. Campbell (ed.), *The Anglo-Saxons* (Phaidon, 1982), and is author of *Kingship and the Making of Law in England: from Alfred to Henry I* (Blackwell, forthcoming).

Index